The Language Loss of the Indigenous

This volume traces the theme of the loss of language and culture in numerous post-colonial contexts. It establishes that the aphasia imposed on the indigenous is but a visible symptom of a deeper malaise – the mis-match between the symbiotic relation nurtured by the indigenous with their environment and the idea of development put before them as their future. The chapters here show how the cultures and the imaginative expressions of indigenous communities all over the world are undergoing a phase of rapid depletion. They unravel the indifference of market forces to diversity and that of the states, unwilling to protect and safeguard these marginalized communities.

This book will be useful to scholars and researchers of cultural and literary studies, linguistics, sociology and social anthropology, as well as tribal and indigenous studies.

G. N. Devy is Founder of the Bhasha Research Centre at Baroda and Adivasi Academy at Tejgadh, Gujarat, India. He writes in three Indian languages – Marathi, Gujarati and English – and has received prestigious awards for his writings. Formerly he taught at the MS University of Baroda and the Dhirubhai Ambani Institute of Information and Communication Technology (DAIICT). He is currently Chair of the *People's Linguistic Survey of India* and received the civilian honour of Padma Shri from the Government of India in 2014.

Geoffrey V. Davis is former Professor of Commonwealth and Postcolonial Literatures at the University of Aachen, Germany. He has been international chair of the Association for Commonwealth Literature and Language Studies (ACLALS) and chair of the European branch. He co-edits *Cross/Cultures: Readings in the Post/Colonial Literatures and Cultures in English* and the African studies series *Matatu*. His publications include *Staging New Britain: Aspects of Black and South Asian British Theatre*

Practice (2006) and *African Literatures, Postcolonial Literatures in English: Sources and Resources* (2013).

K. K. Chakravarty, formerly in the Indian Administrative Services, has held several esteemed positions in his career as Chancellor of the National University for Educational Planning and Administration; Chairman, Lalit Kala Akademi, the national academy for visual arts; and Member Secretary, Indira Gandhi National Centre for the Arts. Educated at Harvard, he has contributed several research articles to books and journals in archaeology, fine arts, philosophy and education.

The Language Loss of the Indigenous

Edited by G. N. Devy,
Geoffrey V. Davis
and K. K. Chakravarty

LONDON AND NEW YORK

First published 2016
by Routledge
2 Park Square, Milton Park, Abingdon, Oxon OX14 4RN

and by Routledge
711 Third Avenue, New York, NY 10017

First issued in paperback 2017

Routledge is an imprint of the Taylor & Francis Group, an informa business

British Library Cataloguing-in-Publication Data
A catalogue record for this book is available from the British Library

Library of Congress Cataloging-in-Publication Data
A catalog record has been requested for this book

ISBN 13: 978-1-138-48872-4 (pbk)
ISBN 13: 978-1-138-12082-2 (hbk)

Typeset in GoudyOldStyle
by Apex CoVantage, LLC

Dedicated to

The memory of the late Prof. Lachman Khubchandani, who ceaselessly brought new questions to the field of sociolinguistics and taught several generations of linguists that speakers are far more important than speech, societies more complex than languages.

Contents

Illustrations

Figures

Tables

Abbreviations

AIDS	acquired immunodeficiency syndrome
AIPA	Association of Itsekiri Performing Artists
DCE	Douglas Creek Estates
ERT	emergency response team
FM	frequency medium
GO	government order
HIV	human immunodeficiency virus
IAS	Indian Administrative Services
ICT	information and communication technology
INEC	Independent Electoral Commission
ISD	Information Services Department
JSS	junior secondary school
LIE	language of the immediate environment
MDG	millennium development goals
MOMA	Museum of Modern Art (New York)
MT	mother tongue
NACA	National Action Committee on AIDS
NCE	National Certificate in Education
NGO	non-governmental organization
NITDA	Nigerian Information Technology Development Agency
n.p.	no publisher
NP	Nigerian Pidgin
NPE	National Policy on Education
OBC	other backward castes
RCAP	Royal Commission on Aboriginal Peoples
RCMP	Royal Canadian Mounted Police
SQ	*Sureté du Québec*
SRC	States Reorganisation Commission
SSS	senior secondary school
SMS	short messaging services
ST	scheduled tribe
TAVA	African Audio-Visual Awards
UBE	Universal Basic Education

UN	United Nations
UNDP	United Nations Development Programme
UNESCO	United Nations Educational, Scientific and Cultural Organization
ZCC	Zion Christian Church

Contributors

Tony E. Afejuku is Professor of English, Literature and Creative Writing at the University of Benin, Benin-City, Nigeria, and a Fellow of the Literary Society of Nigeria.

A. Maria Mercy Amutha is Assistant Professor in the Department of Humanities and Social Sciences, BITS, Pilani – Hyderabad Campus, India.

Rose Oro Aziza is a Professor of Linguistics at the Delta State University, Abraka, Nigeria.

Gomati Bodra Hembrom is Assistant Professor in Sociology at Jamia Millia Islamia, New Delhi.

G. Christopher is Assistant Professor in the School of Social Sciences and Languages, VIT University, Vellore, India.

Perpetual Crentsil is Researcher at the Social and Cultural Anthropology Department, University of Helsinki, Finland.

Digambar Maruti Ghodke is Assistant Professor of English at S.N. Arts, D.J.M. Commerce and B.N.S. Science College, Sangamner (Maharashtra), India.

Lidia Guzy is Lecturer in Contemporary South Asian Religions at the Study of Religions Department, University College Cork (UCC), Ireland. She is also a *Privatdozent* (Senior Lecturer) at the Free University of Berlin.

Nishat Haider is Associate Professor of English at the University of Lucknow, India.

P. I. Iribemwangi is Senior Lecturer in Kiswahili and Linguistics at the University of Nairobi, Kenya.

Banoth Deepa Jyothi is Assistant Professor of English at Kakatiya University, Warangal, Telangana, India.

Lachman Mulchand Khubchandani was Founding-Director of the Centre for Communication Studies at Pune, India.

A. S. Kushwah is Professor and Head of the Department of English at the S.L.P. Govt. P.G. College, Morar, Gwalior Madhya Pradesh, India.

Sonia Singh Kushwah is Associate Professor in the Department of English at the K.R.G. Govt. P.G. College, Gwalior, India.

Keya Majumdar is Associate Professor at Jamshedpur Women's College, Jamshedpur, Jharkhand, India.

Mbulaheni Nelson Musehane is a Research Fellow of the Department of African Languages at the University of South Africa.

Chinenye Nwabueze is Senior Lecturer in the Department of Mass Communication, Faculty of Social Sciences at Anambra State University, Igbariam Campus, Anambra State, Southeast Nigeria.

Ezinwanne Okoli is a Research Fellow with the Department of Mass Communication, Anambra State University, Igbariam Campus, Anambra State, Southeast Nigeria.

Lesibana J. Rafapa is Professor and Chair of the Department of English Studies at the University of South Africa (UNISA).

Shaily Sharma is Assistant Professor in English at Amity University in Noida, India.

Alero Uwawah is at the Department of Theatre Arts and Mass Communication, University of Benin, Nigeria.

Alex N. Wanjala is Senior Lecturer in the Department of Literature and the Sub-Department of French at the University of Nairobi, Kenya.

Maloba Wekesa is Lecturer of Linguistics and Communication Studies in the Department of Linguistics and Languages at the University of Nairobi.

Glossary

accham fear *(Tamil)*
Adivasi tribal or indigenous people *(Sanskrit)*
aguch manyasi medicine pot *(Dholuo)*
Ahomatrofo telephone *(Akan)*
Akan language spoken in Ghana
akasanoma radio *(Akan)*
andiwo millet *(Dholuo)*
anni mirabilis years of wonder *(Latin)*
azeeb very peculiar *(Persian/Hindi)*
Basudhaiba Kutumbaka the entire universe as one's family *(Sanskrit)*
bayede Hail the King! *(isiZulu)*
bhakti devotion *(Sanskrit)*
Bharatnatyam school of dance *(Sanskrit)*
bhasha language *(Sanskrit)*
buoywe grass *(Dholuo)*
chou dance style in *Orissa*
dadieanoma aeroplane *(Akan)*
Dagbani language spoken in Ghana
dakalo, an altar or platform (*Gormati*, language of nomadic Lambadas)
Dalit oppressed class in India *(Sanskrit)*
Deepavali row of lamps; name of a festival (*Sanskrit*)
dokri bronze figure *(Bengali/Hindi)*
Durga name of a goddess (*Sanskrit)*
edziban food *(Akan)*
ekpo firin-firin palm-oil making (*Itsekiri*)
ese-egbele fowl legs (*Itsekiri*)
Ewe language spoken in Ghana
Fanti language spoken in Ghana
Ga language spoken in Ghana
Gauri pooja worship of Shiva's consort Gauri *(Sanskrit)*
Gêneros Híbridos hybrid genres (*Spanish)*
Gestalt shape *(German)*
gutka tobacco *(Hindi)*
Hausa language spoken in Nigeria
Igbo language spoken in Nigeria

in actu enunciation, positionality (*Latin*)
inédit that which cannot be inscribed (*French*)
in situ propositionality (*Latin*)
inyanga traditional healer (*isiZulu*)
Itsekiri the language and name of a Nigerian people
jadhu patua paintings (*Bengali*)
kalagam insurrection (*Tamil*)
karpu chastity (*Tamil*)
kasapa good talk (*Akan*)
kgoši king (*isiZulu*)
khosi chief (*Tshivenda*)
khotsi-munene brother to the ruler (*Tshivenda*)
Kikuyu language spoken in Kenya
kindal panradu ridicule (*Tamil*)
kisumbu pranks (*Tamil*)
Kiswahili lingua franca of East Africa
kodola, stand bent forward with protruding buttocks (*Tshivenda*)
kowaakrataa newspaper (*Akan*)
Kuravar hill man (*Tamil*)
Kutrala Kuravanji genealogy of Kutrala (*Tamil*)
langue language (*French*)
lapse a dish prepared with jaggery and rice (*Gormati*, language of nomadic Lambadas)
locutio prima natural language (*Latin*)
locutio secondaria language studied, learnt at school (Latin)
lok folk, common people (*Hindi*)
Lokayata a school of philosophy in ancient India
Lubukusu language spoken in Kenya
Luo language spoken in Kenya
madam simplicity, innocence (*Tamil*)
magiciens de la terre magicians of the earth (*French*)
mantiram sacred utterance, but also popularly, magic charm or spell (*Tamil*)
mbirni porridge-pots (*Dholuo*)
min ngege mother tilapia (fish) (*Dholuo*)
mukololo prince or princess (*Tshivenda*)
Mundari bolega to bokabanega if you speak Mundari you will become a fool (*Hindi*)
Naik traditional head (*Gormati*, language of nomadic Lambadas)
naanam shyness (*Tamil*)

nanga traditional healer (*Tshivenda*)
nattanaitanam buffoonery *(Tamil)*
nom de plume pseudonym (*French*)
ochuti sorghum *(Dholuo)*
odukkappattor (the oppressed) (*Tamil*)
ojoyes chiefs (*Warri*)
Okwe peace *(Dholuo)*
Olaraja village head (*Itsekiri*)
Olu head of all Itsekiri people (*Itsekiri*)
omajaja free citizens (*Itsekiri*)
oppaari dirge (*Tamil*)
Oton-Oloye descendants of the royal family (*Itsekiri*)
pagait banter *(Tamil)*
paraiyas a subcaste within the Dalit (*Tamil*)
patta legal document of ownership (*Tamil*)
payirppu modesty (*Tamil*)
Penniyam a Dalit feminist perspective (*Tamil*)
pournami lunar days (*Gormati*, language of nomadic Lambadas)
pundo chalk *(Dholuo)*
Purkhauti Muktangan an open-air ancestral heritage site near Raipur in Chhattisgarh
ragi kuzh millet porridge (*Tamil*)
Rashtriya Manav Sangrahalaya Museum of Mankind
Roraattu lullaby (*Tamil*)
Rudraksha holy beads (*Sanskrit*)
sahitya literature (*Sanskrit*)
Sami-Mootai silver Statue of Goddess Kali
Sati-Bhavani name of a popular goddess (*Sanskrit*)
Seetala a religious festival of the Lambadas
Sharad purnima full moon night at the end of monsoon (*Sanskrit)*
siwandha guest's shed *(Dholuo)*
Skanda Purana title of a purana literary genre *(Sanskrit)*
taazhtappattor marginalized or oppressed people (*Tamil*)
Teej a religious festival of the Lambadas
tehsil area, district *(Urdu/Hindi)*
testimonio life writing *(Spanish)*
thanda hamlet (*Gormati*, language of nomadic Lambadas)
theoria a view of the world (*Greek*)
thobela king (Northern Sotho)
timo nyadhi showing your worth *(Dholuo)*

tseaseanam automobile *(Akan)*
tshikona dance (*Tshivenda*)
tshitaka bush (*Tshivenda*)
tshitungulo any object associated with ancestral spirits (*Tshivenda*)
Twi language spoken in Ghana
tyakten bhunjitha enjoy by renunciation (*Sanskrit*)
umale supernatural/immortalized beings *(Itsekiri)*
Umale-okun sea-god *(Itsekiri)*
Vaacha Museum of Voice in Tejgadh
wirkliche Historie effective history *(German)*
Wirkungsgeschichte effective history (*German*)
yagna fire sacrifice (Sanskrit)
Yoruba language spoken in Nigeria
Zamindari landlordism *(Urdu/Hindi)*
zwiaweloni a place of rest (*Tshivenda*)
zwiendeulu royal burial place (*Tshivenda*)
zwifho sacred place (*Tshivenda*)
zwisima spring (*Tshivenda*)

Introduction

Aphasia: the fate of the indigenous languages

G. N. Devy

The present volume of essays by scholars from various continents is the sixth and the last in the series of volumes resulting from the four *Chotro* conferences held in India from 2008 to 2012. Of the five previously published volumes, two – *Indigeneity* (2010) and *Voice and Memory* (2012) – were brought out under the imprint of Orient BlackSwan, and three – *Narrating Nomadism* (2013), *Knowing Differently* (2014) and *Performing Identities* (2015) – under the imprint of Routledge. Those five volumes and the present one feature a total of 130 essays contributed by scholars, artists and activists from over 20 countries. Taken together, they form a comprehensive comment, both generically and specifically, on the current situation of the indigenous communities in different continents.

The scholars and activists who participated in the *Chotro* conferences and contributed their observation and analysis to the collective learning of *Chotro* included persons from various economic classes, a large variety of educational backgrounds and age groups. It will therefore not be any exaggeration if one were to look at the six volumes together as an authentic and comprehensive representation of the condition of the indigenous communities at the beginning of the third millennium. If one were to draw any single conclusion from these volumes, it would be that the culture and the imaginative expression of the indigenous communities all over the world are in a phase of rapid depletion, as they are surrounded by market forces indifferent to diversity, states unwilling to protect and safeguard them and forms of knowledge that look upon the knowledge of the indigenous as being obscure. The involuntary silencing of the indigenous will be remembered in future as the single most crucial 'contribution' of the post-modern global world. As if it were aphasia, it is inscribed as the collective destiny of the indigenous voice in our time.

All over the world there is an anxiety about languages dying or, more accurately, language itself dying. After a history of 70,000 years of communication through various systems of verbal icons, humans seem to have arrived at a crucial turning point in the process of natural evolution.

There are several estimates for the number of dying languages just as there are widely divergent estimates for the total number of languages in use; and while there is a widely shared fear of language disappearance, it is really difficult to assess the precise number of languages on the brink of perishing in the near future. UNESCO has published an *Atlas* of such languages that indicates that the fears of language loss are not unfounded. However, whether or not there are any definitive statistics on dying languages, the indigenous communities in all parts of world have been experiencing the phenomenon of language loss as an everyday reality. The outlines of their particular narratives may vary, but the Maoris in New Zealand, the Aboriginals in Australia, the Adivasis in India, the Canadian First Nations, the American Natives and the tribal communities in South East Asia and South America present similar stories of language loss and cultural erosion. The environment of rapid cultural globalization has been causing the depletion of their word stocks and oral memories, and the involuntary outward migration that has become necessary for their very survival has induced a shift towards a few international languages. At no time in the known history of humans has such a massive reduction in language diversity been experienced, and the indigenous are in the forefront of the crisis in language identity. In India, where the four *Chotro* conferences were held, no one really knows how many languages people speak. That is also the case with Papua New Guinea, Indonesia and Nigeria, the countries whose languages together account for over half of the world's linguistic stock. It is quite frightening to know that against the assumed figure of 6,000 natural languages, it is estimated that two thirds will vanish by the end of this century, and of the remaining 2,000-odd languages a few hundred will function without all their domains intact. The spectre is unnerving for whoever speaks and is human. This book offers a sampling of field studies and action research reports persuasively pointing to the affliction that the indigenous have to bear.

The fourth *Chotro* conference was held in Baroda in January 2012 together with the *bhasha-vasudha* assembly of over a thousand participants representing nearly 900 languages from all parts of the world. This was probably an unprecedented event where so many languages shared a single platform. The representatives had come together to express their distress, but they had also come together to witness the announcement of the *People's Linguistic Survey of India* (PLSI), a language survey of a scale unprecedented in history, carried out by self-funded volunteers drawn from various economic classes, professional backgrounds and age groups. The *bhasha-vasudha* assembly was convened by the Bhasha Research

Centre; the *Chotro* conference was hosted as part of it by the Association for Commonwealth Literature and Language Studies and Bhasha. *Bhasha* means 'voice' or 'language' and *vasudha* means 'the earth'; thus the title implied 'the voice of the earth' as well as 'the language world'. Thus, the context of the fourth *Chotro* conference was a people's movement for addressing a universal concern. It would be difficult to bring together for a scholarly publication all the lectures and presentations given at the conference. The sheer volume of what was stated and transacted would be too enormous to present in a book format. As convenors of the conference and as editors of the *Chotro* publications, we found it desirable to produce a single volume of articles representing the tenor and the tempo of the 2012 *Chotro* in Baroda.

While reading the essays contained in this volume, one should bear in mind that these are not essays in linguistics. They are not essays in language teaching either. These are not philosophical or historical essays on language or philology. These essays are not on the psychological or neurological aspects of aphasia as a disorder. These essays describe the voice of the communities for whom language loss has come to be the very condition of their own survival. They establish that the aphasia imposed on the indigenous is a visible symptom of a deeper malaise. The larger problem is the mismatch between the symbiotic relation nurtured by the indigenous with the environment and the idea of development that is being put before them as the road map of their future. This conflict is not peculiar to any one country or continent. It cuts across nations with divergent economic profiles. One notices now in India, and in other Asian and African countries, an overpowering desire among parents to educate their children through the medium of English, French or Spanish in the hope that these languages will provide a certain visibility for the children who will grow up in the international market of productive labour. This desire has affected the schooling pattern in favour of an education through an international language, which has not been witnessed in any previous era. Over the last two centuries, thanks to the desires triggered by colonialism, imperialism and globalization, the languages of the world appear to have been distributed into two clear categories, the languages of knowledge and the languages of the indigenous, thus turning everything indigenous into 'non-knowledge'. This is a developmental debacle and an economic liability to the productive world and the 'developed' economies.

In India, the language scenario is somewhat perplexing. While India tops the UNESCO list of 'languages in danger' with a good 197 languages that have gone past the danger signal, there are about 850 living languages in sight. The PLSI has identified and described 780 of them. It admits that it may have overlooked about 80 to 100 languages that are still in existence. The survival rate of Indian languages is certainly much higher than that for indigenous languages in other countries that have experienced colonial domination. On the other hand, the rate of decline of languages in the country over the last fifty years is alarming too, for about a quarter of the language stock has been wiped out. If we do not appreciate the complexities involved in the situation and do not go for well-calibrated micro-planning for each of the remaining languages, the loss can easily become twice as much or worse in the coming half century.

When a speech community comes to believe that education in some other language is alone the way ahead for its very survival, the given community decides to adapt to the new language situation. It would be pertinent therefore to consider whether there is something inherent in the dominant development discourse in the contemporary world that requires a diminishing of the world's linguistic heritage, that demands a kind of a *phonocide*. And, if that is the case, which it is the task of political and economic analysts to show, the future for human languages is frightening. The communities that are already marginalized within their local or national contexts, the ones that are already in a minority within their cultural contexts, the ones that have already been dispossessed of their ability to voice their concerns, are obviously placed at the frontline of the *phonocide*.

The conservation or preservation of languages needs to be seen as significantly different from the preservation of monuments. Languages are, as every student of linguistics knows, social systems. They are impacted by all other contextual social developments. Language as a social system has an objective existence in the sense that dictionaries and grammars of languages can be prepared, and languages can be represented in an orthography, transcribed, mimeographed and recorded on tape from documents and objects, but essentially language does not have an existence entirely free of the human consciousness. Therefore, a given language cannot be completely dissociated from the community that uses it. Quite logically, therefore, preservation of a language entails the preservation of the community that puts that language into circulation.

Between the collective consciousness of a given community and the language it uses to articulate that consciousness is situated what is described as the 'world view' of that community. Preservation of a language involves, therefore, respecting the world view of the given speech community. If a community believes that human destiny is to belong to the earth and not to offend the earth by claiming that it belongs to us, the language of that community cannot be preserved if we invite the community to share a political imagination that believes in vandalizing the earth's resources in the name of development. In such a situation, the community will have only two options: it can either reject the utopia that asserts the human right to exploit natural resources and turn them into exclusively commercial commodities or reject its own world view and step out of the language system that binds it with the world view.

Indeed, the situation of the languages in the world, and more particularly of the languages of the indigenous peoples, of marginalized and minority communities and of the cultures that have experienced or continue to experience alien cultural domination, has become precarious. The alarm to be raised will not come even a day too early. Yet, it would be ambitious to hope that this task can be achieved even in a small degree by merely placing the responsibility on the state. The mission will have to be carried out through the agency of the nation states, as well as independently of them, through a large number of civil society actors – universities, literary and linguistic academies, good-will societies and associations, non-governmental organizations, individual scholars, researchers and activists. Creation of texts, dictionaries, glossaries and grammars in the declining languages will be of use; documentation, museumization and archiving too will be of some use; but if the languages are to survive, the speech communities need to be given the dignity and respect that they deserve, not as anthropological others, not as the last and under-developed traces of the self, but in their own right as deserving of respect because of what they are.

The *People's Linguistic Survey* was a huge exercise. My experience of conversing with such a large number of speech communities across all states has taught me humility. The awareness that smaller languages are close to extinction was written large in every conversation; but there was no sense of panic such as one may notice in the websites of language researchers. Rather, in their simple way, many communities tried to convince me of the importance of perpetuating their languages. They taught me respect for the living rather than mourning for the dead. It takes centuries for a community to create a language. All languages created by human communities are our collective cultural heritage. Therefore, it is our collective responsibility to ensure that they do not face the global 'phonocide' let loose in our time.

This was the tone and the general consensus at the 2012 *Chotro* in Baroda.

Bhasha had invited Geoffrey Davis to Baroda in 2006 for a brainstorming on conceptualizing a new kind of conference. The monthly meeting of the migratory labourers from the indigenous communities that Bhasha had initiated at that time had been named 'Chotro' by the community members. We accepted their formulation and their format for the four international conferences that brought together scholars, artists and activists from all continents. The six volumes resulting from those conferences are available in published form for those scholars, artists and activists who could not personally participate in the *Chotro* conferences. With the publication of the present volume, we bring to a close the first cycle of *Chotro*.

1 Symbolic power, nation-state and indigenous language

A sociological analysis of tribes in central India

Gomati Bodra Hembrom

In *The Romance of the State*, a book by Ashis Nandy (2002), he mentions a moving sequence in Werner Herzog's movie *Where the Green Ants Dream*, in which an old Australian aborigine, who does not speak a word of English, barges into the witness box during a court trial that is about to decide the land rights of Australian aborigines vis-à-vis a uranium mining company. The man begins to deliver a long speech in an incomprehensible language. The shocked judge tells the lawyer fighting the cause of the aborigines that he should restrain his client. The lawyer cannot and when he tries to communicate with the trespasser with the help of other aborigines, even they fail. It then transpires that the man in the witness box is the last surviving member of an extinct tribe. Nobody in the world understands him. This moment in the film, according to Nandy, stresses the fact that a lonely death of an individual will finalize the extinction of a cultural species and a community. The moment also symbolizes the bankruptcy of the dominant consciousness complicit with the process of extinction, a consciousness that does not even know that it is impoverished by the death of a cultural strain and is not aware of the brutalization unleashed by that insensitivity. The plight of indigenous languages is of this 'inaudible dissent'[1] in today's context, as depicted in Herzog's movie. Closer to home it is reality. In 2010 an ancient indigenous Bo language of the Andaman Islands died as the last speaker, Bao Sr, died and thus broke a 65,000-year link to the world's oldest culture. There are around 6,800 languages spoken in the world today. The world's languages are currently dying out at the rate of at least two languages each month, and linguists predict that more than half of today's languages will disappear in the next 100 years. Consequently, nobody can deny that the loss of languages will mean a permanent loss of precious traditional knowledge and practices accumulated over thousands of years by indigenous people (Bhattacharya 2010).

Nation-building and the post-colonial situation of indigenous languages

Historically, states have tried to establish and enhance their political legitimacy through nation-building strategies. India has initially adopted assimilationist and integrationist strategies to establish singular national identities through various interventions in which language plays a crucial role such as adopting the dominant group's language as the only official language and making its use mandatory in all public institutions; promoting the dominant group's language and culture through national institutions including state-controlled media and educational institutions; and seizing land, forest and fisheries from indigenous people and declaring them as 'national resources'. But later on such shortcomings were recognized, and nation-states gave way to the state-nation, where various nations – be they ethnic, religious, linguistic or indigenous identities – can coexist peacefully in a single state polity. Successful strategies to build the state-nation can and do accommodate diversity constructively by crafting responsive policies of cultural recognition. India's constitution incorporates this notion (*UNDP Report*).

According to T. K. Oommen (1997), language and territory are the essential ingredients of state-society as well as the basic prerequisite for nation formation. He has pointed out certain propositions about language. First, experience all over the world clearly demonstrates that communication is imperative in order to bring about participatory development. Second, adequate and appropriate communication is very effective through the language of the people, their mother tongue. Third, to be viable and effective, administrative units ought to be coterminous with communication units, that is linguistic areas. Fourth, language is, generally speaking, directly linked to specific territory, and these together provide the basis for a common lifestyle and communication pattern. Fifth, most languages irrespective of their graphemic status are capable of collective communication in everyday life. Sixth, it is desirable to establish separate administrative units (panchayats, districts and states) for the entire linguistic unit, wherever it is feasible (based on population size, financial viability and territorial spread). Finally, the constitutional guarantee of imparting universal, compulsory primary education in the mother tongue will, if faithfully implemented, substantially contribute to the eradication of illiteracy.

Presently the majority of Indians receive primary education in foreign languages, that is languages other than their mother tongue, which is very true for the tribal population. Oommen (2004) also identifies the context in which denial of language rights exists. The subaltern communities (tribes and peasants), even when inhabiting their traditional homelands, are being denied the opportunity to use their mother tongues, either because the languages are spoken by too small a number of people or because they are not developed, development being viewed in terms of the absence of a script and/or the inadequacy of the vocabulary. In another situation, which is also related to the language loss of tribal people, internal colonization of territory is either government-sponsored or undertaken by a dominant enterprise in search of economic opportunities for industrialization and mining and so on, and this leads to the denial of the cultural freedom of the native inhabitants, an important element of which is the decimation and destruction of their language.

In the Keonjhar district of Orissa, large-scale mining has accelerated the process of acculturation and assimilation and has finally led to the destruction of tribal culture as well as of their languages. Oommen (2004) points out that language is the most viable and pertinent of all bases for an authentic cultural renewal of Indian polity. This applies not only to the officially recognized and developed languages but also to the mother tongue and dialects. Oommen also proposed four prevailing perspectives: the traditionalist (which is Hindu hegemonic and whose focus is Sanskrit); the nationalist (which is statist and pro-Hindi); the modernist (which is pro-English and advocates catching up with the West); and the pluralist (which is democratic and egalitarian). The pluralist perspective explicitly endorses the coexistence of different cultures within the same polity with dignity and is best suitable for polyglot India.

The politics of language and the structure of the state

In the 1920s, the Indian National Congress was reconstituted on linguistic lines. Its provincial units now followed the logic of language: one for Marathi speakers, another for Oriya and so on. At the same time, Gandhiji and other leaders promised their followers that when freedom came, the new nation would be based on a new set of provinces organized on the principle of language. However, when India was finally freed in 1947, it was divided. Now when the proponents of linguistic states asked for this promise to be redeemed, the Congress hesitated. This resulted in violent protests in many areas of erstwhile Bombay province, Hyderabad princely state and the Madras presidencies. It also led to the formation of the States Reorganisation Commission (SRC), which in 1956 put the formal, final seal of approval on the principle of linguistic states. According to Ramchandra Guha (2006), the principle of linguistic states helped strengthen Indian unity as it has answered the aspirations of Indian language communities; otherwise the country could have had to face the same crisis that its neighbours Sri Lanka and erstwhile undivided Pakistan had to face.

What happened to the indigenous people and their languages? The Indian state that had finally emerged was a centralized one. The vast stretch of central India where large *Adivasi* homogenous communities with their own languages and ancient cultures existed were cut up into some times as many as five to six linguistic states with the sinister objective of nullifying their cultural and geographical identities. All this was in the interest of the resource needs of the monopoly and bureaucratic bourgeoisie closely linked to metropolitan capital.

It was George Grierson who undertook the monumental *Linguistic Survey of India* and listed 723 major languages and dialects. The 1931 census, the last done by the British, recorded more than 2,000 languages/dialects. Today, the languages spoken in India belong to four linguistic families: Indo-Aryan (73%), Dravidian (25%), Austro-Asiatic (1.5%) and Tibeto-Chinese (0.5%). The speakers of the latter two linguistic families mainly come from the tribes. Only one of the languages of these two families – Manipuri – has been given constitutional status. The reasons often cited for this are that they do not have scripts and the number of people speaking these languages is very small. But neither of these arguments is sustainable. Several of these languages have developed their own script. At the same time one of the popular scripts, Devanagari or Roman, can be adapted for their use. The speakers of six of these languages number one million or more. Of these, two – Bhili and Santhali – have more than five million speakers each. But what is appalling is that the speakers of some of the indigenous languages were divided into two or three states. The Santhali speech communities are divided between Jharkhand, West Bengal and Orissa. Bhils are apportioned between Gujarat, Rajasthan, Maharashtra and Madhya Pradesh. On the other hand Sindhi, Sanskrit (not a living language) and Kashmiri are spoken by a very small number of people, but they are accorded constitutional recognition.

The language policy of free India has created a hierarchical structure of the legitimacy of languages. At the apex of this hierarchy is Hindi, which is a link, official and national language. The intermediary layer of the hierarchy is constituted by regional languages, the languages of those speech communities that wield political clout, and those languages are perceived to be a part of India's ancient heritage. But numerous other languages with millions of speakers are dismissed as dialects; examples are Maithili, Bhojpuri, Awadhi, Santhali, Bhili, Ghondi, Kurukh and so on. Not only are these languages not given any official recognition, but every effort is made to stigmatize them.[2] Only recently, in 2004, was Santhali given constitutional recognition. The regional languages complain of Hindi imperialism, but they indulged in their brand of linguistic imperialism against the languages of subaltern groups. In this process especially tribes and their languages are liquidated; their cultural identity is destroyed. The whole ethos is that of perpetuating the cultural hegemony of the dominant linguistic group at different levels. Linguistic pluralism is the only insurance against this ongoing process of culturocide.

The reorganization of Indian states based on languages conferred the aspired-for cultural identity and bestowed a measure of politico-legal autonomy. But this has created a hierarchy of languages. The non-recognition of tribal languages led to many mobilizations in independent India. Not only were the languages of subaltern indigenous nations not given any recognition, but their homelands were vivisected; for example the Chota Nagpur plateau or the Jharkhand region, which was broken into four parts and was joined with Bihar, Orissa, Bengal and Central Provinces (MP) between 1891 and 1936 by the colonial state. It seems that this was done for two reasons. The first reason was the sight of the numerous tribal rebellions in the nineteenth and twentieth centuries, of which the Kol rebellion of 1831–32, the Santhal rebellion of 1855, the Rampa rebellion of 1879, the Baster rebellion of 1910, the Oraon rebellion of 1918 and the Bhumij revolt of 1932 are well known. To keep these rebellious people together was asking for trouble. The second reason was the rich and natural resources; division apportioned the resources between four states dominated by three important nationalities – Hindi, Bengali and Oriya. The vivisection of Jharkhand economically weakened subaltern nations in pressing for the formation of a viable administrative unit. But the nation-state has continued the same policy for the last half century. However, faced with the irresistible force of mobilization, the Jharkhand state was finally formed in 2000.

The SRC report (1956) had rejected the demand for a separate state, for three reasons: (1) the tribes are in a minority in the region, (2) there was no specific link language and (3) the economic balance of the neighbouring states would be disturbed. The first reason ignored the historical process of minoritization of the *Adivasi* in the region. The second reason could have been easily overcome by prescribing Hindi as the link language. The third reason seems to be the real one. A separate Jharkhand state would have deprived Bihar, Orissa and West Bengal of their metal and mineral resources with the ongoing process of industrialization. But all the three reasons listed by the SRC were reinforced. Jharkhand, which consists of Chota Nagpur and Santhal Pargana (known as Kalkabana), has had a distinct regional and cultural identity since the sixth century BC. By the beginning of the twentieth century this mineral-rich area attracted industrialists; for example the Tata Iron and Steel Company acquired 3,564 acres of land in Jamshedpur in 1917. The process of turning tribal homelands into an industrial hub without bringing any benefits to the local population has disturbed the local people. The Jharkhand movement started in 1915 demanded some level of political autonomy for the region. After independence, industries such as Rourkela, Ranchi and Bokaro as well as the Damodar Valley Corporation, the Patratu Thermal Project and the Koel Karo Hydel project attracted numerous migrants into the region, gradually weakening the claim of the Jharkhandis for a separate state. Thus the economic development of the region not only pauperized the original inhabitants but also eroded their cultural identity. The goal of Jharkhandis to gain complete control over their homeland is unlikely to be realized because the Jharkhand state just conceded will remain an internal colony dominated by non-Jharkhandis, particularly in the economic contexts. Coming back to the language question, for the big and strong nationalities, the SRC was an apt means to confer a separate culture identity; for the weak and smaller nationalities it was a nemesis that eroded both their economic strength and their cultural identity (Oommen 2004).

Symbolic power and language loss

For some three decades, the French sociologist Pierre Bourdieu has been clearing away the cobwebs that encumber our understanding of the relationship between language policy, language use and political, economic and social power in order for us to appreciate the essential point that language policy and language practices in institutions such as schools and universities inevitably either reinforced or countered societal tendencies towards the unequal distribution of resources, opportunities and life chances. To begin with, Bourdieu's notion of symbolic power is similar to the Gramscian concept of hegemony. The term 'symbolic power' refers not so much to a specific form of power as to an aspect of most forms of power. It is an invisible power that suffuses all spheres of social life in such a manner that the very people who are subjected by it are directly complicit in their subjection (Alexander 2001).

Bourdieu's analysis of the relationship of language to social life results in four conclusions:

a Language is not simply a means of communication but also a medium of power.
b Linguistic expressions are the products of the relationship between a 'linguistic market' and a 'linguistic habitus'.
c Individual choices are conditioned by the demands of the target social field/market (audience).
d Consequently, every linguistic interaction displays 'the social structure that it both expresses and helps to create' (cited in Goke-Pariola 2005: 174).

According to Bourdieu's sociology of language, the contention is that, far from being simply a means of communication, language is also an economic exchange that is established within a particular symbolic relation of power between a producer, endowed with a certain linguistic capital and a consumer (or a market) that is capable of producing a certain material or symbolic profit (Bourdieu 1991). Linguistic signs are also meant to be understood and decoded as 'signs of wealth' (or poverty) and 'signs of authority' (or the lack of it); they are intended to be believed or obeyed.

Habitus is a set of dispositions which incline agents to act and react in certain ways. The dispositions generate practices, perceptions and attitudes which are regular without being consciously coordinated or governed by any rule. Linguistic habitus is a subset of the dispositions which comprise the habitus; it is that subset of disposition acquired in the course of learning to speak in particular contexts (family, the peer group, the school, etc.). These dispositions govern both the subsequent linguistic practices of an agent and the anticipation of the values that linguistic products will receive in other fields or markets – in labour market, for example in the institutions of secondary or territory education. The linguistic habitus is also inscribed in the body and forms a dimension of bodily hexis. A particular accent, for instance, is the product of a certain way of moving the tongue, the lips and so on, and is an aspect of what Bourdieu calls, following Pierre Guiraud, an 'articulatory style'. The fact that different groups and classes have accents, intonations and ways of speaking is a manifestation, at the level of language, of the socially structured character of the habitus (Thompson 1991, Introduction, in Pierre Bourdieu's 'language and symbolic power').

Neville Alexander (2001) in the D.C.S. Oosthuizen Memorial Lecture, delivered at Rhodes University, on the issue of 'language policy, symbolic power and the democratic responsibility of the post-apartheid university' refers to the hegemony of the language of Europe, that is English, on the African continent. According to him, it is important, however, to realize that what we are experiencing as one of the most dastardly consequences of colonial conquest and the subjugation of the peoples of the so-called third world is merely a special case of a general phenomenon. In the words of John Thompson (1994), one of the scholars who have popularized Bourdieu's work in the English-speaking world: dominated individuals are not passive bodies to which symbolic power is applied, as it were, like a scalpel to a corpse. Rather, symbolic power requires, as a condition of its success, that those subjected to it believe in the legitimacy of power and the legitimacy of those who wield it. The second decisive concept is that of 'the linguistic market'. As in the case of economic markets and to a large extent coterminously with their evolution, linguistic markets come about as the result of historically determined interaction between peoples who speak different dialects or languages. In the course of struggles, marked by the peculiarities of each individual social formation, one or other dialect, variety or language becomes dominant in such a manner that its native speakers are thereby advantaged over others. This hierarchy of languages or speech varieties apportions differential value to each of the varieties concerned. Those who have acquired competence, in what comes to be viewed as the 'legitimate language', are said to possess a larger measure of 'linguistic capital' than those who lack such competence. On a given linguistic market, some products are valued more highly than others; and part of the practical competence of speakers is to know how, and to be able, to produce expressions which are highly valued on the markets concerned. Different speakers possess different quantities of 'linguistic capital' – that is the capacity to produce expressions *à propos*, for a particular market. The more linguistic capital that speakers possess, the more they are able to exploit the system of differences to their advantage and thereby secure a profit of distinction (Thompson 1994). Crucial to the understanding of how this market subjugates the speakers of language varieties other than the legitimate one(s) is the process by which speakers exercise self-censorship, a fact that arises from their completely rational assessment of what counts in the market concerned. It is this complicity in their own subjugation which is the greatest obstacle to any attempt to change the conditions ruling on any particular linguistic market. In order to do so – and any society involved in a process of radical social transformation has to do so – what Bourdieu calls the 'linguistic habitus' has to change (Alexander 2001).

Bourdieu's problematic assists us in understanding the ways in which language practices and the language policies of states constitute vital connectors between the system of production and the system of social reproduction. It is completely logical, therefore, that the educational institutions, in Althusserian terminology one of the main ideological state apparatuses, should be singled out as the decisive agencies in shaping the linguistic market in any modern capitalist state. It is unnecessary in the present context to belabour this point. Suffice it to say that every member of a university ought to make the effort to understand, besides the manner in which his or her own specialty is transmitted to the next generation, how the particular vocabulary and, *a fortiori*, the language in which that vocabulary is embedded installs, as it were, a particular software into the minds of the students. Given what we understand today of the relationship between the language(s) of tuition and the empowerment of the elite by means of university and other tertiary education, it is essential that, as far as possible, university teachers do a course in the sociology of language (Alexander 2001).

Bourdieu's academic endeavour facilitates the analysis and understanding of the indigenous language situation in post-colonial India as well as the psychology of second-language acquisition and use in each context. The case of Jharkhand clearly demonstrates the nature of language as a critical tool in the acquisition and maintenance of power, as something capable of bestowing upon or denying to the user a great deal of symbolic profit and, by virtue of this, affecting the construction of the social reality of a society. Today the language situation in Jharkhand, Orissa, West Bengal and Chhattisgarh is such that the indigenous populations are forced to acquire a new linguistic habitus in the process of acquiring the dominant languages of mainstream society; likewise the tribal people who understand the dominant language increase their own power, a symbolic capital. This is one of the reasons that recently in Jharkhand when dominant languages were being given official status (second-language status to Oriya and Bengali passed in the new state language bill in the Jharkhand assembly in September 2011), there was no protest from the tribal population.

At the same time the indigenous languages were being pushed into the corner. Given the power constellation in post-colonial India, the dominant nationalities have redefined the linguistic market. As pointed out by G. N. Devy, the absence of livelihood options for tribal people and migration becoming a coping strategy to survival is the greatest threat to any language (quoted in Vasuki 2013: 5). Tribal people are unable to develop their language and literature. D. K. Bhattacharya (2010), in his article 'The dilemma of tribal development', points out that man's experience with his environment accumulates knowledge and, at every step, man starts taking advantage of this knowledge in making a choice for his actions. This is more determining among the indigenous people. The only tool for communicating this knowledge to the future generations is language. Loss of language means a permanent loss of precious traditional knowledge and practices. More than 80 per cent of our tribal population rely on traditional medicines. With languages spoken in these regions dying out, identification of the herbs, their names and their use will be lost. For example, the Birhors of Hazaribagh (Jharkhand) only 15 years ago were the principal suppliers of herbal medicines, but now their main occupation is begging. They are totally addicted to *gutka* tobacco and speak mainly Hindi and sing Hindi cinema songs.

Indigenous language movements in India

The problems faced by tribals during the colonial period in the form of loss of control over land and other resources because of alienation of land from tribes to non-tribes and displacement caused by state-sponsored development projects have continued unabated in the post-independence period. Despite the constitutional provision aimed at securing the development of tribes, it has caused violence to their language and religion. There has been an attempt at an aggressive incorporation of tribes into the language of the dominant regional community. The response of tribal people to state policy and state administration is generally in terms of the increasing demand for the recognition of their distinct language and religion. There has been a new social mobilization for identity assertion among tribes that now have a sizeable middle class. This increasing assertion is precisely for securing rights and controlling land and other resources and also demands for greater political power and autonomy. Along with this there has been a demand for the promotion and revitalization of tribal languages, including the introduction of primers and other literature in schools. A strong Santhali language movement took place in Orissa, West Bengal and Jharkhand. The script developed and used by Santhali is known as Olchiki, and the Ho script is called Barangchitti. In Orissa, the Sahitya Academy has constituted awards for the Santhali language. Kolkata University has also given it recognition as a vernacular language. Recently in the Jharkhand Assembly, a Rajbhasha bill was passed (11 September 2007), which gave the status of second official language to five indigenous languages (Munda, Santhali, Ho, Kharia and Kurukh) and four regional languages (Nagpuri, Panchparganiya, Kortha and Kurmali). The demands by the indigenous communities are that teachers in these languages be appointed at the primary-school level; that the Sahitya Academy be established, so that the literature is promoted and that indigenous language departments be opened in all state institutions.

Conclusion

In conclusion I would like to quote Jeanie Bell, an Aboriginal linguist, who said that 'languages are a precious storehouse of history, experience and culture, a crucial link between the past and the future' (cited in Dhan 2009). In today's era of globalization, the protection of indigenous languages is a big challenge when there is so much exposure (computer/internet, films, radio, TV) of the dominant languages like Hindi and English through media and telecommunication. It is really a threat to the indigenous languages if the promotion is not successful through government; then only Hindi and English will be languages for cultural expression. The idea of tri-lingual education at primary-school level, keeping in mind the geo-ethnic specification, will have another problem, namely that only the major tribal languages will be promoted and the minor tribal languages like Birhor and Malto (Paharia) will be neglected. States like Orissa with 62 officially recognized tribal communities and with as many languages face similar problems. Another issue is the term 'local language', which is not clearly defined as to whether it is an indigenous or non-indigenous language (Dhan 2009). As in Jharkhand, the government made it mandatory for the teachers and officials to have a sound knowledge of the local language. The languages evolved by various social groups to communicate between themselves are the product of culture, and each language spoken or written within a group acquires an ethnocentric characteristic to effect changes in people's opinions, attitudes and values. So the significance of such a strong communication medium should not be undermined in the overall development of that group.

Notes

1 In the film by Werner Herzog, the dissenting ideology used by the aborigines protesting uranium mining in their ancestral land is their belief that uranium mining will disturb the dreams of the green ants and thus threaten the survival of the world (Nandy 2002).

2 This is evident from various responses in which people stated the reasons for their inability to use tribal language/mother tongue in their day-to-day life. When they encounter the larger speech community, they realize that their own language is very different from the dominant language; it sounds very peculiar (*azeeb*) if they speak it; they are being looked down upon and many times they became a laughing stock. So the attempt to stop speaking their mother tongue was deliberate, and they also reprimanded their children, saying 'Mundari bolega to bokabanega' meaning 'if you speak Mundari you will become a fool'. This shows how a language lacks symbolic power in a particular context (urban setting) in comparison to other dominant languages.

References

Alexander, Neville. 2001. 'Language Policy, Symbolic Power and the Democratic Responsibility of the Post-Apartheid University', D.C.S. Oosthuizen Memorial Lecture delivered at Rhodes University. Retrieved from http://146.230.128.54/ccs/files/ruacfree.

Bhattacharya, D. K. 2010. 'The Dilemma of Tribal Development in the Context of Globalized Market Economy', in S. R. Mehta (ed), *SocioCultural Diversities and Globalization Issues and Perspectives*, pp. 307–20. Shimla: Indian Institute of Advanced Studies.

Bourdieu, Pierre. 1991. *Language and Symbolic Power* (ed. J.B. Thompson and trans. G. Raymond and M. Adamson). Cambridge: Polity Press.

Dhan, Jyoti Sonia. 2009. 'Reluctance Towards Indigenous Language', *Jharkhand Mirror*, 8 October.

Goke-Pariola, Abiodun. 2005. 'Language and Symbolic Power: Bourdieu and the Legacy of Euro-American Colonialism in an African Society', in Derek Robbins (ed), *Pierre Bourdieu 2*, pp. 169–90. London: Sage.

Guha, Ramachandra. 2006. 'Linguistic States Helped Strengthen Indian Unity', *Times of India*, 1 November.

Nandy, Ashis. 2002. *The Romance of the State and the Fate of Dissent in the Tropics*. New Delhi: Oxford University Press.

Oommen, T. K. 1997. *Citizenship, Nationality and Ethnicity: Reconciling Competing Identities*. Cambridge: Polity Press.

———. 2004. 'Language and Nation: For a Cultural Renewal of India', in T. K. Oommen (ed), *Nation, Civil Society and Social Movements: Essays in Political Sociology*, pp. 84–104. New Delhi: Sage.

Thompson, J.B. (ed). 1991. 'Editor's Introduction', in Pierre Bourdieu (ed), *Language and Symbolic Power*, pp. 1–31. Cambridge: Polity Press.

Vasuki, Kestur. 2013. 'Ten Tribal Languages on the Verge of Extinction in Karnataka', *The Pioneer*, 12 August, p. 5. Retrieved 3 September 2013, from http://www.dailypioneer.com/nation.

2 Text, subtext and context of Indian culture in the developmental paradigm of globalization

Keya Majumdar

Human history encounters the fundamental issues of the deflected play of all that lies 'between' and 'beyond' human existence and the transformation of culture over the space of history. As Homi Bhabha explains: 'to dwell "in the beyond" is also . . . to be part of a revisionary time, a return to the present to redescribe our cultural contemporaneity; to reinscribe our human, historic commonality, *to touch the future on its hither side*' (Bhabha 1994: 7). Between many transformations, the lost portions of our cultural heritage thus seem to appear, and a sense of possible recuperation arises. To explore and understand those unheard or silenced 'traces', a nativistic approach should be taken. Opening up a text to a nativistic realm of understanding by bracketing together cultural history, ethnography, anthropology and aesthetics involves questions of approximation in order to achieve the layers of meanings of a given text. Moving in and out and away from the myth of boundaries where the indigene and the mainstream 'national' find themselves perennially engaged, the exploratory search for the conceptual nativistic identity is made.

Before an Indian cultural text is appropriated in the post-colonial Indian context, a clear definition of the terms 'region' and 'regionalism' is called for. In India regionalism is defined in linguistic terms. Different regions of India practice their own cultural norms in their own languages and thus become marginalized. All these small-place cultural identities were displaced by the master narrative of India. In the developmental map of India, the cultural presence of these marginalized, ethnic, native texts needs to be given focused space.

The cultural text is viewed as representing a system of signifying potential of cultural practices and heritage subconsciously preserved and specified by the vital potency of temporality and contemporaneity. Yet, it is not the essential meanings of the fixed cultural terms or positions that matter; what matters is how meanings mutate and metabolize in the course of their transportation, translation and transformation.

The text is not merely the book. To read the text merely as a structure of paradigmatic and syntagmatic devices is to divorce the text, which is a cultural act, from the relations of power that produced it. Indian culture represented in different texts of history, religion, ecology, architecture, communication, literature, food-fashion-festival and so on, always had and is still absorbing changes, and thus growing. This process then has to resist the exclusivist ideas of ignoring the different cultural texts of indigene, Dalit, tribal and rural people, whose cultural representation constitutes the important segment of the Indian cultural text, which I will call in this chapter the sub-text of Indian culture. The complex cultural memory of these indigenous people has been made in a fine tension between the narrative of localized language and tradition practiced in their life and the inborn wisdom of the grand tradition of ancient India. And here lies the plenitude and the place of the cultural diversity of India that valorizes the space of the transparent assimilation of a Pan-Indian sign of 'human' culture.

In my present chapter I intend to find out the points of difference and assimilation floating in the main texture of the Indian cultural text in the form of a native exposition of culture. I will try to seek answers to questions such as how pluralistic textualities perform a continuous dialogue between the given and the flow of other subterranean tributaries, how the native system with its indigenous text of Indian culture internalizes and interacts in the formation of an identity called 'India' and how the question of the text and code of culture, too, becomes invested with the context of global vision. At the same time, I shall try to establish that a national consciousness can be enriched into a consciousness of holistic socio-cultural needs and its fulfilment by bridging the gap of divisiveness between the neo-colonial egoism of the mainstream and the inert mass of words and works of the natives.

By proposing to engage in discursive issues about the Indian cultural text, I do not seek a single-factor explanation of Indian culture through an exclusive focus out of a multitude. India's constantly evolving traditions have shaped all the sub-texts of Indian culture, right from the Lokayata and Carvaka traditions of materialism to pragmatic Buddhism to the epic characters of Javala, Aruni and Eklabya to the rich Adivasi cultural expositions and spectacular folk art of all regions. The list goes on. To seek, therefore, a fuller reading of Indian traditions as well as the history of heterodoxy, there is a necessity of investigating the interactions and impacts of different influences that go to make the sub-text of Indian culture.

By embarking on a voyage that looks and examines inside rather than engaging in a backward-looking politics of blame, post-colonial writers should now adopt a form of resistance by engaging their regional/indigene culture in their texts. In the case of the marginalized texts the continual counterpoint and contestation occur within the actual domain of cultural resistance. But we know that culture flourishes in an atmosphere of shared experience and existence. So, with the sub-text of 'difference' and 'divergence', the Indian cultural text hence needs to include marginalized different tribal, indigenous and regional ethnicities because there lies the true India. Marginalization can take place not only in the context of globalization, but equally damaging can be the marginalization that takes place as a result of internal colonization. In many parts of India, including Jharkhand from where I come, which is known as a tribal state, the first inhabitants of the state are bypassed and sidelined not only in economic spheres but in cultural spheres as well by politicizing their physical and cultural space and enunciation. It valorizes the need for intellectual work to contextualize the political reality of society, building an awareness of subterranean history containing the truth behind the reality. The realism of the cultural text is embedded in the very materiality of the matters for which it speaks: dispossession [of land], injustice, marginality and subjection. Texts such as Dalit writing, writing from rural India, dependent on different region's different influences, show a cultural and social history, a political being as well as a range of implicit connections to other texts. To know the world from which the text originates and the world to which it is affiliated is crucial not only for interpretations but also for making an impact on its readers.

In this connection we can refer to Said's perfectly chosen word 'worldliness' (Said 1983: 39) that signifies a crucial factor for addressing such a text, its revelatory power of representation in its way of being in the world. The text is created as a need for intellectual work to contextualize the political reality of the society. The embedding of such a text in its world and the network of its affiliations with that world are crucial to its meaning and its significance. The worldliness also determines the power position of the writer, his own locatedness, which becomes the source of that energy that drives his own intellectual engagements with culture and politics. The worldliness and circumstantiality of the text has 'sensuous particularity as well as historical contingency . . . conveying and producing meaning' (Said 1983: 39).

The counter-discursive representation of regionality becomes necessary to resist the notion of literary universality practiced by the Europeans for the proper development of a global perspective. Here we can have a more effective model to represent the Indian cultural collage than any national grouping that marginalization can offer. So, reading their culture in their own cognitive codes and acknowledging the regional, culture-specific terms, events, thoughts and practices, situated in their determining relations with their material situation, foreground the idea of regionalism and nativism. Helen Tiffin in her essay 'Post-Colonial Literatures and Counter-Discourse' thus carves out the position from where such texts should be read: 'Post-colonial counter-discursive strategies involve a mapping of the dominant discourse, a reading and exposing of its underlying assumptions, and the dis/mantling of these assumptions from the cross-cultural standpoint of the imperially subjectified "local"'(Tiffin 2006: 101).

In fact, the idea of culture itself is an outcome of colonization. Many of our cultural representations were produced by colonial encounter as they went on re-creating Europe and others through its cultural histories of conquest and rule. This malaise has gone so deep that even after colonizers left our shores, through cultural colonization they had consolidated Western control over the development of world capitalism. As a result our native coconut water has many contenders in the market of foreign brands. As Nicholas B. Dirks points out, indigenous culture was their main target, 'Colonialism not only has had cultural effects that have too often been either ignored or displaced into the inexorable logics of modernization and world capitalism, it was itself a cultural project of control' (Dirks 2006: 58).

So, to break this international cultural hegemony, the representations of our national culture with its apt placement, which have already proved to be eco-friendly as well as people-friendly, need to be propagated. Linked to the present by such terms as 'neo' or 'post' there exists both need and priority in our collective interrogation of the colonial past, so that we can create our own allied network of processes to recultivate our own indigenous culture. We can de-recognize the informal continuities between the colonial past and the present new world order by emphasizing the point of 'Nativism'. It is within the continuing process of identity formation that Nativism needs to be sought and practiced. The once colonized race has discovered gradually now the deeply extensive existence of alien cultures subverting as well as overwriting their own cultural text and recognizes the need to reverse the representations ascribed to them, turning negative identities and identity markers into positive images.

There remains however an ambivalent position also. The Westernized India that the modern intellectual is proud of is looked down upon by the indigene people of India, proud as they are of their ancient wisdom and local tradition. Ashis Nandy judiciously brings this ambivalent situation of the Indian cultural text to a pragmatic point of understanding:

> This is the underside of non-modern India's ethnic universalism. It is a universalism which takes into account the colonial experience including the immense suffering colonialism brought, and builds out of it a mature, more contemporary, more self-critical version of Indian traditions.
>
> (Nandy 1983: 75)

The Indian text and sub-text of culture and tradition, Nandy believes, has always 'tried to capture the differentia of the West within its own cultural domain' (Nandy 1983: 76). It is important to remember that 'India is not non West; it is India' (Nandy 1983: 73). Colonization has affected and contributed in many ways to the Indian way of living or Indian culture while those living in the margins were either untouched or very vaguely influenced as far as their indigene culture was concerned. And what Nandy says about the 'ordinary Indian' can be easily extended to the indigene Indian whose 'pressure to be the obverse of the West distorts the traditional priorities in the Indian's total view of man and universe and destroys his culture's unique *gestalt*' [emphasis Nandy's] (Nandy 1983: 73). It becomes important to situate the indigene and the marginalized that live unsullied by the intertextuality of their historical locations and safe in the mythic memory of a unique collective identity in the space of their cultural diversity, which is the articulation process of multi-culturalism. We know that indigenous forms of dwelling cover a range of sites and intensities, which offers a sense of depth and continuity running through all the ruptures and attachments, the effects of religious/political conversion, state control, new technologies and commodities and so on. Cultural diversity operates within the historicity of the text in which action makes a statement that can be overt or covert shaping the indigene into a historical artefact – a remnant of a golden age that seems to have little connection to anything akin to contemporary life. This is how the distance is created between the urban, mainstream people and culture and the marginalized ones as they live and practice their cultural acts encrusting it with a sense of purity, unsullied by city dwellers' profane culture. Though the doubt about incorporation of 'essentialism' disturbs here, Nativism should be practiced in order to establish the Indian cultural text in its proper place of recognition.

We need to shift our gaze from the settled, established dynamics of culture to its decentred energies hidden in the form of native culture. Neither the periphery nor the centre needs to push each other back because exact space is available for everyone on the basis of exchange and interchange. In his poem 'Bharar Tirtha', Tagore wrote about the generous flow of Indian culture based on the idea of 'give and take', 'mingle and intermingle'. Culture being dynamic in its flexible output, it responds to historical, cultural, economic and political factors, as well as to new conditions of community formation. The movement thus between the various texts of Indian culture and the divergent sub-texts of ethnicity and marginality discovers new ways of approaching interculturalism. The 'inter' can include negotiations and translations between cultures, which used to be incommunicable due to language and geographical barriers.

Next, the notion of ethnicity needs to be separated from its equivalence with nationalism, imperialism and racism, which are the points of colonial or European attachment. The essence of ethnicity is seen in values which are cultural, social, moral, aesthetic and not necessarily territorial, notwithstanding all boundary constructing processes that function as cultural markers. The term 'ethnicity' acknowledges the place of history, language and culture in the construction of subjectivity and identity. We can look at the 'Baul Songs' of undivided Bengal, for example and the Baul communities, the nomadic, homeless marginalized people roaming about propagating the aesthetics and essence of human values in homespun tunes, local allegories, metaphors and images in the dialect of Bangladesh. Tagore had modified, expanded and presented the ideas of these songs in many a creation of his *Gitanjali*, thus placing them on the global map. The 'little' spaces and 'little' Indias assume significance in the broad-based cultural geography of India, as the threat of a universalizing transnational culture created by global technologies of material production becomes inevitable. Only a specific locus in time and place can articulate post-colonial difference, which consequently becomes the sub-text of Indian culture. But then, in the various practices and discoveries of ethnic cultural production, a new cultural politics engages the sub-text of 'difference' dependent on the cultural construction of new ethnic identities.

Here the importance of language as cultural capital cannot be overstressed. We know that the written text is a social situation, so the question arises: can writing in one language convey the reality of a different culture, the meaning of which comes through by a process of 'social' communication between the writing and reading participants? Meaning as such is itself a social fact that comes into being within the discourse of a culture. By making a close connection as well as critical interrogation of that particular meaning, native literature should be studied in English honours classes in close relation with the history of modern and traditional literatures of India. This way, a revival of sorts of the regionalism through the broad spectrum of the English language is possible, the sub-text of which will always be Indian cultural motifs. Here, Indian writing in English performs a superb act by bringing into the limelight all those socio-political, community-based writings based on native cultural history, which lay in dormant state, unseen, undiscussed, unheard.

While one acknowledges the multi-traditional basis of Indian English literature, its essential multi-culturality should not be dismissed superficially as a monolithic product of the colonial encounter. Almost all the writers here probe their native roots in their writings in terms of lived experience. Western literary forms and concerns are the points from where they start, but by invoking their native myths and realities, folk traditions, narrative forms they clearly and explicitly stand as mouthpieces of nativism. Second, inspired by the classical Indian tradition internalizing the diverse structures of metaphysics, transcendentalism and ecological awareness, they attempt a discovery of quintessential India within their creative matrix. From Tagore, Aurobindo, Anand, Narayan, Raja Rao to A. K. Ramanujan, Kamala Das, Amitav Ghosh, Salman Rushdie and Arundhati Roy (the list goes on), we find diverse representations of India alive in its nativism in a broad sense of the term. As each writer belongs to a separate regional cultural identity, the picture becomes a formidable collage of multi-cultural perceptions as the base remains the same. True, the texts by these writers have already been included in the curriculum, but the approach of teaching them should be based on the modalities of modern Indian thought. The critical interrogation and evaluation also should be based on Indian historicity and Indian poetics. The organic assimilation and creative transfiguration of Indian poetics in modern critical text has already been initiated, which however needs to be extended to indigenous native forms.

Various traditions in cultural and literary fields in different regions of India still remain in dark oblivion. Their revival is as necessary as their assertion of nativeness. The field of translation should be expanded to smaller units working on regional, long-lost and forgotten texts of native writings, and most important the translators should have knowledge of the local language and culture. These marginalized texts now need to be revived and asserted on a national/global scale. As the text becomes open to the global reader via translation, he or she oversees the continual interaction of discursive textual systems and the power structures that shape broader cultural struggles. This is why all cultural texts should be fixed in actual material circumstances including the events and the physical senses that made it possible. Through translation then, the native writings and *bhasha* literatures should explicate their native positionality with all the pros and cons of power and justice, deprivation and angst, freeing themselves from the rigid colonial constraints of literary paradigms.

At this point, the intervention of native writers in their fiction and non-fiction looking for and establishing a contrary narrative that offers a true picture of native experiences hitherto omitted from imperial and national mainstream history will create a base for their creative expression. Texts like this with a strong sub-text of self-legitimation in different manifestations will provide us with a strong image of Indian culture valorizing the complicity between the historical discourse and the strategies of cultural, social and political dimensions. Thus, in their effort to remap the cartography of the nation's political and cultural past, the aim of the native writers is to retrieve and regroup voices, spaces and identities.

The idea is to know and study native elements in *bhasha* literatures, to know clearly which native elements need to be modernized and simultaneously to choose which external elements from alien culture are to be borrowed and nativized for the efficient functioning of traditional systems. Bhalchandra Nemade thus examines the issue of nativism: 'culture is a network of interacting systems, every living and potent culture has the in-built capacity to convert and absorb all external influences into a native system. The process of such assimilation may be termed nativization. The more efficient the process the more nourishing it proves to the local culture' (1997: 243). This also calls for a process of critical reconsideration of our existing literary culture and practices, and if need be all those alien attributes that corrode our native tradition, moral climate and language of the masses should be obstructed to create a healthy, integrated Indian culture.

Let us not overlook the fact that the institution of Indian English literature influenced by the power politics of a foreign language, foreign critical structures and power relations with publishing houses has marginalized indigene/Dalit writings and rituals of their home-bred culture for a long time. They have rarely made Indian rustic and rural, Dalit and other marginalized peoples and places their subject matter or the space of their critical interrogation. They had their eyes fixed on Euro-American power centres to employ political, economic and cultural manipulation to get published globally, to gain access to the global award list and to win fabulous advances. And then the process of nativization has been doubly threatened by the Brahminical school of thought. Dr Ambedkar tried to nativize Marx *vis-à-vis* Buddhist thought, but the politics of the Brahministic school started playing tricks to canonize his text as simply Dalit writing, ignoring its value as one of the founding texts of Indian economics.

Nativism, without an incisive understanding of history at all levels – local, inter-regional and national – can degenerate into dogma, too. But an efficient non-political discursive body can always oversee these cultural productions through their honest critical perspectives. Translation in its literal and metaphorical presentation can be helpful in bringing out different cultural representations that were unreachable hitherto. Use of English as the language of translation can blur the difference between self and other, thus helping to create a common ground, where difference is recognized, not romanticized.

To relate to history is to discover the complex and intricate network of relationships between literature and its conditions of production characteristic of the age, to see the text in terms of the essential struggles and embattled situations in society, to understand the political, cultural and ideological currents that impact the making of literature and above all to discuss how cultural plurality, multi-lingual situations and intertextuality within culture overlap in the creation of literary traditions. Since heterogeneity and multi-faceted culture across all the regions of India is the basic tenet of our literature/critical abilities, nativism should work its way through a whole range of the arts and human sciences across disciplinary boundaries. And here, history as a regenerative principle can provide an identifiable unity to Indian critical paradigms.

Knowing the significance of history we know that extrinsic and intrinsic cultural influences brought in by history have already been assimilated and integrated in the native writings that maintain their umbilical link with the national master narrative, which is simultaneously replete with the spirit of the local traditions, something very important for a culturally pluralistic society. India has no common language, nor do we have any critical tradition based on a common language. Naturally our literary history and heritage have unique diversities and multi-directional negotiations. Yet, there is a kind of unity visible in the midst of all this plurality and variety. The historicity and cultural orientation of our ancient scriptures and their pragmatic, humanistic essence tend to weave some kind of a texture of unity.

In the Bhakti Period, we see that Indian literary writings tried to grope for the first time to have their stayhold in regional languages tending towards secular historicization and material narrativization. The producers of these literatures had had a deep investment in negotiating the relationship between our regional particularities and our civilizational unity. This movement put in place the democratization of literary language all over India, in the voices and writings of Nanak, Kabir, Mirabai and Chaitanaya, the whole of South and Tamil writings. India started then to witness the emergence of full-scale literary cultures with a regional turn. More important, out of the Brahminical or colonial hegemony, for the first time, cultural forms experienced the sub-text of the cultural symbols of the common people practiced on common ground. Its position between the modern and the mediaeval, emphasizing the perspective and speech of the popular classes, with a cluster of regional specificities, gave it for the first time the right kind of a political and cultural arena all over the country. But for a long time now these literary traditions, the exotic and discrete histories and the myths of the particular regions remained usually within each language and culture, with almost no attempt to connect these to Pan-Indian perspectives.

Now is the time to contextualize culture as a historically constituted domain of significant concepts and practices as well as a regime in which power achieves its ultimate apotheosis. In the present context of the developmental paradigm, our indigenous culture tested and proved through centuries can celebrate its uniqueness that is still strong. All these diverse regional texts of culture exhort us to find the ideological basis for a wider unity. If we examine the canonization of our epic texts like *Ramayana* and *Mahabharata,* we will find that a certain kind of sanctity comes to be attached even to those cognate texts which are not so central in the specifically religious canon, thus emphasizing Hinduism. The narrowness of such canonicity and the substantial overlap of the literary and the religious are based on metaphysical expositions and spirituality. This privileges certain kinds of readings and disallows others based on 'local' experiences, setups, structures, practices, all those secular conditions of production.

In the globalized world now, no single culture can be characterized as dominant. Instead, it is pluralism, the freedom to choose among many different paths and destinations, that is gaining ground due to globalization and greater exchange. The developmental paradigm should register more remote voices, because they constitute the 'real' India. In the contemporary world the politics of culture keeps on constructing and deconstructing cultural identities. In literatures these identities have become very influential in determining the texts and contexts. This is the time to reconsider and consolidate the possibilities of the sub-text of the Indian cultural text in the context of a globalized world. As the nation is becoming an old-fashioned idea, the non-specificity of time and place and the lack of proper historicization of modern Indian English novels where Indian identity is losing relevance, and the tribal, ethnic literatures remind us in their native simplicity that this is the country that valorized the cultural ideal of *Basudhaiba Kutumbakam* long before the idea of globalization was conceived. All our *bhasha* literatures, located as they are in their own cultural tradition, are richer in literary excellence and cultural expositions than many Indian writings in English. Never subscribing to the frills and flounces of neo-colonialism, the politics of publication or editorial jugglery, they enlighten their own milieu with the flickering wick of their earthen lamps. The time has come now to take the light of these 'little local' worlds to the centre stage of global recognition. An open-minded, decentralized appreciation of a literary work as it is, in its own context, is what is expected in true globalization. The idea is to know India in all its shades that many Indians are not aware of either.

Indian culture has always lived with ambivalences and ambiguities, foreign elements and alien myths. Indian culture had never been so self-conscious as to hold on to any particularity as be-all and end-all, be it religion, custom or ritual. This is what Amartya Sen calls 'toleration of diversity' (Sen 2005: 7). India became the first country in the non-Western world to choose a democratic constitution; it has successfully maintained social harmony during the emergence of Buddhism, Jainism, the waves of the Jews' arrival in the fifth and sixth centuries, the early arrivals of Christians, Parsees in the late seventh century, to the last shelter-seeking group of Bahais in the nineteenth century. The Indian cultural text is enriched by all these cultures. A democratic attitude is a basic part of Indian culture. Even religiosity that takes a major part in the Indian cultural text propagates the main strain of democratic tolerance by allowing atheism and materialism to stay side by side with general religious expositions. Carvaka's material exposition 'Enjoy life to the hilt' has found equal space as counter-discourse to the Upanishadic idea of 'Tyakten Bhunjitha' [Enjoy by renunciation]. The heterodoxy of ideas and the inclusion of these ideas in the cultural text of India always leave space for counter-discourse as well as tolerance for the cohabitation of ideas. Underestimation and the relative neglect of the rationalistic parts of these cultural heritages bear importance in the contemporary accounts of India's wholeness as a nation-state.

In the matter of economic growth, identity formation and cultural development in the context of globalization in the post-modern era that suggests celebration of fragmentation, the Indian cultural text with its enriching sub-text of differences can be exported globally to the cultural sphere. The mimic art of 'Chou' thus can gain equal importance with the pure art of Bharatnatyam. From film to food, folk art to furniture, the sub-text of Indian culture can be inscribed in the developmental map of the country. So, Indian culture as a whole as a cultural product can occupy a wide market in the world economic sector, and this strategy of development will be consistent with the championing and promotion of a powerful national identity. Better formulation of patent laws, for example, is something that can protect our local wisdom and ancient heritage like the use of neem, turmeric and scores of other herbs and grains. Sharing the space of the globalized world, through global movements of cultural ideas that expand across different boundaries of the world, the local text of culture should be promoted. Since the global movement of ideas is seen sometimes as ideological imperialism, the marginalized cultural presentations can well be recognized as representative Indian, and thus the asymmetry of power in cultural presentation can be resisted. In this way, both the cultural alienation of the marginalized people rooted in particular locales and isolationist nationalism can be resisted. A new system of mobile relationship between the text and subtext of Indian culture must replace the hierarchies inherited from imperialism, which Said points out as 'a never ending process of discovery and encouragement' (1994: 336).This is how multiple, pluralistic textualities can perform a continuous dialogue between the given culture and the flow of other cultures. As the boundaries of nations are dissolved because of the economic impact of globalization, in this context now the region appears to be providing a fixed locus, from where it can work out an effective strategy to counter the hegemony of the universalizing paradigms of technology-driven networking communication across India. The regional specificity in cultural geography reinforces its organicity as opposed to the nation's imaginary space.

Conclusion

The native texts, traditions and cultural motifs are open to historical transformations and thus have kept fresh and living over the years.

Through this nativism, a process of assimilation starts by which a living and potent culture converts and absorbs all external influences into its system. Among these external influences those that support the basic structure of the native culture are absorbed finally and this process goes on in the cultural as well as the literary text. In this way the native text adds on to the national master narrative to enrich it further and is thus able to avoid the subverting traps and snares of an in-breeding separatist or closed domain. Also, we should note, that, the various cultural outputs and interpretation coming from indigene India can write the 'nation' too without falling into the traps of rigid nationalism to depict in vivid outlines the culture, events, practices and paradigms of Indian collective consciousness.

Now, globalization's homogenizing waves threaten to be inundating waves of neo-imperialism. Therefore, the valorization of regionalism and the indigenous is needed to propose a strategy to counter the homogenizing thrust. This requires a space where 'difference' and 'plurality' are accentuated. Specificities of the social minorities, which are local in scope and form the sub-text of the vast Indian culture, need to be situated properly. Thus the attempt to synthesize the emancipative and progressive local narrative into a totalizing vision is needed that can question and answer the positives and negatives of globalization, defining their own independent path.

Globalizing Indian nativism, the sub-text of Indian culture with all its different flavours would amount to emancipating the obscure traditions, marginal views and non-canonized, yet important, literary texts, thus offering them for close analysis with other non-canonical texts of the world like Aboriginal writings from Australia. By this give and take that can be applied on a global scale, the aesthetics of globalization would enrich the process of global intellectual and cultural interaction. As a result it would present an inclusionary reading of Indian identity that tolerates, nurtures and celebrates diversity within a pluralist India.

With all the gaps and splits between materiality and spirituality, Indianization and Westernization, the Indian cultural text has become mystic and suggestive, making more room for cultural interpreters to theorize the spaces of the signifier and signified, thus bringing out a picture of the Indian cultural text which is opalescent. And, looking from the viewpoint of futuristic ideology, the sub-text of the marginalized Indian culture, rooted firmly in locality, can be transformed into one of the two strains of a single flow of Indian culture, complementary to each other though offering dialectical perspectives. This brings into focus what

Fanon exemplifies as a 'native intellectual's goal' – 'he must go on until he has found the seething pot out of which the learning of the future will emerge' (1963: 225).

References

Bhabha, Homi K. 1994. *The Location of Culture*. London and New York: Routledge.

Dirks, Nicholas B. 1992/2006. 'Colonialism and Culture, Extract From "Introduction", *Colonialism and Culture*. Ann Arbor: University of Michigan Press', in Bill Ashcroft, Gareth Griffiths and Helen Tiffin (eds), *The Post-Colonial Studies Reader*, 2nd ed., pp. 57–61. London and New York: Routledge.

Fanon, Frantz. 1963. *The Wretched of the Earth* (Constance Farringdon, trans.). New York: Grove Press.

Nandy, Ashis. 1983. *The Intimate Enemy*. New Delhi: Oxford University Press.

Nemade, Bhalchandra. 1997. 'Nativism in Literature', in Makarand Paranjape (ed), *Nativism: Essays in Criticism*, pp. 233–54. New Delhi: Sahitya Akademi.

Said, Edward W. 1983. *The World, the Text and the Critic*. Cambridge: Harvard University Press.

———. 1994. *Culture & Imperialism*. London: Vintage.

Sen, Amartya. 2005. *The Argumentative Indian*. London: Penguin.

Tiffin, Helen. 1987/2006. 'Post-Colonial Literatures and Counter-Discourse', extract from "Post-Colonial Literatures and Counter-Discourse", *Kunapipi*, 9(3)', in Bill Ashcroft, Gareth Griffiths and Helen Tiffin (eds), *The Post-Colonial Studies Reader*, 2nd ed., pp. 99–101. London and New York: Routledge.

3 Adivasi art

The convergence of the intangible and the tangible

Lidia Guzy

During a research project on global museum movements entitled 'From Imperial Museum to Communication Centre' from 2006 to 2010, Rainer Hatoum, Susan Kamel and I studied new museum movements in India, Egypt and North America (Guzy *et al.* 2009, 2010). In our research project I investigated anthropological museums and local museum concepts and undertook various documentations of the intangible cultural heritage of marginalized communities from western Odisha. In this chapter I will focus on two issues:

1 On the issue of the *Adivasi*, the indigenous peoples of India and their role in anthropological museums
2 On the issue of the transformation process from collecting to creating art through museums and thus on Adivasi art – as the convergence of the intangible and the tangible

Adivasi and the museum

Since the 1980s the new museum movement in India (see Kalyan K. Chakravarty 2005; Kishor K. Basa 2005), which led to the Guwahati Declaration of 1988, has been formulated with new guidelines for Indian museology (Bhatnagar 1999: 63–65). In these guidelines, the whole of India and its inhabitants were understood as parts and participants of a museum. Inspired by the philosophy of Mahatma Gandhi, local communities were seen as the museum's fundaments. The new museology of India has been conceived as a community-based eco-museology, where local cultures were supposed to act as curators, narrators and teachers of their own cultural heritage. The role of museum professionals was supposed to be restricted to supporting and mediating these activities. In this context, especially marginalized and officially silenced communities such as the Adivasi were to be included in museum representation.

'Adivasi' is a term that derives from the Sanskrit terms *adi* = the first and *vasi* = dweller. This category includes around 100 million people forming more than 600 socio-culturally autochthonous Austro-Asiatic and Dravidian language and kinship groups in India, administratively labelled as 'scheduled tribes'. The diversified, small-scale, pre-industrial communities live either in remote areas as forest dwellers, hunters and gatherers, shifting cultivators and agriculturalists or in urban slums. The socio-cultural systems and religious world views of the Adivasi strongly differ from the hierarchical logic of the Indian caste system (Pfeffer 1997: 3–27).

Adivasi and marginalization

In pre- and post-Independence India, Adivasi groups have been persistently marginalized (Carrin and Jaffrelot 2002: 21–24). Historically, marginalization started with the British colonial empire and the establishment of the land revenue *zamindari* system in 1793. Sociologically, the marginalization of indigenous peoples in India can be seen in relation to the differences between Adivasi cultures, religions and kinship systems and the hegemonic Hindu caste system. Paradoxically, the post-Independence governmental purpose of positive discrimination through administratively constructed categories of 'social backwardness', such as 'scheduled tribes' or 'primitive tribal groups', continued to marginalize Adivasi cultures as tribal, primitive, non-sedentary and non-urban communities, with a pre-industrial way of life. Adivasi cultures continued to be measured by an evolutionary model of urban modernity, sedentariness and industrial development. The Indian nation's industrial boom ultimately continued the pre-Independence colonial exploitation of Adivasi cultures through displacement and industrial environmental destruction of Adivasi territories.

Alternative museum concepts

With the Indian New Museology, which endeavours to integrate marginalized communities into museums, a substantial answer and direction of Indian museums has been given. The Indian New Museology has been inspired by the global theoretical frame of New Museology formulated at the beginning of the 1980s within the circles of the International Council of Museums (Ganslmayr 1989: 79–84; Dodd and Sandell 2001). Inspired by museum professionals from the United States, Canada, Australia and

New Zealand (Wessler 2007:17), the New Museology initiated a critical debate on the necessity of new forms of representation, thus responding to claims for participation put forward by indigenous groups. The New Museology aimed at their empowerment through cooperation between them, the museums and the general public (O'Neill 1999; Watson 2007: 1–23).

New and dynamic forms of encountering and interpreting traditions and proposing alternative museum concepts emerged. Impressive examples of Indian museums appear as creative expressions of the discourse on national heritage:

> The Indira Gandhi Rashtriya Manav Sangrahalaya or Museum of Mankind in Bhopal, the largest anthropological museum in Asia, is an outstanding example. This museum is particularly devoted to the traditions of rural and indigenous Adivasi India with its local knowledge resources.
>
> (see Chakravarty 2005: 25–30; Guzy *et al.* 2009: 78–139)

The Museum of Mankind is distinguished from other museums by its emphasis on open-air exhibitions. The open-air area displays the ecological and socio-cultural diversity of India, and it also embodies a new political and social sensitivity. The long neglected and discriminated rural and Adivasi cultures of India are nationally recognized and symbolically empowered. By focussing upon marginalized social groups in rural India, the Museum of Mankind raises its own 'pre-colonial people' (Chakravarty 2005: 27) to a new notability. Local Adivasi communities are understood as pre-industrial and pre-colonial knowledge cultures, which have accumulated a rich knowledge on sustainability. Such knowledge might gain substantial importance for the survival of India as an accelerated industrial nation (Chakravarty 2005: 29). With its emphasis on the immaterial cultural heritage, the Museum of Mankind is supposed to place marginalized and muted voices of source communities in a position to speak for themselves through their own concepts of exhibits, realized in diverse habitat designs or by the 'Mythological Trail' created by local artists (Shah 2004; Guzy *et al.* 2009: 116). The Museum of Mankind covering 200 hectares of land deconstructs a conventional European/Western museum concept forced into urban architecture and the authority of timelessness. Contrary to the structural inflexibility of a museum, the change of time and its seasons is inherently included into the museum's optic: the monsoon and the winds change nature and the mud houses of the outdoor exhibits. Local representatives from different

Adivasi communities are invited to give workshops on their healing, artistic or religious systems. Representatives of indigenous communities fundamentally shape the architecture of the museum's open-air exhibits: they build and annually restore the houses in their own way. No one gives instruction how to build or decorate. The houses, decorations, paintings and sculptures arise as indigenous creations. The climate and social change simultaneously also change the museum's face. Urban school children as well as middle-class urban visitors from all over India come to the museum's area to re-discover India's rural and Adivasi identity. Change is included in the museum's vision. Changing workshops and local artists are supposed to change their own and the visitors' perspectives. Going back to one's own locality, a new self-awareness as an artist (*kolakar*) is created among representatives of hitherto marginalized and silenced social groups.

The Museum of Mankind in Bhopal constitutes a model for participatory New and Eco-Museology for the whole of India. As an exemplary place it has influenced all the anthropological and ethnological museums of India, which are run by (a) the Anthropological Survey of India (ASI); (b) the Scheduled Castes and Scheduled Tribes Institutes of the respective Indian states; (c) independent organizations, such as the Adivasi Academy and *Vaacha*, its Museum of Voice in Tejgadh (Gujarat) or (d) museums initiated by private persons. However, the new museum movement still seems fragmented and does not have any Pan-Indian museum cooperation or exchange. The only centralized anthropological museum is apparently the Museum of Mankind itself, as it alone displays ethnically and culturally diversified Micro-India. Other museums remain locally anchored.

The creation of *Purkhauti Muktangan*, an open-air ancestral heritage site near Raipur in Chhattisgarh, represents a similar Eco-Area for reflection on the sustainable relationship between earth, man and environment, reflecting thus the threat of globalization and ruthless industrialization. A critique on urban culture is integrated in the Eco-Area idea.

The Crafts Museum in Delhi dedicated to contemporary rural art and handicraft is another example of alternative museum concepts. This was already designed between the 1950s and 1960s as stated in the museum's vision:

> The institution of the museum, aimed at housing objects of antiquity, is of Western origin. Indians themselves did not have a tradition of setting up museums of fragmented sculptures, rusted swords and out-of-context

> paintings. Broken images were immersed in holy water, worn-out objects were left to decay and merge with the earth from which they were created. It is due to this continuous process of abandonment of the old and reproduction of the new that the traditions of craftsmanship have formidably survived in India. As India adopted the ready-made, Western archaeological museum concept in the nineteenth century, it missed out on the fact that, unlike the West, the 'past' and the 'present' were not so severely divided in its case, and it therefore failed to give adequate importance in its museums to the evolving context of its culture – the living practices of rituals; festivals; weekly markets; picture-shows of itinerant storytellers; the materials, techniques and tools of artisans; the cultural changes and the attitude towards the past and the contemporary tradition as such. It is this overlooked dimension of Indian culture which is emphasised in the concept of the Crafts Museum.[1]

The Crafts Museum reveals a national trend towards the recognition of living contemporary crafts arts as Contemporary Art, creating hence the notion of contemporary Indian art. This turn from contemporary handicraft and folk art to contemporary Indian or Adivasi art was especially visible in the exhibition of Contemporary Indian Adivasi Art Collection 'Other Masters – Contemporary Folk and Tribal Artists' presented at the Crafts Museum in Delhi in 1998 and curated by Dr Jyotindra Jain.

This trend has been followed by other museums such as the private Museum of Folk and Tribal Art in Gurgaon, Haryana, founded by K. C. Aryan in 1984 and devoted to 'Neglected Art in India' of indigenous groups.

Besides New Museology, the UNESCO convention of 2003 on the preservation of the intangible cultural heritage has been particularly influential for Indian museums. This convention ascribes the highest priority to the collection and preservation of intangible cultural heritage in the entire world. Through the UNESCO convention, the scientific and administrative organs of the Indian government have in recent years become increasingly aware of the urgent need to document and preserve the country's immaterial cultural heritage.

This transnational shift towards the immaterial side of culture, as well as the academic discourse on literacy and orality (Goody 1968), has strongly influenced the definition of museums and their collections in India. The concept of 'intangible cultural heritage' has overcome the hegemony of the script, which long excluded or marginalized techniques of knowledge transmission and knowledge systems not encoded in script. The unwritten heritage of societies without script has long been overlooked. The lack of script has become a socio-cultural pattern in the sociological and ideological marginalization of societies dominated by orality.

Adivasi cultures are predominantly cultures of orality. This means that the local values and knowledge systems are enshrined in that which is oral: speech, song, acting, drama and ritual performance. Local knowledge systems and meanings can be understood as indigenous theories without any script. One should keep in mind that the Greek term *theoria* once denoted the physical act of regarding as well as the ritual procession or performance that was regarded; it was both the act of looking upon and the action looked upon itself. In a more general and more contemporary sense *theoria* signifies contemplation or a view of the world. Due to the hegemonic script-centred interest of pre- and post-Independence India, many of these indigenous theories of orality were ignored.

India thus possesses an overwhelming richness of oral and performative forms of indigenous theory (Rangacharya 1982 (1971), 2003; Champion 1996). In India, indigenous theories often have a religious character. They create meaning by establishing a relation between human life and the cosmos, thus constructing a particular rationality of individual action. Indigenous theories are often articulated by means of performing arts or music, both vocal and instrumental (see Vatsyayan 1980; O'Flaherty 1981; Guzy 2008).

Since the transnational academic and institutional shift from literacy to orality, the most significant challenge for Indian anthropological museums has become to represent and to collect the ignored intangible cultural heritage.

How did collections in India start?

Systematic collections started in India in British colonial times. Local specimens of crafts, economic artefacts, dress and ornaments as well as objects related to religious activities and musical instruments deriving from indigenous peoples and from local rural contexts were collected by British officers and researchers. In the colonial terminology the collected objects were labelled 'tribal' artefacts, objects and specimens. In this context the problematic term 'tribe' was introduced to India in the mid-nineteenth century as an administrative and ideological category (Guha 1951: 152–190; Hacker 2003: 30–32). By then the colonial terminology was coloured by a racial ideology that categorized the diverse ethnic communities of India according to an evolutionary anthropometric typology (Guha 1926: 1–81).

Colonial administrators and researchers gathered the material and visual culture of indigenous communities of South Asia in order either to send them to numerous European museums or to assemble them in newly founded museums in India.

One good example for the foundation of such a museum is the British colonial research institution of the Asiatic Society in Kolkata, which was created in 1784 by Sir William Jones (Chakrabarty 2008: 2–28). In 1839, the Asiatic Society suggested the establishment of a public museum in Kolkata, which was finally founded in 1875 as the Indian Museum in Kolkata, the oldest public museum in India.[2] In due course important collections of the Asiatic Society were transferred to the Indian Museum. After Independence in 1947 the ethnographic collections of the Indian Museum were administered by the newly created Anthropological Survey of India, which as an autonomous research unit had the explicit aims to document, collect and spread knowledge on local Indian communities.

Since 1945, the Anthropological Survey of India has started vigorous collection activities in accumulating abundant ethnographic material including audio-visual documentations of local communities. Post-Independence internal Indian collections became a matter of post-colonial pride and emancipation.

An outstanding figure from this period was the British anthropologist Verrier Elwin. He substantially influenced the collections and their development in India. With Verrier Elwin's book *The Tribal Art of Middle India* from 1951, a new trend arose in India: it was the focus on the indigenous material and immaterial culture expressions as vernacular artistic forms. As an ardent disciple of Mahatma Gandhi, Elwin supported his call for a separate status of the Adivasi, arguing for the preservation of their unique forms of life. With his book on *The Tribal Art of Middle India*, the rich cultural and aesthetic traditions of the Adivasi are documented in full detail, with a minimum of interpretation by the author. With Verrier Elwin's work, the shift in perspective already started: artefacts and material culture began to be regarded as art. This book thus enhanced the emergence of the category of *Adivasi art* – also popularly known as tribal art.

Besides the influence of ethnographic collections and the work of Verrier Elwin for the formation of the category of Adivasi art in India, museums have played a crucial role for establishing the new category of art.

The union of handicraft and art mediated by museums has thus created a new art market. Today, different styles of individual Contemporary

Adivasi artists appear in Indian modern art galleries. This turn from contemporary handicraft and folk art into contemporary Indian or Adivasi art was especially visible in the exhibition of the Contemporary Indian 'Other Masters' Collection in the Crafts Museum in Delhi in 1998. This turn is also remarkable in the newly created Rabindranath Tagore Cultural Centre in Kolkata, which gives scope for transnational art projects. Today, traditional *jadhu patua* paintings of the itinerant singer of the indigenous Sora community and the bronze *dokri* figures of the indigenous Rana and Khond communities have become very expensive and exclusive examples of contemporary Indian art. One has thus to acknowledge an increasing commercialization and popularization of Adivasi art for urban and transnational markets.

Adivasi art and global contemporary art

Within the global contemporary art market, the trend towards Adivasi contemporary art also reveals traces of a new Orientalism – as the Eurocentric/Western construction of the 'Other' in order to define 'Oneself'. The infamous MOMA exhibition 'Primitivism in 20th Century Art – Affinity of the Tribal and the Modern' in 1984 has become the basis for the creation of global art (Haustein 2008: 83) through the comparing of de-contextualized aesthetics between the constructed 'Modern' and the 'Tribal'. A subsequent notorious contemporary art exhibition *magiciens de la terre* at the Centre Georges Pompidou and the Grande Halle at the Parc de la Villette in 1989 curated by Jean-Hubert Martin tried to counter-present contemporary global art through inclusion of the exotic cultural Other in the global art world. He invited 100 contemporary artists from all continents to represent their art through their presence and personality. Among them were five Adivasi artists from India.

Both discredited exhibitions displayed a most challenging issue for cultural politics and diplomacy, namely how to avert 'racist parochialism' (Cubitt 2002: 3) in order to represent 'otherness' in a post-oriental, dialogical, polyphonic and post-colonial way – an issue that until today remains critical and unresolved.

The discovery of contemporary Adivasi art by the global art market has incited a highly damaging commercialization of Adivasi art. A shocking event in this context was the sudden suicide of Mr Jangarh Singh Shyam committed in a Japanese museum where he was supposed to create his master works. Shyam, being a member of the Gond community of Madhya Pradesh, was a famous representative of Adivasi contemporary art, had taken part in the *magiciens de la terre* exhibition and had been included as one of the five artists in the prestigious 'Other Masters' exhibition. The tragic example of Jangarh Singh Shyam shows the vulnerability of Adivasi art exposed to global art commercialization. It poses serious concerns about the logics of the mass production of art with its commercial exploitation of local artists, and it questions the appropriateness of adequate presentation and re-presentation of fragile art for any kind of museums or exhibitions.

The transformation from culture to art mediated through museums and then through art exhibitions displays on the one hand a trend towards aestheticization and de-territorialization of contemporary Adivasi art. On the other hand the transformation from culture to art also demonstrates the extreme vulnerability of the fragile art exhibited. The Indian anthropological museum that has become an art gallery and art studio of contemporary Adivasi and rural art will henceforth gain a new social and cultural responsibility.

Notes

1 http://nationalcraftsmuseum.nic.in/about_Museum.htm accessed on 29 April 2014; see Jain/Aggarwala/photographs by Shah 1989.

2 cf. http://www.britannica.com/eb/article-9042286/Indian-Museum; and Sabita Ranjan Sarkar 2005.

References

Basa, Kishor K. 2005. 'Humankind Matters', *Humankind. The Journal of Indira Gandhi Rashtriya Manav Sangrahalaya, Bhopal*, 1: iii–vi.

Bhatnagar, Anupama. 1999. *Museum, Museology and New Museology*. New Delhi: Sundeep Prakashan.

Carrin, Marine and Christophe Jaffrelot (eds). 2002. *Tribus et basses castes. Résistance et autonomie dans la société indienne*, Collection Purusartha, pp. 21–24. Paris: École des hautes études en sciences sociales.

Chakrabarty, Ramakanta. 2008. *The Time and the Present*, pp. 2–28. Kolkata: The Asiatic Society.

Chakravarty, Kalyan K. 2005. 'Indira Gandhi Rashtriya Manav Sangrahalaya: The Noah's Ark'. *Humankind*, 1: 25–30.

Champion, Catherine (ed). 1996. *Traditions orales dans le monde indien*, Collection Purusartha. Paris: Ecole des hautes études en sciences sociales.

Cubitt, Sean. 2002. 'Prologue: In the beginning – "Third Text and the Politics of Art"', in Rasheed Araeen, Sean Cubitt and Ziauddin Sardar (eds), *The Third Text Reader: On Art, Culture, and Theory*, pp. 1–8. London and New York: Continuum.

Dodd, Jocelyn and Richard Sandell (eds). 2001. *Including Museums: Perspectives on Museums, Galleries and Social Inclusion*. Leicester: Research Centre for Museums and Galleries.

Ganslmayr, Herbert. 1989. 'Die Bewegung "Neue Museologie"', in Hermann Auer (ed), *Museologie Neue Wege – Neue Ziele*, pp. 79–88. Munich: K.G. Saur.

Goody, Jack (ed). 1968. *Literacy in Traditional Societies*. Cambridge: Cambridge University Press.

Guha, Bijara Sankar. 1926. 'The Comparative Anthropometry of Indian Castes and Tribes', *Man in India*, 6: 1–81.

———. 1994 (1951). 'The Indian Aborigines and Their Administration', in Chandan Roychaudhuri (ed), *The Asiatic Society and Anthropological Studies in India*, pp. 152–90. Calcutta: Asiatic Society.

Guzy, Lidia, Rainer Hatoum, and Susan Kamel. 2009. *Museum Islands*. Berlin: Panama Verlag.

———. 2010. *From Imperial Museum to Communication Centre? On the New Role of Museums as Mediators Between Science and Non-Western Societies*. Würzburg: Königshausen und Neumann Verlag.

Hacker, Katherine. 2003. 'Tribal art', in Margret A. Mills, Peter J. Claus and Sarah Diamond (eds), *South Asian Folklore: An Encyclopedia*, pp. 30–2. New York: Routledge.

Haustein, Lydia. 2008. *Global Icons. Globale Bildinszenierung und kulturelle Identität*. Göttingen: Wallstein Verlag.

Jain, Jyotindra. 1998. *Other Masters*. New Delhi: Crafts Museum.

Pfeffer Georg. 1997. 'The Scheduled Tribes of Middle India as a Unit. Problems of Internal and External Comparison', in G. Pfeffer and Deepak K. Behera (eds), *Contemporary Society: Tribal Studies Vol. I: Structure and Process*, pp. 3–27. New Delhi: Concept Publishing.

Shah, Shampa. 2004. *Anugunj. Catalogue of the Mythological Trail Featuring Folk and Adivasi Myths of India*. Bhopal: Indira Gandhi Rashtriya Manav Sangrahalaya.

Wessler, Adelheid. 2007. *Von Lebendabgüssen, Heimatmuseen und Cultural Villages. Museale Repräsentation des Selbst und des Anderen im (De-)Kolonisierungsprozess Namibias*. Unpublished Ph.D. dissertation, University of Cologne, pp. 8–9. Retrieved from http://deposit.d-nb.de/cgi-in/dokserv?idn=985998385&dok_var=d1&dok_ext=pdf&filename=985998385.pdf.

4 Aesthetics of representation

Media and Canadian Aboriginal resistance

Shaily Sharma

> [A] crisis situation precipitates a moment of truth for the political system. It is also a moment of truth for the mass media. Communications studies have shown that in time of crisis, coverage tends to become more alike, and the many differences are submerged with the filtering out of unimportant political details. The focus is on the common interest and the differences that do show up are seen as being fundamental in nature.
>
> (Siegel 1983: 210–211)

Media, not only as a national institution, but also as a powerful mediating structure, can, on the one hand, play both an enabling and a disabling role in the sense that it can threaten, contain and manage marginal voices (here, Aboriginal voices) and, on the other, facilitate the process of making repressed voices heard and understood in society. According to Robinson and Charron, one of the primary functions of media, besides presenting the living reality of different social groups, is to fashion public consensus on major issues of the day (1989: 147). However, the mainstream Canadian media appears to be essentially integrationist in its approach towards the issues of native autonomy and sovereignty, willing to subsume the native presence under the shadow of the politics of the great mosaic.

This chapter is a direct reflection on the ways in which the media portray the image of the Canadian Aboriginals, how the media discourse serves to further the myths and stereotypes about the indigenous peoples in a way that constructs their biased and opinionated image amidst the mainstream news consumers. In order to elucidate the media's negative, monolithic representations of the Aboriginals and their concerns and constant stereotyping of these peoples in the media discourse, textual analysis of three strategic events in the history of Aboriginal–non-Aboriginal relations within Canada has been looked at (1) the Mohawk standoff at Oka, 1990; (2) the Gustafsen Lake standoff, 1995 and (3) the Caledonia Lake Conflict, 2006. The prominent methodology in the study is discourse analysis, which is an analytical tool for understanding social reality. It is qualitative in approach and focuses on surface structures as well as underlying semantic or latent structures of the text (Van Dijk 1983). According to Hall, discourse analysis 'gives greater attention to uncovering implied meanings that represent ideological positions' (1980). Hall further explicates, 'Discourse analysis incorporates the broader contextual evidence surrounding text allowing an interpretation of the latent or ideological meaning beneath manifest language . . . it seeks out recurring patterns that point to latent meanings and allow inference as to the source' (1975: 15). Applying this methodology to media discourse, one is able to discern specific events, which upon analysis reveal layers of underlying meaning and the context built in the process that reflects a particular ideological stance around the signified event.

In the context of the Aboriginal reportage, the press derives its performance largely from the images that have been floating since the early encounters of the Europeans with the Natives. During the early years of colonization, the indigenous peoples of Canada were understood and represented through the imaginations of the European settlers. The dominant image of the Aboriginals conjured by the whites was that of 'noble savages' and the stereotypes used to establish this image in contrast to the whites were 'primitive', 'extinct', 'vanishing', 'uncivilized' and 'backward'. Such images and stereotypes helped the European colonists to establish their own supremacy over the Aboriginals, which subsequently led to the creation of hierarchy within the society and consequent exploitation based on the polarity thus created. Rob McMahon's essay 'Bringing Peace to Practice? The Need to Consider Journalism Practice when Reforming Aboriginal Media Coverage in Canada' also sheds light on mainstream journalism practice that creates a dichotomy with respect to the Aboriginal–non-Aboriginal relationship:

> much of the coverage of First Nations groups in Canada perpetuates representations of conflict between Aboriginal and non-Aboriginal Canadians. Beyond winners and losers in court, during dramatic events such as protests or standoffs, portrayals of Aboriginal groups are similar to those that appear in wartime news correspondence. Conflict between Aboriginal parties and the state is portrayed as a struggle between enemies, and First Nations groups are framed as being located outside of, and in opposition to, the Canadian nation-state.
>
> (2008: 2)

Though expressions of these images changed with time, they still continue to affect the performance of the press and the general understanding of these peoples in the mainstream society.

Journalists as agents of social and cultural dissemination and as news producers play a vital role in putting the society and nation in a right frame for the general readership. They build a forum through the mass media where each individual and group should be able to access impartial intercultural and completely contextual understanding of events and social groups. Though based on the assumptions and ideals of pluralist, liberal-democratic and multi-cultural ethics, mainstream media fails at delivering its goals. With respect to the coverage of Aboriginal issues, journalists are often lacking in the indigenous historical and cultural knowledge, and the early political treaties and agreements between the Aboriginals and the settler Europeans, which is indispensable for understanding any contemporary event. Chibnall quotes Marx to attest to the importance of the historical context in assessing the validity of contemporary states of affairs: 'without history reality becomes vulnerable to the interpretation of a dominant ideology' (1977: 24). To add to this journalistic malpractice, reporters unthinkingly resort to the use of stereotypes that offer the ease of delivering news since they act as a shortcut to appeal to the common sense of news consumers. As Harding puts it:

> By invoking stereotypes, journalists avail themselves of a ready-made structure that they can hang their stories on. . . . Journalists do not derive their stereotypes based on actual contact with those people who are the object of them, but rather from their stereotypical ideas based on a wide variety of indirect sources, including their immediate work and social circles, and from premises that filter through the organizational hierarchy.
>
> (2005: 325)

Fleras and Elliot observe that the mainstream media portray Aboriginal peoples as a 'social problem', either 'having' social problems that are resolved by the taxpayers' money or 'creating' problems that are a threat to the social order of the nation. Under the weight of such clichéd reporting, media coverage of Aboriginal issues calls for reforms in the daily practice of journalism since it is not all-inclusive and contextually appropriate (1992: 9). Led by these misperceptions, journalists resort to 'sensationalizing unfamiliar religious practices, making simplistic inferences, and insensitively representing Native traditions' (Lambertus 2004: 194). In addition to the latent inadequacy of journalists, Lambertus discovered other inhibiting factors within the structure of the media institutions that allow little space to report Aboriginal issues in the right frames, as appropriate to the context in question. She quotes one reporter who was sent into an Aboriginal camp explaining the constraints put by the editorial practices on the final production of news: 'The editors were going for the drama, they weren't going for the philosophical' (2004: 59–60). Robert Hackett also points to similar practices within the press saying that while journalism 'operates within a nexus of sometimes contradictory forces that may allow scope for agency and alternative practices . . . those spaces are limited, constrained by powerful forces both within and outside the media field' (2006: 5).

Abundant use of stereotypes, labels and symbols in the media discourse, which are required by both the journalists and the audience, respectively, to frame the news and analyse and understand the content of the news, however, serves the Aboriginals damagingly and bears far-reaching consequences for them. These stereotypes feed into the media's construction of the 'common sense', which is used by the audience to interpret news. Common sense, as articulated by Nesbitt-Larking, is 'a closed form of thought, resistant to curiosity, challenge or change' (2001: 79). Once established by social institutions, such as media, it acquires unquestioned, universal authority that overlooks or is unaware of its 'particular and partial reading of the world' (2001: 79). Common sense is greatly bolstered by media imperatives woven in the Aboriginal discourse, such as symbolization, distortion, exaggeration, simplification, sensationalization, titillation, prediction, magnification, melodramatic vocabulary, violence and conflict. These imperatives leave little space for alternative viewpoints and competing perspectives that hold the capacity to put the event in proper context for audiences' perception.

As Harding has observed in his research on 'The Media, Aboriginal People and Common Sense', stereotyping the Aboriginals has long been a feature of Canadian media discourse. However, it is disturbing to find that the new stereotypes are replacing the older ones or are co-existent with the older ones. According to Harding's study, 'the most prevalent emergent stereotype . . . is one which casts into doubt the ability of Aboriginal people to successfully manage their own affairs. This new stereotype appears at a critical juncture in the relationship between Aboriginal and non-Aboriginal people' (2005: 312). The emergence of this new stereotype of Aboriginal people as 'incompetent or corrupt financial managers', 'unable to meet modern standards of governance' and 'taking advantage of the system', can be understood against the background of the highly debated Indian Act of 1876, which aims to institutionalize the Aboriginals under the Canadian political, social and legal system, making them subservient to the Canadian government while losing their sovereignty. Through such stereotypes, media frames the 'common sense' about Aboriginal peoples that naturally leads the audience to believe that Aboriginals are incompetent to look after their affairs. These stereotypes bear destructive consequences for the Aboriginals for they result in 'glossing over critical nuances of issues and the conflation of diverse individuals, communities and First Nations . . . one dimensional, de-contextualized coverage of important issues which further entrenches the "communication gulf" between Aboriginal and non-Aboriginal people' (Harding 2005: 325–326). The conditions of conflict appear from the news coverage of Aboriginal issues, which further distorts their image.

Harding narrows down three major stereotypes in his study, identified by the Royal Commission on Aboriginal Peoples (RCAP), which were present in the early Canadian press and are still in use in the contemporary media discourse: the 'Aboriginal as pathetic victim', the 'Aboriginal as angry warrior' and the 'Aboriginal as noble environmentalist' (2005: 319). Harding further observes that during the 1990s, the mainstream Canadian press used news frames such as 'Aboriginal People as Inferior', 'Heroic White Man Saving Primitive Aboriginal People' and 'The Triumph of Reason over Emotion' in Aboriginal discourse that would further misrepresent the native peoples and distance the audience from capturing the historical depth of the contexts in question. Without ignoring the fact that the contemporary media discourse shows greater sensitivity towards the Aboriginals and their concerns, we can still find ample evidence of outright racism, negative stereotyping and anti-Aboriginal bias in the reportage of Aboriginal issues and 'references such as "Native culture is a mess", "miserable Native culture", "Canada's Aboriginals face a bleak future", and "despair, poverty and hopelessness are norm"' (2005: 317). The articles, headlines, editorials and front-page coverage are replete with similar negative connotations, damaging stereotypes and ahistorical and de-contextualized information that builds the 'common sense' of the mainstream audience and further perpetuates these stereotypes in society. News articles embedded in war-like discourse, set in conflict and loaded with stereotypes leave no space for the Aboriginal cultural and historical nuances in context to be transmitted to the news consumers.

While analysing the media discourse on the Aboriginals and their issues, it becomes essential to understand the news stories in the 'frames' they are woven in. What a 'frame' is and how it affects the public opinion and common sense of the audience needs to be understood for the discourse analysis of Aboriginal reportage. According to Stephen D. Reese, a frame is a multi-sited structure, which moves from textual structures to mental structures (Reese in D'Angelo and Kuypers, 22). Frames are 'embedded in a web of culture, an image that naturally draws attention to the surrounding cultural context and the threads that connect them' (Reese 2010: 18). Framing, as an analytical approach,

> represents a process for organizing information by drawing attention to some aspects of reality as normal and desirable, but away from others as irrelevant or inferior – in the hopes of encouraging a preferred reading consistent with seeing like the media. . . . The interplay of deeply embedded news values and norms with institutional routines and organizational imperatives imposes limits on the boundaries of discourse.
>
> (Lakoff and Ferguson 2006; Fleras 2011: 13)

Thus, frames are specific media constructions that are rooted in ideological hegemony and that further strengthen the status quo of the society. In the context of Aboriginal media discourse, frames serve to further the existing Euro-centric hegemony, deflect facts around Aboriginal land claims, their culture and tradition and mould anti-Aboriginal public opinion in the news consumers, so that hegemony remains unquestioned and voices of dissent silenced. Although framed events can be contested through counter-frames that represent alternative perspective of the event, the dominant frame appears more intelligible because it syncs well with the common sense of the mainstream news consumers. Fleras has identified five major frames laden with layers of latent meanings and symbols that are employed by reporters to pigeonhole Aboriginal issues: (1) political (from unrest to militancy), (2) social justice (defence of rights), (3) racial (discrimination to stereotypes), (4) legal and (5) economic (costs or benefits). In understanding the news coverage of Aboriginal issues, these frames serve to provide a background derived from a common-sense understanding of the events. Within the context of the Aboriginals, Schlesinger notes, 'Inferential frameworks of "law and (dis)order", the "violent society", and the "threat to democracy", reduce complex political events to "commonsense understandings"' (1978: 224).

However, conflict remains central to the building of all and any of the frames. It is important to note that conflict has fundamentally remained a forceful factor in the production of news. Conflict, used in daily journalistic practice, presents different segments of nation as always in a state of turmoil and restlessness. Schultz defines conflict as the key factor in deciding the newsworthiness of any event: 'When the news criterion of conflict is used in the daily construction of newsworthiness, this means selecting stories and angles accentuating conflicts of interest between people, between causes, organizations, etc.' (2007: 197). He further quotes Pierre Bourdieu to articulate that, 'the journalistic field is part of the field of power, not least because the constant cultural production of social discourse not only implies production of categories for "vision" of the social world, but at the same time, categories of "division"' (2006: 192). Therefore, especially with reference to the Aboriginal news reportage, conflict is made prominent and the basis for deepening the dichotomy between the native and non-native communities. It serves to further crystallize the marginal position of the Aboriginals in the social order of Canada and to divert their attempts towards cultural and political expression and self-determination.

The Mohawk Crisis at Oka, Quebec, during the 1990s has been a major flashpoint in media discourse and communications studies. It is also critical in the history of Aboriginal–non-Aboriginal relations in Canada, for the Natives took up arms in protest for the first time ever, and the government too deployed the military for the first time to deal with an internal crisis. The Oka standoff also became a catalyst and precursor for other crisis situations, significantly affecting and altering the nature of Aboriginal–government relations in Canada. Looking back at the history of Oka dating back to 1781, the land has long been contested, with Aboriginals protesting against frequent encroachments. However, this dispute turned into protest and opposition when the municipality of Oka proposed to expand a golf course into the Mohawk's sacred burial ground, 'The Pines', from early 1989. However, things flared up by early 1990, and the agitated Mohawks at Kanesatake erected barricades in retaliation on 11 March 1990. Initially the protests were received and relayed by media in ambiguous categories, such as 'environmental issues', 'internal factions between Mohawks' and 'territorial protection'. It was only by early July, that the whole episode gathered momentum to make way to the front page of media. On 6 July 1990, the French-language newspaper, *La Presse*, announced the story on the front page as 'Resistance Hardens at Oka', accompanied by photographs of masked and armed Warriors. On 11 July 1990, *Sureté du Québec* (SQ) officers attacked the protest site, which was followed by a gunfight that led to the death of a police officer, following which the story gained the status of national news and was redefined as a land claims issue. From then on, media focused on the theme of violence, while the long-standing claim for territory and sovereignty was obscured by the war imagery that dominated the news stories.

Following a series of unfortunate incidents, the Aboriginals erected another barricade on the Mercier Bridge that led to Montreal, which disrupted access to the city for daily commuters. All efforts at negotiations failed as the government was unwilling to accept the land claims of Mohawks and instead handed an ultimatum to the natives to either dissolve the standoff or face military intervention. On 8 August, the SQ was replaced by troops of the Canadian Forces to take charge of the situation.

The Oka crisis has been widely studied under qualitative discourse analysis and news framing to understand the role of media in voicing the silenced subjects. Research indicates that the coverage at Oka was based primarily on official sources and little attention was paid towards the Aboriginal perspective on the happenings. Many commentators have pointed towards evidence that suggested that 'some media organizations were too close to government sources to be objective about the events at Oka' (Harding 2005: 313). Some of the major newspapers put out screaming headlines to magnify the conflict between the Aboriginals and the Canadian government: 'Rough Justice: After Oka Will the Violence Spread?' (*Maclean's*, 6 August 1990); 'The Fury of Oka: After the Showdown, Indian Leaders Promise a Violent Autumn' (*Maclean's*, 10 September 1990); 'Mohawk Militancy' (*Ottawa Citizen*, 15 September 1990); 'The Mohawk Warriors: Heroes or Thugs?' (*Toronto Star*, 24 November 1990); 'The Making of a Warrior' (*Saturday Night*, April 1991) and Aislin's political cartoon of the 'Mafia Warrior' (*Montreal Gazette*, 30 April 1990) (details from Valaskakis 1994). The articles and editorials in *The Gazette* were replete with negative vocabulary, such as 'Mohawks actions are revolting, intolerable'; 'arrest Mohawks, they are despicable, intolerable'; 'gang of criminals', 'Indian organized crime'; 'professional terrorists'; 'masked criminals'; 'vandals'; 'foul-mouthed exhibitionists' and 'militant warriors' (Keller 1996: 45). Such and similar vocabulary was used for the Mohawks in the French newspapers like *La Presse* as well.

During the period of the standoff, media focused solely on framing the Aboriginals as violent warriors, intimidating the peace and order of the state. One particular image that emerged as the most dominant stereotype during the conflict was that of 'bandanna-masked, khaki-clad, gun-toting warriors' (RCAP 1996: 6; quoted in Harding 326). Evidence indicates that such terminology that categorized Mohawks as 'criminals', 'thugs', 'warriors', 'extremists', 'militants' and the entire episode as 'war-like' originated from the government and other elite mainstream agencies, such as bureaucrats and government spokespersons. As Harding observes,

> Rather than inform audiences of the context and history of the complex issues at stake, media outlets cast the story in terms of familiar, marketable stereotypes. While this type of coverage might play into the public's fascination with conflict and violence, it results in an entrenchment of old ways of thinking and represents a missed opportunity to educate the Canadian public about issues that have profound significance for Aboriginal and non-Aboriginal people alike.
>
> (2005: 326)

Some researchers are of the opinion that the reporters were actually campaigning for the official 'law and order' instead of situating the Aboriginal voice in an appropriate historical and political context within the society. The role that the majority of the mainstream media played deflected the exact focus of the crisis and attributed illegitimacy to the Aboriginals' claims of sovereignty and self-determination. *The Gazette* declared the Oka crisis as 'no less than Indian organized crime' (July 28, 1990). The press functioned in a neo-colonial fashion to marginalize the Aboriginal voice and secure the status quo in society, ensuring the monoliths of Eurocentric hierarchy in the so-called multi-cultural mosaic.

The Gustafsen Lake standoff, which took place in British Columbia in 1995 and has been declared the largest paramilitary operation in Canadian history, also reflected similar series of events and media reception. This, too, stemmed from the long history of land claims conflicts between the Aboriginals and non-Aboriginals and violation of treaties. The conflict began with the Aboriginals assembling at a specific site in ancestral Secwepemc near the Gustafsen Lake to perform the traditional ceremony of Sundancing in 1989. The site was also pasture land whose grazing rights were with a non-Aboriginal American rancher, Lyle James. However, the Sundancers had reached an agreement with James that they would assemble on the land every summer for the Sundance cycle period, but would not erect any permanent structures for the ceremony. However, in 1995, during the Sundance performance, the Aboriginals had to put up a fence around the sacred area to keep cattle away from the ceremony, which was unacceptable to James. On being asked to vacate the land, Sundancers refused because they could not interrupt the Sundance ceremony. Tensions escalated as some cowboys harassed the Sundancers one night, and minor incidents of a similar nature followed.

Gradually, the argument between the Sundancers and James over a parcel of land turned into a bigger issue of Aboriginal land rights and treaties. The Sundancers refused to leave the site after the ceremony and decided to claim it back. During the initial stages of the dispute, the RCMP merely acted as observers and mediators. But in August 1995, when the situation turned volatile, it was asked to take direct action. Thereafter, the RCMP first sent a camouflaged Emergency Response Team (ERT) to assess the arms and weapons in the Aboriginals' camp. This move triggered off incidents of firing from both sides. Media were not allowed into the site of direct action, and they were located in a centre called 100 Mile House, away from the disputed land. The RCMP further severed all communications to the camp. Journalists were dependent on the RCMP and other government sources for the coverage of events. Quite obviously, the mainstream newspapers were filled with information that was skewed and that portrayed Sundancers as terrorists, criminals, militants, a threat to law and order and a social problem.

Lambertus describes the RCMP's role in news framing and content manipulation in her detailed and well-investigated case study of the Gustafsen Lake dispute, *Wartime Images, Peacetime Wounds: The Media and the Gustafsen Lake Standoff*. The crux of her research lies in revealing and demonstrating the nexus between the Aboriginal protestors and the Canadian government and how the police and the media negotiate the news content to preserve the existing social hierarchy and delegitimize voices of dissent. According to her, the events at the disputed area 'provided the impetus for the RCMP to shift their interpretation of the situation from a civil dispute to a serious criminal offence. The police defined the shooting incidents and the possession of dangerous weapons as acts of terrorism. This label implied that the social order was under a serious threat' (2004: 45).

The 1996 *Report of the Royal Commission on Aboriginal Peoples* (RCAP), which ironically was running parallel to the Gustafsen conflict, interrogated the negative media representations of the Aboriginal peoples in Canada. It declared that the media are responsible for perpetuating negative and damaging stereotypes that create hostility towards these peoples in the mainstream society. The document further quotes the Canadian

Association of Journalists, which accepts that the characterization of Aboriginals in the mainstream media 'often contains misinformation, sweeping generalizations, and galling stereotypes about native and native affairs' (vol. 3: 634). The report emphasizes that such media discourse deflects the Aboriginal land claims and other issues from their specific context and meaning and treats the various sites of crises as opportunities for disseminating stereotypes, rather than informing and educating the non-Aboriginal audiences about the Aboriginal historical and political specificities (vol. 3: 623).

During the Gustafsen Lake standoff, the RCMP had sabotaged the entire site of action and had barred media and journalists from entering the area. So, the communication of media men was entirely one-sided and solely dependent on the RCMP reportage. The RCMP had set up Williams Lake Press Conference for reporting the events at the dispute and framing the news content from their perspective. Since the RCMP was the only authority physically present during the crisis, their information and leads dominated the news accounts. Interestingly, one journalist, William Johnson, reportedly admitted, 'I'm uneasy about the reporting. Journalists have been kept away from the scene by the RCMP and the native occupiers could not tell their side of the story because Mounties have cut off their means of communication . . .' (*Montreal Gazette*, 29 August 1995). In September as well shooting incidents continued and the RCMP decided to bring in military personnel who later laid land mines in the area surrounding the camp. Heavy police and military intervention created panic among the Aboriginals who were protesting to claim their rights on the contested land. Finally, the stage of negotiation arrived but only against a background of military interference, incidents of shooting and several Aboriginals being arrested and charged. Later, the government was condemned not only for putting excessive police and military pressure on the Sundancers but also for downplaying and under-representing their role in public.

Another major standoff occurred in recent years in Caledonia on 28 February 2006; this was an outcome of years of protests and resentment against the federal government's policy on Aboriginals' land claims settlements. Under the leadership of two Six Nations women, Jamieson and Smith, the Aboriginal peoples of the province of Ontario led a peaceful, informational campaign to educate non-native peoples about the government's encroachment policies and the historical 'Haldimand' Proclamation issued on 25 October 1784, which accorded land rights to natives of the Mohawk nation on the 950,000 acres extending six miles deep on either side of the Grand River. Since then, despite the legal settlement, the government has been encroaching upon the native land, and the natives have been protesting against the injustices. As part of the centuries-old struggle to draw the attention of the mainstream society to the facts surrounding their land claims, and stage their protest against government's coercive practices, the Aboriginals of the district of Caledonia endorsed the 'Six Miles Deep' campaign, which culminated in the occupation of a tract of disputed land. This has remained the longest political direct action ever taken by the natives in Canadian history, wherein the 'members of the Six Nations physically occupied and peacefully halted construction on a housing development known as the "Douglas Creek Estates" (DCE), in Caledonia, Ontario' (Vyce 2010: 8). As the protests and the 'occupation' progressed, many other native communities and the Warrior's Society from all over Canada came in to support the claims and cause of the Six Nations in Caledonia. On the other hand, Henco Industries, whose housing development plans on the now 'occupied' land were thwarted, filed a complaint against the protestors, in response to which the court issued injunctions against the natives and ordered them to vacate the land. But the Aboriginals' disobedience continued, followed by a second injunction and the Ontario Provincial Police's forceful evacuation of the land. Since the protestors did not recognize the jurisdiction of the provincial court, they demanded direct political action from the federal government.

What followed after this happens to reflect similar incidents of Aboriginal protests against the government's unfair handling of lands claim disputes, media's stereotypical coverage of the 'conflict', and the mainstream society's typical reaction framed by 'common sense' knowledge of Aboriginals and their issues. Once again, evoking the memories of the 16-year-old Oka crisis, the local newspapers manipulated facts and utilized government sources to present the coverage of the Caledonia conflict couched in myths and stereotypes.

> Because of the violent acts that were perpetrated by some 'protestors' and the barricades that blocked residents from traveling freely in and around Caledonia, the 'occupation and protest' has been described in local newspapers as: a 'drama', 'terrorism', 'illegal', a 'disruption' to the 'normal' lives of the residents of Caledonia, a 'sad reality of political correctness run amok',

> a 'fiasco', a 'state of emergency', 'idiocy', tearing apart Canada for 'ridiculous reasons', 'wrongheaded', a 'circus', 'stupid and unnecessary', 'violent', 'bogus', an 'intolerable situation', a 'living nightmare', 'chaos and mayhem', activities financed by 'organized crime', 'absolute nonsense', 'a war in our own country', 'the epicenter of a civil "cold war" conflict raging across the nation', the 'Wild West', 'poor and/or shameful behaviour on the part of the Six Nations', and 'inexcusable and immature'.
>
> (Vyce 2010: 11–12)

However, not all residents reacted and responded to the native protests in language that affirmed the stories in newspapers. In a move to support the Aboriginal protests over the land rights, and ensure speedy settlement of long-standing issues, citizens of Caledonia came together with local trade union activists and the Six Nations to form a solidarity group called 'Community Friends for Peace and Understanding with Six Nations'. Since the Oka crisis of the 1990s, the Aboriginal peoples have been able to garner some understanding and solidarity with the non-Aboriginal citizens of the country on issues of indigenous self-representation and land claims. Aboriginal bodies such as the Native Action Committee on the Media have also come into action to counter racism prevalent in the press and the stereotypes and images constructed and perpetuated through the media discourse. Even the mainstream media have begun to employ Aboriginal journalists and reporters to achieve greater validity of coverage on Aboriginal issues. To complement the process of achieving objectivity and factuality in Aboriginal news discourse, mainstream 'white' journalists are systemically trained in especially designed Aboriginal diversity programs, where they learn about the historical and cultural legacy of the First Nations of Canada.

Further, Aboriginal awareness towards the process of mainstream media's representation of them and their issues couched under myths, symbols and stereotypes, devoid of history and context and audiences' one-dimensional perception of Aboriginals has led to the emergence of an indigenous press. In response to the dominant journalism practice of inadequate representation of the Aboriginals, the indigenous media have moved on to appropriate mainstream communication technology to voice their own concerns and set things straight and within a context for Canadian audiences. This transformation in modes of Indigenous representation has enabled the Canadian Aboriginals to meet their own social and political needs and to create their presence in the social spaces within the nation. The indigenous media serve as a weapon to put forth native issues, demand their rights and present the mainstream society with factual, contextual information regarding their problems. Acknowledging the necessity of indigenous media, Prins observes: 'In an intervention that paralleled the post-colonial move to "write back" against colonial masters, Indian activists began to "shoot back", reversing the colonial gaze by constructing their own visual media, telling their stories on their own terms' (2004: 518).

Conclusion

To summarize, today the Aboriginal peoples are not only struggling with the government for their land rights but also with the mainstream Canadian media to create their own aesthetics of representation and rectify their distorted portrayals. Gramsci aptly articulates with respect to the indigenous renaissance that the Canadian Aboriginals 'have passed suddenly from the state of political passivity to a certain activity, and put forward demands which, taken together . . . add up to a revolution' (Gramsci 1971: 210).

Note: In the course of this chapter, I have used the terms 'native', 'Aboriginals', 'First Nations', 'Indians' and 'indigenous peoples' interchangeably, without intending any debate on the critical use of these terms.

References

Bourdieu, Pierre. 2006. 'On Television', in M.G. Durham and D. Kellner (eds), *Media and Cultural Studies: Keyworks*, 2nd ed., pp. 328–36. Malden: Blackwell.

Chibnall, S. 1977. *An Analysis of Crime Reporting in the British Press*. London: Tavistock Press.

Fleras, Augie. 2011. *The Media Gaze: Representations of Diversities in Canada*. Vancouver: University of British Columbia Press.

Fleras, Augie and Jean Leonard Elliott. 1992. *The Nations Within: Aboriginal-State Relations in the United States, and New Zealand*. Toronto: Oxford University Press.

Gramsci, A. 1971. *Selections from the Prison Notebooks*. New York: International Publishers.

Hackett, Robert. 2006. 'Is Peace Journalism Possible? Three Frameworks for Assessing Structure and Agency in News Media', *Conflict & Communication Online*, 5(2): 1–13.

Hall, Stuart. 1975. 'Introduction', in A. C. H. Smith, E. Immirizi and T. Blackwell (eds), *Paper Voices: The Popular Press and Social Change 1935–1965*, pp. 9–24. London: Chatto and Windus.

———. 1980. 'Introduction to Media Studies at the Centre', in S. Hall, D. Hobson, A. Lowe and P. Willis (eds), *Culture, Media, Language: Working Papers in Cultural Studies 1972–1979*, pp. 2–35. London: Hutchinson.

Harding, Robert. 2005. 'The Media, Aboriginal People and Common Sense', *The Canadian Journal of Native Studies*, XXV(1): 311–35.

Keller, Elizabeth Andrea. 1996. *Anglos with Feathers: A Content Analysis of French and English Media Coverage in Quebec on the Oka Crisis of 1990*. Unpublished Ph.D. dissertation, University of British Columbia.

Lakoff, George and Sam Ferguson. 2006. *The Framing of Immigration*. Berkeley, CA: The Rockridge Institute.

Lambertus, S. 2004. *Wartime Images, Peacetime Wounds: The Media and the Gustafsen Lake Standoff*. Toronto: University of Toronto Press.

Montreal Gazette. 1990. 'Editorial: 'Less Like Warriors Than Thugs', July 17.

———. 1995. 'RCMP Should Avoid Waco-Style Shootout in B.C.', August 29.

Nesbitt-Larking, Paul. 2001. *Politics, Society, and the Media*. Peterborough: Broadview Press.

Prins, Harald E. L. 2004. 'Visual Anthropology', in Thomas Biolsi (ed), *A Companion to the Anthropology of American Indians*, pp. 506–25. Oxford: Blackwell.

Reese, Stephen D. 2010. 'Finding Frames in a Web of Culture: The Case of the War on Terror', in Paul D'Angelo and Jim A, Kupyers (eds), *Doing News Framing Analysis: Empirical and Theoretical Perspectives*, pp. 17–42. New York: Routledge.

Report of the Royal Commission on Aboriginal Peoples. Ottawa: Royal Commission on Aboriginal Peoples, 1996.

Robinson, Gertrude and Claude-Yves Charron. 1989. 'Television News and the Public Sphere: The Case of the Quebec Referendum', in Marc Rabbi and Peter Bruck (eds), *Communication for and Against Democracy*, pp. 147–63. Montreal: Black Rose Books.

Schlesinger, Philip. 1978. *Putting 'Reality' Together: BBC News*. London: Constable.

Schultz, Ida. 2007. 'The Journalistic Gut Feeling: Journalistic Doxa, News Habitus and Orthodox News Values', *Journalism Practice*, 1(2): 190–202.

Siegel, Arthur. 1983. *Politics and the Media in Canada*. Toronto: McGraw Hill-Ryerson.

Valaskakis, Gail.1994. 'Rights and Warriors: First Nations, Media and Identity', *ARIEL*, 25(1) (January): 60–72.

Van Dijk, Teun A. 1983. 'Discourse Analysis: Its Development and Application to the Structure of News', *Journal of Communication*, 33(2): 20–43.

Vyce, Amanda. 2010. *Protesting the 'Protest': Understanding 'Non-Native' Reactions and Responses to the Six Nations Land 'Occupation and Protest' in Caledonia, Ontario*. MA thesis, McMaster University. Retrieved from http://digitalcommons.mcmaster.ca/opendissertations/4230.

5 The forgotten tribe

The Kuravars of Tamil Nadu

A. *Maria Mercy Amutha and* G. *Christopher*

Kuravars belong to the nomadic tribe commonly known as Gypsies. It is hard to ignore them as they appear decked with colourful beads, carrying trays filled with small essentials like hairpins, clips, bands and bangles that immediately catch the eye of any woman even during the rush hours in a local train in Tamil Nadu. The Kuravars belong to one of the indigenous tribes who hail from the Kuranji Hills. The Tamil word 'Kuravar' comes from *Kundru+Avan*, that is hill man, which denotes his origin. In addition to this evidence, the song 'Kutrala Kuravanji', which compromises a series of verses written by Thirukuda Rasappa Kavirayar and is said to have been written more than 300 years ago speaks of the Kurava women and men dwelling in the Kurunji Hills. The verses tell the story of a Gypsy who foretells Vasantvalli's destiny, that is her union with Lord Siva; it also portrays women as clever with a taste for beautiful things and men on the 'not so clever' side. Other literary evidence is *Perunkurunji* or *Kurunji Paattu* written by Kabilar (1956).

Our account of Gypsies here is based on the following note:

> The roots of this problem are ancient, dating almost to the first European arrival of the Roma from India, believed to have occurred perhaps as early as the twelfth century. According to the magisterial eleventh edition of the *Encyclopedia Britannica* (1910), the Gypsies were 'a wandering folk scattered through every European land, over the greater part of western Asia and Siberia; found also in Egypt and the northern coast of Africa, in America and even Australia'.
>
> (Cooper 2001/2002: 69)

This short note does seem to give an idea that these tribes belonged to India, although which part of India is not very clear. Kabilar's *Kurunji Paattu* may suggest one answer: they originally belonged to the Kutralam Hills and became nomadic due to the arrival of the Aryans. Furthermore, the tribe was for the first time discriminated against as a low-caste tribe under the Aryans in India. There are also endless studies that have actually proved that Gypsies all over the world originate from this Tamil tribe and that they left their homeland of India 1,000 years ago and began moving into Europe around 1400.

It has been stated that people in this tribe are polyglots capable of speaking more than ten languages. However their main language is Vagriboli. The Kuravars are no longer wealthy or own lands, having been sent away from their ancestral dwelling in accordance to what 'Kutrala Kuravanji' professes them to be. In fact they now even seem to be of the belief that travelling would bring them good health and money for survival. The other sad reality about this community is the fact that they no longer remember that they once belonged to a wealthy tribe and were minor kings. They have now become an outcast group facing major problems like poverty, illiteracy, diseases and discrimination. This chapter focuses on these issues and seeks to voice their cry for identity in the changing environment they live in.

The Kuravars have existed for such a very long time in our community; they have seen the changes and experienced them, yet they have their own culture and regulations with which they live. In order to understand the Kuravars better, it was essential to prepare a questionnaire before we approached them for an interview.

The questionnaire had the following questions:

Questionnaire

1. Can you tell us a brief note of your history?
2. What are the religions followed in your group?
3. We have heard that K. B. Sundarambal is from your clan. Is this information correct?
4. Which gender is dominant in your society? Is there equality?
5. What are the occupations you currently have?
6. Do you have any special occasions you celebrate as festivals?
7. With changes that have come about in your lifestyle, do you still follow the traditions of your past?
8. How far is the statement 'the Gypsies were nomadic because they believed travelling would bring health and good luck, while settling down would bring the opposite' true?
9. Can you tell us something about your marriage?
10. Do you have your representatives in politics? If so what are their postings?

11 Can you explain how the government has played a part in bringing changes in your life?
12 Has the decision of the government to move you from scheduled tribe to backward caste affected you?
13 Do you have a recognized ration card?
14 It was reported that your community people had difficulty voting. How far is this true?
15 How much of reality does the movie *Kurathi Magan* portray with your lifestyle?
16 Do you still follow your culture? How do you manage to preserve it?

The stories that we heard sparked an interest in the Gypsy culture and people; they are the colourful people with a style statement of their own. The Gypsies were interviewed near Thiruvanmiyur railway station on 28 February 2011. The interview lasted from 10.30 am to 11.30 am. The initial plan was to drive up to Besant Nagar and interview Gypsies selling beads, but on seeing those bags of paper neatly stacked up near the signal at Thiruvanmiyur we had to stop and check out the group. They were indeed a Kuravar group willing to share a few moments. To acknowledge the beautiful hearts that helped with this report would be the Kuravars who go by the names Jeeva, Valliammai, Roja, Saradha, Puspha, Muruga, Maliga, Gowri, Walter, Sarath Kumar (fifth std), Surya (fifth std) and Vellan (first std).

They were a happy group who opened up to answer the questions posed to them. From the observations made, their major concern seemed to be being homeless under the hot sun and the torrential rains. They also lacked ration cards or identity cards, which would give them the benefits the other tribal classes enjoyed. They told stories of approaching the government office for the issue of these cards, but they were denied. Inflation seemed to be a major threat to them; they said that they did not know how they would tackle their problem with the minimum income they get from picking papers. Their other problem as we learnt is that this tribe did not register their births and deaths. Most of the children were delivered at home, and due to their lack of education and awareness they do not possess a valid birth certificate. It was brought to our notice that it is only due to the efforts taken by the NGOs that they have some awareness about the above mentioned. This could be the main reason that most people in this community do not possess a valid ration card and voter's ID. More than the facilities they can enjoy under the quota system they are worried about having an identity of their own.

The other major concern after talking to them was that they seemed to be entirely unaware of their tradition and origin. They did not know that they were tribes from the Kurinji Hills and were not aware of their origin or history. This could be a major reason for them to be moved from the scheduled tribe to the other backward community. They identify themselves as people belonging to Chennai and those who live around Mylapore Kapaleeswarar Temple.

Yet, this is not the plight of everyone in the Kuravar community. They did acknowledge that some in the community had managed to get a permanent residence in Chennai and to obtain ration cards. This was possibly due to the outreach of M. G. Ramachandran, a former chief minister of Tamil Nadu, who did show some interest in the welfare of this community. This conversation led us to talking about films, and they did cheer up so much that they even put up a show singing and dancing in the sidewalk near the signal.

They informed us that some of their family members in the past had worked with M. G. Ramachandran in a song that went 'Nanga Pudusa Kattikitta Jodi Thaananga', which starred the then chief minister M. G. Ramachandran and the present chief minister Selvi J. Jayalalitha. They also acknowledge that K. B. Sundarambal, who played the role of Aavayaar in Tamil movies, was a member of their community.

When asked if they followed the same tradition and culture that was followed years back, they informed us that in the early times a man used to disown his wife if she returned after 6.00 pm, but it was no more in practice. They said with urbanization they had to change and adapt their ways. They also have a system of marriage where the dowry is given by the groom; in other words the groom buys his wife. Their marriages take place in the presence of the Goddess Madurai Kali Amman who is their household deity.

They said they did carry a Sami-Mootai, which was considered sacred and was passed on through inheritance in the group. The Sami-Mootai consisted of a silver statue of Goddess Kali or Madurai Meenakshi. The festival they mostly celebrated was Pongal, which most of the Tamilians celebrate in the month of January. They revealed the fact that they drank blood of buffaloes and stirred hot pots of boiling porridge without being hurt as they believed they were possessed by the Gods during their celebrations. One other tradition even dictated that they should not cut their hair and keep it long if they were very conservative by nature. Their long hair, which they maintained in a knot, was a status symbol. The other status symbol of these Kuravars was the red turbans they wore. They did seem to have strict norms that govern them, and they did take ultimate pride in the virtue they had. To quote them they said 'Nanga tooingum poodthu payaapda mattom, panam irrikruvangatan payapadanaum'. Their philosophical nature also emerged as they said,

'The rich have to be sleepless in order to safeguard their wealth. But we are a happy lot; we have no one to fear as we do not have anything worth looting'.

When questioned about education they acknowledged that their children did go to municipal/corporation schools and took pride in them being able to fare well in English. They however did complain that in spite of education some of them had to return to selling beads because being accepted at their new work place was painful as they faced discrimination because of the communities they came from.

They said that their source of beads was chiefly Agra and they did see the process in which the beads were made. It seemed that if taught correctly and enlightened about the process this could be developed into a small-scale industry that could generate its own revenue. They did exhibit knowledge of entrepreneurial skills as they initially tried to show the comparative price of the beads that they brought in Agra for Rs. 100 to those available in Paris (Chennai market) that were sold for Rs. 300.

Asked about what they do for their living, they answered that they sold honey, picked up paper, made and sold remedial medicine for back pain and hair growth and so on. They also sold beads. Some of them also sold seeds and holy beads called 'Rudraksha'. Due to laws banning them from selling fox nails, birds and bats, they did not seem to follow those professions anymore. They did not acknowledge begging. Instead, they had taken to cleaning of homes and roads.

As a follow up of their health and hygiene concerns, when asked they said that whenever they wanted to take a bath they would go to the government bathrooms and used the pay bathrooms available at Rs. 10. There they would wash their clothes and later dry them on the roads.

Having heard of reports of harassment of this community by the police, we asked how far this was true. It was not true. The police took them to task only if they made the place filthy. However, they did have a say about where these Gypsies had to sell their paper and scrap. We must of course acknowledge this community's contribution to society as they were actively involved in the recycling process. They are the ones who make it possible. In a place where conferences are held to speak about global warming, conservation and recycling, this is the community that silently backs up the whole process even when their magnificent contribution to society is not known. The NGOs and government could actually canalize this into a beneficial process. The government with its own paper mills and textbook prints can vouch for recycled paper for its textbooks and notebooks, which can put to use the contribution of the Gypsies, providing them with ample jobs and giving them betterment in life. They did talk about economic conditions and the inflation of food prices. The other problem they had was that even if they managed education, they were not given jobs because of the community they belonged to.

On further exploration of the community's status, it was learnt that the problem has a connection to the revised Constitution (Scheduled Castes) Order Co. 19. The original order, called the Constitution (Scheduled Castes) Order, 1950; PART XVI – Tamil Nadu, had 76 scheduled tribes as shown in Table 5.1 on page 68. The Kuravar community was listed as one among them; it was in the 36th position in the list of 76 tribes.

Later on, the Social Welfare Department issued an order to the Tamil Nadu state government, which reads as follows:

Government orders of interest to citizens government of Tamil Nadu

Abstract

Communities – Scheduled Castes and Scheduled Tribes – The Constitution Scheduled Castes and Scheduled Tribes Orders, 1950 – Amended – The Scheduled Castes and Scheduled Tribes (Amendment) Orders, 1976 – Issued – The Scheduled Castes and Scheduled Tribes Orders (Amendment) Act, 1976 – Published and came into force – Notification – Republished and communicated for general information – Orders Issued.

Social welfare department

G.O.Ms.No.1773 Dated: 23.6.1984

Read:-

1 From the Secretary to Government of India, Ministry of Home Affairs, New Delhi, Letter No.BC.12016/34/76-SCT.V, dated 8th October 1976.
2 From the Government of India, Ministry of Home Affairs, New Delhi, Letter No.BC.12016/34/76-SCT.V, dated 27th July 1977.

Read again:-

1 G.O.Ms.No.709, Social Welfare dated the 7th October 1977.
2 Government Memo No.65226/HW.VIII/77–3, Social Welfare, Dated the 2nd November 1977.

Order:

The Government of India, Ministry of Home Affairs, New Delhi, have informed this Government in their letter first read above that The Constitution (Scheduled Castes) Order, 1950 and the Constitution (Scheduled Tribes) Order 1950 as modified in the Constitution Scheduled Castes (Modification) Order, 1956 and the Constitution Scheduled Tribes (Modification) Order, 1956 have been amended in the Scheduled Castes and Scheduled Tribes (Amendment) Act, 1976, which was passed by the Parliament and received the assent of the President of India on 18th September 1976. They have also informed that the Act has not yet come into force and that the date from which the Act will come into force will be notified in the Gazette of India in due course. Subsequently, the Government of India, Ministry of Home Affairs, New Delhi, have informed this Government that the lists of Scheduled Castes and Scheduled Tribes as contained in The Constitution (Scheduled Castes) Order, 1950 and the Constitution (Scheduled Tribes) Order 1950 have been amended by the Scheduled Castes and Scheduled Tribes (Amendment) Act, 1976 (Central Act 108 of 1976) which has been brought into force with effect from the 27th July, 1977. They have pointed out that it has been brought to the notice of the Ministry of Home Affairs, Government of India, New Delhi that the District Collectors, Heads of Departments certificate issuing authorities, etc., are not yet aware of the revised list of Scheduled Castes and Scheduled Tribes pertaining to the State of Tamil Nadu and have requested that the revised list may kindly be widely circulated to all the concerned authorities and the State.

2. The Scheduled Castes and Scheduled Tribes Order (Amendment) Act, 1976 (Central Act 108 of 1976) was accordingly republished by this Government in the Extraordinary issue of the *Tamil Nadu Government Gazette* in Part IV-Section 4, dated 31st December 1976. The Notification of the Government of India bringing into force of the Act with effect from the 27th July 1977 was also published at page 637 in Part-II Section 1 of the *Tamil Nadu Government Gazette,* dated the 2nd November 1977 according to the orders issued in the Government Order read above. In the Government Memo read above the position was pointed out to all the Collectors and Heads of Departments and they were requested to instruct the certificate issuing authorities under their control to issue community certificates to persons belonging to Scheduled Castes and Scheduled Tribes as per

the revised list in the Scheduled Castes and Scheduled Tribes Orders (Amendment) Act, 1976, with effect from the 27th July 1977.

3. It has been brought to the notice of this Government that certificate issuing authorities still not adopting the list of revised list and correct name of Scheduled Castes and Scheduled Tribes while issuing the community certificate to eligible and genuine persons belonging to Scheduled Castes and Scheduled Tribes. It has, therefore, become necessary to bring to notice of all concerned the list of Scheduled Castes and Scheduled Tribes as contained in the Scheduled Castes and Scheduled Tribes (Amendment) Act, 1976 (Central Act 108 of 1976) which was brought into force with effect from the 27th July 1977. A list of Scheduled Castes and Scheduled Tribes, 1976 is given in Annexure I to this Order. In order to have a first-hand knowledge of the position with respect of list of Scheduled Castes and Scheduled Tribes Orders, 1950 and 1956, a copy of each of those Orders are also given in Annexure II to this Order for information and guidance in such matter. A copy of the Act is also given in Annexure III to this Order.

4. The Collectors and Heads of Departments concerned and the certificate issuing authorities under their control are requested to adopt the list of Scheduled Castes and Scheduled Tribes contained in the Central Act, 1976, strictly. Any deviation will be viewed seriously. The receipt of this order shall be acknowledged.

(By Order of the Governor)
M.K. GOMETHAGAVELU.
Additional secretary to government.

Annexure I The Scheduled Castes and Scheduled Tribes Orders (Amendment) Act, 1976 (Central Act No. 108 of 1976)

The Constitution (Scheduled Castes) Order, 1950 as amended by the Scheduled Castes (Amendment) Order, 1976

In exercise of the powers conferred by clause (1) of Article 341 of the Constitution of India, the President, after consultation with the

Governors, Rajpramukhs of the States concerned, is pleased to make the following order, namely:-

1. This Act may be called the Scheduled Castes (Amendment) Act, 1976. it shall come into force on the 27th July 1977.

2. Subject to the provisions of this Act, the castes, races or tribes, or parts thereof, or groups within, castes or tribes, specified in Parts I to XIX of the Schedule to this Order, shall in relation to the States to which those Parts respectively relate, be deemed to be Scheduled Castes so far as regards members thereof resident in the localities specified in relation to them in those Parts of that Schedule.

3. Notwithstanding anything contained in Paragraph 2, no person who professes a religion different from the Hindu or the Sikh religion shall be deemed to be a member of a Scheduled Caste.

4. Any reference in this Order to a State or to a district or other territorial division thereof shall be construed as a reference to the State, district or other territorial division as constituted on the 1st day of May 1976.

Table 5.1 The Scheduled (Scheduled Castes). Part XVI – Tamil Nadu

1.	Adi Andhra
2.	Adi Dravida
3.	Adi Karnataka
4.	Ajila
5.	Arunthathiyar
6.	Ayyanavar (in Kanyakumari district and Shenkottah taluk of Tirunelveli district)
7.	Baira
8.	Bakuda
9.	Bandi
10.	Bellara
11.	Bharatar (in Kanyakumari district and Shenkottah taluk of Tirunelveli district)
12.	Chakkiliyan
13.	Chalavadi
14.	Chamar, Muchi
15.	Chandala
16.	Cheruman

17. Devendrakulathan
18. Dom, Dombara, Paidi, Pano
19. Domban
20. Godagali
21. Godda
22. Gosangi
23. Holeya
24. Jaggali
25. Jambuvulu
26. Kadaiyan
27. Kakkalan (in Kanyakumari district and Shenkottah taluk of Tirunelveli district)
28. Kalladi
29. Kanakkan, Padanna (in the Nilgiris district)
30. Karimpalan
31. Kavara (in Kanyakumari district and Shenkottah taluk of Tirunelveli district)
32. Koliyan
33. Koosa
34. Kootan, Koodan (in Kanyakumari district and Shenkottah taluk of Tirunelveli district)
35. Kudumban
36. Kuravan, Sidhanar
37. Madari
38. Madiga
39. Maila
40. Mala
41. Mannan (in Kanyakumari district and Shenkottah taluk of Tirunelveli district)
42. Mavilan
43. Moger
44. Mundala
45. Nalakeyava
46. Nayadi
47. Padannan (in Kanyakumari district and Shenkottah taluk of Tirunelveli district)
48. Pagadai
49. Pallan
50. Palluvan
51. Pambada
52. Panan (in Kanyakumari district and Shenkottah taluk of Tirunelveli district)
53. Panchama
54. Pannadi

(Continued)

Table 5.1 (Continued)

55.	Panniandi
56.	Paraiyan, Parayan, Sambavar
57.	Paravan (in Kanyakumari district and Shenkottah taluk of Tirunelveli district)
58.	Pathiyan (in Kanyakumari district and Shenkottah taluk of Tirunelveli district)
59.	Pulayan, Cheramar
60.	Puthirai Vannan
61.	Raneyar
62.	Samagara
63.	Samban
64.	Sapari
65.	Semman
66.	Thandan (in Kanyakumari district and Shenkottah taluk of Tirunelveli district)
67.	Thoti
68.	Tiruvalluvar
69.	Vallon
70.	Valluvan
71.	Vannan (in Kanyakumari district and Shenkottah taluk of Tirunelveli district)
72.	Vathiriyan
73.	Velan
74.	Vetan (in Kanyakumari district and Shenkottah taluk of Tirunelveli district)
75.	Vettiyan
76.	Vettuvan (in Kanyakumari district and Shenkottah taluk of Tirunelveli district)

Source: Ministry of Law, Justice and Company Affairs, New Delhi, 20th September 1976, *The Gazette of India Extraordinary*, No. 151, Part II, 1384-85 and 1394-95.

The Constitution (Scheduled Tribes) Order, 1950 as Amended by the Scheduled Tribes Orders (Amendment) Act, 1976, No. 108 of 1976

In exercise of the powers conferred by clause (1) of Article 342 of the Constitution of India, the President, after consultation with the Governors and Rajpramukhs of the States concerned, is pleased to make the following order, namely:-

1. This Act may be called the Scheduled Tribes Orders (Amendment) Act, 1976. It shall come into force on the 27th July 1977.

2. The tribes or tribal communities, or parts of, or groups within, tribes or tribal communities, specified in Parts I to XVI of the Schedule to this Order, shall in relation to the states to which those parts respectively relate, be deemed to be Scheduled Tribes so far as regards members thereof resident in the localities specified in relation to them respectively in those parts of that Schedule.

3. Any reference in this order to a state or to a district or other territorial division thereof shall be construed as a reference to the state, district or other territorial division as constituted on the 1st day of May 1976.

Table 5.2 The Scheduled (Scheduled Tribes). Part XIV – Tamil Nadu

1.	Adiyan
2.	Aranadan
3.	Eravallan
4.	Irular
5.	Kadar
6.	Kammara (excluding Kanayakumari district and Shenkottah taluk of Tirunelveli district)
7.	Kanikaran, Kanikkar (in Kanyakumari district and Shenkottah taluk of Tirunelveli district)
8.	Kaniyan, Kanyan
9.	Kattunayakan
10.	Kochu Velan
11.	Konda Kapus
12.	Kondareddis
13.	Koraga
14.	Kota (excluding Kanyakumari district and Shenkottah taluk of Tirunelveli district)
15.	Kudiya, Melakudi
16.	Kurichchan
17.	Kurumbas (in the Nilgiris district)
18.	Kurumans
19.	Maha Malasar
20.	Malai Arayan
21.	Malai Pandaram
22.	Malai Vedan
23.	Malakkuravan

(Continued)

Table 5.2 (Continued)

24.	Malasar
25.	Malayali (in Dharmapuri, North Arcot, Pudukottai, Salem, South Arcot and Tiruchirappalli districts)
26.	Malayakandi
27.	Mannan
28.	Mudugar, Muduvan
29.	Muthuvan
30.	Pallayan
31.	Palliyan
32.	Palliyar
33.	Paniyan
34.	Sholaga
35.	Toda (excluding Kanyakumari district and Shenkottah taluk of Tirunelveli district)
36.	Uraly

Source: Ministry of Law, Justice and Company Affairs, New Delhi, 20th September 1976, *The Gazette of India Extraordinary*, No. 151, Part II, 1384-85 and 1394-95.

The Constitution (Scheduled Tribes) Order, 1950, as amended by the Scheduled Tribes Order (Amendment) Act, 1976, No. 108 of 1976, has had a great impact on the Kuravar community.[1] The Scheduled Tribes Order amended in 1976 and passed in 1977 no longer listed the Kuravars as a scheduled tribe; it listed only 36 tribes and the Kuravars were not among them. This is shown in Table 5.2 above. It was unfortunate for them as they had been moved to the other backward castes under the section of the Denotified Communities Act. They are listed in sections as mentioned in Table 5.3: http://www.tnpsc.gov.in/communities-list.html#bc.

Being moved to the OBC category meant a tremendous change for this particular community.

The Hindu reported from Tirunelveli on 5 December 2006 that the Kuravar community people sought SC status:

> A group of people, belonging to the 'Koravar' community, submitted a petition to the Collector, G. Prakash, during a grievance day meeting held on Monday, seeking to categorise them as members of the 'Scheduled Tribe' community.
>
> The petitioners said the members of Kuravan or Koravars or Kuravans living in Shencottai taluk of the district could get the community certificate, confirming them as members of the 'Scheduled Tribe' community, while the

Table 5.3 The Kuravars listed as other backward castes under the section of the Denotified Communities Act

13	Dobba Koravars	Salem and Namakkal Districts
19	Dabi Koravars	Thanjavur, Nagapattinam, Tiruvarur, Tiruchirapalli, Karur, Perambalur, Pudukottai, Vellore and Tiruvannamalai districts
23	Gandarvakottai Koravars	Thanjavur, Nagapattinam, Tiruvarur, Tiruchirapalli, Karur, Perambalur, Pudukottai, Cuddalore and Villupuram districts
25	Inji Koravars	Thanjavur, Nagapattinam, Tiruvarur, Tiruchirapalli, Karur, Perambalur and Pudukottai districts
30	Koravars	Kancheepuram, Tiruvallur, Ramanathapuram, Sivaganga, Virudhunagar, Pudukottai, Thanjavur, Nagapattinam, Thiruvarur, Tiruchirapalli, Karur, Perambalur, Tirunelveli, Thoothukudi, Chennai, Madurai, Theni, Dindigul and the Nilgiris districts
33	Kala Koravars	Thanjavur, Nagapattinam, Tiruvarur, Tiruchirapalli, Karur, Perambalur and Pudukottai districts
37	Monda Koravars	
44	Ponnai Koravars	Vellore and Tiruvannamalai districts
50	Salem Melnad Koravars	Madurai, Theni, Dindigul, Coimbatore, Erode, Pudukottai, Tiruchirapalli, Karur, Perambalur, Salem, Namakkal, Vellore and Tiruvannamalai districts
51	Salem Uppu Koravars	Salem and Namakkal districts
52	Sakkaraithamadai Koravars	Vellore and Tiruvannamalai districts
53	Saranga Palli Koravars	
56	Thalli Koravars	Salem and Namakkal districts
59	Thogamalai Koravars	Tiruchirapalli, Karur, Perambalur and Pudukottai districts
63	Vaduvarpatti Koravars	Madurai, Theni, Dindigul, Ramanathapuram, Sivaganga, Virudhunagar, Tirunelveli, Thoothukudi, Tiruchirapalli, Karur, Perambalur and Pudukottai districts
66	Vetta Koravars	Salem and Namakkal districts
67	Varaganeri Koravars	Tiruchirapalli, Karur, Perambalur and Pudukottai districts

people from the same community living in other parts of the district were not being given ST status.

Along with the petition, they submitted a letter from the Department of Adi Dravidar and Tribal Welfare to the Secretary, Ministry of Social Justice

> and Empowerment, Government of India, which recommends that the 'Koravar' community could be included in the list of Scheduled Tribes.

The demand cited is one among the many such rights this community seeks. Another judgment passed in favour of the tribe is the Madurai High Court Order of 12 March 2011.

> The Madras High Court has made a suggestion to the State Government to amend the Tamil Nadu Panchayats (Election) Rules thereby making it mandatory for the contestants to produce their community certificates in order to prevent non-Dalits from occupying posts reserved for the Scheduled Castes and Scheduled Tribes.
>
> Justice R.S. Ramanathan made the suggestion while setting aside the election of P. Tamilarasi, who belonged to Hindu Vanniyar community, as the president of Palaniyapuri Panchayat in Attur Taluk of Salem district in 2006. The judge held that she had no right to contest for the Panchayat president post reserved for the Scheduled Tribes. Allowing a civil revision petition filed in 2008 by her sole opponent Sannasi, belonging to Hindu Malai Kuravan community (a notified scheduled tribe), Mr. Justice Ramanathan declared the petitioner as the winning candidate as only two candidates contested for the post and one of them (Tamilarasi) had been found to be ineligible to contest.

It can be noted that in spite of the various struggles this community stages, there have been no proper steps taken by the Social Welfare Department to place the Kuravars where they belong, as scheduled tribes.

In fact the lifestyle of this community would become better if the right opportunity comes their way and if the NGOs continue with their job of educating this tribe. During the interview with these tribes, we realized that it was only in places where the NGOs were actively working for this tribe in terms of education and health, their life style improved. Only a small group emerged voicing for their rights.

Now, let us have a look at what educating this community can do. For instance, the Sun Network aired a programme featuring a student from the Kuravar community.

The debate programme broadcast on Deepavali presented a participant from the Narikuravar community who acknowledged that he was from Tiruvannamalai. He started his speech with 'Aiya konjam yosiangal, narikuravarri konjam nesiangal', which translates as 'Sir, give a thought to the Gypsy and love the Gypsy'. He stated that he was the first graduate from their community. To get to this state, there were days when he did go to school hungry and without food. In his speech he praised the womenfolk of his community as the first women to step outside to do business selling beads, ribbons, clips, pins and so on. He stated that if a child has parents who work it would not affect the growth of the child but only raise the child's value, helping him to get a better education. He proved to the audience that in spite of the circumstances in which he grew up, a child always manages to achieve once his mind is set to succeed. This speaker's aim was to become an IAS officer; he is currently doing his BA English literature, first year. Indeed this programme served as an eye-opener and brought the realization that several of the people from this community who availed themselves of the right opportunity at the right time were better off.

It does not end here; here is a look at what a person can come across in a search through one section of Bharat Matrimony's community matrimonial website section Kuravan matrimony: www.kuravarmatrimony.com.

Search

Active

One week (16)
One month (33)
One month and above (83)

Profile type

With Photo (22)
With Horoscope (6)

Age

18 yrs to 30 yrs (83)

Height

4ft to 7ft 11in (83)

Marital status

Unmarried (79)
Divorced (4)

Education

Bachelors – Engineering (20)
Bachelors (17)
Masters (13)

Employed in

Private (44)
Government (10)
Defence (3)

Occupation

Executive (12)
Not Working (7)
Software Professional (6)

Annual income

Rs. 1 lakh to Rs. 3 lakh (14)
Rs. 3 lakh to Rs. 5 lakh (4)
Rs. 5 lakh to Rs. 10 lakh (3)

Country

India (81)
United States of America (1)

Citizenship

India (83)

Eating habits

Non-vegetarian (44)
Vegetarian (6)
Eggetarian (4)

Profile created by

Self (31)
Sibling (25)
Parents (17)

It was truly an interesting lesson reading the identities of brides and grooms, which have not been disclosed in the interest of the privacy of the individuals. It was noted that some of them were in professions related to administration, management, engineering and teaching. Some of these jobs depend on their inherited qualities of entrepreneur and management skills. But the sad factor is that those who have received a collegiate education rarely return to work for the development of the community.

S. Veerangan, the head of one of the groups interviewed near Saarakuttai Village of Katpadi, showed us clips from newspapers of a meeting they had organized at Gandhi Nagar, near Don Bosco School, Katpadi, voicing their claim to be given their proper stand as a scheduled tribe.

They also showed us petitions that they had written to the chief minister of Tamil Nadu Ms J. Jayalalitha requesting *patta* (legal document of ownership) for land. Further they added that they had been given homes on a small hillside not very far from the place they stayed. They had to confront wild animals and snakes. There were no facilities, and they had no means of transportation. The lack of medical facilities and bad roads meant help was always out of reach for them. The community had lost two pregnant women without being able to get help. This was according to their report the very reason they had moved out of the shelter the government had provided for them.

They said, 'We want to live where other people live; be given the facilities extended to the scheduled tribe. Look at our condition. How can we be lifted up to the upper class, when our lifestyle is poor? We require the status of the scheduled tribe to avail the facilities of education and establish ourselves. Nothing good is happening; we have no home; we do not want to be nomadic any more. Give us a proper place to live in with the basic needs'.

They have now become an outcast group facing major problems like poverty, illiteracy, diseases and discrimination. This chapter focuses on these issues and seeks to voice out their cry for identity in the changing environment they live in.

The issue of this Tamil tribe who have been among us for a very long time has gone unnoticed. The main reason could be that we live in a world that is too busy to notice these poor people who struggle for their survival. It has to be noted that they are not beggars but people who belong to a tribal community – a community ignorant of their past and hence unable to make proper claims with evidence that they are tribes. Only when questioned and informed about their ancestry do they acknowledge their ignorance. Their voice goes unheard due to their insignificant status.

A featured article in *indiaenews* reads:

> Under the polythene cover of a photo album that Rakamma carries is a voter ID card and a faded photograph of a street display taken by a newspaper,

> which resulted in the police coming down heavily on the gypsies for talking to the media.
>
> Yet, Rakamma, 41, her sister Sokamma, Padmini, Vijayalakshmi and their bright eyed children Yasmini and Sivaraj have not stopped telling stories of a social justice system that has perhaps passed them by.
>
> (*indiaenews*, 2011)

The groups interviewed for this chapter are from Chennai and Vellore. The information gathered from them is furnished. Ethnographic studies of this community reveal the immense ecological and medicinal knowledge that the community's elders possess. According to them they used to be trappers and hunters, but hunting has now been banned and they have found themselves helpless. They relied more on their traditional handicraft of making of bead garlands. They seemed to have some poultry around them. S. Veerangan, who seemed to be the head of the group, informed us that they had inherited their elders' knowledge of medicine and treated diseases related to gastric disorders, piles, headache and so on. They showed a tub of herbal powder and capsules in which these were filled to prevent the bitter taste.

They had a segregated place fenced with clusters of medicinal roots hanging around it. The place was clean with a hut in which their deity's pictures hung. This was a place where they followed the ritual of preparing their medicine.

This group of Kuravars considered themselves superior compared to those who pick papers and clean homes for their living in Chennai. They had knowledge of their community being given the OBC status and are clearly not happy about it. Moreover they do not have a representative in the state as they do not actively participate in elections as a contestant. The groups interviewed acknowledge the contribution of Dr M. G. Ramachandaran (the former chief minister of Tamil Nadu) as he had recognized and helped the community voluntarily.

To conclude with a few suggestions that could help this community: first would be to educate them on their history, as it needs to be preserved. This serves as authentic evidence of them being scheduled tribes. Moreover in the discussions seen there is also authentic proof that there are still judgments passed in their favour, which consider them as scheduled tribes. Clarity about their actual status as a community has to be determined. One easy solution to this problem would be to have a representative from this tribe as a member in parliament. Politicians should refrain from showing short-term interest in them during elections.

It should also be remembered that this community should not be treated as untouchables and given homes far away, preventing them to get their basic amenities and help.

There is no denying that there are rehabilitation centres set for the welfare of this community, missionaries reaching out to them and NGOs educating them. Also, the government is extending its services to them. But how are they benefited? They have lost their identity as tribes. They embrace education for a better living. Some survive by letting go of their identity, never to return to the group, and others return to their bead-selling work due to the discrimination as a low caste. They are confused about their status. They could not fight because of their forgotten past and are unaware of how to make a claim. The Kuravars of Tamil Nadu have to be acknowledged and preserved for what they are. This chapter is presented as an attempt to revive their identity and claim their status as a tribe, so that they too can avail themselves of the facilities extended to other tribes by the government.

Join hands and fight to revive the privilege for the forgotten tribe of the Kuravars.

References

Constitution (Scheduled Castes) Order, 1950. (1950). Retrieved 12 September 2011, from Government Orders of Interest to Citizens: http://lawmin.nic.in/ld/subord/rule3a.htm.

Cooper, Belinda. 2001/2002. '"We Have No Martin Luther King": Eastern Europe's Roma Minority', *World Policy Journal*, 18(4): 69–78. Retrieved from http://www.jstor.org/stable/40209780.

6 Tesu and Jhenjhi

A festival celebrating cultural life

Sonia S. *Kushwah and* A. S. *Kushwah*

Indian folklore encompasses a wide diversity of ethnic, linguistic and religious groups due to the heterogeneity of Hinduism. Folk tradition not only explains the existence of local and religious customs but goes beyond this, taking into account the entire body of social tradition whose chief vehicle of transmission is oral.

The word 'folk' carries larger, multiple and varied connotations with reference to the Indian context. According to the Sanskrit scriptures folk indicates the internal realization of the time consciousness. The Hindi word for 'folk' is *lok*, but it refers to a multiple and diverse range of meanings such as *lok-alok* (darkness-light), *bhu-lok*, *swarg lok*, *bhuvar lok* (the three worlds – earth, heaven and hell). Philosophical studies relate *lok* to *lokdhatu* in Buddhistic studies, *lokdharmi* in dramaturgy and *lok purush* in Jainism. Besides this, *lok* has its unification with *lokyatra*, *loksangrah*, *lokachar*, *lokantar*, *lokpal*, etc. All these associations with *lok* indicate its specific usage but, if we generalize the word *lok*, then *lok* refers to this world comprising the ordinary and common people.

The English word 'folk' has limited significance as per anthropological and Western social studies. It specifically stands for the rural and natural rather than the cultivated and civilized. The Western researchers are unable to give folk a wider significance, whereas we Indians do not present folk and classical, oral and written or folk and classical behaviour as polarities. They are in a continuity shaping and defining our thought process and behaviour patterns. Herein lie the strength, identity and originality of the Indian folk. The folk culture is in a state of flux, acquiring new references and meanings beyond the ancient culture. Culturization is a live process that germinates in the ground of folk. Culture at the level of folk is folk culture comprising the ideals, faiths and customs of common man. Folk, when specific, gains standardized and accomplished values to constitute classical culture. Folk culture depends upon folk art and literature, and is shaped by the folk mind and folk behaviour which are constantly acting and reacting with contemporary situations. It is our firm belief that an effort to record the folk history of a nation may give us the real history as this would be the history of the masses.

Although efforts have been made to collect, record and chronologically arrange folk tales, songs, stories and festivals to depict the effect of orality on the process of culturization, much more needs to be done, as folk literature may be an illuminating source for rewriting history which otherwise has gaps. We all are a part of some folk tradition or other which unites us internally. The passage of time has definitely changed the social structure but the seeds of folk traditions remain constant in the form of the pivot on which the entire wheel of civilization revolves.

We all have a rich past to discuss. The folk festival we have taken for our study is an elaborated festival taking into account the entire social community of northern India. The festival has no historical or scriptural validity, but it pierces deep into the social context, cultural configurations and moral viewpoints. The complete performance encompasses a period of approximately one month and involves rituals, songs and exuberant dances.

Our acquaintance with this festival goes back to our childhood days. We have reminiscences of groups of boys and girls performing the festival which filled us with awe and wonder. This conference gave us an opportunity to relink ourselves to Tesu and Jhenjhi folklore. It is a regional festival celebrated in the states of Uttar Pradesh and Madhya Pradesh, but its vibrant manifestation is in the Bundelkhand region comprising the Jalon, Jhansi, Lalitpur, Hamirpur districts of Uttar Pradesh along with some *tehsils* of Banda district. Districts like Panna, Chattarpur, Tikamgarh, Datia, Sagar, Damoh, Narsinghpur, Jabalpur and Hoshangabad are also part of the Bundelkhand region. This geographical area of land is known for its rich folk cultural heritage. The Tesu Jhenjhi festival is one such jewel studded in the glorious folk tradition of Bundelkhand.

The festival begins simultaneously with nine-day worship of Durga during which the adolescent girls participate in *Gauri pooja*. In the seventh lunar month (September–October), during the moonlit fortnight, girls erect a mud platform on nine steps. They consecrate the mud idols of Gauri-Mahadev on this platform. The image of Suatta, the demon, is painted on the wall with the images of sun and moon on either side. Suatta is embellished with various small pieces of mirror and shells. It wears a string of shells with large ear-rings.

Figure 6.1 Suatta the Demon

Source: Courtesy of the author.

There are numerous versions of the folklore associated with Suatta. According to one popular folk belief he was a demon who kidnapped and devoured adolescent girls. Thus the girls prayed to Gauri for nine days to save them from this demon. The goddess killed the demon, relieving the girls from the terror of Suatta. Gauri prayed to get Lord Shiva, and so the girls pray to her to find a suitable match for themselves.

The scriptural references to Skanda are closely linked to Suatta as Skanda was the overlord in the form of evil. His wife Vemata is known to trouble the infants and cause other family mishaps. The foundation of their worship lies in the protection against their destructive nature. Later on Skanda may have been transformed to Suatta.

This ceremony of *Gauri pooja* is followed by the girls and boys playing the marriage rituals of Tesu and Jhenjhi. From the ninth day of the bright half of the seventh lunar month, girls and boys make two groups. The boys carry the image of Tesu in the evening to almost all the homes in a community. They sing Tesu songs and ask for money for the marriage of Tesu. Similarly the group of girls carries Jhenjhi door to door collecting finances to arrange the marriage. They sing and dance while doing so in the houses.

Figure 6.2 The image of Tesu

Source: Courtesy of the author.

The image of Tesu is made of wood and mud. A tripod of wood is prepared on which to place the head of Tesu, which is decorated by the boys. The image is that of a handsome young man with a big moustache, turban, a royal costume and ornaments, and it reflects chivalric knighthood. The songs sung by the boys narrate the heroic deeds of Tesu. There is an element of humour in the songs of Tesu which makes him resemble the eccentric Sir Roger de Coverley of Addison's essays or Shakespeare's Falstaff.

Jhenjhi is made of an earthen pot with geometrical or floral cuttings. A handful of rice or wheat is put in the pot on which is lit an earthen lamp whose light reflects out from the holes in the pot. Girls carry Jhenjhi and ask everyone for grains or money. They sing and dance elaborating the pain of an adolescent girl who has to leave her parents and go to her in-laws. Both the groups deliberately avoid each other while going around in the community.

Figure 6.3 Jhenjhi

Source: Courtesy of the author.

Here are a few Jhenjhi songs.

1

A water pot without a headrest is hard to balance, oh dear parrot.
Without a calf, a cow brays day and night, oh dear parrot.
Without a son, a mother suffers day and night, oh dear parrot.
A sister with seven brothers travels in a brightly decorated palanquin, oh dear parrot.

2

My Jhenjhi asks for rice.
She asks for a bowl full of grain and a cake of raw sugar.
She asks for red dye for her feet and red powder for the part of her hair.
She asks for bangles for her wrists and a red dot for her forehead.
She asks for toe-rings for her feet.
Oh dear parrot, my Jhenjhi is preparing for marriage.
Tesu has left for the marriage; my Jhenhji is lagging behind.

3

Oh moon of Kvara, shine brightly.
No one in this world is as pure as you are.
May the daughters of the whole world enjoy themselves,
So that my mind will feel pleasure.

4

I had forgotten, ta tatha ta thei thei.
Keep the father-in-law in the house, ta tatha ta thei thei.
By tying him to the cot, ta tatha ta thei thei.
Keep the husband's elder brother in the house, ta tatha ta thei thei,
By tying him to a peg, ta tatha ta thei thei.
Keep the husband's younger brother in the house, ta tatha ta thei thei,
By tying him to a peg, ta tatha thei thei.
Keep your husband in the house, ta tatha ta thei thei,
By tying him near the drainage, ta tatha ta thei thei.

5

My Jhenjhi is in the courtyard.
In the courtyard all decked up
When will Tesu come.
Be not late thou O Tesu be not late

Why is it late for mandap
Priest is here
Be not late O Tesu.
Wish not to be here in my father's home
Hastily fetch me be not late, thou.
Hastily fetch me.

6

My Jhenjhi's name is Jehenjhiriya O jehenjhiriya O
I am going to my home.
My paro's name Parvatiya O parvatiya O
I am going to my home.
Bring danglers for my Jhenjhi O danglers O
I am going to my home.
Bring stole for my Jhenjhi O stole O
I am going to my home.
My Tesu will fetch me in the dole O
I am going to my home.

One girl puts lighted Jhenjhi on her head and dances around, while other girls circle round her clapping and singing. All the songs are sung without accompaniment.

A few Tesu songs are also worth mentioning:

1 My Tesu stands here
Wish to eat dahi bada here
Dahi bada is nasty
give me son fifty
fifty paisa will give you coat
give me son twenty rupee note
twenty rupee note is fake
grandpa will put you to stake
Tesu came to marry
Jhenjhi will he carry.

2 My Tesu naughty
daily drives fat fati
fat fatti is of Tesu's grandpa
All hail mother India.

3 In my court yard Tesu stands
With him all his friends stand

Made us all to beg for him
Jhenjhi waits to marry him.

4 I have five silver pan
From them came a gentle man
Gentleman's name is Tesu
We have come to beg you.

On the full moon night (*Sharad purnima*) the last day of the festival, the marriage of Tesu and Jhenjhi is accomplished with great fun, enjoyment and partying. The group of boys and girls is accompanied by the adults of the community performing the marriage rituals. After the ceremony the images of Tesu and Jhenjhi are thrown in a water tank with fireworks.

The Tesu songs are on broad subject-matter taking episodes from *Ramayana*, *Mahabharata* and other glorifying epics. It is sung in the couplet style, which makes it significant.

The girls sing a variety of songs. The subject-matter relates to in-laws, marriage, the parental house and longing for Tesu. The word *savanna* is often repeated at the end of each line. The symbolism implied is that like a *savanna* (parrot) the girl will leave her home and would be caged in the in-laws' house forever.

According to a folk oral narrative Jhenjhi was the daughter of Suatta, the demon. Tesu allured by her beauty decides to marry her, but he had to first fight Suatta to get Jhenjhi as his bride.

There is yet another reference to an ancient King Bhimsen, who performed an elaborated *pooja* prayer to get a child. He was then blessed with a son whom he named Tesu. Tesu was a poet by nature, least interested in the royal administrative work. He used to wander in the forest reciting poetry. A tribal girl named Jhenjhi was inspired by his songs, and once she repeated his lines. Tesu was highly impressed, and they fell in love. Suatta was the minister in King Bhimsen's court. The king sent Suatta to separate Tesu and Jhenjhi, but finally Suatta was killed and the two lovers were united forever.

These were the folk origins of this festival, but folk people find its origin in the epic *Mahabharata*. Babhruvahana was a famous archer. One day Lord Krishna asked him to shoot all the leaves off one tree using only one arrow. Krishna craftily plucked one leaf and put it under his foot. Babhruvahana's arrow pierced all the leaves on the tree and then came towards Krishna's foot. Krishna lifted his foot and the arrow pierced that last leaf also. Krishna realized that Babhruvahana was a great archer and feared that he would challenge Arjuna and change the entire result of the war, so he decided that Babhruvahana must be killed somehow. Krishna therefore asked Babhruvahana for a boon; when Babhruvahana gave his consent, Krishna asked for his head. Babhruvahana willingly agreed, but requested that he be allowed to see the Mahabharata war. Krishna said, 'Your head will live until the end of the war'. And thus Krishna put Babhruvahana's head up on three sticks of *sirkanda* (a kind of reed), so that he could watch the war.

Yet another reference says that Babhruvahana met the daughter of Narakasur, Jhenjhi, and both had promised to marry. When Babhruvahana donated his head to Krishna, Jhenjhi killed herself. After the war, Krishna made puppets of them and married them. The festival of Tesu and Jhenjhi has been celebrated ever since then.

A few villagers say that first before the beginning of the Mahabharata war, Bhishma *pitamaha* wanted to test the strength of Kauravas. Barbarika, the grandson of Bhima and son of Ghatotkacha, proclaimed, 'There is no warrior among the Pandavas and Kauravas, who is as brave as I am.' To prove this, he took out a powder which a yogi had given him. He sprinkled the powder on the people and as a result all fainted. Since Krishna feared that he might destroy both Kauravas and Pandavas, Krishna cut off his head. Bhima and Ghatotkacha requested Krishna to restore life to Barbarika. Krishna put his head on a hill so that he could see the war.

All these citations are from the *Mahabharata* epic and were recorded orally by the present authors while working on this subject. Some faint connections can also be traced to the written records in the *Skanda Purana*. We could not gain any information as to how the name Tesu was acquired. In the Bhind district of Madhya Pradesh, we were informed orally by a group of children participating in this festival that it has its links to the epic *Ramayana* too. Shurpanakha, sister of Ravana, was in love with a tribal man named Vidhutjuha and looked for the conjugal unification. Ravana was against this marriage so he cut Vidhutjuha's head off. Shurpanakha felt offended and decided to avenge his brother by becoming the cause of the war between Ram and Ravana.

Whatever may be the originating text, it is evident that the festival has great social significance. It prepares the girls for leaving their homes after marriage as per the Indian tradition. The songs sung by the girls for Jhenjhi are full of pathos exhibiting the great anxiety and grief at the departure of a girl loved and cared for by her family since childhood.

The girls learn the rituals of marriage and the family customs in a playful manner. The symbolic marriage of Tesu and Jhenjhi paves the way to accept the girls' leave-taking with enthusiasm and happiness. Boys do not have to undergo such a transition as they inherit family property and wealth, so they enjoy the festival by being happy and humorous. We think this is the reason why we have humorous songs of Tesu and sad songs of Jhenjhi.

The festival provides an apt situation for all the people irrespective of their age to participate. It also releases the taboos associated with caste, as all play in a group. It is a festival that provides an outlet for emotional feelings. The psychological release is encouraged, because many socio-cultural standards are relaxed. It trains all the youngsters in the customs of marriage and promotes harmonious interaction between young and old and rich and poor. The Tesu and Jhenjhi festival serves as a mood builder and enhances the enthusiasm of the folk for celebrating Dussehra, Diwali and finally the arranged marriages as per the Hindu calendar. It trains the young girls and boys to manage an event, to arrange the finance and accomplish the whole programme with a feeling of oneness.

Festivals of this kind are the epicentres for cultural awareness providing a suitable atmosphere for social gatherings. The joy of the festival rejuvenates the folk to work with higher spirits. It enhances the feeling of brotherhood, giving a democratic outlook to the occasion. Festivals of such a kind arouse the people's interest with their celebration and need to be preserved. Very few groups are seen nowadays participating in such kinds of activities, as children nowadays have 'n' numbers of means to entertain themselves and are hardly conscious of the need to preserve their cultural roots. These festivals involve the entire folk-depicting folk psychology. It would not be an exaggeration to state that the history of national unity originates from folk festivals, and so they must be carefully preserved for coming generations.

In the end, we would like to say that the lit lamps placed in the images of Tesu and Jhenjhi symbolize the life and spirit of the body. This suggests the consciousness of the male and female needs to be enlightened before they enter into the sacred relationship. Cutting off Tesu's head at the end of the whole ritual has philosophical implications which relate to the shedding of the male ego for a happy marital life. On the whole the festival is like a preface to the future life of an adolescent girl so that she can prepare herself for married life. This marriage ritual is also thought to take all evil with it, so that a girl may be freed from the spell of witchcraft and sorcery before she enters the new phase of her life. Witchcraft, sorcery and necromancy are still a vital part of folk life. All these references have been orally transmitted, suggesting the wide significance, cultural importance, entertainment value and moral implications of this festival, which is on the verge of extinction and needs to be preserved.

7

Articulating tribal culture

The oral tradition of Lambadas

Banoth Deepa Jyothi

The Lambadas are a nomadic tribe, one among the scheduled tribes of India. The versatile and colourful Lambadas are the most populous and widely dispersed tribes in Andhra Pradesh. The Lambadas originally belong to Rajasthan. They had adopted the nomadic way of life and originated as a caravan trading community in South India. They are called by different names, such as Banjaras, Lambadas and Sugalis. Though called by different names in different parts in accordance with the place of their settlement, they all refer to themselves as the Lambada community. They are found scattered among other ethnic groups persistently maintaining their cultural and ethnic identity.

The Lambadas have a rich tradition of oral literature which has been preserved in their community from time immemorial: 'The oral tradition is that process by which the songs, myths, legends, tales and lore of people are formulated, communicated and preserved in language by word of mouth' (Momaday 1970: 167). The oral songs and tales of the Lambadas are the distinct ways of knowing their culture. The knowledge of the Lambadas is reproduced, preserved and conveyed from generation to generation through their oral tradition.

The festivals of the Lambadas have their own identities, distinct culture and traditions. The values and principles embodied in their traditions are based on their life and reality: 'They worship the seven sisters goddess called "Sati-Bhavani". Individually known as Tolja, Kankali, Hingla, Mantral, Dholangar, Samba and Meramma' (Bhukya 2010: 204). Besides celebrating their own religious festivals, they also celebrate all the main Hindu festivals such as Dusshera, Diwali, Holi and Ugadi according to their cultural style.

The festivals, which symbolize the feelings of the whole community, are social and religious in nature. They involve either a single ritual or a conglomeration of rituals and commemorate many of their social customs. The rituals are intended for the social and physical welfare of the community. The main religious festivals of the Lambadas are *Seetala* and

Teej. They believe that the world is full of a multitude of spirits. As a result, sacrifices are made to propitiate the gods during their festival time. The main aspects of Lambada religious festivals are production (fertility) and protection of their animals and crops.

The *Teej* festival known as the 'fertility festival' is an important ceremony of the Lambadas. According to Pratap, 'The Teej ceremony was celebrated as a festival of fertility during the beginning of the monsoon. The rituals are performed with utmost religious fervour for nine days' (Pratap 1972: 10). The ceremonial rituals symbolically represent the function of man and woman in the procreation of the race and in eking out a livelihood. The fertility festival provides splendour and decoration blended with dance and song. The Lambada women, whose colourful dresses are embroidered with small mirrors, dance ceremonial dances. The Lambada girls dance rhythmically to the melodious tunes that bewitch the spectators. The meditative mood, the sacred feelings and the holy atmosphere descend upon the Lambada *thanda* (hamlet).

The festival is exclusively meant for young maidens. The married men, women and widows are prohibited from performing the rituals. B. Chinya Naik records a myth about *Teej* in his book, *Banjara Charitra-Sanskruthi Pragathi*. Pratap writes: 'The goddess Bhavani or Parvathi is reunited with her consort Lord Shiva after a long and trying period of stern austerity on the day of Teej. The goddess declared that whoever invokes their desires will be fulfilled' (Pratap 1972: 11). The unmarried girls believe that if they invoke the goddess with sincere devotion, they will obtain good and virtuous husbands. The rituals are performed for nine days with variations. The first and final day rituals are the most important because they are specially intended for the god Sevabhaya and the goddess Meramma.

Battu Ramesh writes about the origin of the 'Teej':

> There were two brothers named Abdu and Gabdu. They had five hundred cows. One day their cows grazed in the field of wheat, and on their return they had put their dung on a rock. On that rock the seeds of wheat in the dung had sprouted as plants and the roots of the plants entered into that rock. Abdu and Gabdu observed that their deity 'Meramma' had appeared in those plants and they decided to worship and offer sacrifices to their goddess who was in the form of 'Teej'.
>
> (Ramesh 1998: 131)

This is a popular belief of the Lambadas regarding the celebration of the 'Teej' festival.

The Lambadas celebrate the fertility festival with splendour and enthusiasm. The *Naik* (traditional head) of the *thanda* takes the initiative for the participation of other members in the community. Small wild, date-twig baskets are bought from the basket weaver for every young maiden. In the name of the goddess Meramma, the girls fill baskets with earth and manure, and the unmarried boys sow wheat seeds in the baskets while singing the following song:

Chandanema gayhu gallayo re! Sevavo
Chandanema gayhu gallayo re! Sevavo
Chandanema oladi gunthayo re! Sevavo
Chandanema gayhu chankayo re! Sevavo
Chandanema dakalo nakayo re! Sevavo
Chandanema bokada katayo re! Sevavo
Chandanema jhuralo nachayo re! Sevavo
Chandanema teej borayo re! Sevavo (Jhamku.Tejavath)

Oh! Sevalal. The wheat seeds are soaked on full moon day.
Oh! Sevalal. The baskets are weaved on full moon day.
Oh! Sevalal. The wheat seeds are sown in the baskets on full moon day.
Oh! Sevalal. An altar is erected on full moon day.
Oh! Sevalal. Sacrifices are made on full moon day.
Oh! Sevalal. Dances were performed on full moon day.

The young Lambada maidens perform the ceremonial rituals on the lunar days (*pournami*). The wheat seeds are soaked and sown in the baskets. *Dakalo*, meaning an altar or platform, is erected to place the *Teej* baskets on it. They express their joy by saying that they would do everything for the *Teej* festival. The song also reveals the invocation of God Sevabhaya. The *thanda* sports a colourful look with dances and melodious religious songs. The whole atmosphere is replete with joyous expectations and excitement.

The *Teej* baskets are watered before sunrise by the girls singing songs. The following is a song sung during the watering of the wheat baskets:

Sevaro teej borayo re
Panni ghalena
Kuvalo khodalo re
Panni Na ra tho
Meramma ro teej borayo re
Diyala la gada lo
Raatha andarema

Sevabhaya ro teej borayo re
Koda kata li Jo re
Dhoo vala lagadena (Jhanki Bai)

Sevabhaya's *Teej* was planted
Dig the well if there is no water
To water the wheat saplings (*Teej*)
Meramma's *Teej* was planted
Light a lamp if the night is dark
Sevabhaya's *Teej* was planted
Burn the sacred fire
And raise smoke.

The song suggests that the *Teej* planted by the god Sevabhaya and the goddess Meramma is sacred. The *Teej* baskets should be watered with water fetched from a well or stream. The sacred burning fire and the smoke raised are intended to thwart the evil spirits. The sowing of the seeds by the boys and the watering of the seed beds symbolically represent the respective roles of male and female in the procreation of the race.

The Lambada young maidens sing a song praising the beauty of the tender wheat saplings grown in the *Teej* baskets:

Sevabhaya byato soneri gudima
Gudi zankiye chari malekema, chari malakema
Dapada vajiye chari malekema, chari malakema
Malavo byatiye chari malekema, chari malakema
Dandiyadi byati soneri gudima
Gudi zanki ye chari malekema, chari malakema
Kadavo kide ye chari malekema, chari malakema
Jhuralo nachi ye chari malekema, chari malakema
Teeja thuti ye chari malekema, chari malakema (Ami Bai)

Sevabhaya was seated in a golden temple
And the temple is glowing like gold
The people gathered everywhere
Drums were beaten everywhere
Dandiyadi was seated in a golden temple
The temple is glowing like gold
The rituals were performed everywhere
Sheep were sacrificed and
Dances were performed everywhere
Teej is plucked everywhere.

The rituals are performed regularly till the seventh day. On the seventh day of the ceremony, they perform a ritual called *Dhamoli*. They prepare *lapse* (a dish prepared with jaggery and rice) and offer it to the sacred fire with the rising smoke before the *Teej* baskets in the name of Sevabhaya. On the eighth day, the girls prepare a fanciful clay figure called *Gangoar*. The girls and the women make fun of *Gangoar*, which symbolizes the males. The boys and men feel that it is an insult to their sex and try to spoil the inscription of *Gangoar*.

The final ceremony on the ninth day is very important for it marks the mass performance of rites. It is a moment of grief and melancholy as the tender sapling nurtured with care is to be distributed and thrown into the waters. The men wear their traditional long turbans sitting in front of the *Teej* baskets. The Naik offers a prayer by reciting the following words:

Ya sevabhaya bappu! Bachya maharaj
Sai ve jayes yadi! Meramma
Gor garib asami se
Petena patto bhand thani
Nav daad taro chakiri karthani
Ganga nadhi ma lejarecha
Gor garibena andhara chandanema
Sena bhar pur rakades bapu
Savukarena samanak
Kacherer pachen rakades yadi
Yi varase dadero panduga tona
Bhar pur kidecha bapu. (Severi Bai)

Oh! God Sevabhaya Maharaj
Bless us and save us
We the poor Lambadas have celebrated
The rituals for nine days and today
We are taking *Teej* to immerse in the Ganga
Bless us and protect us from police. (Translation by author of the article)

The girls weep as an outward expression of their affection and love for the saplings they nurtured. Subsequently, the *Teej* is immersed in a nearby well or pond.

The oral tradition defines the life patterns of the Lambada people. It imposes a great responsibility on the people to revere their ethics. The indigenous songs, dances and rituals express the community's way of life in the physical and spiritual environment. The oral tradition of the

Lambadas is suggestive of the tradition-bound community. In this regard Rustom Bharucha writes: 'Folklore which constitutes oral tradition is always contemporary, when it deals with cultures and communities who continue to live outside of modernity. If the past continues to have any meaning in societies, it survives; otherwise it disappears' (2003: 25). In spite of variations from place to place, the rituals remain an abiding force for most of the indigenous communities. Oral traditions form the foundation of indigenous societies connecting the speaker and the listener and uniting the past and the present in the collective memory.

References

Bharucha, Rustom. 2003. *Rajasthan: An Oral History*. New Delhi: Penguin India.

Bhukya, Bhangya. 2010. *Subjugated Nomads: The Lambadas Under the Rule of the Nizams*. New Delhi: Orient BlackSwan.

Momaday, Scott N. 1970. *The Remembered Earth*. Albuquerque: University of New Mexico Press.

Pratap, D.R. 1972. *Festivals of Banjaras*. Hyderabad: Tribal Cultural Research and Training Institute.

Ramesh, Battu. 1998. *Society and Culture of Banjaras in Andhra Pradesh*. Unpublished dissertation, Potti Sri Ramulu University, Sri Sailam.

8 Micro and macro intergenerational oral communication in the Zion Christian Church

Lesibana J. Rafapa

Introduction

This chapter looks at the cultural significance of poetry that is presented orally within the Zion Christian Church (ZCC). While such poetry belongs to the African-Initiated Church's oral tradition, my method of analysing this mode of oral tradition is one that assumes that as a source of oral history, oral data are situated within specific cultures. It is as a result of this vantage point that historians like Prins (1991: 119) could observe that historians should not presume serial time in dealing with oral traditions of different peoples. He cautions that 'serial time is not the only sort of time that men use' (1991: 119). The other Western hegemonic approach of history writing that Prins (1991: 119) would like to see changing is one in which change is seen as the main index of historical content because 'there are other things than change to explain'.

My approach is thus a close analysis of the poetry aspect of the ZCC oral tradition, using the oral historical method. Leavy (2011: 4) separates the oral tradition from other kinds of traditions that people may have by stressing that 'an oral tradition is one in which stories are passed down through the generations'. Oral history is 'a method of collecting narratives from individuals for the purpose of research' (Leavy 2011: 4). Ontologically oral history as a research method assumes that 'research is a *process*, not an event' where 'we build meaning through the generation of an interview narrative, and the analysis and interpretation of that narrative' (Leavy 2011: 7). Epistemologically, in the oral history method 'researchers and participants are placed on the same plane' and researchers are 'not conceptualized as "the knowing party" with full authority over knowledge production' (Leavy 2011: 8).

Prins (1991: 120) makes a helpful distinction between two major types of oral source. The first is 'personal reminiscence' which he describes as 'oral evidence specific to the life experiences of the informant' (1991: 120). The second is oral tradition that is 'systematically and dependently related to the reproduction of social structure', which he adopts from the theorist Durkheim (Prins 1991: 121). As the ZCC is an organization and not an individual, my focus in analysing the content of its oral tradition will be on its usefulness in reproducing the social structure of the organization. It is from looking microscopically at the ZCC social structure as it is reflected in its oral tradition that I shall proceed macroscopically to look for reflections of the culture of the people who belong to its majority membership and thus give the organization a specific cultural identity.

Oral tradition can be further subdivided into four types according to whether it is free and formulaic as in names and proverbs, free and narrative as in recollections of historical and other information by research participants, frozen and poetic as in poetry learnt by rote and passed from generation to generation, or free and epic as in poetry composed by a creative mind using data from the oral tradition (Prins 1991: 121). The ZCC oral poetry I shall be looking at as preserved in audio recordings and transcriptions published in its official newsletter named ZCC *Messenger* will be analysed using the criteria outlined earlier. It is important to note that 'the main problems of use and misuse of oral tradition relate to traditions not learned by rote: epics and narratives' (Prins 1991: 123). Narratives transmit 'traditions of genesis, dynastic histories and accounts of social organization' (Prins 1991: 125).

It will be interesting to check the content of the narrative parts of the oral poetry of the ZCC against the authoritative historical accounts by writers such as Mafuta (2010), Lukhaimane (1980) and Anderson (2001), which employed 'modern' historiography. In order to check the modern historical accounts by the writers mentioned here, oral accounts by elderly members of the ZCC, narrative in their form collected by ZCC leadership and published in ZCC *Messenger*, will be explored. ZCC poetry analysed in this chapter was recorded by the church across the three generations of its leadership since its founding in 1910.

Signs of continuity in the praise poem of the current ZCC bishop

The title of this poem recorded on audio tape and published in the official newsletter by the ZCC is 'Ramarumo Mohwaduba'. Ramarumo is a praise name for the current ZCC head, His Grace the Rt. Rev. Bishop

Dr Barnabas Lekganyane. Mohwaduba, too, is not the bishop's surname. It is a clan name of a broad cluster of Sotho families who venerate the buffalo, whose domestic equivalent is a cattle head. For this reason, when the Lekganyane family members are praised in a manner aligned to Northern Sotho cultural practice, references to them by the totems of cattle head and buffalo are used interchangeably.

Such a traditional emphasis on the clan name or totem in praising African leaders of outstanding stature like each of the ZCC bishops coming from the Lekganyane dynasty serves seamlessly to superimpose the lauded attributes of earlier leaders on to those succeeding them. For this reason, traditionally praise poems do not belong to individuals. Although some parts may be added or subtracted as the praise poems pass down generations, some formulae remain constant, thus paying tribute not only to the individual but also to the entire clan or dynasty. The very same poem now used to pay tribute to the current ZCC head was used to pay homage also to his father, Bishop Edward Lekganyane, except for a few lines that the gifted praise singer adapts from time to time. The praise singer, Petrus Molelemane, lived from the days of the founder Bishop Engenas Lekganyane, through to Bishop Edward Lekganyane's reign, up to the early parts of Bishop Barnabas's period. The lines of the oral epic alluding to the founding of the church in 1910 by Bishop Engenas Lekganyane bear testimony to the fact that the same praise poem was used to praise Bishop Engenas during his days, followed by minor adaptations when Bishop Edward Lekganyane assumed leadership of the ZCC in 1948 upon his father's death.

When I compared the taped (ZCC *Church Choir Volume 1 & 2*, 1990) and printed (ZCC *Messenger*, September 1985: 4–5) versions of the praise poem, I noticed that three lines from the original oral rendition were omitted in the printed version. These are:

Gola mogolo ramalala a gola,	Grow, one who grows all night, 23
Ramahlwa a gola,	One who grows all day,
Ramahlwa a bolelela ditšhaba go loka.	One who teaches right all day to nations, 25.

These omitted lines are preceded by and organically expand on the lines:

Ge e le go thakga o thakgile,	As for doing good you have done good, 13
O thakgetše Molepo le Mamabolo,	You did good to Molepo and Mamabolo,

O thakgetše le Makgowa a Mahwibidu,	You did good even to the red whites,
Mohwaduba' Mmaphaka' Monare;	You a Hwaduba of Mmaphaka of buffalo;
Mokgoši wa gago,	Your surging presence, 17
O kwetše Moše wa mawatle,	Reverberates across the seas,
Amerika le Yuropa di a lla,	America and Europe groan,
Ge e le Jerusalema o gakilwe,	You Jerusalem are petrified,
Maphutha ditšhaba,	By he, nations' sanctuary, 21
Ke ra makgoka a kgokolla.	He who ties to untie.

The beginning of the praise epic, entitled 'Ramarumo Mohwaduba' ('Ramaruno of Hwaduba Clan'), up to the lines reproduced earlier, has these lines:

Re a go lotšha Morena Lekganyane,	We salute you King Lekganyane, 1
Lekganšha ditšhaba,	Luminer of nations,
Morena wa kganya ya Sione,	King exuding Zion glory,
Re re thobela Morena.	We say *thobela* King.
Re re Morena Lekganyane,	We say, King Lekganyane, 5
Golela godimo;	Tower skyward;
Mogolo wa go gola re robetše,	Elder who sprouts while we slumber,
Magoši le marena,	With rulers and kings,
Ba re ba tsoga ba hwetša o nabile;	Waking in your mazy spread;
Ga ke go roriše Morena Lekganyane,	I am not lauding you, King Lekganyane, 10
O rorile –	You are lofty –
O rorišitšwe ke mošomo wa gago.	Exulted by own toil.

The praise singer whose performance was recorded first on vinyl in the 1960s and later on audio tape in the collection ZCC *Church Choir Volume 1 & 2* in 1990 performs the praise poem of the ZCC head in the same fashion used in oral literature by praise singers of traditional African leaders. Lines 1 and 4 salute in terms similar to the Zulu *bayede* used traditionally in praising Shaka and other Zulu kings, this time using the Northern Sotho equivalent *thobela*. This is because the ZCC headquarters are in an area where the overwhelming majority is Sotho-speaking black Africans.

For a leader in the northern province of South Africa heading a Christian religious organization with a stronghold in southern Africa to be associated with the holiness of Zion/Jerusalem in Israel is significant. This not only reveals that the ZCC headed by the bishop is, as Lukhaimane (1980) observes, a supra-tribal structure. It stretches the influential sphere of the bishop and ZCC globally, though with an African identity exemplified by words like 'king' and 'thobela', whereby the notion of a great leader cannot be divested of majestic supremacy similar to that of a traditional king. Hence, we have references by ZCC followers to the three generations of bishops starting with Engenas Lekganyane both as bishop and as *kgoši*/king (see Lukhaimane 1980).

When in line 20 the praise singer describes the huge Israeli city of Jerusalem as baffled by the transference of Christian glory historically associated with her to a tiny city in rural Mamabolo in the northern recesses of South Africa, cohesion weaving the long praise epic together is achieved. Allusions to Jerusalem of biblical fame cohere with images elicited by phrases from earlier lines like 'exuding Zion glory' and 'sprouts while we slumber' in lines 3 and 7, respectively. After lines 14 and 15 have credited the bishop and ZCC with use of the Gospel to banish darkness from South African blacks and whites, represented respectively by the phrases 'Molepo and Mamabolo' and 'red whites', the lines 'Reverberates across the seas' (18), 'America and Europe groan' (19) and 'By he, nations' sanctuary' (21) yield an overriding image of the ZCC as expanding her mission inexorably from the soil of King Molepo and King Mamabolo to America and Europe. From being a supra-tribal black South African Christian church, the ZCC is now painted as a multi-racial, multi-national organization.

After the ZCC praise singer has charted the demographic constituents and contours of the ZCC thus, the lines that follow revert to the beginning of the ZCC in 1910 by its founder Engenas Lekganyane. Makgoka is the praise name by which Bishop Engenas Lekganyane is known immortally.

E re nka be o be Makgoka	O that you had been a Tier, 23
Wa go kgokela ruri;	Who ties for ever;
O tla šala le bafe Makgoka,	With what people shall you remain, Tier,
O tla boela gape dithabeng tša Sione,	Shall you clamber again the mounts of Zion, 26
Go yo rapela, go phuta setšhaba,	To supplicate, to amass the throngs,
Ge e le mo setšhaba se timela,	For congregants go astray,
Go timela baetapele?	It is leaders who wander away? 29.

The central lines 26 and 27 state the historical fact of Engenas, after his call in 1910 (see Lukhaimane 1980; Mafuta 2010) praying on the mountain of Zion in Moria, South Africa. Zion is not the original name of the mountain. Engenas renamed the mountain Zion after founding the church to signify Christian ties with Zion in Israel. In the ZCC founder's prayers on Mount Zion, he asked God to send him people that he could teach the Gospel of Jesus Christ to (Lukhaimane 1980; Mafuta 2010). As congregants (line 28) and leaders (line 29) within the congregation typically veer into aberration despite the ZCC founding bishop's hard work to show them the way of the Lord, the performer expresses a paradoxical wish that after the ZCC bishop had converted people to Christianity such people would not have remained with a choice either to continue following Christian ways or to revert to dark ways. It is an aspect of the Christian Gospel that human beings differ from all other creation by virtue of having a choice. The praise singer's complaint thus serves to reveal a thorough knowledge by the ZCC bishop of Christian principles.

The previous lines are followed by the oral performer's request for forgiveness from God, trusting this to the ZCC bishop's prayers. He advances as a mitigating factor the fact that unlike heaven, the earth is a place of sin, tempting the children of God to forsake the teachings of Christianity:

Re rapelele Morena Lekganyane,	Pray for us, King Lekganyane, 30
Legodimo le lefase ga di tshwane;	Heaven and earth are not the same;
Re a go lotšha;	We humble ourselves before you;
Tebernikele ya Sione re re e tlile,	The tabernacle of Zion is here with us,
Tebernikele ya Sione e tlile e se na sebopego,	Tabernacle of Zion came without form,
E tla bogwa ke bohle,	To be beheld by all,
E tla bogwa ke meloko le meloko,	To be beheld by this and coming generations,
E tla bogwa le ke ngwana wa lesea.	It shall catch even the eye of a babe, 37.

The oral performer's metonymic hallowing of the ZCC bishop to the point of bestowing on him a halo of holiness should be interpreted in the African cultural convergence of respect for a good leader with a god-like worship, as explicated in Lukhaimane's (1980) study of the ZCC. From an African cultural perspective such a regard for the king or any leader accorded the stature of a king is ethical. That is why Shai's (2006) biographical study of the Rain Queen Modjadji points the reader to the traditional belief of Modjadji's subjects that the Queen's unhappiness could lead to famine or other kinds of pestilences plaguing the nation, for a benevolent African monarch is traditionally seen to possess god-like supernatural powers. The praise singer understandably asks the ZCC bishop vicariously to forgive congregants' sins.

Pervading biblical allusions continue to tie the black South Africa–founded Christian denomination to the mission of Christ and sanctity embodied in Israel's Jerusalem/Zion, seen in the repeated word 'tabernacle'. According to the oral performer the new tabernacle of South Africa–based Zion is of mystical beauty perceived more by the human soul than physical eye (shown in the phrase 'catch even the eye of a babe' in line 37), with supernal power to rivet all mankind due to its quality to transcend physical form. As the ZCC tabernacle is 'to be beheld by this and coming generations' (line 26), through its historical Christianity is heightened to invoke the ideal in order to satisfy the human need to hope for a paradise by means of which the frailties of this world will be defeated. According to Africanist writers like Abraham (1962) and Mphahlele (2002), the African cultural view of human life and death is that of life continuing beyond death, wrongdoing being corrected by intervention of ancestors during the carnal life of the ancestors' progeny, and an afterlife that is fantastically of ever-lasting bliss. It is not difficult to see that the ZCC notion of an afterlife portrayed by the oral performer is the Africanist one in which sins are cleansed from the congregation by the bishop while the congregants are still alive, so that in their idea of death there is no alien cultural notion of hell.

The redeeming nature of ZCC-style Christian Gospel is depicted in hopeful terms that lean on the traditional mission of the Gospel to banish darkness. Lines 38 to 76 that follow testify to this.

Taba yena	May this matter 38
A e ke e ngwalelwe meloko	Be written down for generations
Ye e sa tlago go tswalwa,	Yet to be born,
Le re go bona,	Tell them,
Bošego bo fedile,	Night is finished, 42
Ga bo sa tla hlwela bo e ba gona;	It won't be any longer;
Bohlale bo hloka maelelo,	Wit is frozen stagnant,
Ditau di fedile meno,	Lions' teeth are filed,
Kganya e retwa ke bohle;	All extol light;
Morena Lekganyane,	King Lekganyane,

Ke molato wa gago;	It is your doing;
O tla re ruta go loka,	You shall teach us righteousness,
E seng ka bobe le ge e le kgalefo,	Not through evil or bluster, 50
Gobane modiša wa dinku ga a bolaye,	For a good shepherd does not kill,
Ka mehla o bofa tše šohlago,	He ties those that break the kraal,
O bofa a hunela digwahla matolo,	He bandages tightening knees of the invalid,
O kgoka tše šohlago,	He ties those that break the kraal,
Makgoka Morena Lekganyane,	Tier, King Lekganyane,
Thobela Morena.	*Thobela* Lord. 56
Hlaba letšatši le legolo,	Rise high o great day,
Magola a hlaba,	Rise you who grows with dawn,
Letšatši magoletša le legodimo,	Sun that kindles the heavens,
Letšatši mahloka sereto;	Sun defying praise;
Letšatši o senyetša batho boroko,	You sun spoil people's sleep, 71
Mola e se ke ya ba wena,	Had it not been you,
Batho nka be re robetše,	We would be fast asleep,
Go buša bošego bja ga malala a putuka,	Letting rummaging night reign,
Bošego bja go re bo e sa,	Night that as it fades,
Lefsifsi ka katakata ntweng.	Makes dark recede battle 76.

Lines 48 and 49, respectively, attribute the ascendance of light to Bishop Lekganyane's teachings and organization as well as describe the world with such light as a paradise in which 'Lions' teeth are filed' (line 45), where without the ZCC bishop's diligent guidance the followers will be disorientated. In line with what Shai (2006) observes about the pragmatic and visionary ascriptions of a traditional ruler, traditionally the African king is expected to possess extraordinary genius that enables him or her to guide and protect his or her followers as a parent does with his or her children. The image of Bishop Lekganyane here tallies with such an African conception of a king or any significant leader.

Congruous with the feature of African cultures hinted earlier, to expect ancestors and the Supreme Being to recompense the wrongdoing of mortals while they still live in the physical world, the oral praise singer of the ZCC counterpoints the pleasant invocation of worldly paradise with that of a vividly drawn worldly purgatory:

Nto ye nngwe e etla,	Some chimera is looming, 77
Ke nto ye e se nago lebitšo,	Thing without name,
Ke mantšhekgedile,	Thing of spiky tinklings,
Wa bošego le mosegare,	Pounding by day and by night,

Ke nto ya go ja bana le batho ba bagolo,	Thing gorging young and old, 81
Yo e tlago mo feta,	One whom it spares,
O tla ba le lehlogonolo,	Will be lucky,
Gobane o tla dula le bahu,	For he will live with the dead,
Empa badimo ba sa dule le motho	Though the dead live with no one. 85

Apart from these lines conjuring up the shape of an anthropomorphic monster sent by the ancestors and Supreme Being to bring back balance among human beings with the harmony of the universe they also paint a picture true to the Africanist understanding of a reality that does not separate the physical from the spiritual, the animate from the inanimate, the empirical from the mystical, etc. That is why line 84 contains the phrase 'live with the dead' bridging the phenomena of life and death, normally known to exist in mutual exclusion. The phrase 'live with the dead' not only defies western Manichean binaries, but reveals that the world view represented by the oral performer is steeped in African cultures that put human beings and the 'living dead' at the centre of their cosmology (see Mphahlele 2002). This, according to African writers like Rafapa (2010), is the fabric of African cosmology which leaders of South African African-Initiated Churches are known to invoke in order to show Christianity is devoid of an African outlook.

In the lines that follow, the oral rendition sketches the anguish caused in non-ZCC members of ambient African communities, whose unmediated belief in traditional religion leads to temperamental anguish. The combined effect of the phrases 'an *inyanga*' (line 89) and 'we have lost it' (line 90) is that of associating unmediated traditional religion with loss, in the light of the advent of the new Jerusalem of ZCC and the gospel heralded by it. This is seen when a visit to the traditional healer yields no respite from rampant deaths dealt human beings by the God-decreed monster:

O ile go e kwa a tlala pelo,	Someone got vexed to hear this, 86
A hlanola dinao,	And then hurried,
Moroma a gara thogwana,	Till speed tossed up the skirt,
Ra re ge e le ngaka,	And we opined if an *inyanga*,
E ka hlolela re paletšwe;	Were to stop the deaths we have lost it;
Mme a boa a nyamile pelo,	Yet he returned with a sad heart,
Gobane a hlokile motlatši,	For he had not found one in agreement,

mothetši a ditaba,	One with agreeing ears to listen, 92
A ditaba tau ya go ja e sa kgore,	News of lion eating with leaping hunger,
Sebata se se nago boya;	Predator without body hair;
Tseba legodimo,	Know that heavens,
Ga le a ka la ahlolwa le batho.	Can never be judged with men.
Re a go lotšha,	We salute you, 97
Morena wa kganya ya Sione,	King exuding Zion glory,
Re re thobela Morena,	We say *thobela* King,
Marobathota a kgomo	Breaker of bull hump
Lepelle la Mmamogodi,	In Lepelle River of Mmamogodi, 101
Ba ile ba re ge ba go bona,	As those nearby witnessed,
Ba ikhurumetša difahlogo ba re,	They hid their faces saying,
Kgomo mma 'a ditšhaba o ye tla.	One with Cow totem, mother of nations, is coming.

The imagery of motherly love and protection in the words 'Cow' and 'mother of nations' in the closing line of the long oral praise epic signifies that if human beings were to defer to the conquering crusade of God's new kingdom coming through the ZCC leader, a paradise would be experienced on earth.

The content of this praise epic departs from some deeds of the present generation leader of the ZCC in order to recall the history of how the Church was founded in 1910 and later heightened during the reign of the second bishop. Timeless formulae that transcend individual ascription are a vehicle for transporting the memory of the audience to the past. These are what Prins (1991: 123) describes as 'crystal of wording' that 'remain unchanged within a changing kaleidoscope of structures adapted to particular purposes'. These are words like 'Mohwaduba' 'Mmaphaka' 'Monare' (line 16); 'Sione' (lines 26, 33 and 34); 'Makgoka' (lines 22, 23, 24, 25, 54, 55 and 98); 'Morena Lekganyane' (lines 1, 2, 4, 5, 10, 30, 47 and 55); 'Thobela Morena' (lines 4, 5, 10, 56 and 99); 'Re a go lotšha' (lines 1, 32 and 97); 'Morena wa kganya ya Sione' (lines 3 and 98) and 'Kgomo' (lines 100 and 104).

With regard to narrative parts of the epic that by their nature are not constant but vary in keeping with the purpose of the poem's structure that is adapted to the present times of an organization, these stand out and perform a separate function from that of the history conjuring formulae. The present-reconstructing narrative parts of the ZCC praise epic below distinctively dwell on Bishop Edward Lekganyane's second-generation segment in the continuum of ZCC leadership now in its third generation. Clearly there are bound to be in the praise epic individual leader-specific qualities that set the achievements and character of the specific leader apart from his predecessor and successor. These are parts that offer the performer leeway to apply his or her creativity and expertly compose lyrics of his own, which the historical formulae should only serve to frame within the epic mode.

Continuity and rupture during the second-generation ZCC leadership of Bishop Edward Lekganyane

The poem below has not been reduced to writing by the ZCC, forcing me to transcribe from a taped oral rendition of it. The oral performer starts by naming it 'Sereto sa Bishop Edward Lekganyane' ('Praise poem for Bishop Edward Lekganyane'). Bishop Edward is the second-generation ZCC leader who took over after his father's death in 1948 (Lukhaimane 1980; Anderson 2001). When Bishop Edward died in 1967, his son, the current ZCC bishop ascended the throne (Lukhaimane 1980; Anderson 2001; Mafuta 2010).

Ga e le ka direto,	With praises,
Re a mo phopholetša,	We merely grope for him,
Re re ke Edward ke Morena Lekganyane,	We say he is Edward he is Lord Lekganyane,
Ke Mohwaduba wa Mmaphaka Monare,	He is a Hwaduba of Mmaphaka of buffalo,
Re re a a ratana marena,	We say rulers lick each other, 5
Bošego a a etelana,	Paying each other visits by night,
A a rera sephiring,	They conspire underground,
A rera ka lebitšo la gago.	They rue your name.
Morena Lekganyane,	Lord Lekganyane,
Re re ka mahlo ke e bone kgoši,	We say I saw a ruler with naked eyes, 10
E apere lesaka e tšama e letša lenkga,	Clad in sack and blowing plaintive horn,
E re batho re tshwenyegile,	Declaring anguish among people,
Re tshwentše ke pitša e tala mafapanya,	Cursing the green pot sowing gulfs,
E re fapantšha le batswadi,	Ripping us from parents,
Ke phefo ye kgolo mahube,	Blasting wind dawn,
Ye e tšamago e kgobakantšha ditšhaba,	Raking in nations,

Ditšhiwana ga re holege re kokobetše,	We orphans too low to gain,
Re emetše go phetha diporofeto,	Shelved to live prophecies,
Ditšhabeng tša Sione,	Amid Zion throngs, 19
Gobane re mo dumetše motho	
yo moso Lekganyane;	For we believe in black man Lekganyane;
Gobane ba bašweu ba e tlišitše nnete,	For whites came with truth,
Ya mmakgodi 'a kgookgoo,	Nothing but the truth,
Re re dumela Morena Lekganyane,	We greet you Lord Lekganyane,
Kgoši maaga a rutla,	King that erects and breaks,
O agile sefateng sa Kwenane,	Resident in the Kwenane pass, 25
Mokgahlong ga Molepo le Mamabolo;	Between Kings Molepo and Mamabolo;
O duletše go hloma sefoka,	With mission to hoist laurels
Folaga ye tala ya boReuben Lekgasa,	Green flag of Reuben of Makgasa regiment,
Ngwanabo seahlola ka pula le maru,	Sibling of judge wielding rain and clouds,
Re re ahlola Morena Lekganyane,	We prostrate to your verdict Lord Lekganyane,
Mohlala wa pula o go wena,	Trail or rain rests in you,
Re gana phefo fela,	Only storms we loathe, 32
Phefo matšama a roba dihlare makala,	Storms of broken boulders,
Naga ya šala e apotše.	Stripping land naked.
Mola e se ke ya ba go ja thapo ye ntsho mogolo,	Were it not of eating and dark string gullet,
Nka be a re porofetela mangaka 'a koma,	Initiation healers would prophesy to us,
A phulakanya mašoba,	Tearing ground to pitted furrows,
A re epela dihlare re alafa;	Digging herbs for our healing;
Ge e le ditaola di gakile barei ba tšona,	Diviners' bones baffle their namers,
Di bolaile namane,	They predict defeat, 40
Pheko ya dithebele e re,	Remedy bones point to,
E yong botšiša Bibele selo sa go seba,	Is perusal of Bible of cautions,
E sebile Kgoši Moraswi e sebile Setlakalane,	Cautions for King Moraswi,
cautions for Settlakalane	
Ya re ge e seba ya šupetša marena bophelo,	Pointing the rulers towards life,
Ya re Kgomo e tšwa Leboya,	Speaking of Cow totem from the north,

E a getlagetla e phutha se hlotšago,
Le se omeletšego ditho,
E se bokelela GaLeshasha,
Ga Willie ga morwa lekgowa;
white man;
Kgomo e buša ka go etiša leje pele;
Ge e le yena Engenase o bolela
ka lentšu,
O boelela GaMamabolo Bopedi
Thabakgone,
Thabakgone of Pedi,
Go yo phetha dikano.
Re re Edward Morena Lekganyane,
Go tla ba lehlogonolo,
Ba 'a tlang go o bona mmušo wo
wa gago,
Gobane batho re a bitšwa re bitšwa
ke lehu,
Lehu madula a bogwa lehu nka
be le tlwaelwa,
Nka be re le aparela diala,
Mohla re tlogang lefaseng ra lokelela,
column, 60
Ra bina kgotso mpogo koša ye mpsha,
Koša ye e se nago leepo.
Edward Morena Lekganyane,
A o tla re rapelela go yo fihla
Le wena mafelelong Morena,
Ge e le mona re eja ke seja,
Lehu madula a bogwa Morena?
Ge e le sebe sona mphapantšha,
Se mphapantšha le wena,
Morena wa kganya ya Sione,
Ge o re bileditše go loka,

Se re ntšha lešakeng la gago;
Mmušo wa gago morwa Khutane,
Re be re o letetše ka go sa feleng,
Empa ge e le lefase le re thetsitše,

Le re fapantšha le wena morwa
Khutane.

Actively saving that which limps,
And those with stiff joints, 47
Gathering all at Leshasha's abode,
At shelter of Willie son of the

The Cow reigning with the rock;
As for Engenas he speaks through
the word,
Turning back to Mamabolo in

To live the covenant.
We say Edward Lord Lekganyane,
Blessed are those,
That will see your kingdom,

For we are beckoned by death,

Death ever puzzling were it
scrutable,
We would adorn in trophies,
Upon departing earth and wind in

And chant born song *mpogo*,
Song with no vile tail.
Edward Lord Lekganyane,
We beseech, pray for us to reach
With you the end of time's Lord,
For we fall in the eater's mouth,
Death living always with us?
As for divider sin,
It makes me differ with you,
King exuding Zion glory, 70
After you have redeemed us to
righteousness,
It pulls me out of your kraal;
Your kingdom son of Khutane,
We have always awaited,
Yet as for the world, it has tempted
us,
It makes you cross with us son of
Khutane.

In the preceding praise epic, dedicated to the second-generation ZCC bishop Edward Lekganyane, there are formulae already encountered in the analysis, earlier, of the praise poem for the third-generation ZCC bishop Barnabas Lekganyane. Some of them are 'Morena Lekganyane' (lines 3, 9, 23, 30 and 54); 'Mohwaduba wa Mmaphaka Monare' (line 4); 'Kgomo' (lines 45 and 50); and 'Morena wa kganya ya Sione' (line 70). The bulk of Bishop Barnabas's praise epic, except for the narrative sections that are attributed specifically to him, was also used to praise the first and second-generation ZCC bishops. The present poem, though dedicated to second-generation Bishop Edward, was used to praise the founder Bishop Engenas, but for the narrative parts referring specifically to him. That this is the case is borne out by the presence of the same formulaic phrases that are in Bishop Barnabas's praise poem.

In the same way as third-generation Bishop Barnabas is uniquely credited with expanding the church beyond South Africa and the continent of Africa in non-formulaic parts of his praise poem, similarly non-formulaic parts of the present poem spell out second-generation Bishop Edward's specific achievement. Lines 1 and 2 of this poem reveal that there is more than meets the eye in Bishop Edward Lekganyane. Although this quality of inexplicable spiritual power is true also for Bishop Edward's predecessor, it has heightened and intensified during Bishop Edward's rule. Hence the content of the two opening lines of the poem. Bishop Edward's reference as 'morwa Khutane' (lines 73 and 76), using second-generation Bishop Engenas's nickname of Khutane instead of the formal Engenas, signifies such a deepening of inscrutable spiritual power, for the meaning of Engenas's nickname is 'One who hides'. In other words, Engenas and Edward prefer to appear in front of their followers like ordinary men while they are actually masking their true, celestial identity. Parts of the taped poem that single out Edward's most outstanding achievement of drawing his followers away from the spell of traditional healers known also for their use of divining bones are lines 35 to 49. One reason for traditional healers having lost their former noble role in society, now overtaken by the ZCC leader, is that they started lying to their patients and spreading unwarranted malice to thrust battles in the midst of society, as long as they extorted money to satisfy their own greed. This is revealed in the lines 'Mola e se ke ya ba go ja thapo ye ntsho mogolo' ('Were it not of eating and dark string gullet') and 'Nka be a re porofetela mangaka 'a koma' ('Initiation healers would prophesy to us').

In the way described earlier, both rupture and continuity are represented by parts of the praise epic dedicated to Bishop Edward Lekganyane.

Conclusion

Rafapa (2010) describes the Zion Christian Church mores at the least as an abrogation of Western Christianity to imbue it with African Humanist values that have, through history, proven to be the survival kit of Africans whose identity was being smothered by the alien cultural sensibility of the protagonists of apartheid. Hence the basic commonness with Shembe's Church of the Nazarites, which Pongweni (2000: 195) and Anderson (2001: 101) credit with attempts at spiritual and cultural survival of the underprivileged in its heyday. Anderson (2001: 101) furthermore highlights this culturally and economically affirming tenet of the ZCC throughout its existence in his observation that 'the ZCC has emerged from the fear of a powerful and oppressive regime to attempt to play a role in the radical changes that have taken place'. As a result of this place of the ZCC on the fringes of power and its holistically salvaging message for the underprivileged, Mafuta (2010: ii) is able to describe the consequences of this in his remark that

> empowering its adherents economically through a religious soteriology, the ZCC has become an example of a trend that is shaping the Global South and is reviving the interest of social scientists and theologians to further investigate the impact of religious and theological formulations on the economic conduct of individuals.

Because the ZCC is a church, all the social and nation building roles described earlier start with spiritual salvation borne of a distinct African cultural identity that excludes the traditional use of healers, drinking of traditional and other beer and taking of any drugs including smoking. The reality constructed by the ZCC among Africans is forged through adjustment towards insights the praise epics discussed earlier contain. As a researcher my approach was that of reconciling my horizon, categories and values with those of the poets and the organization they present. A horizon is 'a set of cultural and personal categories and values' which any researcher shapes an understanding of researched entities 'based to a certain extent on them' (Michrina and Richards 1996: 28). Values reveal to a person what his or her culture 'prefers, what is allowed, rejected, or is forbidden; they indicate what is beautiful, good, fun, helpful, distasteful, bad, boring, or destructive', while 'categories indicate the most important qualities of things' (Michrina and Richards 1996: 28).

This is the oral history approach outlined at the beginning of this chapter, which in my view is reconcilable with what Michrina and Richards (1996: 28) refer to as a 'systematic investigative method called dialogical hermeneutics'. According to Michrina and Richards (1996: vii), the word 'dialogical' refers to 'the use of dialogue – dyadic conversation, negotiation of an understanding' – while the word 'hermeneutics' refers to 'the construction of a description of a whole scene or phenomenon through an incremental analysis of information', leading to a holistic description through incremental analysis of dialogue. Dialogue in this case is the semantics of the formulaic parts of the praise epics signifying historical and cultural continuity, as well as the meanings of the lyrical parts of the poetry performances defining the character and achievements of a specific ZCC leader and the body of the ZCC at a certain juncture. These complementary functions of ZCC epic poetry coincide with Prins's (1991: 123) definition of the epic as 'heroic poetry composed orally, according to rules . . . written down subsequently' with a structure that is 'strong enough to transcend' the process of writing and later oral modifications, having a 'fixed form'. In keeping with Prins's definition, the ZCC oral poetry analysed in this chapter performs the category of researched data called the 'narrative' in the oral tradition analysed by means of the oral history method.

Of significance is the achievement of ZCC micro intergenerational communication by means of the endemically recognizable epic structure of the poems analysed above to magnify into a macro intergenerational communication that is an index of the evolving cultural outlooks of the African communities in its ambience, who are not necessarily members of the church. This is achieved by means of the extraorganizational cultural content of the ZCC oral poetic performances, hinted at by the descriptions of the ZCC represented by the writers Lukhaimane (1980), Mphahlele (2002), Mafuta (2010), Rafapa (2010) and Anderson (2001). It becomes clear from the writings of these researchers on the ZCC that to talk about the evolving cultural identity of the ZCC is to talk about the cultures of the African communities around it that have evolved across generations. The communication of these cultural traits internally within the ZCC by means of the oral tradition is tantamount to macro intergenerational oral communication of the greater community within which the ZCC operates.

References

Abraham, W.E. 1962. *The Mind of Africa*. Chicago: University of Chicago Press.

Anderson, Allan. 2001. *African Reformation: African Initiated Christianity in the 20th Century*. Trenton: Africa World Press.

Leavy, Patricia. 2011. *Oral History: Understanding Qualitative Research*. Auckland: Oxford University Press.

Lukhaimane, Khelebeni Elias. 1980. *The Zion Christian Church of Ignatius (Engenas) Lekganyane, 1924 to 1948: An African experiment with Christianity*. Unpublished Master's dissertation, University of the North.

Mafuta, L. 2010. *Religion and Development in South Africa: An Investigation of the Relationship Between Soteriology and Capital Development in an African Initiated Church (AIC)*. Unpublished doctoral thesis, University of South Africa, Pretoria.

Michrina, Barry P. and Cherylanne Richards. 1996. *Person to Person. Fieldwork, Dialogue and the Hermeneutic Method*. Albany: State University of New York Press.

Motolla, E.M. (ed). 1985. *ZCC Messenger* (September): 12–13, 22–5.

Mphahlele, E. 2002. *Es'kia*. Johannesburg: Kwela Books in association with Stainbank and Associates.

Pongweni, Alex. 2000. 'Voicing the Text: South African Oral Poetry and Performance', *Critical Arts*, 14(2): 175–222.

Prins, Gwyn. 1991. 'Oral History', in Peter Burke (ed), *New Perspectives on Historical Writing*, pp. 114–39. Cambridge: Polity Press.

Rafapa, Lesibana. 2010. *Es'kia Mphahlele's Afrikan Humanism*. Johannesburg: Stainbank and Associates.

Shai, M. 2006. *Bogoši bja Kgošigadi Modjadji*. Thohoyandou: Ditlou Publishers.

ZCC Church Choir Volume 1 & 2 (music cassette). 1990.

9 Sacred places as traditional heritage for the Vhavenda indigenous community of Limpopo Province, South Africa

Nelson Mbulaheni Musehane

Introduction

Before embarking on research of this magnitude, it is imperative to define what sacred places are. Failure to do this would not do justice to the topic. Hornby (1989: 1113) defines a thing as sacred when it is

> connected with or dedicated to God or a god; connected with religion: a sacred rite, place, image, a sacred building, e.g. a church, mosque, synagogue or temple.

By this definition Hornby believes a sacred object is anything that is connected with praying to God or gods. For example, in India, a cow is considered to be a sacred animal. Tulloch (1991: 1354) goes further to explain what a sacred thing entails. She defines it as follows:

> Exclusively dedicated or appropriated (to God or to some religious purpose); made holy by religious association – connected with religion; used for a religious purpose – safeguarded or required by religion, reference or tradition.

According to her definition a thing is sacred if it is dedicated, concentrated, hallowed, holy, blessed, sacrificed, revered, divine, venerable, venerated, blest, religious, spiritual, church, chapel, ecclesiastical, priestly, hieratic, ritual, ceremonial, solemn, sacramental, liturgical, votive, inviolable, inviolate, untouchable, protected and sacrosanct.

In the Tshivenda language such a place is called *zwifho*<*tshifho* 'gifts from' <*-fha* 'to give'. It is a place where rituals are given. Van Warmelo (1989: 398) defines *zwifho* (sacred place) as follows:

> Sacred place or grove of aboriginal inhabitants of the country, where ancestor cult rites or others involving offerings are in many cases still performed.

Such a place is also known as *zwiendeulu* (royal burial place) of the ruling *khosi* or chief. He referred to Lake Fundudzi as *tshiendeulu tsha vha Tshiavha,* meaning that Lake Fundudzi is a sacred place of the ruling family of *Tshiavha.*

Sinclair (1992: 1278) in the *Collins COBUILD English Language Dictionary* indicates the following:

> Something that is sacred is believed to be holy and to have a special connection with God; connected with religion or used in religious ceremonies; regarded as too important to be changed or interfered with.

He goes on to indicate things that can be sacred such as sacred cows or sacred owls. One describes a belief, custom or institution as a sacred cow. When one thinks that people regard something with too much respect and never criticize or question it or show disapproval, it is sacred.

Davidson *et al.* (1996: 874) define 'sacred' as follows:

> Consecrated, devoted; set apart or religious; entitled to veneration.

This definition is supported by the *Cambridge International Dictionary of English* (1995: 1247) which considers something to be sacred when it is

> holy and deserving respect, especially because of a connection with religion.

According to Pearsall (2001: 1634) something is sacred as long as it is

> Connected with God (or the gods) or dedicated to a religious purpose and so deserving veneration, religious rather than secular, regarded with great respect and reverence by a particular religion, group or individual.

In conclusion, sacredness includes all the above-mentioned definitions. We can have a sacred cow, sacred heart, sacred kinship, sacred society, sacred scriptures, sacred pipe, sacred baboon, sacred clown, sacred river and sacred places, as long as each of these has been connected or dedicated to God or gods of the aborigines of the country.

Fundudzi sacred lake

Lake Fundudzi is located in the Soutpansberg in the Vhembe District of the Limpopo Province of South Africa. It is found on the eastern side of the N1-road that connects Musina and the Beit Bridge border post between South Africa and Zimbabwe. According to Van Warmelo (1989: 429) the word *tshitungulo (-tungula)* refers to

> Any object associated with ancestral spirits or ancestor cult, esp., heirlooms handed down in the family and used in the rites to pour libations over them, or to wear as a protective amulet of the inhabitants.

The lake is the *zwifho<-fha* at a sacred place of the Tshiavha clan. The lake distinguishes itself from other lakes found in the whole world because of the following aspects.

Mutale River floating on the lake

The water of the Mutale River can be seen floating through the sacred lake. Water from other rivers, if poured from one utensil, would mix freely, and no one would be able to distinguish it from other water. However, the water from the Mutale River does not mix freely with that of the sacred lake. Mutale River is known to be a river that floats over a sacred lake, hence – *tala* 'float or swim'. The water from the sacred lake is also thicker than the water in the Mutale River; hence Mutale River water floats on Lake Fundudzi.

Supernatural powers

The lake is known for its supernatural powers and things happening in its surroundings, which are known to the inhabitants of the district. It is believed that during the night a *tshikona* dance can be heard in the sacred lake without anyone seeing the people who are participating in it. When people proceed to the lake to take a look, it stops. This lake is a sacred place for the Vhavenda of Tshiavha.

Type or species of fish and crocodiles in the lake

The Fundudzi sacred lake contains numerous species of fish and is infested with crocodiles. It is believed that some of the fish species are not found in most other local rivers. There are also crocodiles that are different from those in local rivers. Notably, the crocodiles in local rivers take people, beasts, goats and dogs. However, people find the crocodiles in Lake Fundudzi harmless. When people fish on the lake, crocodiles swim past them without harming them.

Rites performed on the banks of Fundudzi sacred lake

After visiting the sacred lake, one does not then leave as one pleases. One has to perform certain rituals first. Before one leaves the sacred lake, one should *kodola,* that is stand bent forward with protruding buttocks; hence, the other name of Fundudzi is *Dzivha la Nyankodolela,* meaning the sacred lake where one should stand bent forward with protruding buttocks before one leaves.

Reasons for performing the rituals

It is believed that if one visits the sacred lake and fails to perform the rituals before one leaves, bad luck would befall one.

In addition, before one visits the sacred lake area, one should report to the local *khosi* (chief). If one does not do so, it is believed that bad luck would befall one. It is said that some white tourists once visited the sacred lake without reporting or announcing their mission so that the lake could be 'fenced off'. The visitors went to work the first day and knocked off without a problem, hoping to restart their work the following day, and retreated to their tents. It is said there was a sudden loud noise and whirlwind that night. The tourists feared for their lives. When they woke up the following morning, they were shocked to find all the poles of the fence had been removed, as if the tourists had not done any work. They could not believe it. They resumed their work and knocked off as usual. The following day they returned to work. However, they found everything uprooted again. The local people had to inform the whites that the place was sacred and should not be 'fenced in'. They realized late that the lake is not to be fenced in or tampered with. To date, until the local *khosi* Netshiavha is informed and he in turn speaks to the gods, requesting permission to visit the lake, one cannot just go there. Sometimes permission is not given. When it is not, one should not dare to visit the lake. If one insists on doing so, it is believed that bad luck may befall one.

Protection of Lake Fundudzi as a sacred heritage

In the *Limpopo Mirror* of 2 December 2011, an article appeared entitled 'Sacred Lake Fundudzi to receive formal protection status'. According to the article

> Lake Fundudzi at Tshiavha, outside Thohoyandou, the only inland lake in South Africa and a sacred burial shrine for the Netshiavha royal family of the Vhatavhatsindi clan of the Vhavenda people, will at last receive formal protection status from the South African Heritage Resources Agency.

This was a statement issued by Victor Netshiavha, who is the royal family spokesperson and a government heritage resources manager at the Freedom Park. He said this in consultation with all interested parties, in particular, the Netshiavha royal family.

'The declaration of Fundudzi Lake as a National Heritage Site is the most appropriate decision, as the lake will at last receive the protection it deserves', commented the *Limpopo Mirror*. This was after the Netshiavha family had very painful experiences in fighting for the respect and observation of the indigenous practices that had made the lake a venerated landscape for decades; it was these practices that had kept the lake sacred and preserved. Netshiavha was concerned about reports in the media that some members of the public, in particular among the Vhavenda people, were suspicious of the move, as they thought that the lake would be commodified and commercialized. According to him Fundudzi is their identity and who they are is important. No circumstances will push them to commercialize their identity. 'Fundudzi will remain sacred and a secret for the Netshiavha royals', he said, and it is 'through processes like these that its sacredness can be respected. People should not confuse the declaration of the site with tourism, as the primary objective of such a declaration is to protect the site'.

He went on to state that 'the only challenge we have is that there are many people who claim to know more about the spiritual significance of Fundudzi than the Nestshiavha themselves. These people have distorted and misrepresented our heritage, for us. It is very derogatory' (*Limpopo Mirror*). If people want to get accurate information about the spiritual significance of the place, Mr Netshiavha advises them to enquire from the family. What is important is that 'a site is declared a national heritage site because of its special significance or other special values and its importance in the community patterns of South Africa's history'. Another factor is whether it possesses any uncommon, rare or endangered aspects of South Africa's natural or cultural heritage according to the National Heritage Resources Act.

Zwiawelo ('resting place') as sacred places

In Tshivenda culture, the rulers are posted far away from each other. When one dies, they bury the person in a hut built in one day. In the hut they put a bed made of poles. The person rots in the house or in the grave for a couple of years. When the time for the removal of bones from the charred body comes, they dig out the bones and move them to the burial place for senior chiefs, which will be his final resting place. They bundle the bones and carry them to the grave. When on the way, they find a place to rest when they are tired. Whilst resting, they put the load of bones on the ground. The place is demarcated by putting a bunch of leaves to form a heap. From that day any person who passes on that path will take a leaf from a tree and put it on that heap. It does not matter what type of tree it was, as long it is a green leaf. The place would be called *zwiaweloni*, 'a place of rest'.

Sometimes people who want to get good fortune make a request by throwing the leaf. It is believed that the gods would answer their prayers.

Sometimes when a hearse is carrying a corpse en route to the graveyard, it will also be expected to stop and rest. This stopping of the hearse is to enable the corpse to rest and then move on. It is not known how a corpse should rest because corpses are carried by a hearse. When a person was involved in an accident the corpse is also carried in a hearse. The hearse that takes him to the mortuary may sometimes be running at a high speed. Sometimes the corpse is taken in the morning on the day of burial and driven at a high speed to make up for lost time for burial services. But from home to the cemetery the cortège travels at a snail's pace, sometimes stopping and resting. This is known as *zwiawelo* in Tshivenda culture.

This tendency is passed on from generation to generation orally. It is a traditional heritage that is sacred to the Vhavenda community. The community does not do away with the practice because it is intangible. If it is not done in this way they feel that burial rites are not fulfiled.

Zwisima ('spring') as sacred places

Sometimes springs can be found where it is dry. This could be near a mountain. The spring is a source of a river. The water from the spring does not dry up. Sometimes there could be water surrounded by reeds, which are used for making mats. Near this well or spring there could be snakes. When these snakes see people, they hide. It is believed that if one kills the snakes, the spring would dry up. That is why the place is sacred for people are not supposed to interfere with the snakes. The well is considered sacred because the grass, the snakes and all the things surrounding the well are intangible.

Burial place for royal blood

People from the royal family are buried differently from other people. The *mukololo,*[1] which means 'prince' or 'princess', refers to a child of a reigning chief or his brothers. When one of their generation succeeds, one of the *vhakololo* becomes the *khotsi-munene* or 'brother to the ruler'. When these people die, only people of royal blood should go to the burial site. At the grave side the *vhakololo* remove their shoes while the women are topless. When the coffin of the deceased is lowered, the rituals that are performed include kneeling down at the grave side; men *kumela* (which means 'growl' or 'grunt' to signify one's assent or approval as in a court case, to make oneself heard in thanking for something, or to pass by while ululating). Sometimes the *tshikona* dance or performance of a reed-flute ensemble or *nanga* (traditional healer) is accompanied by *ngoma, thungwa* and *mirumba* drums, with music specific to solemn and other important occasions.

Zwitaka ('bushes') as sacred places

Sometimes the clans have their *tshitaka* ('bush') as a sacred place where their people are buried. In Venda there are many such places where clan members are buried; these are known as *Tshitaka tsha Vhutanda, Tshitaka tsha Mulangaphuma, Tshitaka tsha Nekhwevha* (i.e. bush of the Nekhwevha family). These are fenced-in places where they bury their people. Everything found there is intangible. The trees, snakes and animals found in this area are not to be interfered with. This is intangible heritage because the burial site has been passed on from generation to generation.

Conclusion

Sacredness is an integral part of the lives of the Vhavenda people in South Africa. Not even the arrival of the missionaries has stopped these practices, although they had a negative impact on the continuation of some of the practices of the Vhavenda community. Whereas most of the practices are still intact, *zwiawelo* are not often seen. The *zwifho* of Fundudzi sacred lake is still respected by elderly people. Young people who do not respect sacred places do so out of ignorance. The rituals at graveyards (burial sites) are still intact, while springs inhabited by snakes do not exist anymore. It is presumed that if these were still in existence, young people would attack and kill the snakes out of ignorance. Most of these sacred places are therefore observed and respected by the Venda communities. It is recommended that such places should be protected and respected as heritage sites.

Note

1 The Tshivenda word *mukololo* is derived from the Karanga words *manyika, mukororo, mukorori* (= son) and *mukorore* (=grandson). The plural form of *mukololo* is *vhakololo*.

References

Davidson, G. W., M. A. Seaton and J. A. Simpson, *et al.* (eds). 1996. *Chambers Concise Dictionary*. Edinburgh: Chambers.

Hornby, A. S. (ed). 1989. *Oxford Advanced Learners Dictionary of Current English*, 4th ed. Oxford: Oxford University Press.

Limpopo Mirror. 2011. 'Sacred Lake Fundudzi to Receive Formal Protection Status by Mr Netshiavha', 2 December, p. 3.

Pearsall, Judy (ed). 2001. *The New Oxford Dictionary of English*. Oxford: Oxford University Press.

Procter, Paul (ed). 1995. *Cambridge International Dictionary of English*. Cambridge: Cambridge University Press.

Sinclair, John (ed). 1992. *Collins COBUILD English Language Dictionary*. Glasgow: HarperCollins.

Tulloch, Sara (ed). 1991. *The Reader's Digest Oxford Complete Wordfinder*. London: Reader's Digest Association.

Van Warmelo, N.J. (ed). 1989. *Venda Dictionary. Venda-English*. Pretoria: J. L. Van Schaik.

10 Translating power, gender and caste

Negotiating identity, memory and history: a study of Bama's *Sangati*

Nishat Haider

Bama, the nom de plume of Faustina Mary Fatima Rani, is one of the first Tamil Dalit women writers to be translated. Her first novel *Karukku* (1992) is not only the first autobiographical work of its kind but is written in a dialect that is spoken by the *paraiyas*, a sub-caste within the Dalit[1] community. Her narrative marked a milestone both in Tamil fiction writing and in the use of orality and the spoken language. The autobiography also upset the Roman Catholic Church in Tamil Nadu because it exposed to the public that the church epitomized the interests of upper-caste converts and discriminated against the *paraiya* community that had converted to Catholicism to escape caste exploitation (McNamara 2009: 268). Bama has subsequently written two more novels, *Sangati* (1994) and *Vanmam* (2002), and two collections of short stories, *Kusumbukkaran* (1996) and *Oru Tattavum Erumaiyum* (2003). Engaging in an ideological debate on contextual feminism, Bama moves from the story of individual struggle in *Karukku* to a startling revelation of the lives of Dalit women who face the triple jeopardy of oppression by double patriarchies – the 'discreet' patriarchy of their own caste and an 'overlapping' patriarchy of the upper caste – as well as poverty in *Sangati*. Through the act of articulation as a Dalit woman writer, Bama not only transgresses caste and gender boundaries but also demolishes the conventional exclusions of language and genre. In her translations of Bama's *Sangati* and *Karukku* (originally written in Tamizh, i.e. Tamil) into English (in 2000 and 2005, respectively), Lakshmi Holmström,[2] a female translator, accomplishes the audacious task of rendering in English the essence and flow of Bama's original prose, the Tamil Dalit dialect. It is a fact that in India major texts of Dalit literature[3] are available only in Indian regional languages and they can be accessed in different languages through English (and in some cases French), and these exchanges are crucial to investigating a critical awareness of the issues of gender and caste liminality. The most common difficulty in translation studies has traditionally been the dilemma between the historical and synchronic approaches in the analysis and description of the culture of translation. Describing the asymmetrical relationship between women and language in terms of the 'muted group', Mary Crawford and Roger Chafin (1986) argue that to some extent, the perceptions of the muted group are unstable in the idiom of the dominant group (which Michèle Causse terms 'androlect'). A natural corollary to this means a submission that the translator too is gendered and that he or she cannot be an 'impersonal' or 'transparent' medium. Therefore, Gayatri Chakravorty Spivak, Michael Cronin and Kwame Anthony Appiah argue for a more creative understanding of the role of the translator. In this chapter it will be my endeavour through a reading of Bama's *Sangati*:

a. To probe the role of translators, linguistic and cultural specificities of the Dalit narratives; what is foregrounded and what gets occluded in translation?
b. To explicate, through a Bakhtinian reading of the text, the broad picture of cross-cultural communication. An attempt will be made to map out the processes that are at work in translation rather than to focus on morphological, syntactic and semiotic aspects of translation.
c. To delineate Dalit feminism and to unwind the helix of class, caste and gender by analysing the specificity of Dalit women's experience with patriarchy and oppressed sexuality.
d. To interpret the 'oral', 'collectivist', 'repudiative' character of these writings, 'cultural catharsis' and the oppositional and/subversive element latent in these writings.

Throughout the chapter, my discussion functions in all the registers – philosophical, linguistic and political – in which translation as a practice works in India. If at any point I seem to dwell on only one of these, it is for a purely strategic purpose. Before embarking on the analysis of the translation of gender caste and identity in Bama's *Sangati*, I will map out the major issues involving literature as one of the institutionalized sites of historical memory and identitarian politics.

History, memory and identity

The philosopheme of translation positions a multiplicity of discourses that emerge out of the systemic collaboration of the discourses of historiography, philosophy, education, theology and literary translation that inform the hegemonic apparatuses that belong to the ideological structure of India. The academic discourses, of which literary translation is theoretically emblematic, through the production of hegemonic texts help preserve the power of the upper-caste Hindus that sanctions them to secure the 'free acceptance' of subjection via the interpellation of its 'subjects'. Though over the last few decades there have been some notable renderings of non-Brahmanical reconstructions of historiography (Omvedt 1993, 1994, 1998; Aloysius 1997) and feminist history of modern India (Omvedt 1976; Patil 1982; Bhagwat 1990; Geetha 1992; O'Hanlon 1994; and Chakravarti 1998), the relationship between the construction of gender, caste and memory and their combined influence on the recuperation, documentation and evolution of voices and narratives so crucial to the emancipatory discourse on caste and gender has been overlooked (Rege 1998). Sangeeta Ray in her book, *En-Gendering India*, an important contribution to post-colonial, feminist, cultural and Asian studies, challenges 'the androcentric bias of most modern national imaginings', specifically 'the assumptions behind the masculinist, heterosexual economy hitherto governing the cultural matrix through which an Indian national identity has become intelligible' that exclude the voices of the subaltern and women (2000: 3–4).

Post-independence studies of India, to a great extent, as Inden (1990), Arjun Appadurai (1986), Kancha Illaih (1996), Veena Das (1995) and others have pointed out, have tended to place caste at a remove from history rather than at its shifting frontiers, consigning Dalits to play the role of the ontological, political, economic, cultural and other (Ganguly 2000). This created a patriarchal, Brahmanical normative mode of reference by which the Dalits were accorded marginalized position. To counter such oppressive historical and literary constructions, Indian feminist historiographers and Dalit women writers have engaged with the creation and compilation of contesting histories and narratives re-inscribing and re-encrypting themselves in the nationalist, socio-political and religious movements, 'the voice of a defiant subalternity committed to writing its own history' (Guha 1997: 12). These 'alternate' narratives recuperate the silenced/occluded voices, re-interpret culture and history, construct/wrench out their own creative/intellectual space and use it to express dissent and subvert the dominant narrative. There is no doubt that the humanities have been richly fertilized by the political insights and intellectual inquiries of Indian feminism. However, even after two decades of sophisticated feminist scholarship, opportunities are found for retrieving Dalit women from the 'enormous condescension of history' (Nair 2008: 177). Gayatri Spivak, drawing upon Gilles Deleuze and Felix Guattari, opines that we produce historical narratives and explanations by transforming the *socius* in which the various discursive productions of caste circulate as 'common sense' and 'popular'. As an alternative to the Hegelian and positivist Rankean model of history, Stoler and Strassler indicated that 'memory as a repository of alternative histories and subaltern truths', which resists the totalizing impulse of 'official memory' (Nair 2008: 169), what Guha describes as 'historiography powered by statehood', is increasingly becoming significant as a potential, oppositional archive that allows access to elided/muted voices. In recent years, the readings of C. L. R. James, Chakrabarty, Guha, Koselleck, Spivak and others reveal that there has been a growing disquiet among the 'new humanists' in post-colonial studies to place at the foreground the imperial will-to-power and the subjugation of non-Western knowledge forms/narratives that inhabit the disciplinary domain of academic humanities.

Many historians have written comprehensively on such interrelated subjects as 'social memory' (Fentress and Wickham 1992), 'historical memory' (Le Goff 1992), 'history as the art of memory' (Hutton 1993), 'history as the phantasm of oblivion' (Geary 1994), 'history constructed through traumatic memory' (Roth 1995) and 'history as memories of symbols and myths' (Isnenghi 1996, 1997a, 1997b). Historical memory to a large extent is constituted by and through 'institutionalized sites of memory' like literature. Narrative is often implicated in the functioning of memory. Elaborating on what is often called the 'narrative turn' in social sciences (Bruner 1991; Kreiswirth 1992, 2000, 2005; Currie 1998; Richardson 2000; Brockmeier and Harré 2001; Ryan 2005), narrative solves the problem of translating knowing into telling; it is a human universal – 'international, transhistorical, transcultural' (Barthes 1977: 79). What is true of the natural history of India is also true of its literary history, given the privileging of Indian writing in English in contemporary multi-lingual India. It is imperative for the national literature to be inclusive of all voices. The narrative of *Sangati* is a fine example of what Guha, in a recent book, has called 'historicality' which he describes as 'the narrative of being-with-others', which evokes the ways in which 'characteristic moments of . . . particularity and individuality, complexity and volatility, chance and change tend to cling to the worldhood of being in its grassroots' (2003: 73). He contrasts this with conventional 'history', which he describes as 'historiography powered by statehood' (2003: 73). Dalit personal and collective memory narratives make visible the collusion of rationalist epistemology with the process of modern nation-building, a collusion that delimits the ways in which subaltern/authorized communities can draw on their repertoire of cultural memories to articulate/contest their multiple pasts (Ganguly 2000). In this essay, for the purpose of reading Bama's *Sangati* and its translation in English, I take historicity to imply 'effective history' (Nietzsche's *wirkliche Historie* or Gadamer's *Wirkungsgeschichte*), or that 'fraction of the past that is even at this instant operative in the present' (Niranjana 1992: 37). As Foucault declares, 'effective history affirms knowledge as perspective'; it may be seen as a radical kind of 'presentism', which we may be able to work from (1997: 156). Thus the study of the historicity of Bama's *Sangati* and its translation in English includes questions about how the translation worked, why the text was translated, and who did/does the translating. This approach recognizes a dialectical relationship between the intratextual sphere (modes and strategies of representation within the textual form and its translation) and the intertextual sphere (social and political contexts that include both national discourses and gender and caste relationships of power within which texts circulate).

Sangati is a powerful critique of Indian society itself: the caste system, patriarchal attitudes and the church, and it highlights the complicity between class and caste in post-independence India. Though *Karakku* dealt chiefly with casteism within the Roman Catholic Church, *Sangati* critiques the church on broader issues. Bama mentions how the *paraiyas* (excluding other Dalit communities who remained Hindus) of her grandmother's generation converted to Christianity influenced by the proposal of free education and a good life to their children by the missionaries. Much to the chagrin of Bama, the church itself is beset with the problem of gender and caste bias: church rules, particularly those dealing with marriage, widowhood and divorce that, by and large, militated against women and aimed to keep them under control; denial of 'choice' to women to decide their own life partner; forcing of women and children to do the meanest jobs in the church in lieu of 'reward in heaven'. The word *Sangati* implies events, and thus the novel narrativizes the events that take place in the life of the women in the *paraiya* community through individual stories, anecdotes and memories. Bama's *Sangati* underscores what G. N. Devy calls 'social epiphanies', pointing out to us the key role of 'memory' (1995: 163). Elucidating the current popularity of women's autobiographies and personal/collective memory narratives in feminist research as a counter-hegemonic narrative to the mainstream, patriarchal discourse, Carolyn Steedman opines, 'once a story is told, it ceases to be a story; it becomes a piece of history, an interpretative device' (1986: 143). On the assumption that in the works of post-colonial women writers, memory and sites of memory are especially significant since they represent the possibility of creating a counter-narrative/history as an alternative to the historiography dominated by the majoritarian/national/official/patriarchal discourses, Bama's *Sangati* creates a site of collective 'counter-memory' of Hinduism and its caste system. By reading caste as a string of articulations at sites of overlapping discursive realms, one could comprehend it in terms of oral practices, performance and enunciation.

Present-day enunciations of alterity bring to light the phallocentric and majoritarian tendencies of narratives/historiographies that produce Dalit women as the silenced, backward and eventually invisible 'other' of the normative modern (read upper class/caste, Brahmin). In *Sangati*, Bama has refunctionalized features of the oral tale in the written text in order to reiterate Gopal Guru's[4] (1995) opinion that Dalit women talk differently. Orality in Dalit women's narratives, usually comprehended as an alternative, non-Brahminic and/or culturally resistant form of writing, has been used to posit cultural and political representation to the subjugated castes and has become the primary rhetorical means by which to counter-hegemonic narratives of nationhood and modernization in India. Representations of orality in *Sangati* figure as tropes of social and cultural difference, serving not only as a linguistic marker of historical subordination to modern, lettered culture but simultaneously as a metonym for alternative (again, primarily indigenous) modes of being persisting in external relation to, and uncontaminated by, upper class/caste/Brahminic categories and reason. Bama's Dalit, polyphonic women's narrative, *Sangati* (2005) evocatively synthesizes the two positions of orality and textuality: recording (writing) personal and social memories (the literate/textual tradition predicated on the principle of linearity) and telling (performing) Dalit muted voices (traditional oral tradition privileging circularity) (Ermarth 1981; Fludernik 1991, 1996). The awareness of the voices of 'others', the plurality of stories to tell, has produced, as Foucault describes it, a 'new form of history [that] is trying to develop its own theory' and one in which one works 'to specify the . . . concepts that enable us to conceive of discontinuity'. And, one might add, difference. History cannot be 'reversed or erased out of nostalgia.

The remaking of history involves a negotiation with the structures that have produced the individual as agent of history' (Kruger and Mariani 1998: 282). In *Sangati,* this negotiation involves the rewriting of caste and women in narrative, and the recuperation of the Dalit muted voices without annihilating its concrete particularity and its singularity as a fragment of lived experience. Among oral forms present in *Sangati* are conversational storytelling (experiential narrative), songs, gossips and jokes. All these types of narrative, written and oral, share one prominent feature: they are structured on an episodic pattern that operates in a recursive manner, whereby a series of episodes is strung together one after the other (Ermarth 1981; Fludernik 1991). To counter the 'aporia of the aesthetic' in the reading of *Sangati,* it is particularly pertinent to investigate the enunciative markers (e.g. frequent shifts in narrator from first to third person and vice versa, second-person narrators, the layering of several situations of enunciation) with which the text is highly imbued.

A key issue in the research on gender is the ongoing debate, beginning in the mid-1970s, between scholars who foreground gender and those who emphasize the intersection of religion, class, caste and gender (Purkayastha 2003: 505). Making linkages between the production of knowledge on Dalits and on women, Aditya Nigam says,

> Dalit histories, dalit accounts of the past, like feminist ones, raise a fundamental question about the possibility of the 'knowing subject' who stands outside the so-called object whose history she writes and about whom this subject 'produces knowledge'. . . . That no dalit histories could be produced till dalits themselves started writing their own history – much like the feminists – points to a deeper problem with academic histories written from the distance of a scientist, ever unable to share the experience of oppression.
>
> (2000: 4256)

Dalit women's ways of knowing and ways of seeing the world have rarely been acknowledged (Karlekar 1982, 1983; Bhave 1988), let alone celebrated (Paik 2009: 175). The narrative of *Sangati* intersects multi-layered complexities of difference and identity formulated within an interlocking matrix of caste, class and gender that are mediated in such a way as to form a politics of difference, which can neither be disconnected from social relations of power nor be de-coupled from the anxieties and resistances that originate from those relationships. Women scholars, in response to current debates over the problems of representing 'other' groups distinct, for instance, by class, cultural or national difference, have attempted to devise particular types of textual strategies that can subvert the power dynamics inherent in textual representations of subalternity (Behar 1993; Visweswaran 1994; Fernandes 1997). The narrative of *Sangati* marks a shift between the generic codes of individual life-writing/*testimonio* (Henke 1998; Beverley 1992; Nayar 2006) to collective biography in this text. What is at once distinctive about Dalit women's narratives in general, and Bama's *Sangati* in particular, is its interlocutory, or dialogic, character, reflecting not only a relationship with the 'other(s)' but an internal dialogue with the plural aspects of self that constitute the matrix of Dalit female subjectivity. A Bakhtinian reading of *Sangati* is particularly significant in revealing the processes of dialogism that give vent to marginalized feminine voices to be heard above the din of the monologic, authoritative and hegemonic voice. According to Mikhail Bakhtin

> A verbal-ideological decentering will occur only when a national culture loses its sealed-off and self-sufficient character, when it becomes conscious of itself as only one among other cultures and languages . . . there will arise an acute feeling for language boundaries (social, national and semantic), and only then will language reveal its essential human character; from behind its words, forms, styles, nationally characteristic and socially typical faces begin to emerge, the images of speaking human beings. . . . Language (or more precisely, languages) will itself become an artistically complete image of a characteristic human way of sensing and seeing the world.
>
> (Bakhtin 1981: 370)

Following Bakhtin's optimistic hope for a state of 'decentring', where a manifold of voices comes about with 'social, national and semantic' changes, an attempt is made in this analysis to extend and re-read Bakhtin's theory from the standpoint of gender and caste, categories absent in Bakhtin's original system of social and linguistic stratification. Dale Bauer, a proponent of feminist dialogics, argues that Bakhtin allows 'the feminist voice (rather than the male gaze) [to] construct and dismantle the exclusive community [of dominant ideology] and patriarchal critical discourse', so that the woman's voice that has been silenced or excluded by hegemonic narrative strategies can be read 'back into the dialogue in order to reconstruct the process by which she was read out in the first place' (1991: 673).

The narrative of *Sangati* weaves the narrative around several generations of women: the older women belonging to the narrator's grandmother Vellaiyamma Kizhavi's generation downward to the narrator's own, and the generation coming after her as she grows up. The narrator is, in the earlier chapters at least, a young girl of about 12 years, and in the last three or four chapters, a young woman; but the thoughtful voice is that of an adult retrospectively meditating upon her lived experiences. The reflections that may seem instructive are a way of connecting experience and analysis, concluding with a practical call for action. The conversations between the generations map out the changing perspectives and aspirations as well as the gains and losses over the years. *Sangati* examines the differences between women, their different needs, the different ways in which they are subject to oppression and their coping strategies (*Sangati* xix). The more educated tend to move away, seeking different lives. With growing industries, child labour is recruited from the village. In the end, it is Bama's admiration for the women of her community, from the little girl Maikkanni who supports her mother and her family by working in a matchbox factory to the old woman. These individual stories, anecdotes and memories of personal experience are narrated in the first person, then counterpointed by the generalizing comments of the grandmother and mother figures and later still by the author-narrator's reflections. Speech, as gossip, as private communication among women works upon language anarchically, shattering everything. But from this rupture may come meaning on a new order, not that of coherence but of plurality. In the to-and-fro movement (mobility is evident in the way women's discourse circulates from speech to writing), writing is rupture and plurality. Anchored in the collectivity of women, Bama's narrative problematizes language and subjectivity, which gives rise to a polymorphic quality. Dialogism in *Sangati*, the-one-within-the-other in the Bakhtinian sense of the polyphonic text, works to subvert the monologism of the dominant discourse. The form of each chapter, Holmström says, is therefore 'exploratory, and the structure of the book as a whole seeks to create a Dalit feminist perspective' (*Sangati*, "Introduction" xvi). Thus, through *Karukku* and *Sangati*, Bama has pioneered a Dalit *Penniyam*, a Dalit feminist perspective in Tamil. Both the works are an overt criticism of the patriarchal, caste-ridden society. They are also reflective of the changing attitudes of Dalit women (Geetha). The contributors to *Dalit Penniyam* (Dalit Feminism) point out repeatedly that the Dalit struggle has tended to forget a gender perspective. Talking about power imbalances, which exist between different groups of women, under the blanket notion of gender, the Dalit feminist critic, Sharmila Rege, writes,

> The Dalit Feminist Standpoint is about historically locating how all our identities are not equally powerful, and about reviewing how in different historical

> practices similarities between women have been ignored in an effort to underline caste-class identities, or at other times differences ignored for 'the feminist cause'.
>
> (2000: 15)

Feminist scholars within post-colonial studies have analysed the processes of re-colonization, which unfold through the production of a homogenized 'third-world woman' who is depicted either as a silent victim (of Mohanty 1991) or as a speaking subaltern responding to (Spivak 1988) various structures of oppression. Lamenting the suppression and sufferings faced by Dalit women, the narrator in *Sangati* says

> The position of women is both pitiful and humiliating, really. In the fields they have to escape from upper-caste men's molestations. At church they must lick the priest's shoes and be his slaves while he threatens them with the tales of God, Heaven, and Hell. Even when they go to their own homes, before they have had a chance to cook some kanji or lie down and rest a little, they have to submit themselves to their husbands' torment.
>
> (35)

Adding to their woes, the narrator decries, 'upper caste women show us no pity or kindness either, if only as women to women, but treat us with contempt, as if we are creatures of a different species, who have no sense of honour or self-respect' (66). This experience of suffering is a collective one, where social, historical and political structures oppress all Dalit communities. Bama suggests that one suffers as a Dalit, even though the pain is singular to the suffering individual body. There is thus a critical narrative tension here, where descriptions of localized, individual corporeal suffering are located within larger historical contexts of collective pain. However, the ideals Bama admires and applauds in Dalit women, Holmström says, are 'not the traditional Tamil "feminine" ideals of *accham* (fear), *naanam* (shyness), *madam* (simplicity, innocence), *payirppu* (modesty), but rather, courage, fearlessness, independence, and self-esteem' (*Sangati*, 'Introduction' xix). *Sangati* renders a positive identity to Dalit women highlighting their inner strength and vigour. It celebrates the grit and determination of the Dalit women to stamp their existence in a male-dominated, caste-structured society.

Bama's world, personal as well as creative, is filled with the binaries of Dalit/non-Dalit, male/female, rich/poor, Christian/non-Christian, married/single and so on (Sivanarayanan 2009: 144). Dalit women's discourse is double; it is the echo of the self and the other, a movement into alterity. In negotiating the discursive dilemma or their characters, the Dalit woman writer accomplishes two objectives: the self-inscription of Dalit womanhood and the establishment of a dialogue of discourses with the other(s). The self-inscription of Dalit women requires disruption of the conventional generic forms that convey these narratives. Through this interventionist and revisionary activity, Dalit women writers enter into dialogue with the discourses of the other(s). Disruption – the initial response to hegemonic and ambiguously (non)-hegemonic discourse – and revision (rewriting or rereading) together suggest a model for reading Dalit and female literary expression. Responding to the growing attention being paid to questions of subaltern aesthetics and narrative form (Rege 2006; Nayar 2009; Kumar 2010), Pramod Nayar proposes that the 'dialogic' nature of Dalit texts is embodied in their radicalization of the genre through the appropriation of different registers, a process one could think of as 'narrative appropriation' (Nayar 2006, 2008). In her paper 'Gêneros Híbridos' (Hybrid Genres), Pagano (2001), who has devoted herself to the study of genre and its hybrid characteristics by analysing underlying discursive patterns in texts within the scope of CDA (critical discourse analysis), translation studies or genre analysis itself, advocates that whenever one genre moves from its common, taken-for-granted, textual instance and locates itself into another discursive texture, a tension is formed in order to cause a specific effect upon the text in which other genres are being inserted. In addition, Chouliaraki and Fairclough (1999) also posit that it is through genre moves that moments of struggle are perceived, in a clear-cut linkage between texts, discourses and ideological and power relations. As a result, through this textual manoeuvre the language analyst is able to perceive the several discourses that dialectically form the text and its message (Bakhtin 1986), which suggests that translation analysis should focus itself upon interdiscursivity (Chouliaraki and Fairclough 1999) and interdisciplinarity (Munday 2001: 181–196). *Sangati* flouts conventional concepts of what a novel as a genre should be by mingling the registers and discourses of the folkloric, political, sociohistorical and personal. *Sangati* captures the continuous fluidity of domination and resistance in the lives of women belonging to Dalit caste asserting an identification of both subordination and expressions of defiance, imprinted in the micro-histories of biographies, oral traditions, legends and myths. Bama's Dalit text is replete with references to and the tropes and images of storytelling, textuality and the processes of signification – narrative, in short. The narrative hybridization achieved through the merging of three distinct registers in Bama's text – the mythic, the historical and the immediate – is a political project, reflecting a radicalization of consciousness itself (Nayar 2011: 365). The characters in the text create a language of the self (personal), which interacts with and draws upon the language of the community (oral) and, finally, the language of history itself. The opening line of Bama's *Sangati* is a proverb, a mythic voice appropriating the collective memory of the community. While the grandmother was combing the narrator-protagonist's hair and giving her all the gossip of the village, she says, 'If the third is a girl to behold, your courtyard will fill with Gold' (3). Bama reveals the communal power of a community's 'narrative' when Mariamma is dissuaded and warned by her friends about not reporting about the incident when upper-caste landlord, Kumarasami Ayya, tries to pull her into a shed. Bama draws our attention to the facts that the women who begin to protest are 'silenced' (23) and there is a differential allocation of treatment and grieving based on gender and caste. When Bama's protagonist is outraged at her grandmother for not protesting, she (grandmother) alludes to the story of Tiruvalluvar and his docile wife and says: 'From your ancestors' times it has been agreed that what the men say is right. Don't you go dreaming that everything is going to change just because you've learnt a few letters of the alphabet' (28–29). Realigning the mythic, historical and the contemporary while commenting on the Indian politicians and electoral process, the grandmother proclaims: 'Whether it is Rama who rules or Ravana, what does it matter? Our situation is always the same' (99). The Dalit men too face oppression by the upper castes, but once they return home they 'control their women, rule over them and find their pleasure. Within the home, they lay down the law; their world is scripture' (*Sangati* 59). Thus Dalit women have to bear the brunt of double patriarchy. This destabilization of form by the infusion of the radical narrative forms and linguistic registers is cultural and aesthetic engagement as a political act, which is tied in with the larger social movement for emancipation, relief from traditional structures of oppression and the quest for new routes to state their subjectivity and history (Nayar 2011: 367). The narrative of *Sangati* essentially subversive in character, bringing both content and forms that challenge, received literary norms. Making a forceful plea for reclaiming and reinforcing a special Tamil Dalit usage, Raj Gauthaman says that Dalit writing

> should set out to outrage, by choosing as subject matter, the lifestyles of Dalits, who by definition, stand outside caste-proprieties. It should offer a totally different world view to Tamil readers. Dalit literature describes the

> world differently, from a Dalit perspective. Therefore it should outrage and even repel the guardians of caste and class. It should provoke them into asking if this is indeed literature.
>
> (qtd. in 'Introduction', *Sangati* xxii)

Translating power, gender and caste

Although language and translation inevitably are tools for gender subjugation or liberation, yet, in today's globalized world it is important 'to ask whether a dialogue between academics working in the field of gender and language and in that of gender and translation has yet taken place; and if so, how fertile these interdisciplinary debates have been' (Castro 2013: 6). In fact, not all academic work done in these two realms stems from a feminist perspective (Mills and Mullany 2011: 2). The link connecting translation, gender and power works at a variety of levels and on diverse registers. The choice of texts to be translated, the choice of languages involved, the choice of method in translating and the entire paraphernalia of the circulation of translated texts have their own narratives of power to narrate. Writing/reading translation may not always be a transparent act. Gender consciousness in translation practice, in effect, has generated many issues about linguistic and social stereotypes, the ideology and politics of language and the significance of milieu in which the translator lives and works. Before delineating the gender-specific orientation of *Sangati's* translation, it is important to acknowledge that although my decision to analyse the translation of Bama was explicitly grounded in a feminist commitment to expand the range of Dalit women's written literary texts available in English translation, feminism as a named, explicit and politicized response to oppression was not expressed in the same terms in the source text. My articulation of the implications of the gendered/feminist translation of *Sangati* thus suggests that writing practice predates theory, so that the 'feminism' voiced by Bama's fiction is the ground for a subsequent explication of a feminist agenda within a Dalit discourse in the post-colonial framework. Explicating gender-conscious translation of Dalit texts as a form of activism, I argue that Dalit feminism manifests in translation not only informatively, through linguistic and cultural representation, but also through formative processes that are constitutive of texts. Taking a cue from Tejaswini Niranjana, the post-colonial interpretations of Bama's *Sangati* will not be readings of a hermeneutic or exegetic kind, but somewhat political interventions in the political rewriting of the text and its destination (1992: 172).

The interaction between gender studies and translation studies points to a fascinating arena of discursive conflict in which our intimate desires and identities are established or rejected, (re)negotiated or censored, sanctioned or tabooed. The notion of discourse has exerted great influence on translation studies (Blum-Kulka 1986/2000; Venuti 2000: 215–220; Munday 2001: 89–107). It is my contention that discourse of any kind is a site of struggle. It is a dynamic, linguistic and, above all, semantic space in which social meanings are produced and challenged. Bearing this in mind, translation is culture, politically and socially bound, shaped by ideologies that sustain, perpetuate or challenge existing power relations present in particular discourses (Olk 2002). In other words, the space of literature is one appropriate discursive site within which Dalit women's voices can be heard and understood by the reader. While gender and class analysis in translation studies have uncovered the bourgeois and patriarchal interests that underwrite the humanist subject, we have been unable to critically confront inequalities of caste or community implicit in that subject or its worlds (Tharu and Niranjana 1996: 235). During the last three decades, Dalit feminism has increasingly positioned itself as a differential politics. Dalit praxis seeks to think through this gap, this difference, to explore the positioning of the obsessions and desires of translating caste and gender. Women translators have added some new dimensions to the Dalit feminist discourse pointing to gender as a new axis around which writing relationships are created.

In spite of the fact that the figure of the translator has been rendered invisible in literary and academic spheres, it can be extremely instructive to look for, glean or extrapolate the characteristics and even the ideological agendas that this figure embodies through the looking glass of two of recent history's most prominent (certainly in Europe and the Americas) schools: those of feminist translation theorists and post-colonialist translation theorists (Wallace 2002: 65). Feminist translation has explored the combined potentialities of translation and gender in order to investigate issues of identity that seeks to make the feminine subject visible through language. It is a political activity that aims to reverse women's position of inferiority in discourse and in translation. Susan Bassnett argues for an 'orgasmic' theory of translation, the result of 'elements [that] are fused into a new whole in an encounter that is mutual, pleasurable and respectful' (Bassnett 1992: 72). In particular, Berman emphasizes the creative role of the translating subject. The translator, for Berman, is far more than a passive relay through which the norms of the receiving culture are reproduced (2009: 50–63). The subjectivity of the translator must be understood as part of a complex overlay of mediating activities, which allow for active and critical intervention. One is reminded of Appiah's calls for translations that are not merely word for word correspondences but a 'thick' translation that 'seek[s] with its annotations and its accompanying glosses to locate the text in a rich cultural and linguistic context' (Appiah 2000: 399). Michael Cronin (2004), too, argues for a more creative understanding of the role of the translator. As regards the Indian theory of translation, Shibani Phukan opines, 'If there is an Indian theory of translation, perhaps its distinction lies in its refusal to posit an overarching universal theory of translation' (2003: 27). Gender and post-colonial identity are not necessarily mutually exclusive as is shown in Gayatri Spivak's 'The Politics of Translation' (Spivak 1993: 200). She criticizes the lifeless 'translatese' that comes from a translator of third-world feminist texts who is not fully at one with the 'rhetoricity' of the languages in question. Giving voice and body to the figure of the post-colonial feminist translator, Spivak reminds us that 'translation is not just the stringing together of the most accurate synonyms by the most proximate syntax', and hence the translator must attempt to inscribe the 'trace of the other, the trace of history, and even cultural spaces' (1992: 189). Since postcolonial subjects already exist 'in translation,' opines Tejaswini Niranjana,

> our search should not be for origins or essences but for a richer complexity, a complication of our notions of the 'self', a more densely textured understanding of who 'we' are. It is here that translators can intervene to inscribe heterogeneity, to warn against myths of purity, to show origins as always already fissured. Translation, from being a 'containing' force, is transformed into a disruptive, disseminating one. The deconstruction initiated by re-translation opens up a post-colonial space as it brings 'history' to 'legibility'.
>
> (1992: 186)

Women and translation are no longer subordinated terms, but rather growing sites of alternative textual/sexual power. Locating all traditions of literature in the act of translation, Devy says, 'An act of translation holds two or sometimes more different traditions momentarily together for cross fertilization, and in that sense all translations are *sahitya* (literature)' (1997: 402). Focusing on issues of gender and identity as signs that can be traced in language, I have used the term 'feminist translation theory' as a subset of/alternative to 'woman interrogated', 'gender-conscious' or 'woman-identified' interventions in translation studies. I have used the phrase 'gender in translation theory' interchangeably with 'feminist translation' because it serves as a wider rubric to my reading of Bama's *Sangati* explicating the act of translation as a means to underscore issues of gender inequality and to reveal female social contexts in other cultures. Gender-specific or feminist translation theory is not a unified body of concepts or arguments, but is rather a domain characterized by a growing diversification, constant redefinition and hence it is always open to criticisms or re-articulations. 'Women', 'feminist' and 'translation' are constructed categories, and are in need of continual scrutiny and challenge. Emphasizing the need for a 'redefinition' of feminist translation, Martín Ruano says,

> The acknowledgement of differences among women goes hand in hand with the recognition of a plural meaning in 'translating in the feminine', or at least with a sceptical attitude about the universal validity of 'canonical' or 'established' feminist practices – that is to say, those used and supported by the first paradigm, including the emblematic claim for feminizing language whenever possible.
>
> (2006: 37)

Massardier-Kenney, too, has proposed a redefinition of feminist translation theory and practice and puts forth a new typology that overlaps with some of the strategies identified by von Flotow (1997) and Barbara Godard (1990), but which has a different focus. Her objective is 'a reassessment of translation strategies in terms of their capacity to open up a space for a woman's voice' (Agorni 2005: 822). Massardier-Kenney offers a more universal and/moderate variation of feminist translation strategies. She categorizes feminist translation strategies as 'author-centred' and 'translator-centred'. Author-centred categories include collaboration, commentary and resistancy. Translator-centred strategies include recovery, commentary and parallel texts (1997: 58). This solidarity with gender-conscious translators and feminist interventions in translation, however, is not free from ideological departures. I concur with them on the fact that fidelity and equivalence are extremely relative and problematic concepts which have undergone innumerable shifts throughout history. In the 'metaphorics of translation' operating within translation studies, 'fidelity is defined by an implicit contract between translation (as woman) and original (as husband, father or author)' and this betrays 'real anxiety about the problem of paternity and translation' (Chamberlain 1988: 455–456). Gender-conscious translation theory offers an adequate, critical framework to expose and reverse these time-old sexist metaphors by empowering women as translators and creators of women's narratives, bodies and texts. My consideration of 'woman-identified intervention' in translation, however, does not reject 'fidelity' altogether, but hypothesizes as an alternative a 'new axiomatics of fidelity', a somewhat problematic idea: feminist translators are devoted, at the same time, to production and reproduction, to manipulation and fidelity. Though Indian scholars like Ganesh Devy (1999: 187) have asserted that Western theories of translation do not seem appropriate in the Indian context, if we probe the execution of these gender-specific strategies in the translation of texts in general, and Bama's *Sangati* in particular, we will find that these approaches are not Western in themselves and if used strategically they put the spotlight on issues of gender, caste and identity as retraceable signs in language. To further allay fears of 'hijacking'/manipulation of the text associated with Western feminist translation, I will describe how some of these techniques partially (and not in entirety) foregrounded in *Sangati* reveal how gender itself is translated and produced. Thus, it also seeks to call attention to translators' identity and ideological 'positioning' in the translation project and aims to reveal a perceived patriarchal thought underlying language. This means that the translation of Bama's *Sangati*, on the one hand, becomes a political/identitarian and/ideological act where the translator is entirely conscious of historical, social and political implications of gendered context, text and languages and, on the other, the attention to the translation process emphasizes how the practice can be considered as a creative form of 'collaboration', a feminist strategy that rejects the opposition between author and translator and reinforces the collective, creative nature of translation.

The problematic of the power/representation relationship (Foucault 1980) in narratives raises the task of confronting the (un)translatability of difference particularly when the borders of difference are marked by the figure of the 'Third World woman' (Fernandes 1999: 123). In the essay 'The Politics of Translation' (1992), Spivak has suggested the possible methodological strategies that can begin to confront the politics of translation. Her call for modes of linguistic translation that do not just focus on grammatical rules but 'surrender to the linguistic rhetoricity of the original text' begin to point to a conception of cross-cultural translation that does not simply focus either on a rejection of 'the real' or on 'getting the reality right' through increasingly sophisticated methods of empiricism (187). Dalit women's writing and its translation in the context of the need for a poetics of identity meet in their common desire to foreground female subjectivity in the production of meaning. *Sangati* constitutes both textual (preface, acknowledgement and glossary) and extra-textual (commentary in 'Introduction') strategies that contribute to the effective feminization of the text and context and to the visibility of both author and translator. Though in Bama's stories one does not encounter the terms feminism, casteism or patriarchy, she mentions the words caste and patriarchy only in the 'Acknowledgements'. However, it needs to be pointed out that there are distinctions to be made between actual words spoken or written and the action and context of speech itself. It is in the 'action' of speaking and the context within which speech takes place that, according to Foucault (1977), enunciation is realized. As Sheridan (1990) explains, 'by enunciation . . . Foucault means not the words spoken or written but the act of speaking or writing them, the context in which they are uttered and the status or position of the author' (99). Enunciation as a process of resistance and caring for the self is grounded in the marginalized (individual and collective) self's articulation of the structural effects of the violence that is mapped on and through their body in a socio-political way that indicts the social political structure rather than the individual and or collective self. Emphasizing that there's no enunciation without positionality, Hall says, 'You have to position yourself somewhere in order to say anything at all. . . . The past is not only a position from which to speak, but it is also an absolutely necessary resource in what one has to say' (1989: 18). Positioning herself as a Dalit woman writer, Bama says,

> We have all come across news, broadcast widely and everywhere, telling us of the position of women in our patriarchal society; and of the rights that have been plucked away from them. But news of women who have been trapped not only by patriarchy but also by caste-hatred is often sidelined, hidden, forgotten. Occasionally, we hear the sound of a few suffering women weeping. Then we forget it.
>
> ('Acknowledgements', *Sangati* ix)

Foregrounding Foucault's framing of enunciation and speaking of the production of what he calls 'routines of normalization', it could be argued that in the novel Bama describes the forms through which Dalit women are silenced and 'made' silent. This politics of enunciation is grounded in interrogating the dis/connections and fissures between 'truth,' 'to speak,' knowledge and power. Making her intention very clear in the 'Acknowledgements' in *Sangati*, Bama says

> My mind is crowded with many anecdotes: stories not only about the sorrows and tears of Dalit women, but also about their lively and rebellious culture; their eagerness not to let life crush or shatter them, but rather to swim vigorously against the tide; about the self-confidence and self-respect that enables them to leap over their adversities by laughing at and ridiculing them; about their passion to live life with vitality, truth and enjoyment; about their hard labour. I wanted to shout out these stories.
>
> (ix)

One of the techniques most successfully exploited by women writers and translators is collaboration, which is consistent with the theorizations of feminist translators. As Agorni states,

> [. . .] collaboration effectively explodes the notion of translation as a unitary activity, breaking it down into a set of parallel practices and corresponding roles – those of translating, editing, promoting, but also mentoring, supporting the translator, and so on. Not only does this perspective emphasize the notion of negotiability of meaning and interpretation, as Massardier-Kenney (1997) has argued, but it also demonstrates that the roles and activities involved in translation are also essentially negotiable, in a very creative way.
>
> (2005: 827–828)

The influence of gender-specific translation of *Sangati* is most apparent in the metatext (preface) that accompanies the English translation by Lakshmi Holmström. Elaborating on the close collaboration between the translator (Lakshmi Holmström), editor and publisher (Mini Krishnan) and herself, Bama says

> Today, information about Dalit women is being widely discussed in many places by many people. Mini Krishnan who edited and published the translation of *Karukku* into English (1999) approached me in 2001 for the English translation of *Sangati* through Oxford University Press. It was she who introduced my work to French publishers. It was through her that L'Aube translated *Sangati* into French (2002) and it was well received in France. Without Mini's interest, backing and hard work it can be said that *Sangati's* present form would not have been possible. I am delighted to render my affectionate thanks to her. My gratitude also to Lakshmi Holmström who spent years translating, revising, and redrafting the English version of *Sangati* without disturbing the essence and flow of the original.
>
> ('Preface', *Sangati* viii)

This is 'closelaboration', a term derived from translator Suzanne Jill Levine suggesting that the working bond between author and translator is unique. The term was coined by Guillermo Cabrera Infante, a Cuban author with whom Levine worked closely. In *Sangati*, Lakshmi Holmström uses 'the preface as metadiscourse accompanying the translation to make explicit the importance of the feminine or of woman/women (either in terms of structural constraints or in terms of women's agency) in the translated text'. It is a strategy that not only 'reminds the reader that translating is an activity which creates authority for the writer translated' but also that 'the translator is a critic responsible for introducing and marketing a specific image of that writer' (Massardier-Kenny 1997: 60). It is easier and more visible to make gender-specific (theoretical) statements in a preface than to do it through each and every (practical) translating option.

In India, since 'the bulk of literature to us comes through translation', Devy insists that these exchanges are crucial to investigate, for they have become the site of an 'overwhelming zeal' in the Indian literary context as the 'polylingualism inherent in Indian culture is seeking to express itself through [. . .] literary translation' (Devy 1993: 134–135). Mapping a reconfigured relationship in post-independence India between some Indian languages and the English language, Rita Kothari locates the context for accommodating translation. She opines that we see in this period both the 'strengthening of a regional literary and linguistic tradition' and 'the rise of English as an Indian language' (32). Though Tamil Dalit texts have not received significant visibility in the other Indian languages, they have been translated into English and French, spawning several debates and controversies with regard to the various issues about translation of Dalit texts into English. The major challenge for anyone translating Tamil Dalit writings into English, says G. J. V. Prasad, is the inherent seemingly untranslatable resistance of the language of this literature, which remains close to its oral roots, full of proverbs and chants and songs (Prasad 2007, 2011). The linguistic nuances of this literature are of paramount importance and translation can erase the locational differentiations, cultural oppressions and the resistance. Talking about the performative nature of cultural communication inhered in translation, Bhabha opines, 'it is language *in actu* (enunciation, positionality) rather than language *in situ* (*énoncé*, or propositionality). And the sign of translation continually tells, or "tolls" the different times and spaces between cultural authority and its performative practices' (1994: 326). The translator has to convey all this layering and this is made insidious by the translator's non-Dalit identity. Talking about the challenges in translating Bama's works, Lakshmi Holmström says,

> The most difficult aspect of translation, for me, is conveying the individual voice and style of the original. This means paying attention to the way the author uses language (the 'rhetoricity' of the original text, in Gayatri Spivak's language) and trying, imaginatively, to recreate it. . . . So it was both a challenge and a privilege to work . . . and to have the opportunity to meet and talk to Bama. It [*Karakku*] speaks very directly from its anger and its pain and I wanted desperately to convey something of that. I wanted to convey something of its colloquiality and the way it speaks directly to the reader. But also its dignity, its hard-won self-respect.
>
> (2001: *Outlook Magazine*, 5 April)

But the translator also has a voice or 'discursive presence' as it is called by Theo Hermans (1996: 27). For Hermans, 'it is only . . . the ideology of translation, the illusion of transparency and coincidence, the illusion of the one voice, that blinds us to the presence of [the translator's] voice' (1996: 27). Talking about the translator's discursive presence, as a distinct voice and speaking position, what Folkart calls a 'differential voice' (always present in the text itself), Hermans says

> Marginal, paratextual comments by translators on their own performance are bound to rupture the apparently seamless web of the translated discourse. Wordplay sometimes calls for such interventions. In exploiting the economy of a particular language, wordplay constitutes that language's 'signature' (Davis 1997), referring metalinguistically to the particular system onto which it is felicitously grafted. In rendering wordplay, translators may be able to handle the matter entirely in terms of the receptor language, without the reader of the translation being in a position to detect that a semantically very different constellation has been erected. In some cases however translators admit defeat and intervene in paratextual asides such as footnotes or bracketed comments. In so doing they disrupt the discursive flow by pushing to the fore the voice we as readers were not supposed to be conscious of.
>
> (2002: 12)

In the English translation of Bama's *Sangati*, for example, we often encounter Tamil phrases interspersed in the English text. However, in order to convey to the reader the meanings of Tamil words, the translated version inserts the English equivalent word in parenthesis and glossary (provided by the translator at the end of the text), informing the reader that those particular words were originally in Tamil – which then reminds the reader that the rest of the text was not originally in English, so that it cannot have been Bama who wrote all those other English words that have been explained in the glossary at the end of the narrative. Owing to differences in cultural and linguistic location and locution between the writer and the translator, Holmström clarifies that her initial norm[5] is not to be disloyal to the source text but to transfer it, making the translation to some extent more accessible than the original. In the 'Introduction' to Bama's *Karakku*, Holmström says,

> There is often a layering of meaning in certain words, where a Tamilized Sanskrit word is given a new Catholic meaning. For example, Tamil *mantiram* (sacred utterance, but also popularly, magic charm or spell) from Sanskrit *mantra* becomes 'catechism' in Catholic use. Hence often there is a spin or a turn-around of meaning; a freshness in some of the coinages, and different routes and slippages in the way Catholicism has been naturalized (and sometimes not) into the Tamil of the text. Bama uses neologisms and puns to parody and attack conventional language. Other strategies included the fragmentation of language, the disregard for grammatical or syntactical structures. (xx)

In *Karukku* and later in *Sangati* as well, Bama lets loose an inventive, local language that illustrates free play with the limits of spoken language. She trusts the dialect to do the work of personalizing the narrative for her. Wordplay in particular appears to be culturologically effective and valuable, in that it destroys the spatially organized logical system of language. In ancient oral cultures, language is not a symbolic, instrumental system of signification; rather, communication is a tactile-corporeal act. The production of meaning and the expression of truth are not formal constructions, but organic-corporeal dramas. The rich, imaginative and ingenious language of the Dalit women gives way to proverbs, folklore and folksongs. The women have an innate talent to give appropriate nicknames to others. Seyarani is called *maikanni* because she has ensnaring eyes. Sanmuga kizhavi is called *maikuzh kizhavi* because she takes only *ragi kuzh*.[6] Gnaanambal is called *dammatta maadu* because she goes round like a young bullock dragged and dazed without knowing what is going on (Geetha). But the other aspect of this language of women is its vigour and its closeness to proverbs, folk songs and folklore. Vellaiyamma Kizhavi's retellings of the stories of Esakki who becomes a *pey*, a spirit who possesses young women, and of the Ayyankaachi troupe are evocative episodes in the text. In the introduction to *Karakku*, Holmström says that Bama 'reclaims and remains close to an oral tradition made up of work-chants, songs sung at rites of passage, as well as proverbs and some of this tradition belongs particularly to the woman's domain' (xx). Bama writes, 'From birth to death, there are special songs and dances. And it is only the women who perform them. *Roraattu* (lullaby) to *oppaari* (dirge), it is only the women who will sing them' (78). Bama records a number of these. A song sung at a girl's coming of age, with a chorus of ululation at the end of every four lines begins:

> On a Friday morning, at earliest dawn
> she became a *pushpavati,* so the elders said –
> her mother was delighted, her father too,
> the uncles arrived, all in a row.
> (chorus of *kulavai,* ululation) (*Sangati* 17)

Bama pays particular attention to oral gestures, acts of eating and drinking and their social and communicative effect. Bama also gives several examples of witty rhymes and verses made up on the spur of the moment to fit an occasion. Once, while the girl was grinding masalas in the middle of the street, her cousin, to whom she was promised in marriage, went past. At once, Mogurkari, who was playing a dice game makes up a song to tease her:

> In front of a house made of plaster and lime
> You were grinding turmeric for a curry.
> What magic powder did he cast on you
> You cannot move the grindstone anymore.
> (*Sangati* 77)

The corporeal origin of language leads to Bakhtin's special interest in laughter as a corporeal event on the one hand and as a reaction to semantic processes on the other. Bama recognizes and applauds the ability of certain women in her community to undermine authority figures by ridiculing them or playing tricks on them. In his foreword to the collection, *Kusumbukaaran* (1997), Raj Gauthaman says,

> Their customary habit of joking and lampooning finally gives Dalits the strength to stand up courageously against caste oppression. Dalit jokes and arid banter *(pagait)* lead the way to the language of insurrection *(kalaga mozht)*, and so, finally, to insurrection *(kalagam)*. But the stories say this, not overtly; but very naturally and easily, with their own rhetoric.
> (qtd. in 'Introduction', *Sangati* xxi)

Talking about Bama's linguistic leap in reclaiming/retrieving/recuperating the 'muted speech'/register/language, Holmström (2005) says,

> In her latest work, the collection of stories called *Kisumbukaaran,* she has developed this aspect of Dalit language even further. *Kisumbu* or *kusumbu* means pranks, making mischief. Other key words in Barna's stories are *kindal panradu* or *pagadi panradu,* to ridicule or lampoon, and *nattanaitanam* or *nat-natanam,* buffoonery; but also rashness or recklessness. Between them, these words cover a range of meanings: teasing or leg-pulling between comrades and friends, a sending-up or ridiculing of authority figures within the community, and then by extension, invective in defiance of upper-caste landowners.
>
> ('Introduction', *Sangati* xxi)

Sangati reveals the inexplicable and unarticulated bond that strengthens the spirit of the Dalit women. In the midst of all the misery there is an inseparable liveliness in the Dalit women. They would always laugh and chatter 'even though they left at dawn and hardly ever came back until after dark, they still went about laughing and making a noise for the greater part' (Bama 2005: 76).

Sangati is in the voices of many women speaking to and addressing one another as they share the incidents of their daily lives. Each social group speaks in its own 'social dialect' – possesses its own unique language – expressing shared values, memories, perspectives, ideology and norms. These social dialects become the 'languages' of heteroglossia 'intersect[ing] with each other in many different ways. . . . As such they all may be juxtaposed to one another, mutually supplement one another, contradict one another and be interrelated dialogically' (Bakhtin 1981: 292). Bama brings to her text a diversity of languages or 'world views' in a way that recalls Bakhtin's conceptualization of each language as 'a kind of ideology brought-into speech' (1981: 294). Bama explored Dalit women's experiences that had not been put into words before and tried to write *l'inédit*. She sought to create a new idiom with which to express these experiences of the body and write a women's utopia. *Inédit* is a privileged term in Nicole Brossard's writing referring to that which cannot be inscribed for lack of appropriate language. In this way, Bama opens up possibilities to read *Sangati* as a site of conflicting and possibly liberating

> languages-in-use, which unsettles the patriarchal myth of one monologic language of truth. These voices, sometimes shrill in anger or in anguish as they lash out at each other, or against their oppressors, are reported verbatim. Such a language is full of expletives and profanities quite often with explicit sexual references. Sexual language is a privileged area to study the cultures one translates or gets translated into – it is a site where each culture places

> its moral or ethical limits, where one encounters its taboos and its ethical dilemmas.
>
> (Santaemilia 2008: 228)

Bama suggests several reasons for the violence of this language and its sexual nature. In *Sangati*, the narrator says

> No matter what the quarrel is about, once they open their mouths, the same four-letter words will spill out. I sometimes think that because they have neither pleasure nor fulfillment in their sexual lives, they derive a sort of bitter comfort by using these terms of abuse which are actually namers of their body parts.
>
> (68)

Sometimes a sharp tongue and obscene words are a woman's only way of shaming men and escaping extreme physical violence. At other times, the use of non-official/subversive speech by Dalit women helps them to overcome fear of authoritarian power by emptying the words of meaning and the content of speech, thus uniting the collective. These speech acts allow autonomy, an autonomy that is not 'made in heaven', but that is rather always in a process of negotiation through an aesthetic cognition of the other's inner and outer specificity, repeated endlessly in the world and history, in existence, and transformed and potentially heightened in artistic creation. Or it might be the result of a desire to propose a new, experimental and subversive language in order to reinscribe women's subjectivity in language. From the earliest times, traditional Tamil grammarians have distinguished between '*sen*-Tamil' (the literary) and '*kodun*-Tamil' (the colloquial). In fact, a Bakhtinian analysis reveals that Bama takes the colloquial approach to the extreme by using a dialectal Tamil full of profanities and invectives and thus subverting the strictures of traditional discourse. Bama's dialectal language functions to cast phallogocentrism loose from its moorings in order to return the masculine to its own language, leaving open the possibility of a different language. Arguing that this is a calculated step that brings Bama to her community's fold, M. S. S. Pandian says

> Bama's conscious choice of spoken Dalit Tamil, ungoverned by the tyranny of elaborate grammatical rules, as the medium to voice the story of her community is indeed instructive. In a spirit of defiance, it obviously challenges the authority of literacy over orality, a divide which was ratified and nourished by Tamil Saivism or Tamil nationalism of different hues, including mainstream

> Dravidianism during this century. But at an equally important plane, it is an effort by Bama to break free from her proficiency in standardized written Tamil, a result of her privileged education in schools and colleges, and to lose herself in the community of Dalits.
>
> (2003: 132–133)

Berman's statement that for translation 'everything is "dialect" ' is another way of reaffirming that if individual languages (*langues*) are all manifestations of our essence as human beings, that is are 'dialects', then the task of translation is to uncover what he calls 'orality', the originary elements of language, that are hidden in the different strands of these dialects. Emphasizing the 'insurmountable' problems entailed in the translation of such a dialectal use of language, Sivanarayanan says

> Lacking a lexicography – a practical model of moving from the usage to a literary semantic version – the translation is forced to summarize into prose what, when translated back, would be into a literary Tamil. Thus, rather than reading . . . [it] as a Tamil novel translated into English, it would be more accurate to read it as a Tamil Dalit novel translated into literary Tamil and then into English.
>
> (2009: 148)

Mini Krishnan[7] says that it was not easy at all to find a new third language that was neither mainstream Indian language in English nor the unusual 'dialect' of Dalit writing. For instance, Lakshmi Holmström used phrases like 'He ran hell for leather' in the first draft of *Karukku*, and Krishnan had to gently suggest that it was too Western, as in the case of the word 'briars' for 'thorny' and so on. The Tamil *thanni-ginni* (in Hindi *paani-vaani*) in *Sangati* is rendered 'water and geeter'. Unidiomatic usage abounds, like 'he was born alongside four or five brothers'. On the most literal level, 'code-switching', which refers to shifts in linguistic and cultural codes designating gender, religious, class or caste norms, posed a challenge to the translator to find ways of calling attention to a novel and freer form of communication idiom in Tamil, which expresses more accurately the experiences of women rather than reinforcing popular and conventional images. Talking about the challenges of representing the cultural differences in *bhasha* (vernacular, regional) texts and negotiating the differences in linguistic registers when translated into English, Mini Krishnan says

> In attempting to translocate India's tremendous linguistic complexities, every text is a challenge, and I don't think there are norms. . . . The challenge is to

> make the text beautiful, clear, without embellishments, over-writing or losses. You're translating not just words but a whole culture. English is from a land where there is no such thing as a yagna or caste system or rambling, complicated kinship terms. We have to find a third language – it isn't Kannada/Hindi/Oriya, it isn't wholly English. You have to 'throw' voices . . . you know . . . it's literary ventriloquism.
>
> (2009: 126–127)

The loss of a regional, spoken dialect transforms the novel in significant ways. The emotional complexity and the linguistic dexterity that comes to a point in the lyrical, exploratory form of Bama's Tamil *Karukku* are absent from its English translation. The translation adopts an adaptive strategy – it makes the complex circular narrative structure, the immediacy of the local language, the looping, gesturing and figurative language of the regional Tamil lack of boundaries drawn between reported speech and dialogue simple – as a way of dealing with the heterogeneous richness of Bama's Tamil (Sivanarayanan 2009: 147).

Sangati maps the trajectory of Dalit women's consciousness from 'subjugation to celebration' (Geetha) by problematizing what it means to speak as a minoritized[8] Dalit from a 'marginal' caste and gender positionality, wherein the hegemonic nation-state's collective voice is determined by the constraining and paralyzing frameworks of dominant majoritarian (patriarchal and brahmanic) discourses sustained and disseminated by and through institutionalized authoritative power and knowledge production. In *Sangati*, Bama exemplifies an individual and collective mode of transformative anti-hegemonic enunciation that acknowledges (a) the caste oppression in nation-state contexts and (b) the role and presence of collective implicatedness in continuing and replicating oppression. Bama challenges Tamil cultural codes that continue to regulate Dalit women's bodies and behaviour, requiring them to be chaste, self-effacing, pliant and, above all, respectable, in the name of their *karpu*, or chastity, and Tamil culture.[9] Bama's code-switching extends to the discursive codes of nationalism and representation, as her work complicates a unitary sense of Indian national identity, fragmented as it is along ethnic, regional, linguistic, religious and caste lines. Bama's *Sangati* is a Dalit narrative text bearing witness to the collective testimonies of the caste-based exploitation and violence rather than a single woman's resistance against caste, class and gender prescriptions (Nayar 2006). Both *Karukku* and *Sangati* exploit autobiographical material and Dalit personal/social/collective memories to create remarkably new literary forms; they trace the trajectory of Dalit subjectivity 'from subjugation to celebration' (Geetha) with real-life stories of risks taken and of challenge, agency and change. In *Sangati*, Bama accomplishes the rare creative feat of blending autobiography, fiction, polemics and praxis. *Sangati* not only explodes/subverts the mainstream majoritarian upper-class, upper-caste *brahminical* aesthetic, but also offers a new one that is fundamental to her ideological and identitarian politics. The differences in the English and Tamil versions both point to the ways the subject herself becomes produced within the narrative in certain ways. In order to appreciate her writings and praxis, it is expected and/desired of the translator and reader, to quote Gayatri Spivak, a 'surrender to the special call of the text' (Spivak 1993: 183). The ways in which multiple forms of feminism manifest in the translation of *Sangati* illustrate and exemplify that 'beyond the discursive presence of identity markers associated with feminist practices, a feminist understanding of processes of becoming through joints and connections within subjectivity-as-encounter contribute to the shifts in position and new narratives that are essential for change' (Flotow *Translating Women*, 2011: 300).

Notes

1 The word 'Dalit' comes from Marathi and means 'oppressed' or 'ground down'. It was first used by Dr B.R. Ambedkar in preference to his own earlier term 'scheduled castes'. The term began to be used by politically awakened ex-Untouchables in the early 1970s when the Dalit Panthers, a youthful group of activists and writers in Bombay, came on the scene to protest injustice (Michael 2007: 33). The Dalit Panther Organization is now scattered and important only in a few places, but the pride and militancy that accompanied the name has created a category of culture in India (see Zelliot 1996: 1–4). The term 'Dalit' is not merely a rejection of the very idea of pollution or impurity or 'untouchability'; it reveals a sense of a unified class, of a movement toward equality. In Tamil Nadu, the term had been used intermittently along with *taazhtappattor* (those who have been put down) or *odukkappattor* (the oppressed) during the 1980s, but it is only since the 90s that it has been used widely, not only by Tamil Dalit writers and ideologues in order to identify themselves but also by mainstream critics. Today its usage includes socially suppressed caste groups in India. Its semantic scope has been extended to include tribals, landless farm-labourers, so-called criminal

tribes and the exploited. On the Indian caste system, see Louis Dumont, *Homo Hierarchicus: The Caste System and Its Implications*, New Delhi: Oxford University Press, 1980; Gail Omvedt, *Dalit Visions*, New Delhi: South Asia Books, 1998; and Sagarika Ghose, 'The Dalit in India', *Social Research*, 70(1) (2003): 83–109.

2 Lakshmi Holmström, the founder-trustee of South Asian Diaspora Literature and Arts Archive, is an Indian-born British writer, literary critic and translator into English of Tamil fiction by contemporary writers in Tamil like Ashoka Mitran, C. S. Lakshmi, Pudhumaipithan, Mauni, Sundara Ramasami and Imayam. Her translation of Bama's *Karakku* won the Hutch Crossword Award (2000) in the Indian Language Fiction Translation category. Pointing to the prestige of the Crossword Award as an indication of the enormous influence wielded by the field of translation, Rita Kothari, in *Translating India* (New Delhi: Foundation Books, 2003), talks about the rapidly spawning translating industry. Holmström was appointed Member of the Order of the British Empire in the 2011 New Year Honours for services to literature.

3 Though the first Dalit literary conference was held in Bombay (Maharashtra) in 1957, Dalit literature, which expresses the suffering of the Dalit community in pre- and post-independent India, began to carve a niche for itself only during the 1960s. For further information, see Dangle (1992: 242–244).

4 Gopal Guru, a professor of social and political theory in the Centre of Political Science at Jawaharlal Nehru University, drawing attention to the formation of a pan-Indian group known as the National Federation of Dalit Women, wrote a piece in the *Economic and Political Weekly* on 'Dalit Women Talk Differently' (1995).

5 Initial norm determines, by and large, the translator's choice to adhere 'either to the original text, with the norms it has realized, or to the norms active in the target culture, or in that section of it which would host the end product' (Toury 2000: 201). Toury, however, rejects the obligation of total compliance between an overall decision made and every single decision made in the lower levels of translation process and, therefore, refutes the existence of absolute regularity in translational behaviours (201). The alternatives that are offered to the translator by Toury's initial norm are almost analogous to those which Venuti (1998: 240) elaborates in his foreignizing and domesticating strategies of translation.

6 The English equivalent of the Tamil word *ragi kuzh* is millet porridge. Since Sammuga Kizhavi loves eating *ragi kuzh*, her actual name is playfully fused with porridge to create a humorous nickname *Maikuzh Kizhavi*.

7 Mini Krishnan has worked in the publishing industry in India for over 20 years. Currently, she is an editor with Oxford University Press and oversees its translation program. Previously, she worked at Macmillan and was its series editor for Modern Indian Novels in Translations. Several of the translated works that she has edited have been winners of the Hutch Crossword Prize. She has also won Sahitya Akademi prizes for translation. Three of her projects, Bama's *Karukku* (2000), Chandra Sekhar Rath's *Astride the Wheel* (2003) and, most recently,

C. S. Lakshmi's *In the Forest, A Deer* (2006), have won the Hutch Crossword Prize for Translation. She is also the founder-editor of the South Asia Women's Writing website hosted by the British Council. (For further information, see Sivanarayanan 2009: 123–134.)

8 The three characteristics of minor literature are 'the deterritorialization of the language, the connection of the individual and the political, the collective arrangement of utterance. Which amounts to this: that "minor" no longer characterizes certain literatures, but describes the revolutionary conditions of any literature within what we call the great (or established)' (18). For more information, see 'What Is a Minor Literature?' by Deleuze, Guattari and Brinkley.

9 For further discussion of *karpu*, going back to the Tamil epic *Silapathikaram*, see Mala Kadar, 'The Myth of Kannaki: The Concept of Chastity and Power', sangam.org (13 October 2003). http://www.sangam.org/articles/view/?id=27.

References

Agorni, Mirella. 2005. 'A Marginal(ized) Perspective on Translation History: Women and Translation in the Eighteenth Century', *Meta*, 50(3): 817–30.

Aloysius, G. 1997. *Nationalism without a Nation in India*. New Delhi: Oxford University Press.

Appadurai, Arjun. 1986. 'Is Homo Hierarchicus?' *American Ethnologist*, 13(4): 745–61.

Appiah, Kwame Anthony. 2000. 'Thick Translation', in Lawrence Venuti (ed), *The Translation Studies Reader*, pp. 331–43. London: Routledge.

Bakhtin, M. M. 1981. 'Discourse in the Novel', in Michael Holquist (ed), *The Dialogic Imagination* (Caryl Emerson and Michael Holquist, trans.), pp. 269–422. Austin: University of Texas Press.

———. 1986. *Speech Genres and Other Late Essays* (Vern W. McGee, trans.). Austin: University of Texas Press.

Bama, 2000. *Karukku* (Lakshmi Holmström, trans.). Chennai: Macmillan.

———. 2005. *Sangati* (Lakshmi Holmström, trans.). Chennai: Oxford University Press.

Barthes, Roland. 1977. 'Introduction to the Structural Analysis of Narratives', in Stephen Heath (ed. and trans.), *Image-Music-Text*, pp. 79–124. New York: Hill and Wang.

Bassnett, Susan and Harish Trivedi (eds). 1999. *Post-Colonial Translation: Theory and Practice*. London: Routledge.

Bauer, Dale. 1991. 'Gender in Bakhtin's Carnival', in Robyn R. Warhol and Diane Price Herndl (eds), *Feminisms: An Anthology of Literary Theory and Criticism*, pp. 708–20. New Brunswick: Rutgers University Press.

Behar, Ruth. 1993. *Translated Woman: Crossing the Border with Esperanza's Story*. Boston: Beacon Press.

Berman, Antoine. 2009. *Toward a Translation Criticism: John Donne* (Françoise Massardier-Kenney, trans.). Kent: Kent State University Press.

Beverley, John. 1992. 'The Margin at the Center: On Testimonio (TestimonialNarrative)', in Sidonie Smith and Julia Watson (eds), *De/Colonizing the Subject: The Politics of Gender in Women's Autobiography*, pp. 91–114. Minneapolis: University of Minnesota Press.

Bhabha, Homi. 1994. *The Location of Culture*. London and New York: Routledge.

Bhagwat, Vidyut. (1990). 'Man–Woman Relations in the Writings of Saint Poetesses', *New Quest*, 82: 223–32.

Bhave, Sumitra. 1988. *Pan on Fire: Eight Dalit Women Tell Their Story* (Gauri Deshpande, trans.). New Delhi: Indian Social Institute.

Blum-Kulka, Shoshana. 2000. 'Shifts of Cohesion and Coherence in Translation', in Lawrence Venuti and Mona Baker (eds), *The Translation Studies Reader*, pp. 298–313. London and New York: Routledge.

Brockmeier, Jens and Rom Harré. 2001. 'Narrative: Problems and Promises of an Alternative Paradigm', in Jens Brockmeier and Donald Carbaugh (eds), *Narrative Identity: Studies in Autobiography, Self and Culture*, pp. 39–58. Amsterdam and Philadelphia: John Benjamins.

Brossard, Nicole. 1977. *L'amer: Ou, le chapitre effrite* (Barbara Godard, trans.). Montreal: Quinze.

———. 1983. *These Our Mothers, or, The Disintegrating Chapter*. Toronto: Coach House Press.

Bruner, Jerome. 1991. 'The Narrative Construction of Reality', *Critical Inquiry*, 18(1): 1–21.

Castro, Olga. 2013. 'Introduction: Gender, Language and Translation at the Crossroads of Disciplines', *Gender and Language*, 7(1): 5–12.

Chakravarti, Uma. 1998. *Rewriting History: The Life and Times of Pandita Ramabai*. New Delhi: Kali for Women.

Chamberlain, Lori.1988. 'Gender and the Metaphorics of Translation', *Signs: Journal of Women in Culture and Society*, 13(3): 454–72.

Chouliaraki, Lilie and Norman Fairclough. 1999. *Discourse in Late Modernity: Rethinking Critical Discourse Analysis*. Edinburgh: Edinburgh University Press.

Crawford, Mary and Roger Chafin. 1986. 'The Reader's Construction of Meaning: Cognitive Research on Gender and Comprehension', in Elizabeth A. Flynn and Patricinio P. Schweickart (eds), *Gender and Reading: Essays on Readers, Texts and Contexts*, pp. 3–30. Baltimore: Johns Hopkins University Press.

Cronin, Michael. 2004. *Translation and Globalization*. London and New York: Routledge.

Currie, Mark. 1998. *Postmodern Narrative Theory*. Houndmills: Palgrave.

Dangle, Arjun. 1992. *Poisoned Bread: Translations from Modern Marathi Dalit Literature*. Mumbai: Orient Longman.

Das, Veena. 1995. *Critical Events: An Anthropological Perspective on Contemporary India*. New Delhi: Oxford University Press.

Davis, Kathleen. 1997. 'Signature in Translation', in Dirk Delabastita (ed), *Traductio: Essays on Punning and Translation*, pp. 23–43. Manchester and Namur: St. Jerome.

Deleuze, Gilles, Félix Guattari, and Robert Brinkley. 1983. 'What Is a Minor Literature?' *Mississippi Review*, 11(3): 13–33.

Devy, G. N. 1995. 'Translation Theory: An Indian Perspective', in G. N. Devy (ed), *In Another Tongue: Essays on Indian English Literature*, pp. 162–7. Chennai: Macmillan.

———. 1997. 'Literary History and Translation: An Indian View', *Meta: Translators' Journal*, 42(2): 395–406.

———. 1999. 'Translation and Literary History: An Indian View', in Harish Trivedi and Susan Bassnett (eds), *Postcolonial Translation Theory*, pp. 182–8. London: Routledge.

Dumont, Louis. 1980. *Homo Hierarchicus: The Caste System and Its Implications*. New Delhi: Oxford University Press.

Ermarth, Elizabeth. 1981. 'Realism, Perspective, and the Novel', *Critical Inquiry*, 7(3): 499–520.

Fentress, J. and C. Wickham. 1992. *Social Memory*. Oxford: Blackwell.

Fernandes, Leela. 1997. *Producing Workers: The Politics of Gender, Class and Culture in the Calcutta Jute Mills*. Philadelphia: University of Pennsylvania Press.

———. 1999. 'Reading "India's Bandit Queen": A Trans/national Feminist Perspective on the Discrepancies of Representation', *Signs*, 25(1): 123–52.

Flotow, Luise von. 2011. *Translating Women*. Ottawa: University of Ottawa Press.

Fludernik, Monika. 1991. 'The Historical Present Tense Yet Again: Tense Switching and Narrative Dynamics in Oral and Quasi-oral Storytelling', *Text*, 11(3): 365–97.

———. 1996. *Towards a 'Natural' Narratology*. London and New York: Routledge.

Foucault, Michel. 1977. 'Nietzsche, Genealogy, History', in Donald Bouchard (ed), *Foucault, Language, Counter-Memory, Practice*, pp. 139–64. Ithaca: Cornell University Press.

———. 1980. *Power/Knowledge: Selected Interviews and Other Writings, 1972–1977* (Alan Sheridan, trans.). New York: Pantheon.

Gadamer, Hans-Georg. 1975. *Truth and Method* (Garrett Barden and John Cumming, trans.). New York: Crossroad.

Ganguly, D. 2000. 'Can the Dalit Speak: Caste, Postcoloniality and the New Humanities?', *Journal of South Asian Studies*, 23: 43–62.

Geary, P.J. 1994. *Phantoms of Remembrance: Memory and Oblivion at the End of the First Millennium*. Princeton: Princeton University Press.

Geetha, V.1992. 'Gender and Logic of Brahmanism: E V Ramaswamy Periyar and the Politics of the Female Body'. Paper presented at the Seminar on Women's Studies, IIAS, Shimla.

Ghose, Sagarika. 2003. 'The Dalit in India', *Social Research*, 70(1): 83–109.

Godard, Barbara. 1990. 'Theorizing Feminist Theory/Translation', in Susan Bassnett and A. Lefevere (eds), *Translation: History and Culture*, pp. 87–96. London: Frances Pinter.
Guha, Ranajit. 1997. 'The Small Voice of History', in Shahid Amin and Dipesh Chakrabarty (eds), *Subaltern Studies: Writings on South Asian History and Society* (Vol. 9), pp. 1–12. New Delhi: Oxford University Press.
———. 2003. *History at the Limit of World History*. New Delhi: Oxford University Press.
Guru, Gopal. 1995. 'Dalit Women Talk Differently', *Economic and Political Weekly*, October 14–21: 2548–50.
Hall, Stuart. 1989. 'Ethnicity: Identity and Difference', *Radical America*, 23(4): 9–21.
Henke, Suzette. 1998. *Shattered Subjects: Trauma and Testimony in Women's Life-Writing*. London: Macmillan.
Hermans, Theo. 1996. 'The Translator's Voice in Translated Narrative', *Target*, 8(2): 23–48.
———. 2002. 'Paradoxes and Aporias in Translation and Translation Studies', in Alessandra Riccardi (ed), *Translation Studies: Perspectives on an Emerging Discipline*, pp. 10–23. Cambridge: Cambridge University Press.
Holmström, Lakshmi. 2001. 'A Number of Great Indian Writers Are Not Known in the Rest of the World', *Outlook Magazine*, 5 April. Retreieved 3 December 2015 from http://www.outlookindia.com/article/a-number-of-great-indian-writers-are-not-known-in-the-rest-of-the-world/211410.
———. 2005. 'Introduction', in Lakshmi Holmström (trans.), *Sangati by Bama*, pp. xi–xxiii. Chennai: Oxford University Press.
Hutton, P.H. 1993. *History as an Art of Memory*. Hanover: University Press of New England.
Illaih, Kancha.1996. *Why I Am Not a Hindu: A Critique of Sudra Philosophy*. Calcutta: Samya.
Inden, Ronald.1990. *Imagining India*. Oxford: Blackwell.
Isnenghi, Mario. (ed). 1996. *I luoghi della memoria: simboli e miti dell'Italia unita*. Bari and Rome: Laterza.
———. (ed). 1997a. *I luoghi della memoria: strutture ed eventi dell'Italia unita*. Bari and Rome: Laterza.
———. (ed). 1997b. *I luoghi della memoria: personaggi e date dell'Italia unita*. Bari and Rome: Laterza.
Kadar, Mala. 2003. 'The Myth of Kannaki: The Concept of Chastity and Power', *sangam.org* (13 October 2003). Retrieved from http://www.sangam.org/articles/view/?id=27.
Karlekar, Malavika. 1982. *Poverty and Women's Work: A Study of Sweeper Women in Delhi*. New Delhi: Vikas Publishing House.
———. 1983. 'Education and Inequality', in A. Beteille (ed), *Equality and Inequality: Theory and Practice*, pp. 182–242. New Delhi: Oxford University Press.
Kothari, R. 2003. 'Two World Theory', in Kothari (ed), *Translating India*, pp. 26–35. Manchester: St. Jerome Publishing.

Kreiswirth, Martin. 1992. 'Trusting the Tale: The Narrativist Turn in the Human Sciences', *New Literary History*, 23(3): 629–57.

———. 2000. 'Merely Telling Stories? Narrative and Knowledge in the Human Sciences', *Poetics Today*, 21(2): 293–318.

———. 2005. 'Narrative Turn in the Humanities', in David Herman, Manfred Jahn and Marie-Laure Ryan (eds), *Routledge Encyclopedia of Narrative Theory*, pp. 377–82. New York: Routledge.

Krishnan, Mini. 2009. 'Publishing Translations: An Interview with Mini Krishnan, Oxford University Press', in Nalini Iyer and Bonnie Zare (eds), *Other Tongues Rethinking the Language Debates in India*, pp. 123–31. Amsterdam and New York: Rodopi.

Kruger, Barbara and Phil Mariani (eds). 1998. *Remaking History*. New York: The New Press.

Kumar, Raj. 2010. *Dalit Personal Narratives: Reading Caste, Nation and Identity*. Hyderabad: Orient BlackSwan.

Le Goff, Jacques. 1992. *History and Memory* (Steven Rendall and Elizabeth Claman, trans.). New York: Columbia University Press.

Levine, Suzanne Jill. 1991. *The Subversive Scribe: Translating Latin American Fiction*. St. Paul: Graywolf.

Massardier-Kenney, Françoise. 1997. 'Towards a Redefinition of Feminist Translation Practice', *The Translator*, 3(1): 55–69.

McNamara, Roger. 2009. 'Towards a Dalit Secularism: Bama's *Karakku* and the Possibilities of an Internal Critique', *South Asian Review*, 30(1): 269–85.

Michael, S.M. 2007. *Dalits in Modern India: Vision and Values*, 2nd ed. New Delhi: Sage Publications.

Mills, Sara and Louise Mullany. 2011. *Language, Gender and Feminism*. London: Routledge.

Mohanty, Chandra. 1991. 'Under Western Eyes', in Chandra Mohanty, Ann Russo and Lourdes M. Torres (eds), *Third World Women and the Politics of Feminism*, pp. 51–80. Bloomington: Indiana University Press,

Munday, Jeremy. 2001. *Introducing Translation Studies: Theories and Applications*. London and New York: Routledge.

Nair, Janaki. 2008. 'The Lateral Spread of Indian Feminist Historiography', *Journal of Women's History*, 20(4): 177–84.

Nayar, Pramod K. 2006. 'Bama's *Karukku*: Dalit Autobiography as *Testimonio*', *The Journal of Commonwealth Literature*, 41(2): 83–100.

———. 2008. 'Dalit Writing, Cultural Trauma and Pedagogy: The Testimony of Omprakash Valmiki's *Joothan*', *Haritham*, 19: 51–65.

———. 2009. 'Postcolonial Affects: Victim Life Narratives and Human Rights in Contemporary India', *Postcolonial Text*, 5(4). Retrieved from http://journals.sfu.ca/pocol/index.php/pct/article/view/1078/1027.

———. 2011. 'The Politics of Form in Dalit Fiction: Bama's *Sangati* and Sivakami's *The Grip of Change*', *Indian Journal of Gender Studies*, 18(3): 365–80.

Nietzsche, Friedrich. 1957. *The Use and Abuse of History* (Adrian Collins, trans.). Indianapolis: Bobbs-Merrill.

Nigam, Aditya. 2000. 'Secularism, Modernity, Nation: Epistemology of the Dalit Critique', *Economic and Political Weekly*, 35(48): 4256–68.

Niranjana, Tejaswini. 1992. *Siting Translation: History, Post-Structuralism, and the Colonial Context*. Berkeley: University of California Press.

O'Hanlon, Rosalind. 1994. *A Comparison Between Women and Men: Tarabai Shinde and the Critique of Gender Relations in Colonial India*. Chennai: Oxford University Press.

Olk, Harold. 2002. 'Critical Discourse Awareness in Translation', *The Translator*, 8(1): 101–15.

Omvedt, Gail. 1976. *Cultural Revolt in Colonial Society: The Non-Brahman Movement in Western India 1873–1930*. Mumbai: Scientific Socialist Education Trust.

———. 1993. *Reinventing Revolution: India's New Social Movements*. New York: Sharpe.

———. 1994. *Dalits and Democratic Revolution: Dr Ambedkar and the Dalit Movement in Colonial India*. New Delhi: Oxford University Press.

———. 1998. *Dalit Visions*. New Delhi: South Asia Books.

Pagano, Adriana Silvina. 2001. 'Gêneros Híbridos', in Célia Maria Magalhães (ed), *Reflexões sobre a Análise Crítica do Discurso*, pp. 83–104. Belo Horizonte: FALE/ UFMG.

Paik, Shailaja. 2009. 'Chhadi Lage Chham Chham, Vidya Yeyi Gham Gham (The Harder the Stick Beats, the Faster the Flow of Knowledge): Dalit Women's Struggle for Education', *Indian Journal of Gender Studies*, 16(2): 175–204.

Pandian, M.S.S. 2003. 'On a Dalit Woman's Testimonio', in Anupama Rao (ed), *Gender and Caste*, pp. 129–35. New Delhi: Kali for Women.

Patil, Sharad. 1982. *Dasa-Sudra Slavery*. Mumbai: Allied Publishers.

Phukan, Shibani. 2003. 'Towards an Indian Theory of Translation', *Wasafiri*, 40: 27–30.

Prasad, G.J.V. 2007. 'Translating Tamil Dalit Literature into English or How to Resist One's Self', *Language Forum*, 33(1), 65–71.

——. 2011. *Writing India, Writing English: Literature, Language, Location*. New Delhi: Routledge.

Purkayastha, Bandana, Mangala Subramaniam, Manisha Desai and Sunita Bose. 2003. 'The Study of Gender in India: A Partial Review', *Gender & Society*, 17(4): 503–24.

Ray, Sangeeta. 2000. *En-Gendering India: Woman and Nation in Colonial and Postcolonial Narratives*. Durham and London: Duke University Press.

Rege, Sharmila. 1998. 'Dalit Women Talk Differently: A Critique of "Difference" and Towards a Dalit Feminist Standpoint Position', *Economic and Political Weekly*, 33(44) (October 31–November 6), WS39–46.

———. 2000. '"Real Feminism" and Dalit Women: Scripts of Denial and Accusation', *Economic and Political Weekly*, 35(6) (February 5–11, 2000), 492–95.

———. 2006. *Writing Caste/Writing Gender: Reading Dalit Women's Testimonies*. New Delhi: Zubaan.

Riccardi, Alessandra. 2002. *Translation Studies: Perspectives on an Emerging Discipline*. Cambridge: Cambridge University Press.

Richardson, Brian. 2000. 'Recent Concepts of Narrative and the Narratives of Narrative Theory', *Style*, 34: 168–75.

Roth, Michael S. 1995. *The Ironist's Cage: Memory, Trauma and the Construction of History*. New York: Columbia University Press.

Ruano, Martin. 2006. 'Gender(ing) Theory: Rethinking the Targets of Translation Studies in Parallel with Recent Developments in Feminism', in José Santaemilia (ed), *Gender, Sex and Translation: The Manipulation of Identities*, pp. 27–37. Manchester: St. Jerome.

Ryan, Marie-Laure. 2005. 'Narrative', in David Herman, Manfred Jahn and Marie-Laure Ryan (eds), *Routledge Encyclopedia of Narrative Theory*, pp. 344–48. London and New York: Routledge.

Santaemilia, José. 2008. 'The Translation of Sex-Related Language: The Danger(s) of Self-Censorship(s)', *TTR: Traduction, Terminologie, Redaction*, 21(2): 221–52.

Sheridan, A. 1990. *Michel Foucault: The Will to Truth*. London and New York: Routledge.

Sivanarayanan, Anushiya. 2009. 'Translation and Globalization: Tamil Dalit Literature and Bama's *Karukku*', in Nalini Iyer and Bonnie Zare (eds), *Other Tongues Rethinking the Language Debates in India*, pp. 135–54. Amsterdam and New York: Rodopi.

Spivak, Gayatri Chakravorty.1988. 'Can the Subaltern Speak?' in Cary Nelson and Lawrence Grossberg (eds), *Marxism and the Interpretation of Culture*, pp. 271–97. Urbana: University of Illinois Press.

———. 1992. 'The Politics of Translation' in Michèle Barrett and Anne Phillips (eds), *Destabilizing Theory: Contemporary Feminist Debates*, pp. 177–200. Stanford: Stanford University Press.

———. 1993. *Outside in the Teaching Machine*. London and New York: Routledge.

Steedman, Carolyn. 1986. *Landscapes for a Good Woman: A Story of Two Lives*. London: Virago.

Tharu S. and T. Niranjana. 1996. 'Problems for a Contemporary Theory of Gender', in Shahid Amin and Dipesh Chakrabarty (eds), *Subaltern Studies IX*, pp. 232–60. New Delhi: Oxford University Press.

———. 2000. 'The Nature and Role of Norms in Translation', in Lawrence Venuti (ed), *The Translation Studies Reader*, pp. 198–211. London: Routledge.

Venuti, Lawrence. 1998. 'Introduction', *The Translator* (Special Issue: 'Translation and Minority'), 4(2): 135–44.

Venuti, Lawrence and Mona Baker (eds). 2000. *The Translation Studies Reader*. London and New York: Routledge.

Visweswaran, Kamala. 1994. *Fictions of Feminist Ethnography*. Minneapolis: University of Minnesota Press.

Von Flotow, Luise. 1997. *Translation and Gender: Translating in the 'Era of Feminism'*. Manchester: St. Jerome.
Wallace, Melissa. 2002. 'Writing the Wrongs of Literature: The Figure of the Feminist and Post-Colonialist Translator', *The Journal of the Midwest Modern Language Association*, 35(2): 'Translating in and across Cultures', 65–74.
Zelliot, Eleanor.1996. 'Dalit Movement', *Dalit International Newsletter*, 1(1): 1–4.

11 Historiography or imagination?

The documentation of traditional Luo cultural memory in Kenyan fiction

Alex N. Wanjala

In accordance with the conference theme 'Imagining the intangible', this chapter seeks to demonstrate how some female Kenyan writers have chosen to perpetuate their local communities' intangible heritage through the use of the novel as a cultural tool. The chapter will demonstrate how, in a manner somewhat similar to the situation that Victorian romance writers faced, such writers have had their novels frowned upon by critics who would have preferred that they occupy themselves with texts that espouse 'Aristotelian canons of mimetic probability' (Duncan 1992: 3). My argument is that critics who hold such views fail to see the richness of texts written in such a manner and therefore miss out on harnessing the traditional knowledge to be found within such texts that would be helpful when analysed as a commentary on contemporary social issues and that these elements are derived from what Abiola Irele refers to as the African Imagination (see Irele 1990). The chapter will focus on one such text: *Miaha* (1983) by Grace Ogot – published originally in Dholuo and translated into English as *The Strange Bride* (1989) – to study whether Grace Ogot, in reinterpreting a traditional Luo myth in her novel, documents indigenous culture or whether the memory of the traditions (re) presented in her text should be dismissed as fantasy.

The chapter is in itself an attempt to preserve intangible cultural heritage and is guided by the United Nations Educational Scientific and Cultural Organisation's views on the links between cultural heritage and intangible heritage.

> UNESCO's work in the field of 'cultural heritage' was initially limited to the protection and conservation of heritage such as historical monuments, objects or cultural sites, Over the years, the international community called

> for taking into account intangible heritage as an essential component of cultural heritage, giving rise to a novel approach that recognizes communities and groups as the main protagonists of cultural heritage. Intangible or 'living' forms of cultural heritage are the traditions or living expressions inherited from our ancestors and passed on to our descendants, such as oral traditions, performing arts, social practices, rituals, festive events, knowledge and practices concerning nature and the universe, and skills involved in producing traditional crafts.
>
> (2009: 11)

Through sharing knowledge on the intangible cultural heritage of the Luo community internationally, the chapter seeks to promote intercultural dialogue amongst the several indigenous groups that were represented at the conference.

In this chapter, I treat the novel as a tool that serves in passing on information from one generation to the other on the world view of a people and thus preserves and perpetuates intangible culture. In this I am guided by the approach used by Edward W. Said in *Culture and Imperialism* (1994). Said provides us with a working definition of culture that is applicable to our study:

> As I use the word, 'culture' means two things in particular. First of all it means all those practices, like the arts of description, communication, and representation, that have relative autonomy from the economic, social and political realms and that often exist in aesthetic forms, one of whose principal aims is pleasure. . . . Second, and almost imperceptibly, culture is a concept that includes a refining and elevating element, each society's reservoir of the best that has been known and thought.
>
> (1994: xii, xiii)

Said sees in the novel an important tool, because first of all one can derive pleasure from reading it, and second because it is written by people in society who have an elevated position in that they harness the best thoughts and practices in society and represent this in the novel; thus one can study a society's culture through the novel.

Said goes on to explain his method of analysis:

> The novels and other books I consider here I analyse because first of all I find them estimable and admirable works of art and learning, in which I and many other readers take pleasure and from which we derive profit. Second, the challenge is to connect them not only with that pleasure and profit but also with the imperial process of which they were manifestly and unconcealedly a

> part; rather than condemning or ignoring their participation in what was an unquestioned reality in their societies, I suggest that what we learn about this hitherto ignored aspect actually and truly *enhances* our reading and understanding of them.
>
> (1994: xv)

Said's method calls for the enjoyment of a work of art for its literary qualities that the critic should be able to bring out. However, the critic's reading should, apart from enjoying these artistic qualities, connect the work of art to the culture it belongs to in order to study the society presented through the text. Said in his analysis is using the novel to study the process of Imperialism and how it was related to the culture of Western societies. His intention is to read in the silences of such a text the presence of the voice of the colonized. My intentions are similar in a way. My analysis of *The Strange Bride* will bring out the literary qualities of the text and at the same time link it to the Luo society. By extension, my study intends to read in the silences of the text, the presence of the voice of the woman to determine her position in the traditional context of Luo society and thus determine her struggles in the present.

Grace Ogot is Kenya's best-known female writer. She has published several novels and short stories both in English and in Dholuo, a language spoken in East Africa. Her first novel was *The Promised Land* (1966). Florence Stratton explains how a critic, Gerald Moore, harshly condemned this novel: 'Grace Ogot', he opines, 'would be advised to return to [the short story] form, which she has handled with some skill, and to abjure all attempts to give the visions of her essentially fantastic imagination a realistic dress' (1994: 60). Commenting at a time when masculine Kenyan writers such as Ngũgĩ wa Thiong'o were adhering to mimetic canons of writing the novel – that they had borrowed from their Western counterparts – such a review must have had the effect of a bias in the critical reception of Ogot's text, especially because, as Stratton demonstrates in her analysis, the condemned novel was written in an attempt to subvert the Manichean allegory of gender. Meanwhile the novels praised by critics for adhering to the mimetic canon perpetuated a conventional male narrative tradition.

It should thus be with resilience that Grace Ogot comes up with *Miaha* (1983), a novel that still follows the same mode of writing as *The Promised Land* but, unlike the earlier novel that was written in English, is written in an indigenous language: Dholuo. Coming at a time when the issue of writing in indigenous languages had been popularized by the arguments fronted by Ngũgĩ wa Thiong'o, one would expect that Ogot's novel would be received with, if not as much, at least some critical acclaim as had Ngũgĩ's *Devil on the Cross* (1982) that had been published just a year before in an indigenous language, Kikuyu. Stratton points out how Ogot had a similar point of view to Ngũgĩ's on the debate on writing in indigenous languages:

> Ogot's stance on the language issue is not essentially different from Ngũgĩ's. As early as 1968 she stressed the need for African writers from 'an urban environment' to attempt to bridge the 'great cultural gulf' which separates them from 'the overwhelming majority of the population who live in the villages'. And in 1983, she stated that she was prompted to start writing in her first language by her mother's remark on the publication of *The Graduate* that 'if only you could write in Luo you would serve your people well'. She also indicates that she has remained committed to writing in Dholuo so that her work can 'be read by all my people' and her language preserved and not 'swallowed up by English and Kiswahili'.
>
> (1994: 59)

If treated at the time of its publication as part of the ongoing debate in what was then developing as post-colonial studies, Grace Ogot's *Miaha* should have made a very important contribution in demonstrating that Ngũgĩ was not the only person carrying the torch in terms of turning away from writing in English and embracing indigenous languages in written literature in Kenya. That critics were quiet on this development goes a long way in demonstrating the continued silencing of women's voices even in the 1980s. It is more than a decade later that Stratton addresses the text. Surprisingly though, Florence Stratton, in her analysis of *Miaha*, does not treat the text as a novel. As she states,

> Ogot has had a fairly productive career as a writer. She has to her credit two novels – *The Promised Land* and *The Graduate* (1980) – as well as three volumes of short stories – *Land without Thunder* (1968), *The Other Woman* (1976), and *The Island of Tears* (1980) – in English. But the critical establishment as well as feminist critics have tended to ignore these works.
>
> (1994: 59)

Stratton's failure to list *Miaha* (which in 1989 had been translated into English as *The Strange Bride*) could be excused if we surmised that she did not list it simply because it was not originally published in English. However, in her analysis she places it on the same plane as a short story because it is carried out alongside that of the short story 'Elizabeth' and another short story, 'The Green Leaves', clearly demonstrating that Stratton shares Gerald Moore's views that such a text could at best be analysed as a short story. Suffice it to say, her analysis of *The Strange Bride* is quite laconic relative to that of *The Promised Land* and *The Graduate*. Another critic, Oladele Taiwo, talks of *Miaha*'s popularity as a dramatic piece when performed in Luo-speaking areas of Kenya, demonstrating that the play could be used as a medium of transmitting indigenous culture (quoted in Stratton 1994: 59). It seems therefore that for Oladele Taiwo, the text would be relevant only when transmitted orally but not as a novel.

Stratton in her text carries out an extensive critical analysis of *The Promised Land*, insisting that it should be read for its merits as a novel. Because it is written in the same mode as *The Strange Bride*, one wonders why she does not consider the latter text as a novel in the same vein as the former. Eileen Julien interrogates the fact that critics of African literature see a disjuncture between indigenous forms of African verbal arts and the novel form (see Julien 1992). Indeed, as she demonstrates in her text, African literary practitioners, often with the aid of Western anthropologists, have tended to search for genres that existed before colonization in order to find their continuity in modern forms of literature that are written in European and African languages:

> For many practitioners of African literature and criticism, continuity has meant more often a search for a heritage from oral traditions to the new literatures written in European and African languages, the 'passage from orality to writing'. Orality is a complex concept to which we shall give considerable attention, but here let us note simply that scholars of written African literature generally have looked for the origins of continuity in those genres which existed centuries before the colonial period and the writing of novels: poetry, proverbs, riddles, narratives, epics articulated and performed orally the so-called indigenous and authentic genres.
>
> (1992: 4)

As Julien states, most of these practitioners emphasize orality as the source from which continuity between orality and written arts must flow. She sees the danger inherent in this view as being in the intellectual categories that are used when constructing the differences between orality and writing. It creates essentialism in which orality is seen to be part of a traditional African heritage and by extension the natural way of doing things and the written text is seen to be Western, modern and contiguous with that culture. As such, the accidental fact that writing and printing did not exist in Africa before the advent of colonialism is shown to demonstrate that the novel form is not for Africans.

Following Julien's argument, one could argue that Florence Stratton does not view *Miaha* as a novel due to her essentialist view of orality as metonymy for traditional Africans and therefore to her, a text that is written in an indigenous language and furthermore bears traces of orality cannot be seen as a novel as it represents what to her would be a closed past that should exist only in a verbal art form. It would therefore be natural to Stratton then, that apart from Ogot's novels written in English, she should concentrate only on other texts written in European languages by such African writers as Flora Nwapa, Buchi Emecheta and Mariama Bâ, in order to bring out the features of the emerging female tradition in African fiction. Obioma Nnaemeka, publishing in the same year as Stratton, also sets out to do a study of texts written by more or less the same writers Stratton studies, namely Flora Nwapa, Buchi Emecheta and Mariama Bâ (see Nnaemeka 1994). Like Stratton, Nnaemeka is interested in studying female traditions in African fiction. Like Florence Stratton, Nnaemeka sees a situation whereby African women writers have been silenced through the gaze of male critics on the kind of work they produce:

> By the time Flora Nwapa's *Efuru*, the first published novel written by an African woman was published in 1966, a uniquely male literary tradition was already in place in Africa. The impact of this masculinist literary tradition on African women writers can hardly be overstated. One of the consequences of this situation was that, thematically and stylistically, African women writers and particularly those of the first generation showed close affinities with their male counterparts.
>
> (1994: 140)

Nnaemeka sees this condition as having resulted from colonization and the advent of written literature in Africa. Indeed, in her analysis, she talks about an African past in which through the oral tradition, women were quite visible, not only as 'performers and disseminators of beliefs, cultural ideals, and personal/collective history, but also as composers who sometimes, transformed and re-created an existing body of oral traditions in order to incorporate women-centred perspectives' (1994: 138). Nnaemeka sees the voice of African women as having disappeared from modern African literature, first of all through a re-invention of the African reality via a colonial discourse that denigrated the place of the

African in literature. This led to a reaction by African writers that had the effect of creating a centre-margin paradigm in attempting to readdress the issue of the marginalization of the African through post-colonial scholarship. Nnaemeka describes how this new post-colonial paradigm is deceptive in that it sees uniformity in the margins that in her study refers to African literature. It therefore does not cater for what should really be the heterogeneous nature at that end of the continuum of the paradigm. Thus the African woman, who should be a composite part of that margin, has been blanked out (1994: 141). This circumstance leads to a situation whereby African women writers are not only marginal but liminal figures, edgy about the place in which they have been confined and also aware of the fact that they are writing under the powerful gaze of usually male readers and critics. According to Nnaemeka, this situation that women writers find themselves in forces them to 'negotiate' the creation of their fictional characters. In so doing, they create characters in line with the conventional male narrative literary tradition. Nnaemeka sees the second reason for the silencing of women as the disappearing of orality that privileged women in literature:

> In African oral tradition, women were very visible, not only as performers, but as producers of knowledge, especially in view of oral literature's didactic relevance, moral(izing) imperatives and pedagogical foundations. Researchers in the field of African oral tradition have documented the active participation of women, at professional and non-professional levels, in the crafting, preservation and transmission of most forms of oral literature.
>
> (1994: 138)

Clearly Nnaemeka sees a disjuncture between the oral tradition of African literature and the written form that she refers to as the modern form of literature. By seeing the oral tradition as a closed tradition in which one cannot fit the modern form of the novel, Nnaemeka makes the same mistake that she has castigated the male critics for in that just as the male critics' gaze had created an aspect of positioning that places women at the periphery, so her method of analysis sees the novel as a text that should strictly adhere to what she sees as the conventional narrative tradition of modern writing; texts that constitute orality do not belong in this type of art but belong to a closed form that has no place in contemporary literature. It follows therefore that she would place literature written in indigenous languages in the same peripheral position. Indeed, in her analysis, though mention of Grace Ogot as a writer is made, no attempt to analyse any of her texts or any other female writer's writing using features of orality or writing in an indigenous language is evident.

In the novel *The Strange Bride* (1989), Grace Ogot interprets a Luo myth that explains how the people of Got Owaga started cultivating using their own hands and carrying out economic activities such as the rearing of cattle, the growing of tobacco and fishing. It narrates how Nyawir, a girl from a village neighbouring Got Owaga who had disappeared into the underworld as a child, came back and got married to Owiny, the son of the chief of the village of Got Owaga. This chief was known as Were Ochak. It is demonstrated that the marriage was conducted without due diligence being conducted in finding out about the girl's background.

Nyawir is described as a beautiful, but strange bride, who is driven by a strange and evil impulse to change the status quo in Got Owaga, the village into which she marries, which is the seat of communal power in Luo land. Got Owaga is an idyllic society by the time of her marriage, and members of the community do not engage in manual labour as cultivation of their farms is done for them automatically using a special hoe given to them by their god Were Nyakalaga who dwells nearby on Mount Owaga.

The political organization of the community is spelled out, and it is demonstrated that every member of the community had a role to play. The community's leader, Were Ochak, is the intermediary through whom prayers from the people of Got Owaga are offered to Were Nyakalaga. He also carries out daily prayers and sacrifices on Mount Owaga to their deity to perpetuate this peaceful existence. Were Ochak's wife, Lwak, also has special duties that include brewing of beer for sacrifices and taking out the community's hoe to the farms early in the morning during the cultivation season.

This idyllic life in the community that is reminiscent of life in the Biblical Garden of Eden is brought to a halt by Nyawir's machinations. As a newlywed bride, she uses her wiles to coax information out of her husband on the secrets of how the community tills its land. When she is informed that there is an automatic hoe that is taken out by her mother-in-law early every morning during the cultivation season, she puts her plan into action. She wakes up very early the following morning and waylays her mother-in-law on her way to the farm. She then cajoles her into allowing her to take the hoe to the farm on her behalf. Lwak, who is perturbed by her behaviour, eventually gives in to her demands when she realizes that the day would break without her daughter-in-law, allowing her access to the farms. Another reason that she acquiesces is that there are rules that relate to how people should interact during the season of cultivation and one of them is that they should not engage in arguments. As a result of this, Lwak gives the hoe to Nyawir, with strict instructions that once she gets to the farm, she should simply place the hoe on the ground, then turn around and leave.

However, when Nyawir gets to the farm, rather than do as her mother-in-law had asked, she strikes the ground with the metal-headed hoe. Big fire flames come out of the spot on which the hoe made contact with the ground and the metal-headed hoe breaks. This action has immediate repercussions. Even the monkeys and the birds are shocked into silence. Life will never be the same again in Got Owaga.

Retribution comes swiftly. Were Ochak can no longer intercede to Were Nyakalaga who has been so angered by Nyawir's actions that he places a curse on the community and moves away from his abode on Mount Owaga to a site further up where he cannot be reached. From that moment on, the people of Got Owaga will have to cultivate with their own hands and reap what they sow.

Owiny, who stands by his wife despite her evil actions, is ostracized from Got Owaga together with his bride. They plead with the community to allow them to carry the community's axe, which has the same powers as the destroyed hoe in that it is able to fell trees automatically and is what the community relies on when they want to build houses. The people of Got Owaga after deliberations reluctantly hand over the axe to them. The ostracized couple soon discover that the axe too had lost its magic powers as it fails to cut any tree. Owiny, who had left his wife asleep to go and check on the axe, then decides to cut the trees manually using the same axe, but the head breaks off, falls into a hole and disappears. Distressed by the fact that he has lost his community's axe, he decides to get into the hole to retrieve the axe. It turns out that this hole is the entrance to the underground world. He stays there for a long time, learning their ways.

Meanwhile, on waking up, Nyawir goes in search of her husband but cannot find any trace of him. After a long and futile search, she decides to go back to Got Owaga and inform Owiny's kinsmen of his disappearance even if it would mean that they kill her. They give her a hut in which to stay for a while as she mourns the disappearance of her husband. Later, against the advice of her father-in-law, she goes to the top of Mount Owaga to see the face of Were Nyakalaga and to confront him on the disappearance of her husband. She disappears and is never seen again. It is said that Were Nyakalaga used her as a sacrifice to cleanse the community of the curse she had bestowed on them.

In the underground world, Owiny is taught how to fish and shown the beauty of beads that are vomited by the mother tilapia *min ngege*; the people of the underground world use the beads to adorn themselves and to decorate their clothes. Eventually, the king of the underground world decides to allow Owiny to go back home to Earth, as his body is seen to be unable to survive in the underground kingdom. He is given some beads from *min ngege* as gifts, together with cattle and tobacco, and guided back to Got Owaga. He returns home in glory due to his great wealth and his knowledge of the skill of fishing. Were Nyakalaga instructs Were Ochak to anoint him as the next chief of Got Owaga despite the fact that he is the second-born son and traditionally the chiefdom should go to the first-born son. Were Nyakalaga shows, through this anointing, that even he is happy with the changes that Owiny has brought to the community and thus he has given him his blessing.

It is very easy to dismiss the novel as a simple tale, especially if we glossed over it as I have done in the analysis given earlier. However, a closer reading of the text reveals that there are important issues raised that can be studied. Stratton identifies this in her analysis when she comments: 'In *The Strange Bride*, Ogot combats one of the major orthodoxies of male literature: the representation of women as outside history' (1994: 64). Just for this reason, the text should be studied alongside other texts that are identified as part of the canon of African feminist fiction. It seems, therefore, that although Ogot is making an important comment on contemporary social issues through her text, it is her source of inspiration, the myth, which may be problematic to critics. This argument may be seen to be paradoxical, considering that many practitioners of African literature see the authenticity of an African novel as being as a result of the incorporation of orality within it. As Mohamadou Kane states, 'It is . . . opportune to show that the originality of the African novel must be found more particularly in its relationship to forms of oral literature from Black Africa' (1974: 537). Mohamadou Kane's argument has shown the thread along which the critical treatment of the continuity in orality in written literature has been perpetuated. It focuses on forms rather than what one may refer to as traditions and world views indigenous to Africa.[1] As Eileen Julien explains, this attitude stems from the fact that Western anthropologists who earlier studied African oral narratives were influenced by evolutionary theories that placed contemporary nineteenth-century Europe at the apex of civilization and traditional Africa at the bottom of the same scale. Therefore to people influenced by this school of thought, African oral narratives would be carriers of a culture that was too rudimentary to be studied in literature. As Eileen Julien quotes from Hegel

> The Negro exhibits the natural man in his completely wild and untamed state . . . What we properly understand by Africa is the unhistorical, undeveloped spirit, involved in the conditions of mere nature and [only] on the threshold of the World's History.
>
> (Quoted: 1992: 11)

This attitude seems to have had a lasting effect on African literature in that it locked out some tales from being collected by early practitioners of African literary studies, and also when it came to written literature, the biases manifested themselves in creating a scale in which the traditional African elements were seen as belonging to the periphery while those of the West belong to the centre. As Julien elaborates

> With regard to African oral traditions, [Ruth] Finnegan hypothesizes that evolutionist biases manifested themselves in the very selection of oral materials made by collectors, in the kinds of thematic interpretations that poems and tales were given, in the lack of attention to literary qualities and effectiveness, and in the preoccupation with 'traditional' tales as opposed to 'new' innovative, or idiosyncratic ones that would have challenged the view of oral art as communally created. Written literature was an implicit norm against which oral literature was judged. The latter was seen as simple, uncrafted, and generally the product of the communal mind, whereas written literature, especially the novel, was held at the opposite and final end of the developmental process: it was complex, deliberate, and the work of a single author.
>
> (1992: 12)

It therefore follows that the study of a writer who uses myth in the novel would therefore be problematic to the critic of 'modern' African literature, not because of the fact that the novel incorporates orality, but because 'modern' African literature is seen to link the European and African traditions. A novel such as Grace Ogot's *The Strange Bride*, which reinterprets myth, locks out European tradition even while exploiting the written form. Therein lies the problem that makes critics such as Florence Stratton leave it out of their analysis of novels and similarly the reason that Obioma Nnaemeka sees orality as belonging to a closed past.

Ogot in *The Strange Bride* describes a society in which traditions are observed strictly and rituals are carried out daily to appease Were Nyakalaga who lives amongst the people. The person closest to Were Nyakalaga is the community chief Olum Ochak to whom the duty of carrying out the daily sacrifices to their deity falls.

> Olum Ochak's duties as a chief were both administrative and religious. Every morning, at day-break, he climbed to the peak of Mt. Owaga to pay homage to Were Nyakalaga when the eye of the sun first shone over the mountain to wake up the mortals, who believed that the power of Were Nyakalaga was expressed in the heat and the dazzling rays of the sun. Thus they referred to the sun as the eye of Were Nyakalaga. So, when the sun made its magnificent appearance over the horizon, Olum Ochak would spit in its direction saying: '*Thu!* May you bring good to us, and may your eye shine blessings on us for the whole of this day'. After that he came back home and waited until evening when he went back to the peak of the mountain. At sunset, when the sun turned red, he bid it farewell by spitting and saying: '*Thu!* May peace be with us until we see your eye again when you wake up tomorrow'.
>
> (1989: 2)

Olum Ochak is also endowed with supernatural abilities through which he interprets the messages sent by Were Nyakalaga through thunder, wind and songs of birds. He also reads secrets that are carried by clouds, the moon and the stars and is capable of interpreting dreams (1989: 2). All these elements make him a great leader, and eventually he is referred to by his people as Were Ochak or first ruler of the nation. Grace Ogot demonstrates to us that traditional Luo society was not a pre-political society and that it had a form of social organization and religion even before the advent of the colonization of East Africa by the British. She further demonstrates the social organization through describing the division of labour within the Ochak homestead. While Were Ochak is out for prayers, his sons Opii and Owiny set traps for catching quail; when Were Ochak comes back, he joins Opii in making cages for their chicken while Owiny goes to trap and collect ants that will be used to feed the chicken. The womenfolk Lwak and Achola also occupy themselves in preparing food for the quail by germinating millet grains used to feed the birds (1989: 5).

Apart from the daily rituals to appease their god and ancestors, Ogot describes others that are undertaken at specific times and the significance of such rituals. When Nyawir disappears from her homestead at an early age, she is believed to be dead. Ogot describes the rituals that happen at the 'burial' of a person who disappears in such a manner:

> They took an unripe fruit of a sausage tree and dressed it like the corpse of a child who had died out in the forest. They made a passage through the fence of her father's compound and brought the 'corpse' into the compound through that passage. Then they dug a grave close to the fence and buried the 'corpse' there, according to the rules governing the burial of people who died outside their homes. After that, all the funeral rites were performed.
>
> (1989: 9–10)

Later on, when Nyawir reappears, her parents have to cleanse her through a ritual before she enters back into the homestead. They therefore fetch a diviner *Min* Ogisa to carry out the ritual:

> She gave Nyawir *manyasi* to drink. Then she sprinkled ash on her. After that she led Nyawir to the gate, into the compound, and took her to the grave where the fruit of the sausage tree had been buried to represent her body. She then gave her some more *manyasi* to hold in her mouth and sprinkle on the grave. When Nyawir had done that, *Min* Ogisa gave her a hollow reed full of ash and said to her: 'Shake the ash out of the reed onto the grave!' Nyawir did as instructed. That done, *Min* Ogisa took Nyawir to her mother's house.
>
> (1989: 25)

Min Ogisa also carries out a divination ritual through which she validates the circumstances of Nyawir's disappearance. She discovers that it was indeed Awinja – Opolo's mother – who came and took away the girl because she was lonely and had no one to run errands for her. She got tired of Awino's daily lamentations and decided to return her daughter to her (1989: 26). There is also a thanksgiving ritual that is carried out. The family offers thanks to Awinja and Were Nyakalaga for the miracle of their returned daughter.

The community is observant of signs through nature, and when the people feel that it is time to open the season of cultivation, specific rituals are carried out. At an appropriate time the community gathers at Mount Owaga. Were Ochak then carries out a ritual in which he goes to the shrine and comes out carrying a hoe with a piece of metal in his right hand and an earth dish containing a roast chicken in his left hand. As the sun sets, Were Ochak spits towards it and recites an incantation asking for a blessing from its eye, which is the eye of Were Nyakalaga. He then dips a fly whisk into a medicine pot (*aguch manyasi*) and sprinkles the medicine onto the roof and the whole of the wall of the shrine while chanting that he is keeping evil forces at bay by sprinkling medicine on Were Nyakalaga.

He then sprinkles the same medicine on the assembled crowd and thereafter picks the roasted chicken and tears it into pieces, which he throws in different directions while chanting that the people have roasted the chicken to share with Were Nyakalaga and their ancestors. Lwak then plays her part in the ritual. She stirs the medicine in the pot and then prays that the medicine may flow downhill towards their farms and give them a good harvest. When she sees that the medicine is boiling, she interprets that as a sign of a blessing and thanks Were Nyakalaga through prayer. The crowd also joins in the thanksgiving.

After that, Were Ochak announces to the people that the work that took them to the mountain has ended well. He asks them to go back home in peace and observe certain taboos at this special time. They should not fight or offend anyone. No man should spend the night alone in his *dwol*, so that they should flourish and multiply. The multitude thanks him, and they disperse and head back towards the village. Were Ochak and other elders remain behind to eat the sacrificial chicken and also to have some of the beer that Lwak had brought for the ceremony. They pour out what remains to the ancestors and throw the bones of the chicken to the four corners of the Earth before proceeding down the mountain (1989: 68).

From the description of the ritual carried out at the beginning of the season of cultivation, we can ascertain that the traditional Luo community exercised some form of democracy in that the entire community was involved in interpreting nature for signs that the season of cultivation was nigh. It also was ordered politically in that the most important sacrifices are left to the leader of the community, Were Ochak. It is evident also that women were not left out of these important rituals as it is shown that Lwak takes over in performing the ritual of sacrifice at one point. The significance of these rituals is that they perpetuate harmony within the community by ensuring that the people do not anger their god Were Nyakalaga and that they also maintain peace with their ancestors whose retribution would harm their peaceful existence, as is demonstrated by what happens when Nyawir goes against the societal norms. Grace Ogot, by explaining how the rituals are carried out and giving their significance, preserves Luo indigenous culture through her novel.

The novel also brings out various practices among the Luo community such as courtship and marriage. The courtship of Owiny and Nyawir is elaborately presented in the text. In preparation for his proposal of marriage to Nyawir, Owiny picks three other boys who, like him, are very handsome: his brother Opii; Oyoo, the brother of Ajwang; and Waga, a handsome dark boy. They dress up and set off to ask for Nyawir's hand in marriage.

> Owiny and his friends decorated their bodies with chalk, and put red ochre on their hair. They wore animal skins which were beaten soft to be used as clothes. These skins covered their bodies well. In addition, Owiny, being the star of the occasion, wore a band of skin around his head and used it to hold beautiful long feathers round his head. When they arrived, they found the girl equally prepared, together with her beautiful cousins. Nyawir's head was decorated with cowries while that of her cousins was decorated with red ombulu seeds. They wore clean, white sisal skirts, which went down to their knees. In addition, they wore beads on their necks and decorated their legs and arms with chalk.
>
> (1989: 40)

It is demonstrated that the young men are welcomed well and the prospective bride is given a chance to see the prospective suitor and decide on whether she likes him, a factor that shows that marriages in this community were not forced upon women.

> When the boys arrived, Nyawir's cousins met them at the gate and led them to the shade of a big *siala* tree where chairs had been arranged for them. And when the visitors were all seated, the girls went to Awino's house and brought Nyawir from where she had been waiting, to greet her visitors. Walking gracefully, the daughter of Opolo went to her visitors and greeted them one by one, feeling a mixture of pride and fear. When it came to Owiny's turn to shake Nyawir's hand, he held her hand and kept it in his for some time. And as their eyes met, each of them sighed. Nyawir even felt her lips trembling. They both knew at once that they were in so much love with each other that only death would separate them. Owiny's friends' and the girls who surrounded Nyawir witnessed this immediate union of souls.
>
> (1989: 40–41)

It is indeed love at first sight between the couple a positive indication for their future relationship. Grace Ogot brings out the negotiations that are undertaken during such a ceremony through the behaviour of the suitor and his companions.

> After noticing that the girl liked him, just as he liked her, Owiny together with his companions refused to eat or even drink porridge before they got an opportunity to put their request to the parents of the girl whose hand they had come to ask for. The matter was quickly taken up by the elders, where they

> were sitting with Opolo around the dung-heap fire. They came under the tree and sat on their side, each on his stool. Since their culture did not allow them to shake hands with this category of visitors, they only greeted them verbally saying: *Okwe uru* (Let there be peace). And the boys replied in a similar manner, saying: *Okwe* (peace). After that, they went straight into serious business. Opii, Owiny's elder brother, put the matter before the elders telling them that the major reason for this visit was to discuss Owiny's wish to engage Nyawir.
>
> (1989: 40)

It is established in the novel that taboo prevents the elders from discussing the marriage proposal with the young men who have come to ask for their daughter's hand in marriage. All they can do at that point is to ask their daughter whether she accepts the proposal. Nyawir agrees, and the suitor and his companion go back to their clan a happy lot (1989: 42–43).

The marriage preparations go on when a visit by the elders from Owiny's family to Nyawir's family takes place and discussions on the bride-price are undertaken. Each party uses their oratory skills to negotiate the bride-price.

> When the elders arrived at Opolo's clan in the morning hours of the day, they found their fellow elders from Opolo's clan already seated, waiting for them. After the elders had greeted one another, Nyawir and her sisters also greeted the visitors. She realized, from the happy expression on their faces, that the visiting elders were impressed with her appearance. After that the visitors drank finger millet porridge; and then the negotiations started. Each side presented their case thoroughly and persuasively.
>
> (1989: 45)

Once the negotiations are done, both parties share a drink and a meal (1989: 46). Owiny has to pay more in bride-price than had been paid for by any suitor in the history of Got Owaga. Indeed, due to the large volume of food required as the bride-price, several women have to come together to help in airing, thrashing and pounding the sorghum so that it may be ready to be packed in baskets and delivered. When they are done, Were Ochak, accompanied by two male elders, prays to Were Nyakalaga thus

> Oh Were Nyakalaga
> A woman, indeed, is a mystery to the world!
> She is the mother of the land
> And she is the man's eye
> With which he sees things.

A bachelor feels uneasy in his bed
And turns from side to side
Until the day breaks
Because there is no one
To light a fire in his cold house.
Aa Were Nyakalaga,
A woman surely is the strength of a man
Because a woman is the house
And a woman is the home.
Bless these sorghum grains
So that tomorrow
Owiny's house may also find a fire-lighter
The potent fire which does not die out
Until the day breaks.
Aa . . . a woman, indeed, is a mystery of the world.
(1989: 49–50)

The process of the preparation of the bride-price as well as the prayer offered by Were Ochak to Were Nyakalaga as he asks to bless the bride-price further demonstrate the division of labour according to gender roles within the Luo community. The song further explains the place of woman in a man's life in Luo society and the importance of marriage.

After the preparations, some girls and boys are sent to deliver the bride-price. This ceremony is also described in detail in the text. A message is sent to the Nyawir's kinsfolk telling them to expect visitors in four days' time who will bring the bride-wealth. After receiving the message, they also start preparing themselves for the ceremony by decorating themselves. A bridal party is selected from Owiny's side. It comprises three strong boys who accompany a number of strong girls and women responsible for assuring the safe delivery of the bride-price at the girls' home. They are blessed by Were Ochak before they set off for their journey. Owiny and a friend escort them for a short distance before returning back home.

Nyawir's relatives have meanwhile placed scouts strategically along the way in order for these scouts to alert them of their visitors' approach. They pass word on by whistling to each other until word gets to the scout nearest the homestead who dashes off and informs the host family that their guests are about to arrive. A group of women who have been awaiting word thus set off to welcome the party through song. They are dressed attractively. They sing *sigweya*, to which the visiting party respond in song too (1989: 52). The songs and ululations put both parties in a festive mood by the time they come to meet each other.

The ceremony of awarding bride-price is not an occasion for speeches, unlike the bride-price negotiation ceremony. It is a day for *timo nyadhi* (showing your worth to the other party), and the bride's family is ostentatious.

> After the initial stage of greetings and introductions, the visitors were treated to porridge brought in about five porridge-pots, *mbirni*. The porridge was served in clean calabashes with decorations on their backs. After the visitors had drunk the porridge, there were further celebrations consisting of singing and eating until late in the afternoon. All the time the bride sat quietly among the other girls, without doing any work, because it was her day of showing off her dignity. Her body was beautifully decorated with chalk, *pundo*, and her hair with white cowries
>
> (1989: 53).

There is also some etiquette to be observed during such ceremonies. For example, the visitors are not supposed to gawk at their prospective in-law.

> There is no doubt that Achola and all her companions in this journey greatly appreciated the beauty of the girl Owiny had chosen. But they did not reveal it while they were still visitors in the home, because marvelling at a person's beauty in their presence can bring them misfortune. That was why the people of those days did not like someone who publicly marvelled at others' achievements. Praising someone's beauty was done secretly between lovers.
>
> (1989: 53)

For the host family, it is the bride's mother and young married women who are in charge of preparing and serving the food. After feasting, the party leaves for Got Owaga in the late afternoon. They are escorted part of the way by their hosts, who sing *sigweya*. The party, on arrival back home, gives a report on their visit, all being in agreement that the bride is beautiful and that they were treated well on their visit (1989: 53–54). The descriptions given on the courtship and marriage negotiations are important as they document the etiquette to be observed during such ceremonies and their significance. This is important because such ceremonies are carried out in Luo culture to date.

Ogot goes on to narrate the marriage ceremony between Owiny and Nyawir. It takes place immediately after the paying of bride-price. Nyawir is hidden in *Min* Ogisa's, her grandmother's, house. There she is fed on good food, and her body is massaged with fine sesame butter to make it soft and reveal her natural beauty, as for Owiny, he thatches his cottage with fresh *buoywe* grass and decorates the floor with drawings. He also plasters his walls, both inside and outside, with white chalk soil (1989: 55).

Preparations are made by the entire village to receive the bride. Boys and girls dress up for the occasion. Lwak and Achola supervise young married women who cook the food. Lwak brews for the elders. While awaiting the bridal party, the hosts divide themselves into groups. Lwak and other elderly women seat at the foot of a *siala* tree. Owiny and his friends sit at the front yard of his cottage. Achola and the other young married women who are preparing the food work close to the guest's shed, *siwandha* (1989: 56).

The visitors' arrival is announced through song. The hosts hear the singing and respond in kind; led by girls and women, together with boys, they go to the gate of the homestead to meet their visitors. Their joy is appreciated by the visitors, who sing *salu* songs, as they approach the gate to the homestead (56). At the gate, however, the bride refuses to enter and her companions stop and dance around the gate. Achola sends a colleague to inform Lwak that the bride has refused to enter. Lwak passes on the message to Were Ochak, who instructs her to send a gift of various kinds of millet to the gate to offer to Nyawir.

> Lwak was happy to hear that because it was said that the girl who had looked after herself well must be received with dignity so that her husband's people would know that she had not come from an ordinary home. So Lwak took some women in her house and gave them *ochuti* sorghum which was well thrashed in two medium-sized baskets. She also gave beans and the *andiwo* millet also of the same quantity, and one such basket of sesame.
>
> (1989: 57)

It is evident, therefore, that such behaviour was expected from the bride on arrival at the homestead, in order to show *timo nyadhi*. The bride however still refuses to budge despite the generous gifts that she has received so far. This prompts Were Ochak to leave the rest to Owiny, who swings into action. He takes a present that he had kept for the bride and proceeds to present it to her. It is a chain of small beads of various colours. Owiny's presence, coupled with the gift he imparts to her, works the magic needed, and Nyawir can no longer resist entering the homestead. The couple walks in together much to the joy of all present.

> Then the bride's co-wives (wives of her brothers-in-law) and her husband's sisters, who all this time, had been waiting with the sesame in calabashes,

> started to throw the sesame on the bride and groom, as they walked along together, until they reached the visitors' reception shade [sic], *siwandha*.
>
> (1989: 58)

On the day following the wedding, four girls in Nyawir's bridal party are chosen to stay behind while the rest leave to go back home. Those who leave sing, signalling joyously that their sister had kept herself well and been married a virgin (1989: 61). Owiny rewards his wife with an armlet, and Achola presents her with a beautiful water pot, a balancing coil and two calabashes. All these gifts signify how important the concept of a virgin bride was to the traditional Luo. As a newly wed wife, Nyawir is not allowed to do any work for four days. Thereafter, she is assigned light duties by Achola.

Although, these practices may not be carried out in the same way today, Ogot's narration of their cultural significance goes a long way in preserving indigenous Luo culture.[2] This gives the novel a strong cultural significance that not only serves to bring women into history but actually perpetuates the historiography of the Luo people through conserving their traditional cultural practices and rituals in a written form, the novel.

As an oral tale, *The Strange Bride* would be in the category of an explanatory tale. Isidore Okpewho explains this as being a tale that 'sets out primarily to explain the roots of a society's traditions, customs, morality, or else natural phenomena' (1983: 62). He sees such tales as part of a mythical continuum, which through variations in categories such as time frame – Mbiti's 'sasa' and 'zamani' set the tale in either the near or distant past – and through a variation in the use of fact and fiction, can be categorized as historic legend, mythic legend, explanatory tale and fable. In terms of the historicity of the text, the closer it is to what is perceived in the patriarchal tradition as the reality, the higher up the scale it is placed. Tales such as Grace Ogot's, which give the history of a community but incorporate elements that would today be seen as externally analogous, are thus placed lower in the scale, hence the category explanatory tale.

Scholars working on subaltern studies have deconstructed the notion that history is always what is received as the hegemonic discourse and brought in the element of the narratives from below, narratives of counter-insurgency as valid accounts of history that should be taken into consideration. As Dipesh Chakrabarty explains

> Subaltern Studies . . . was in principle opposed to nationalist histories that portrayed nationalist leaders as ushering India and her people out of some

> kind of 'pre-capitalist' stage and into a world-historical phase of 'bourgeois modernity', properly fitted out with the artefacts of democracy, citizenly rights, market economy, and the rule of the law.
>
> (2000: 22)

Even though Chakrabarty is explaining a situation that affects India, one may draw parallels and refer to Africa in general and Kenya in particular. The idea of the explanatory tale as being part of a continuum, in which it re-enacts a backward consciousness whereas the historical legend is depicted as being more related to the truth, is elitist and perpetuates a patriarchal ideology. Grace Ogot counters this in her writing by rejecting the notion that the consciousness of the peasant is pre-political through bringing this consciousness out as the best that is known and thought in the society through her writing it into her novel. In so doing, she counters hegemonic discourse that is Western fomented and sees the traditional African society as being pre-political, just like the work of the subaltern studies historians does.

Following this account, *Miaha* should be read as a historical novel, without distinguishing between the aspects of culture presented in a mimetic manner and the externally analogous elements. In so doing, we would be subjecting the text to a reading that takes into consideration the continuity of the oral tradition in the written form of the novel. We would also be countering the hegemonic discourse perpetuated by patriarchal historic legends, an element that allows the bringing in of feminist criticism to texts written in such a manner and also a way of destabilizing conventional Eurocentric criticism in the study of the African novel.

Indeed, one sees in the writing of the novel by Grace Ogot a form of palimpsestic writing in that the text translates a Luo myth into a form that is foreign to its tradition (the novel) and also a language that is 'foreign' to the novel form in Kenya (Dholuo).

In studying the text as a novel, one discovers that some of the concerns addressed in Obioma Nnaemeka's text cited earlier are addressed by Grace Ogot in her own terms. One of these concerns is representing the history of the traditional Luo society. The other is demonstrating that women like Nyawir, the central character in *The Strange Bride,* have been subjects of change. Nyawir challenges the god and wins. She is shown to have had an ideology for which she is prepared to die. This is brought out from the fact that she had lived in the underground world and seen a different society. She is thus driven by a wish to bring the same changes to

Got Owaga. She explains her philosophy to Owiny after they have been expelled from their village:

> I agree that I sinned and now I've brought a big problem for Were Ochak, my father-in-law, and Lwak, my mother-in-law. But, look, Owiny, the people of Got Owaga have a saying that generations replace one another in the enjoyment of the pleasure of life. In my own mind, that saying means there must be a change on the world, meaning that when our elders' days are finished and they die, then those who are born after them become elders and take their places, and the youth also go through the various stages of growth until they become adults and assume leadership. Now if those growing children only follow the practices of their forefathers, without bringing any changes, how can the world develop, if man does not use the intelligence which Were Nyakalaga gave him? Didn't Were Nyakalaga give man intelligence and strength for his own good?
>
> (1989: 120)

In a traditional society where change almost never takes place, Nyawir's ideas are seen as revolutionary and indeed are alarming to Owiny, who when learning of his wife's philosophy becomes scared and advocates (weakly so) for the conservative stand taken by his community.

> *Rapudo*, Were Nyakalaga gave our forefathers many laws with which to guide the world, and it is by the use of those laws that our fathers have ensured the welfare of the world for all these years. And there has always been peace in the world, and that peace has enabled our community to live in love and harmony, wanting in nothing. Now, if our generation begins to change the customary laws with which our forefathers established the world, it will look as if we are rejecting our forefathers. It will appear as if we are belittling the good deeds which our forefathers performed here in Got Owaga, so that our children may forget them. And if the children forget their forefathers, or if we make them despise the good things their forefathers did here, we'll be like people who are slowly cutting the roots of a tree. Since our childhood we've known that a community is big like a fig tree. The roots of that tree are our forefathers; our parents are its stem, and our generation its branches which bear fruits when it rains tomorrow. Those fruits are the children who are not yet born. And, as the roots are the strength of a fig tree, giving it life and energy, so our forefathers are the strength of our nation, because Were Nyakalaga put all the commandments which govern our nation in their hands. That is why when we try to alter our customs, we are breaking the commandments of Were Nyakalaga; and we are destroying the earth.
>
> (1989: 120–21)

As Stratton suggests in her analysis, this discussion between Owiny and Nyawir shows women as advocates for change and men forming a conservative part of the African society. Without recreating the Manichean categories that Stratton inadvertently falls into, promoting women over men, I would argue that the textual politics used by Grace Ogot in her reinterpretation of a Luo myth in *The Strange Bride* allows Nyawir to be depicted as 'strange' and 'evil' because of her machinations to put into place the things she had learnt while in the underground world. Her endeavours are indeed punished by her death. However, her actions lead to Owiny's visiting the same underground world and learn a new way of doing things and this leads to changes in his society. His actions are celebrated as worthy and he is fêted and rewarded with the chieftainship. A deeper understanding of the narrative demonstrates that it is indeed Nyawir who instigated the change, although at face value the change would be credited to Owiny. Obioma Nnaemeka concludes the essay cited earlier by suggesting that women writers can and should use their characters to re-position themselves as the purveyors of African traditions and culture: 'For the African woman writer to take advantage of this vantage position, she must assume this position on her own terms. She must reinscribe herself in history on her own terms' (1994: 154).

As our analysis demonstrates, Ogot subtly hints that it is indeed women who are behind major changes in society although due to its patriarchal nature, men would want to be credited with them. Through oral narratives such as that of *Miaha* in which the central character is a woman, women tease out their influence in a nuanced manner that inscribes them into history on their own terms.

By demonstrating that the central character in the novel, Nyawir, is an advocate for change, while acting as a custodian of Luo culture by conserving the communities' language, history and traditions through the novel form, Grace Ogot demonstrates to us that women, though hardly ever celebrated in historic legends, are major players in African history and the conservation of Africa's indigenous culture.

Notes

1 The Senegalese literary critic Mohamadou Kane, having been the first African literary critic to analyse tales as literary texts in his doctoral thesis

(1968), goes on in 1974 to analyse narrative structures in the African novel as having been influenced by the tale ('Sur les formes') and in 1982 examines how the African tale informs the tradition of the African novel (*Roman africain et tradition*), an area yet to be further exploited by literary critics. For more on this critic, see Lambert (2001).

2 Betrothal and marriage customs amongst the Luo community have been presented at length in anthropological texts such as Simeon H. Ominde's *The Luo Girl from Infancy to Marriage* and Paul Mboya's *Luo Kitgi Gi Timbegi.*

References

Chakrabarty, Dipesh. 2000. 'Subaltern Studies and Postcolonial Historiography', *Neplanta: Views from South*, 1(1): 9–32.

Duncan, Ian. 1992. *Modern Romance and Transformations of the Novel: The Gothic, Scott, Dickens*. Cambridge: Cambridge University Press.

Irele, Abiola. 1990. 'The African Imagination', *Research in African Literatures, Critical Theory and African Literature*, 21(1) (Spring 1990): 49–60.

Julien, Eileen. 1992. *African Novels and the Question of Orality*. Bloomington: Indiana University Press.

Kane, Mohamadou. 1974. 'Sur les "formes traditionnelles" du roman Africain' in *Littératures francophones de l'Afrique noire*, 3–4 (juillet-décembre): 536–68.

Lambert, Fernand. 2001. 'Un leader de la critique africaine, Mohamadou Kane', *études françaises*, 37(2): 63–77.

Mboya, Paul. 1938. *Luo Kitgi Gi Timbegi*. Nairobi: Atai Joint.

Ngũgĩ wa Thiong'o. 1982. *Devil on the Cross*. London: Heinemann.

Nnaemeka, Obioma. 1994. 'From Orality to Writing: African Women Writers and the (Re) Inscription of Womanhood', *Research in African Literatures*, 25(4) (Winter 1994): 137–57.

Ogot, Grace. 1966. *The Promised Land*. Nairobi: East African Educational Publishers.

———. 1989. *The Strange Bride*. Nairobi: East African Educational Publishers.

Okpewho, Isidore. 1983. *Myth in Africa: A Study of Its Aesthetic and Cultural Relevance*. Cambridge: Cambridge University Press.

Ominde, H. Simeon. 1952. *The Luo Girl from Infancy to Marriage*. Nairobi: Kenya Literature Bureau.

Said, Edward W. 1994. *Culture and Imperialism*. London: Chatto and Windus.

Stratton, Florence. 1994. *Contemporary African Literature and the Politics of Gender*. London and New York: Routledge.

12 Tackling endangered languages in the midst of diversity[1]

Lachman Mulchand Khubchandani

The relationship between language and culture is interwoven in a unique manner in different traditions. One of the major consequences of technology-driven globalization has been the increasing *marginalization* of less-populated language communities and the *intimidating hegemony* of larger socio-economic networks. This phenomenon acquires more visibility through the excessive control of widely used languages in everyday life communications, notoriously identified as 'killer' languages (Fishman 2000).

Being and becoming

There has been a lurking fear that the forces of globalization will wipe out languages used by smaller populations, particularly those that do not have a written tradition (Crystal 2000). The issues of language endangerment acquire a greater salience under the premise that language is a crystallized being, insulated within well-defined enclosures and conceived around normative entities as cultivated in school education. Language as *being* is built through conventions. Verbal communication bound within the milieu of literate tradition is often viewed as a standard ripened product legitimized in the domains of literature, education and administration.

At the same time, one cannot ignore that a living language with its openness undergoes perpetual change along with its usage, just as reality changes. Language as an ongoing process in everyday life communication remains in a state of *becoming*, a characteristic of open systems. Speech activity in oral tradition, depicting robust grassroots reality, operates on multilayers of memory and interprets verbal and pictorial space by *tentativeness* and *fluctuality*, that is 'what is customarily said' (Wittgenstein 1973), through constant negotiations. In an oral milieu, both thought and expression tend to be aggregative and concrete (i.e. context-determined), as if 'the texts were inscribed almost into the body's motor memory' (Ramanujan 2001: 84). A written discourse, in contrast, is viewed as a reflective contrived reality. In a sense, oral varieties of speech represent the 'avant-garde' face of language: 'Main languages are . . . banks [of the stream], the dialects are the flow of the stream' (Devy 2006: 94).

There is an interplay of centripetal and centrifugal factors prevailing in a speech community that contributes to the natural growth of a living language. It is demarcated by flexible framing and by transient elements of its self-organization, informally presented in Table 12.1. Various aspects of a living language – as a communication device, as a strategy of control and as a repertoire in totality – reveal diverse characteristics of *speech process* and *normative entity* as a social artefact promoted by the custodians of language. This distinction makes us aware of the apparent paradox in the speech behaviour of plural societies marked by the complementarity of speech varieties and, at the same time, striving for language standardization apparatus in a speech community. Braga (1972: 7–58), projecting the dialectal premise for developing a comprehensive model in sociolinguistic studies, introduces a distinction between *expectations* concerning linguistic behaviour and *actual performance* (cf. Khubchandani 1983).

Table 12.1 Speech as living phenomena

	Speech process	*Normative entity*
I	**Communication device**	
1.	An organic process, potentially diverse and heterogeneous.	A formalized entity, emphasizing uniformity and homogeneity.
2.	Registered as a non-autonomous device, communicating in symphony with other non-linguistic devices; its full signification can be explicated only from the imperatives of context and communicative tasks.	Ideally aiming at the targets of being an autonomous and unambiguous tool of communication.
3.	Interpretation dependent on the focus of communication 'field' and the degree of individual's sensitivity towards it.	Interpretation relying heavily on explicit formulas-grammars, dictionaries and so on; efforts for consistency made through the standardization apparatus.

	Speech process	*Normative entity*
4.	An effortless integral activity, discourse centres around the event with the support of ad hoc 'expression' strategies.	An ideal-oriented representation requiring directed effort; discourse concentrates on 'expression', which measures the 'event'.
II	**Strategy of control**	
5.	Guided by implicit identity pressures – a sort of etiquette agreed-upon *ad hoc* by those participating in it.	Characterized by explicitly defined value system – a prescriptive code with sanctions from the language elite in the community.
6.	Regulated by 'situation-bound' propriety in which ecosystems, constituting the social reality 'here and now', claim a prominent share.	Conditioned by 'tradition-inspired' profiles in which time-honoured standard practices (spelled out through grammatical accounts, lexicons and style sheets) dominate the scene.
7.	Permissive towards inherited variations linked with region, class and so on.	Less tolerant towards such ascribed deviations; assimilatory pressures in favour of the elitist standard variety.
III	**Total repertoire**	
8.	Total verbal repertoire is malleable, responsive to contextual expediencies, resulting in un-inhibited convergence between speech varieties with the contact pressures of pidginization, hybridization, code-switching and so on.	Total verbal repertoire is demarcated for the demands of different normative systems (specified by a distant elite) stressing on maintaining divergent development of a different system; and insistence on exclusiveness or 'purity' of tradition.
9.	Greater scope of functional fluidity leading to innovations and creativity of expression in negotiating the 'event'.	Restrictions over the scope for spontaneity and creativity due to the pressures of exclusive conformity to different systems.
10.	Fuzzy speech boundaries; interlocking variations responding to covert stratificational and situational differences.	Sharp language boundaries; compartmentalization through overt linguistic differentia.

Source: Lachman M. Khubchandani. 1983. *Plural Languages, Plural Cultures: Communication, Identity, and Sociopolitical Change in Contemporary India*. East-West Center, Honolulu: University of Hawaii Press.

In this regard, Saussure's dichotomy of *parole* and *langue* (1959), Pike's etic and emic approach to language (1967) and Chomsky's model of language distinguishing performance from competence of the ideal speaker (1965) provide useful insights concerning the plurilateral facets of speech community. Dante, a leading architect of Italian standard language during the Renaissance, distinguished between:

- *locutio prima*, a natural and living vernacular for emotional and interior life of people, particularly for art and identity and
- *locutio secondaria*, a refined and more precise vernacular responding to clear social purposes such as for court and state, sharing the communicative load of a community, although ranked in diglossic hierarchy (cited in Lo Bianco 2005: 109–133).

Physical and social scientists have been debating over the methods for building a bridge from *being* to *becoming*, providing insights for tackling the issues distinguishing closely knit systems from relatively open-ended systems in 'live' fuzzy reality (Prigogine 1980). The presentation here focuses attention on initiating a dialogue to identify the phenomenon of fluid and fuzzy enclosures in plural societies resulting from the changed scenario, with a particular reference to South Asia.

In recent years, economic and commercial factors of globalization have tilted the balance in favour of languages that dominate the physical space, as the empowerment of English has done on the electronic media, particularly in international forums in the postcolonial era. At the same time, human interactions conducted through demographically and economically 'weaker' languages can assert their utility in less glamorous, but vital, domains known as the communitarian space in everyday life reality (Khubchandani 2003):

> In a paradigm of *fair* communication, rising above petty interests and narrow loyalties in a transcendental sense, the prestige and dignity (and not powerlessness) should go with the language networks encouraging *complementation* (such as lingua francas), and not with those aspiring to promote exploitative and *hegemonistic* networks of communication (through 'majority' pressures and market forces) on the local, national, regional and global scenes.
>
> (7)

In the communication landscape of the Bhili group of languages in Gujarat and Maharashtra, one notices ancestral vernaculars remain intact for intimate (in-group) domains of kinship, rituals, festivals and folklore. At the same time, one or more dominant languages (Gujarati, Marathi, Hindi) complement one another in intergroup public domains.

Depending upon the language attitudes of interacting groups, one cannot rule out a gradual shift in favour of the dominant language(s).

The phenomenon of maintaining ancestral languages among subaltern cultures (such as tribal communities in the Central belt, Saurashtrans in Tamil Nadu, Dalits in Maharashtra) has not yet been given serious attention (Pandit 1969; Khubchandani 1983, 1992). Of course, in such milieus, boundaries between languages remain fluid, calling into question our ability to separate one language from another. One can cite the case of Kangri that is counted as a variety of Punjabi in the 1961 Census, but is re-classified as a variety of Hindi in the 1971 Census. A majority of the people in Kangra district (Himachal Pradesh) are at variance in claiming their mother tongue as Kangri, Hindi or Punjabi in census enumeration.

Multiple identities get strengthened by a measure of fluidity in their manifestation. Chatterjee (1943) views Indian heterogeneity of speech within an overall organic unity of communication. Gandhiji (1906) explains the *interdependence* of individual units in a society through an analogy of concentric circles in an ocean. Describing an ideal community with multiple identities, he states, 'There will be ever-widening, never ascending circles. Life will not be a pyramid with the apex sustained by the bottom. But it will be an oceanic circle whose centre will be the individual'. In a plural pattern, the 'inner circle' forms an integral unit of the 'outer oceanic circle', it cannot be crushed by the overwhelming power of the outer periphery. On the contrary, each should give strength to the other (Kripalani 1959: 100).

A Slovenian rebel poet Srečko Kosovel (2010), representing the aspirations of a minority community in the erstwhile Yugoslav federation, has beautifully expressed this relationship, his intimate belongingness to the world community:

> 'I am a broken arc of the circle'.[2]

He presents a poignant recognition of *individuality* and, at the same time, of *entirety*.

Language as an institution

Perceiving language as an institution moulded during the course of history, the endangerment and death of many minor languages with diminishing numbers of speakers across the world is a matter of widespread concern under the increasing pressures of globalization:

> By some counts, only 600 of the 6000 or so languages in the world are 'safe' from the threat of extinction. On some reckonings, the world will, by the end of the twenty-first century, be dominated by a small number of major languages.
>
> (Crystal 2000: i)

This phenomenon, like the large-scale destruction of environment, is both peculiarly modern and increasingly global (Krauss 1992: 4–10).

Some linguists and anthropologists view the *reduction in functions* of many minority languages and their subordinate or complementary roles in cross-cultural settings, a typical feature of societal bilingualism, with great concern. In the classical paradigm, lexical transfers from neighbouring languages, blending patterns of code-switching/mixing, code-neutralization and pidginization, when not legitimized by language custodians, are viewed as language degeneration, such as the emergence of lingua francas *Hindustani* and *Angrezi* (grassroots English) on the South Asianscene.

One notices a greater respect for variation in speech among the tribals and consequently less premium on the values attached to language purism. Illiterate tribals seem to carry heterogeneity in everyday life communications very lightly on their shoulders, unlike the conflicts over diversity of language use visible among literate cultures in the contemporary milieu (cf. Khubchandani 1992). Many tribals belonging to Austric (*Santali, Ho, Munda)* or Dravidian (*Kurukh, Kui, Kisan)* families in the Chota Nagpur plateau appear to be at peace with the *grassroots* grasp of creolized vernaculars of Indo-Aryan origin; these are identified under different labels *Sadri/Sadani, Khortha, Kurmali* or *Nagpuria* – a large section of tribals have even adopted these as their mother tongue. Similar is the case of *Halabi* – a hybrid of *Gondi* (Dravidian) and *Chhattisgarhi* and *Marathi* (both Indo-Aryan) languages in Madhya Pradesh and Maharashtra.

In the midst of cultural and linguistic heterogeneity in the North-East, it is interesting to note parallel efforts being made to form new alliances among erstwhile hostile language groups in Nagaland. In recent years a new language acronym, *Zeliangrong*, has emerged by clustering tribes speaking *Zemi* in Nagaland, *Liangmei* in Manipur and *Nruanghmei* (Rongmei) in Cachar district of Assam. Tribes identified with *Chokri,*

Khezha and Sangtam languages in and around Kohima district (in Nagaland) are also welding a common identity under the acronym *Chakesang*. Recently Angamis in the southern part of Nagaland have initiated a movement to bring together all allied tribes in the region covering Angami, Chakesang, Zeliangrong and a few other minor tribes, namely Rengma and Pome, under a single umbrella called *Tenyedie*, the language of Tenye people. A monthly journal *Urauze* is brought out from Kohima under this banner.

Nagaland represents an area of dialectal confrontation where many small groups have been asserting privileges based on parity for respective languages in education, administration and public media. Twenty four exclusive Naga languages (*Ao, Konyak, Angami*, etc.), claimed by nearly two million speakers (in 2001), are a characteristic of this phenomenon.

In Arunachal Pradesh, the Tagins earlier identified with Nissis, later with Adis, now claim their identity as distinct from both. In Manipur, the Anals, Aimols and Chirus earlier identified with the Kuki tribe now prefer affinity with the Nagas.

Language development

The quest for a new paradigm of language development questions the enclosures conceived around normative entities as chaperoned by language custodians. A linguistic initiative needs to be taken to identify the domains where ancestral language(s) are retained and to take into account the *contact processes* by which domineering languages creep in specific domains. By this exercise, a linguist could *win the trust* of the endangered language community and, as a language planner, become one of the stakeholders in the changing scenario.

The so-called objective approach of a fieldworker or researcher usually focuses on documenting linguistic structures (phonology, grammar, lexicon, etc.), for posterity, as inherited from colonial anthropology. Such concerns do not directly match the immediate needs of the members of these communities, who *continue adjusting* their communication needs through various strategies of language contact, conditioned under the eco-pressures of language diversity. A sensitive fieldworker will be alive to unique communication processes being adopted by an individual in the endangered community to cope with the demands of changing times. His or her mind-set constructively responds to such cultural transfer through the contact of two or more languages by blending ancestral language with the prevailing major language(s) (pejoratively described as pidgins). He or she is not so much concerned about *language purity* as such.

Many technological devices designed to facilitate the mode and range of communication, which transcend historical traditions, do not always lead to a better understanding among humans. Several processes such as manipulation and acculturation through the mass media and information technology have been dubbed indoctrination and cultural invasion – a kind of domineering *communication imperialism* (Khubchandani 1986). To reverse this trend, one needs to reflect on the issues in a holistic manner in tackling the phenomenon of endangered languages. The following questions can serve as a guideline:

1. How is the Tower of Babel syndrome applicable to threatened language varieties? Is diversity of speech in a community or in a space (i.e. societal multi-lingualism) an asset or a hindrance to growth of language?
2. Should revitalization strategies of vanishing voices be guided by language autonomy or language purity on the lines of well-knit systems or by language complementation or language blending, a characteristic of lesser-used languages?
3. Who bears the socio-economic burden of revitalizing such endangered languages or vernaculars? Does it amount to the poor to perpetuate in poverty and the privileged to define and dictate the course of development?
4. Can one promote a *universal* model of language plurality, or should we recognize the flexible plural ways of understanding plurality? How crucial are the issues concerning the space- and time-bound *unique* reality of speech communication, in the context of globalization pressures (i.e. market forces, pervasive technologies and pass the pole mechanisms of counting majorities/minorities)?
5. How real are language boundaries in plural societies? Is language a benchmark, an abstract social construct on a heterogeneous speech spectrum at a particular stage in history *vis-à-vis* the live robust ground reality of the vernacular (inclusive of threatened species)?
6. Can one transcend the bounds of language tradition when striving for quality in communication in consonance with the uniqueness and the dignity of the individual in a communication dyad? Are thought processes in individual speakers in a plural society *insulated* within the bounds of a particular language?

7 What do we mean by integral human communications and the issues of language *empowerment* along with language competition (in favour of the dominant) and language attracting *trust* in a communication event (the term *amae* in Japanese) along with language cooperation between the so-called majority and minority?
8 Do we need to separate *short-term* strategies adjusting to immediate imbalances created/instigated by globalization and *long-term* reflections over the phenomenon of living together, as vividly portrayed in the Oriental doctrine *vasudhaiva kutumbakam* ('All the universe is family'.) In what manner does the quality of communication in plural societies transcend *physical* language boundaries in education and other public domains?

A linguist's preliminary task could be to identify the domains where ancestral language is used and to take into account the domains in public where major languages creep in. By this exercise a linguist will be winning the trust of the endangered language community as one of the stakeholders in the changing scenario. In this milieu expansive and hegemonistic networks are regarded as attributes of powerful strong languages and accommodating networks of minority languages are viewed as powerless weak languages.

Notes

1 Some of the issues were earlier discussed in the Keynote address on 'Languages Threatened in a Plural Framework – Dialectics of Speech Variation & Globalization' delivered at the Tenth International Conference of the Foundation for Endangered Languages held at Mysore, India, October 2006.

2 See *Look Back, Look Ahead. The Selected Poems of Srečko Kosovel*, trans. Ana Jelnikar and Barbara Siegel Carlson. Brooklyn: Ugly Duckling Presse, 2010.

References

Braga, Giorgio. 1972. 'Norme e comportamento linguistico come dialettica fra aspettazione ed attuazione' [Linguistic Norms and Behaviour: The Dialectic of Expectations and Performance]. *Sociologia*, 6(1): 7–58.

Chatterjee, Suniti Kumar. 1943. *Languages and the Linguistic Problem*. London: Oxford University Press.

Crystal, David. 2000. *Language Death*. Cambridge: Cambridge University Press.

Devy, G. N. 2006. 'Language and Reality', in G.N. Devy (ed), *A Nomad Called Thief: Reflections on Adivasi Silence*, pp. 90–4. New Delhi: Orient Longman.

Fishman, Joshua A. 2000. 'The New Linguistic Order', in Howard D. Mehlinger, Matthew Krain and Patrick O'Meara (eds), *Globalization and the Challenges of a New Century*, pp. 435–42. Bloomington: Indiana University Press.

Gandhi, Mohandas. 1959 (1906). *India of My Dreams*. Ahmedabad: Navajivan.

Khubchandani, Lachman M. 1986. 'Identity and Communication in Plurilingual Societies: A South Asian Experience', in François Lo Jacomo (ed), *Plurilingualisme et communication*, pp. 85–100. Paris: UNESCO and Société d'études linguistiques et anthropologiques de France.

———. 1992. *Tribal Identity: A Language and Communication Perspective*. Shimla: Indian Institute of Advanced Study.

———. 2003. 'Language Harmony and Language Collisions: Dynamics of Diversity at the Grassroots', in Brian D. Joseph, Johanna DeStefano, Neil G. Jacobs and Ilse Lehiste (eds), *When Languages Collide: Perspectives on Language Conflict, Language Competition, and Language Coexistence*, pp. 296–323. Columbus: Ohio State University Press.

Kosovel, Srečko. 2010. *Look Back, Look Ahead. The Selected Poems of Srečko Kosovel* (Ana Jelnikar and Barbara Siegel Carlson, trans.). Brooklyn: Ugly Duckling Press.

Kripalani, Krishna (ed). 1959. *All Men Are Brothers, Collected Papers of Mahatma Gandhi*. Ahmedabad: Navajivan.

'Living Together in a Multilingual World: Exploring a New Communication Order'. Online Interaction Dialogue Information Society and Sustainable Development. WFIS 2003 Geneva. Retrieved 14 December 2015, from www.irfd.org/events/wf2003/vc/papers/. . ./R12.pdf.

Lo Bianco, Joseph. 2005. 'Globalization and National Communities of Communication', *Language Problems and Language Planning*, 29(2): 109–33.

Pandit, Prabodh B. 1969. 'Logistics of Language Development', in A. Poddar (ed), *Language and Society in India, Transactions*, Vol. 8, pp. 112–17. Shimla: Indian Institute of Advanced Study.

Prigogine, Ilya. 1980. *From Being and Becoming: Time and Complexity in the Physical Sciences*. San Francisco: W.H. Freeman.

Ramanujan, A. K. 2001. 'The Ring of Memory: Remembering and Forgetting in Indian Literatures', in Molly Daniels-Ramanujan and Keith Harrison (eds), *A.K. Ramanujan: Uncollected Poems and Prose*, pp. 83–100. New Delhi: Oxford University Press.

Wittgenstein, Ludwig. 1973. *Philosophical Investigations* (G.E.M. Anscombe, trans.). Oxford: Blackwell.

13 Language shift among the Waddar speakers

Digambar Maruti Ghodke

Introduction

The French essayist and moralist, Joseph Joubert (1754–1824) says: 'Genius is the ability to see things invisible, to manipulate things intangible, to paint things that have no features' (1838).[1] However, there are some people who, despite having their own features, that is culture, traditions, language, customs and practices, remain invisible. They are simply neglected or discarded as crude, barbaric and vulgar. In fact this pessimistic and negative perspective, which has lasted for centuries, has shoved these groups away from the pages of human cultural history. And their cultures and languages too have been kept away from the domain of systematic studies. The positive thinker should see the invisible, feel the intangible and try to achieve the impossible. The present chapter is an attempt to see and feel such an invisible and intangible group of people who have their own customs and practices, belief system, skills and heritage language. I believe that Waddar, one such culture and language, urgently needs to be studied and archived before it vanishes from the galaxy of cultures and languages. The Waddar language is one of the 'vanishing voices' (Nettle and Romaine 2000). It has not been seen or taken notice of by linguists and researchers. According to R. Amritavalli and K. A. Jayaseelan most popular attention and a sizeable section of scholarly debate is restricted to the 'major' languages, which in coverage is practically almost synonymous with the set of 'literary' languages (2007).

Who are the Waddars?

Waddars are one of the many nomadic communities of India. Its members are spread across various parts of the country, but they are mainly concentrated in Andhra Pradesh, Maharashtra and Karnataka. According to the *Ethnologue Report* (2009), Waddars are found not only in India but also in Pakistan, Nepal and Sri Lanka. They are scattered both in rural and in urban areas. They wander from place to place in search of manual work like digging wells or canals, building dams and bridges, quarrying and breaking stones, constructing roads and making grindstone and millstone for sale. Although a few of the Waddars have managed to raise themselves to a good economic position, by and large they are a very poor community with a hand-to-mouth existence.

Waddars are known by different names in different linguistic regions. For instance, in Andhra Pradesh they are referred to as Woddollu and in Tamil Nadu as Ottan-Nayakan and Oddars. In Maharashtra, they are known as Vadars (Bhat 1984). In North India and Pakistan, they are known as Od. The other alternate names for Waddar mentioned in *Ethnologue* (2009) are Orh, Vadari, Vadda Beldar, Werders, Wodde and so on. The Waddar ethnic population of India, Pakistan, Nepal and Sri Lanka is 3.2 million (Indian Missions Association 2003). According to a 1991 report from the Dr Ambedkar Research and Training Institute in Pune, the population of Waddars in Maharashtra is around 4.35 lakhs. As to their origin, there is no written evidence except for a few mythological stories shared by the elderly people of this community. According to some records, they were very actively involved in criminal activities and so the British government had notified them as one of the 'criminal tribes' under the so-called Criminal Tribes Act of 1871. However, in 1952 they were denotified by the Indian government. Hence, in Maharashtra they are officially a Denotified Tribe. Unfortunately, no substantial efforts have been made to place them firmly on the social and cultural map of Maharashtra by the scholars working in the fields of sociology, anthropology, ethnography, sociolinguistics or anthropological linguistics.

Heritage language

All Waddars, irrespective of the states from which they come, speak Waddar or Waddari (as known in Maharashtra), a dialect highly influenced by Telugu and to some extent by Kannada and Marathi languages. Because of the presence of a large number of Telugu words in their dialect, one can trace back its origin to Andhra Pradesh. Tracing its linguistic lineage, *Ethnologue* (Lewis 2009) identifies it as a Dravidian, South-Central, Telugu language. In the absence of a written script, the intergenerational transmission of the language has been oral. It is this heritage language which distinguishes this group remarkably from the other groups previously existing in the barter system of Maharashtra.

The other ethnic groups in Maharashtra, although named by different caste names, might feel a sense of integration to the local traditions and cultures because of their common linguistic inheritance. But Waddars are often considered outsiders because of their different linguistic identity. Being nomads, they are neither insiders nor outsiders anywhere. In Maharashtra, for example, their distinct linguistic and cultural traditions have kept them away from the mainstream of the Marathi-speaking population. Similarly, their language cannot easily be accepted as one of the dialects of Telugu because it does not have much affinity to Telugu language or culture. In other words, a monolingual Telugu speaker and a Waddar speaker will remain mutually unintelligible. On the cultural ground, the Waddar is also unlike the cultural affinity between Padmashali and Telugu, Marwari and Rajasthani or Sikh and Punjabi.

Is it a language or a dialect?

While stating the problem of language identification, *Ethnologue* (2009) admits that how one chooses to define a language depends on the purposes one has in identifying that language as distinct from another. Some scholars base their definition purely on linguistic grounds. Others recognize that social, cultural or political factors must also be taken into account. In addition, speakers themselves often have their own perspectives on what makes a particular language uniquely theirs (Lewis 2009). No expert studies, to my knowledge, have yet been undertaken to establish whether Waddar is a language or a dialect. The commonly held notion is that it is one of the dialects of Telugu. This notion may be the outcome of the extensive lexical and syntactic borrowings in the language from the Telugu. However, this borrowing does not help us conclude that it is a dialect because similar extensive syntactic and lexical borrowing from Sanskrit can be seen in the major Indo-Aryan and Dravidian languages as well. Nonetheless, a close analysis of this language (I prefer to call it so and I shall try to establish it eventually) on different grounds helps us to establish that it is not simply a dialect, but a language with its own linguistic features. Like any other language, it too has an abstract system that generates utterances. These abstract systems, according to linguists, consist of sets of units and principles, which are selected and applied differently from one language to another, despite many similarities (Mufwene 2004: 1–2). Sastry's (1994) discussion of Telugu dialects does not cover Waddar and the other three languages mentioned in the earlier statement in it.

Features of the Waddar language

The attribution of the status of language to any variety depends on the number of speakers, the linguistic features such as syntax and grammar, social perception and so on. In terms of speakers Waddar has a large number of speakers and they are not restricted to any particular region; the language used by this community, irrespective of the geographical locations, is Waddar only. For instance, Waddar is spoken in Maharashtra and Karnataka by this community. Like any other language it has its regionally and socially varied varieties, that is regional and social dialects. In the context of Maharashtra, it is noticed that the Waddar language spoken in Solapur district differs from that of Latur district. For instance, the Waddar word for 'ear' in the Solapur variety is *GuMMa* and in the Latur variety is *ShaVVul*. For 'pull' the words *JaGGu* and *GuNJJu* are used, respectively. Similarly, there are three subgroups in the Waddar community of Maharashtra, namely Gadi or Bandi Waddar or Bandallore; Mati or Mannu Waddar or Manttior; and Patharvat or Ralavor. Waddar language varies according to these subgroups. For instance, for the English word 'meat' they use *nAnjAr* in the Gadi Waddar dialect and *mUrya* in the Patharwat dialects. Nevertheless, there is a high degree of mutual intelligibility within these subgroups, and this division in the Waddar community is more or less the same everywhere in India.

On the linguistic front, Waddar is a distinct language. Especially the Maharashtrian variety differs from Telugu. This is not to deny the syntactic resemblances between the two languages. For instance, the SOV structure is used in both these languages and both are verb-final languages and many of the syntactic features are common to Indo-Aryan languages. However, on the phonological, morphological and lexical levels both the languages differ considerably. Of course, if there are some similarities, it is a common phenomenon in many Indo-Aryan languages (e.g. *bAhIn* in Marathi and *bAhAn* in Hindi or *cchAdd* in Punjabi and *cchOd* in Hindi). Similarly, the word *nAAm* stands for 'name' both in Hindi and in Gujarati languages whereas in Marathi there is a slight variation in the final consonant; the word *nAAv* is used for it. The point is that such variations affect the mutual intelligibility of the speakers of the aforementioned languages. Hence, Telugu and Waddar too have these minor similarities and large variations on different linguistic levels. For instance, the difference in pronunciation is apparent in the use of the consonants *r* and *d* in the words *Raa* and *Daa*, meaning 'come' and *p* and *f* in the words *Po* and *fo* meaning 'go' and the vowel /a:/ is used in Telugu *mAAmU* and /I/ is used in Waddar *mIm(U)* to mean 'we'. The morphological differences can easily be understood in the words *vastunnAva* and *vaccAkanAv*. *Nenu ippudu office ki vellali. . . I have to go to the office now. . . . Nak ippudu office ka yellabek. Vellali* (Telugu) *and yellabek* (Waddar) mean 'have to go'.

There are innumerable examples to illustrate these phonological, morphological and lexical differences between Waddar and Telugu. However, the detailed discussion of it would not go with the main concern of this chapter.

Language shift among the Waddars

While referring to the views of Brenzinger (1992), Craig (1992), Grinevald (1997, 1998), Grenoble and Whaley (1998) and Nettle and Romaine (2000), Anju Saxena (2006) expresses the view that the term 'language shift' refers to a situation where the use of a language is replaced by the use of another (usually a socio-economically or numerically dominant language). The end product of language shift is a complete replacement or language death, but it is normally a gradual process, where a shift in progress can affect a language in terms of the number of its speakers, the functional domains in which it is used and the degree of competence in the language (2006). While attempting a modest survey, I noticed that with upward social mobility and acceptance of sedentary life language shift is becoming a prominent strategy used by the Waddars, especially the educated ones. This shift is occurring through the bilingual behaviour of the second-generation speakers (The phrase 'second generation' in this context is used in terms of upward social mobility of these members). The second-generation speakers of this language prefer Marathi, the official language of Maharashtra, not only for their in-group communication but also for communication within the family, that is between their spouse and children. Waddar is used only to communicate with their parents and some elderly members of the group, if they are illiterate and not well-versed in Marathi. Thus, despite knowing the language they are unwilling to use and transmit their heritage language to the next generation. Once the language is thrown out of the family and in-group social communication, there is hardly any possibility of its survival.

Reasons and necessity for language shift

Why the speakers of certain languages tend to abandon their heritage language has to be understood empathetically. According to Nettle and

Romaine, language shift and death occur as a response to pressures of various types – social, cultural, economic and even military – on a community (2000). Grenoble and Whaley (2006) also support this view. They think that language shift occurs because of unique historical, economic, societal and political factors. Nettle and Romaine (2000) emphasize that language shift and death occur under duress and stressful social circumstances, where there is no realistic choice but to give in. Many people stop speaking their languages out of self-defence as a survival strategy. David Crystal (2000) states that the arguments that support the need for biological diversity can be applied to language as well. His defence of his view rests on two aspects, namely first, the damage to any one of the elements in an ecosystem can result in unforeseen consequences for the system as a whole and, second, if diversity is the prerequisite for successful humanity, then the preservation of linguistic diversity is essential, for language lies at the heart of what it means to be human.

However, it is becoming increasingly difficult for the disadvantaged groups to maintain their languages and cultures in this discriminatory socio-economic and political environment and hence the concept of the 'linguistic diversity' seems to be a false assumption. The social, economic, educational and political factors contribute either to the upliftment or the marginalization of language and culture. The analysis of the linguistic and cultural behaviour of the selected members from the Waddar community provides some insights in understanding the crucial factors responsible for the linguistic and cultural subordination of certain 'disadvantaged communities'. It would not be proper to call them 'minority communities' because some minority communities in Maharashtra such as Gujarati, Marwari, Punjabi, Padmashali, Sindhi, and Kannada have successfully maintained their languages and cultures. The members of these linguistic communities, despite being minority groups, take pride in transferring their heritage languages and cultures to the subsequent generations and use their language in the domains of family and in-group communication and assert their distinct cultural identity without 'shame or guilt' (Mohanty 1994). This particular observation alone makes it clear that the attitude of speakers is one of the major factors: 'The survival and revival of any language solely depends on its speakers' attitude towards it' (Abbi, Som and Das 2007: 345). If people take pride in using their language for social communication and enjoy listening to others using it well, conditions would become favourable for maintenance. On the other hand, if people feel embarrassed to use their language and avoid contacts with those who speak it, the language is bound to move towards extinction. It was observed that the second-generation speakers of the Waddar language view their heritage language, as Crystal says, as a sign of backwardness and as an obstacle in their path to social advancement (Crystal 2000: 84). These members have a vital role to play in the maintenance of their language and culture. However, painfully, they have neither any loyalty nor emotional attachment to their language and culture. They are less interested in keeping contact with the main language group and are also detached from their traditional socio-economic ways of life.

But are they born with this negative attitude for their language and culture? The question cannot be answered affirmatively because it originates, consciously or unconsciously, in the dominant economic and socio-cultural environment.

The interconnection between poverty and language

There is a complex interconnection between language and poverty; poverty affects language survival (Robinson 1996; Nettle and Romaine 2000). According to Ania Loomba there is no doubt that neither local nor global culture, neither nation nor hybridity, can be thought about seriously without considering how they are shaped by the economic system (Loomba 2005). During this case study it was observed that the selected members of the Waddar community find Marathi, the language of the dominant groups in Maharashtra, to be the medium providing an access to socio-economic opportunities, prestige and progress. The illiterate and deprived masses from the Waddars always showed reverence to these 'Marathicised brethren', who presume that 'modernization and upward social mobility demand from them the sacrifice of their cultural and linguistic identity' (Wayne Harbert *et al.* 2009: 45) and their Marathi-speaking children became a matter of curiosity and discussion among them. The fact that knowledge of the heritage language does not earn them bread is one of the causes of the second generation's reluctance to learn or pass on the Waddar language. Thus the very need to use their heritage language is vanishing. On the other hand, the members from certain socio-economically strong groups, although raised in Marathi surroundings, have not allowed their languages to be reduced to a marginalized state. Their languages have been stable for generations together, and Marathi has not entered their home domains or domains of in-group communication.

The attitude of other linguistic communities to the Waddari language and culture

Of course, poverty is a very crucial factor in the marginalization of language. But the attitude of the privileged linguistic communities, too, has an important role in shaping the negative attitude towards the disadvantaged language among its speakers. Being a member of this community, I have personally experienced people mocking at this language as 'a cluster of shapeless sounds creating useless and irritating noise'. Whenever they happen to hear the language spoken by any disadvantaged group, they simply name it 'waddari'. Thus Waddar, in Maharashtra, has been associated with filth, vulgarity and abusiveness, and their culture is reduced to superstition, illiteracy and barbarism. The dominant groups 'stigmatize their language as ignorant, backward, deformed, inadequate, or even a creation of the devil' (Crystal 2000).

The negative attitude of other linguistic communities forces these 'achieved status' members from this linguistic group to feel ashamed of not only their heritage language and culture but also of the people speaking this language. Consequently, they get detached from their heritage language and culture. Once the language ceases to be the home language and stops being transferred, it cannot be saved from the threat of extinction.

Misconceived representation of the language in literary works and books

Literature is popularly studied as 'a reflection of society'. The way the characters in a literary work walk and talk is often perceived as the representation of those of real-life people. Literary books can be helpful in disseminating information about linguistic and cultural diversity among the general public. The Waddar community and its language and culture have long remained out of the pages of literary books. However, recently some of the writers from the community are trying to voice their feelings, ironically, in Marathi because their language does not have a written mode. Their efforts to bring to light the pathetic condition of their community are, undoubtedly, worth appreciating. But, sadly, in an attempt to give a realistic touch to their works, the writers indiscriminately use some Waddar vocabulary in their narrations. These words are often abusive and vulgar, helping to confirm the negative attitude of others towards the writers' own language and culture.

Language and educational policies

According to Ajit Mohanty (2008), nearly 80 per cent of Indian languages, most of them tribal languages, are endangered. In the Indian multi-lingual scenario many languages coexist and certain languages become 'victims of discrimination, social and political neglect and deprivation'. The language policies of the government aim at homogenization, and they are devised and implemented at the cost of 'marginalization' of the languages and cultures of the powerless and disadvantaged groups. It is an attempt at homogenization in favour of the adoption of dominant group language identities (Skutnabb-Kanga *et al.* 1995: 305–314). In this attempt for the establishment of the so-called welfare state, these groups 'lose their linguistic identity; they lose their cultural identity, but do they lose their caste identity?' The language policies of the government centre on the languages of powerful groups, whereas 'the less powerful languages are often dubbed as "dialects" and weak voices for recognition are suppressed in the political and power dynamics' (Harbert *et al.* 2009: 102–124). As mentioned earlier, the Waddars are nomads scattered all over Maharashtra and their number is 4.35 lakhs (1991) and politically they are unorganized and are not influential. Apart from the generosity of including this community in the list of reserved categories (as Denotified Tribes along with 13 other tribes) for some educational concession, the Government of Maharashtra has scarcely shown any interest. Of course, due to their poverty and ignorance there has been no such demand from the community for the maintenance of their language and culture. Their language has no place in the education system. The group, too, accepts the low status and exclusion of their language uncomplainingly. It must be noted that if enough individuals use it and want to maintain a language and if they have enough power and status, they can prevail upon institutions to provide schooling in the language. This will change the societal structure which in turn will affect the language behaviour of the next generation. However, the mismatch between the home and school language makes it difficult for the children of the disadvantaged members of this group to survive in the education system and they remain cut off from the academic environment. This is one of the crucial factors that force the educated Waddars to keep their children detached from their heritage language and culture.

Media representation

The media play a significant role in the representation of language and culture. They are the source through which the information regarding different cultures and their distinct features becomes known to the general audience. Being Indians we all know the crucial role of Doordarshan and Hindi cinema in the spread of Hindi language among the non-Hindi speaking population of India. It is through this medium that the local cultures in many states of India have come largely under the influence of Hindi lifestyle and nomenclature. Not to mention the vested concern of the political leadership for their local culture and language. This superficial anxiety of powerful groups is often hailed as heroic but when the marginalized dare to assert their identity, it is looked down upon as a rebellion against the system.

The Waddar language and culture seldom get any representation in the media. No record of any movie, documentary films, serials or other visual programmes related to this language and culture can be found. Surprisingly, no member of the community is enthusiastic about maintaining their culture by revitalizing it through theatre and the performing arts and through cultural festivals at different levels. This kind of presentation might prove useful in generating some sympathy for their heritage language and culture among the Waddars who aspire for the 'achieved statuses' at the expense of their linguistic and cultural identity.

Civilization and urbanization

Apart from the aforementioned factors, factors such as urbanization and migration are also causing a considerable reduction in the function of the Waddar language in formal settings. It has no role to play in the major domains of power and resources such as official, legal and formal use, education, trade and commerce. While attempting to participate in progressive and developmental activities, Waddar speakers are often confronted with the fact that modernization and upward social mobility demand sacrifice of their cultural and linguistic identities (Harbert *et al.* 2009: 37–50).

What is the extent of language loss and language shift?

I do not presume that the Waddar language is heading towards its extinction immediately. Nonetheless the signs of language attrition are evident in the loss of basic vocabulary as well as change in the word order among the second-generation speakers of the Waddar language. For instance, instead of *rOttyA tIntIv Em?* they use *jEvan AyyA Em?* The word *jEvan* in the latter sentence is the Marathi substitute for *rOttyA tIntIv* in the former. In comparison with the first generation, the second-generation speakers of the language are not fluent in their heritage language, and they do not show any remorse about it. Indeed, they take pride in speaking Marathi, the dominant language of Maharashtra, to their spouse and children. Thus, they are blocking the way for intergenerational transmission of their heritage language. Once, the first-generation members pass away, there is much less hope for language survival among these socially advanced members (!) of this 'disadvantaged and underprivileged' community.

Why is the language potentially becoming extinct?

Linguists like Stephen Wurm (1998) and Michael Krauss have given a framework or schema for classifying languages according to the degree of endangerment. Wurm, in his five-level classification, places potentially endangered languages at the first level and describes them as languages which are socially and economically disadvantaged and under heavy pressure from a larger language, and beginning to lose child speakers. Krauss gives his seven-level ('*a*+' to '*e*') classification according to the degree of viability, from 'safe' to 'extinct', and refers to the languages which are spoken by some children or all children in some places as *instable/eroded* and places them at level 'a' after *safe* ('a+' level) and *stable* ('a−' level). He comes out with one more level of endangerment, that is *definitively endangered* ('b' level), where the language is spoken only by the parental generation and up. The status of Waddar in Maharashtra, if placed in Krauss's classification, is between 'a' and 'b'. It may be placed at level 'a' because it is still spoken by 'some children' of those people who are at the starting point of their 'upward mobility, and 'all children in some places', that is by the children of illiterate and economically disadvantaged members (especially those who are still engaged in their traditional occupations) of this community and at level 'b' because among those who are educated and who have reached 'the achieved status' from this community, the language is spoken only by parental generation, that is first-generation speakers. Hence, the Waddar language in Maharashtra, in Krauss's terms, is both *instable/eroded* and *definitively endangered.* And the Waddar language, in Maharashtra, can also be considered as 'potentially endangered' if we try to place it in the five-level classification given by Wurm because, as mentioned earlier, it is spoken by 'a socially and economically disadvantaged' (Crystal 2000) group in Maharashtra and it is 'under heavy pressure from a larger language' (Crystal 2000), that is Marathi, the official language of Maharashtra.

Suggestions for preservation

Nettle and Romaine note the significance of cultural diversity, which is fostered by language diversity, in stimulating innovative thinking, and encoding alternative ways of seeing the universe (Nettle and Romaine 2000). With growing language contact and cultural assimilation the Waddar language is fast losing its vocabulary and grammar. The analysis of the linguistic behaviour of these members selected for this study indicates the increasing tendency of using Marathi suffixes and words in their heritage language among the second-generation speakers. Hence, there is an immediate need for the documentation of the language used by the first-generation speakers so that at least some features of this language which might be lost with their death may be archived and retrieved for future studies or at least for the sake of preservation.

At present the Waddar language has no script or writing system; hence revitalization and preservation of this language through literacy is out of the question. Linguists like Mufwene question the adequacy of a writing system in the maintenance of language by referring to the dead languages such as Sanskrit and Latin, which, despite their rich literary traditions, have failed to sustain themselves as living languages. So the best way to preserve and revitalize the Waddar language, in my view, is to create awareness among the speech community regarding the consequences of the growing language shift and also the need to maintain their heritage language for their distinct linguistic and cultural identity. Of course, this is not to state that they should stop using the dominant language, which would certainly block their way towards 'upward mobility', but to limit it to the 'macro level' (Grenoble and Whaley 2006) that is to use it only for official and educational purposes and also for intergroup communication; for in-group and family communication they must strictly rely on their heritage language. The Waddar speakers must get rid of their negative attitude towards their own language and encourage their children to learn it. Only then will the intergenerational transmission continue. Otherwise it is for sure that no trace of their language will be left even for the archaeologists, who dig out history and culture from the debris of the past. And these people, who have unearthed stones and constructed historical monuments, will not have any history, and their cultural identity too will vanish with their 'vanishing voices' (Nettle and Romaine 2000).

Note

1 In Joseph Joubert, *Recueil des Pensées de M. Joubert*, ed. and publ. François-René de Chateaubriand. Paris: Imprimerie de Le Normant, 1838.

References

Abbi, Anvita, Bidisha Som and Alok Das. 2007. 'Where Have All The Speakers Gone? A Sociolinguistic Study of the Great Andamanese', *Indian Linguistics*, 68(3–4): 325–48.

Amritavalli, R. and K.A. Jayaseelan. 2007. 'India', in Andrew Simpson (ed), *Language and National Identity in Asia*, pp. 55–83. New York: Oxford University Press.

Bhat, Chandrashekhar. 1984. *Ethnicity and Mobility: Emerging Ethnic Identity and Social Mobility Among the Waddars of South India*. New Delhi: Concept Publishing.

Craig, Colette G. 1992. 'Language Shift and Language Death: The Case of Rama in Nicaragua', *International Journal of the Sociology of Language*, 93: 11–26.

Crystal, David. 2000. *Language Death*. Cambridge: Cambridge University Press.

Grenoble, Lenore A. and Lindsay J. Whaley (ed). 2006. *Saving Languages: An Introduction to Language Revitalization*. New York: Cambridge University Press.

Grinevald, Colette. 1997. 'Language Contact and Language Degeneration', in Florian Coulmas (ed), *The Handbook of Sociolinguistics*, pp. 257–70. Oxford: Blackwell.

———. 1998. 'Language Endangerment in South America: A Programmatic Approach', in Lenore A. Grenoble and Lindsay J. Whaley (eds), *Endangered Languages*, pp. 124–60. Cambridge: Cambridge University Press.

Harbert, Wayne, Sally McConnell-Ginet, Amanda Miller and John Whitman (eds). 2009. *Language and Poverty*. Clevedon, UK: Multilingual Matters.

Joubert, Joseph. 1838. *Recueil des Pensées de M. Joubert*, ed. and publ. François-René de Chateaubriand. Paris: Imprimerie de Le Normant.

Khubchandani, Lachman. 1995. '"Minority" Cultures and Their Communication Rights', in Tove Skutnabb-Kangas, Robert Philipson and Mart Rannut (eds), *Linguistic Human Rights: Overcoming Linguistic Discrimination*, pp. 305–23. New York: Mouton de Gruyter.

Krauss, Michael. 2007. 'Classification and Terminology for Degrees of Language Endangerment', in Matthias Brenzinger (ed), *Language Diversity Endangered*, pp. 1–8. Berlin and New York: Mouton de Gruyter.

Lewis, M. Paul. 2009. *Ethnologue: Languages of the World*, 16th ed. Dallas: SIL International.

Loomba, Ania. 2005. *Colonialism/Postcolonialism*, 2nd ed. New York: Routledge.

Mohanty, Ajit K. 2008 'Perpetuating Inequality: Language Disadvantage and Capability Deprivation of Tribal Mother Speakers in India', in Wayne Harbert, Sally McConnell-Ginet, Amanda Miller and John Whitman (eds), *Language and Poverty*, pp. 102–24. Clevedon: Multilingual Matters.

Mufwene, Salikoko S. 2004. *The Ecology of Language Evolution*. Cambridge: Cambridge University Press.

Nettle, Daniel and Suzanne Romaine. 2000. *Vanishing Voices: The Extinction of the World's Languages*. New York: Oxford University Press.

Robinson, C.D.W. 1996. *Language Use in Rural Development: An African Perspective*. Berlin: Mouton de Gruyter.

Sastry, Venkateswara J. 1994. *A Study of Telugu Regional and Social Dialects: A Prosodic Analysis*. Mysore: Central Institute of Indian Languages.

Saxena, Anju and Lars Borin. 2006. *Lesser-Known Languages of South Asia: Status and Policies, Case Studies and Applications of Information Technology*. Berlin and New York: Mouton de Gruyter.

Wurm, Stephen A. 1998. 'Methods of Language Maintenance and Revival, with Selected Cases of Language Endangerment in the World', in K. Matsumura (ed), *Studies in Endangered Languages*, Vol. 1, pp. 191–211. Tokyo: Hituzi Syobo.

14 Towards a revitalization of Urhobo

An endangered language of Delta State, Nigeria

Rose Oro Aziza

Introduction

Nigeria is a highly multilingual nation with well over 400 indigenous languages in addition to English, which is the main official language; French, which is a second official language; Arabic, which is spoken in parts of the north as a mother tongue; and the Nigerian Pidgin (NP), which is an Indo-exogenous language spoken extensively, especially in the Niger Delta region and in urban centres across the country.

English is the language of the nation's colonial masters and has the highest linguistic value; it is the language of power used for all government business, politics, education, the mass media, as well as national and international relations. For socio-economic upward mobility in any field in Nigeria, one requires a good performance in English, not in any of the indigenous languages. As a result, Nigerians have a positive attitude towards it.

Nigerian Pidgin (NP) is the lingua franca in most parts of the Niger Delta region which includes Urhoboland. It is English-related; English is its superstrate language and provides the bulk of its vocabulary, but its syntactic structure is that of Nigerian languages. As an ethnically neutral language, NP is a bridge between English and the indigenous languages and is used by both the educated and uneducated, the rich and the poor, and for most informal discussions within and outside the home. Although NP does not exist officially in government circles, it is the most widely spoken language in Nigeria and has acquired mother tongue status for many young people who live in the Niger Delta region and especially in the towns and cities in Urhoboland.

Of the over 400 Nigerian languages, three, that is, Hausa, Igbo and Yoruba, enjoy the status of 'major/national' languages and the federal government has invested and continues to invest heavily in their human, material and infrastructural development, but not much emphasis is placed on the other over 397 languages, among which is Urhobo.

The Urhobo people are found mainly in southwestern Nigeria, precisely in Delta State, which is one of the nine states that make up the oil-rich Niger Delta region that accounts for some 90 per cent of the nation's wealth. The language of the people is also called Urhobo and is a southwestern member of the Edoid group, a sub-branch of the Benue-Congo branch of the Niger-Congo languages. Urhobo is the native language of well over two million people according to the 2006 population count, but most of its people own the language only in name; they do not use it for most of their communication needs even within the home, while most of those who do so are mainly the older population. The younger generation, who should carry on its intergenerational transfer, prefers to use Pidgin or English. From our research, the reasons for this shift are many but include government's faulty language policies which do not favour the nation's nonmajor languages, the extensive use of NP that has led to a language shift for the young people in the area, the open social network of the people with their neighbours and the negative attitude of the people towards their language and culture.

In this chapter, we discuss these problems and their effects and suggest ways by which Urhobo can be revitalized and made more relevant to the people and their environment as an instrument for development politically, socially, economically and otherwise.

Causes of Urhobo endangerment and their effects

The Nigerian government's faulty language policy

The Nigerian government recognizes the multilingual nature of Nigeria and so in both the constitution and the National Policy on Education (NPE), the two documents where government's position on language use in the polity is spelt out, and provision is made for the use of English and the indigenous languages.

Section 55 of the constitution states that

> The business of the National Assembly shall be conducted in English, and in Hausa, Igbo and Yoruba when adequate arrangements have been made therefor

while Section 97 of the same constitution states

> The business of a House of Assembly shall be conducted in English, but the House may in addition to English conduct the business of the House in one or more other languages spoken in the State as the House may by resolution approve.

However, implementation is always a different matter. Even though Urhobo is the single largest language in Delta State and is homogenous to eight of the 25 local councils of the state which, in compliance with Section 97, qualifies it to be used for conducting legislative business at the State House of Assembly and for governance in the eight local councils, English is the language that plays this important role.

The NPE (1977, revised 1981, 1998, 2004) is the official document that spells out the philosophy and objectives that underlie education in Nigeria and in it, provision is made for the use/teaching of the learner's mother tongue (MT) or the language of the immediate environment (LIE), one of the three major Nigerian languages, Hausa, Igbo or Yoruba other than the learner's MT, English, French and Arabic in the school system. The main tenets of the NPE as far as Nigerian languages are concerned are as follows:

(a) the medium of instruction at the pre-primary level and the first three years of primary school shall be the MT or LIE while English features as a school subject;
(b) from the fourth year of primary school onwards, the medium of instruction shall be English, while the MT or the LIE, French and one of the three major Nigerian languages, Hausa, Igbo or Yoruba other than the learner's MT shall be taught as a school subject up to the end of the Junior Secondary School (JSS) level, but the major Nigerian language shall be studied throughout the senior secondary school (SSS) level.

Section 1(10a) of the NPE (2004) states:

> Government appreciates the importance of language as a means of promoting social interaction and national cohesion, and preserving culture. Thus, every child shall learn the language of the immediate environment. Furthermore, in the interest of national unity it is expedient that every child shall learn one of the three Nigerian languages: Hausa, Igbo, and Yoruba.

A major problem with these policies of government is that they do not favour the nonmajor languages like Urhobo for, while speakers of nonmajor languages are encouraged to learn at least one of the major languages, no such provision is made for the converse, that is for speakers of major languages to learn any nonmajor language, because of the erroneous belief that the promotion of many indigenous languages in the polity can encourage division and affect national unity and integration. Thus, although the NPE states that government will provide both infrastructure and specialist teachers to enhance learning in all Nigerian languages, the reality is that the federal government commits huge funds to the development and production of qualified teachers and materials only in the major languages. As a result, the nonmajor ones cannot feature effectively in education or the mass media, two major domains for effective language use.

To worsen the situation of the nonmajor languages, in 2004, the Nigerian government introduced the Universal Basic Education (UBE) programme as a strategy towards the attainment of the United Nation's Millennium Development Goals (MDGs). This led to a modification of the educational system from the 6–3–3–4 system (six years primary, three years junior secondary (JSS), three years senior secondary (SSS) and four years basic university) to the UBE 9–3–4 (nine years basic education, three years senior secondary and four years university). One major fault with the UBE Act 2004 curriculum is that it makes no provision for the use of the languages of the environment throughout the nine-year duration, the period when the MT languages were supposed to feature most in education either as a medium of instruction (pre-primary to first three years of primary) or as a school subject (last three years of primary and JSS). Rather, the languages approved to be taught at the UBE level and for which government has produced materials and organized numerous seminars and workshops to train and retrain teachers are Arabic, English, French, Hausa, Igbo and Yoruba.

Such flawed policies are not only against natural justice and a violation of the UN linguistic right which states that it is the right of a child to be taught in his or her mother tongue, but they also create linguistic tension among speakers of the various languages within the polity and give the impression that nonmajor languages have no value beyond their immediate environment. Yet, it is a linguistic fact that competence in the MT enhances learning in every field provided the social, cultural and logistic variables are in place and properly utilized.

Facts from data collected for this chapter from 30 schools in Urhoboland (3 pre-primary and 10 UBE public schools and 7 pre-primary and 10 UBE private schools), to ascertain the level of use of Urhobo in the school system, reveal that no school, public or private, urban or rural, uses Urhobo as the medium of instruction, while 15 schools (i.e. 50 per cent), comprising 10 public and 5 private, teach it as a school subject but without much seriousness; it is done either to satisfy the requirements laid down by the Ministry of Education or because the school head or proprietor is an interested native speaker who sees value in the teaching of Urhobo. The medium of instruction throughout the school system is generally English with a heavy mix of Pidgin in urban schools and Pidgin and Urhobo in rural public schools. In the private schools, English is the only medium of instruction, French is taught with some seriousness but in some of them, children are penalized for speaking Urhobo within the school premises.

What happens in schools in Urhoboland is an anomaly because research has shown that the best medium of instruction, at least for initial education, be it formal, informal or nonformal education, and whether the learning content is in the humanities, science, technology or the social sciences, is the child's mother tongue. Education has always been the bedrock of any developmental process whether for the individual or the society at large. It is a known fact that a good education is one that develops the power and character of the learner and equips him or her to appreciate his or her ancestral environment not one that leads to his or her alienation.

Some problems identified as militating against the teaching and learning of Urhobo include the following:

a) lack of teachers both in quality and in quantity. Urhobo is an academic programme in two tertiary institutions in Delta State: the Delta State University runs a four-year BA Linguistics/Urhobo programme, and the College of Education, Warri, runs a three-year National Certificate in Education (NCE) programme in Urhobo combined with another teaching subject. Between them they turn out only about 30 graduates per year but most of them prefer to find jobs in areas other than teaching.
b) the lack of a well-defined curriculum/syllabus to guide teaching, the dearth of learning materials, especially books, supplementary readers and texts in non-literary areas as well as teaching aids. Urhobo is in the category of developing languages, that is those with a recent but settling orthography, a fairly recent tradition of writing, an incipient standard variety, a nascent metalanguage and some amount of written texts that include primers,

four dictionaries, three short story books and a collection of folk poems. There are no novels, drama books or epics not to mention materials written in the language on science, economics or technology.

c) the negative attitude of learners, teachers and parents to the study of Urhobo. We shall return to this later but in the course of this work, it was observed from interaction with parents that whereas most of them were eager and made it a duty to find private lesson teachers to help their children with English and even French, and bought books, games and other aids to supplement school work, they did not even have films in Urhobo with subtitles in English at home, even where these were available, to help their children become more proficient in the language.

Since government policy does not favour the use of Urhobo in education, and since education should equip people for good jobs, the language hardly has any relevance in the job market beyond teaching in schools in Urhoboland. Good jobs and upward social mobility in Nigeria are still tied to proficiency in English. Even in community services or customer care or related departments in the oil companies or banks that throng the land, Urhobo has no utility value and so young people who should carry on the intergenerational transfer necessary for language survival find its use and study unattractive.

The results from a recent survey involving 1,000 young people aged between 15 and 35 years which was carried out in ten localities in Urhoboland to find out about language use revealed that only 8 per cent said they could speak Urhobo very well and preferred it for their communication needs outside school; 82 per cent preferred to use Pidgin outside the classroom; 100 per cent wanted to study English while only 3 per cent wanted to study Urhobo beyond the primary school level. The results indicate that there is a shift from Urhobo to Pidgin or English. The effect of this shift is that presently there is a communication gap between the old and the young; the common native language that should bind them together is fast disappearing and this has led to conflicts in value systems between the two groups.

The extensive use of Pidgin

A language thrives when there are domains within a society where it is the primary channel of communication. Such domains include the home, school, church, market place, social gatherings, the mass media.

Unfortunately, in Urhoboland, Pidgin has encroached into virtually all these domains both in the urban and rural areas. Urhoboland is in the heart of oil exploration and exploitation in Nigeria and so there is high social mobility and an open social network occasioned by the large number of people from all walks of life who come there for work or business with the oil companies and other government and nongovernmental establishments. There are also other ethnic groups such as Edo, Isoko, Itsekiri, Izon and Ukwuani within the same geographical area. All these have resulted in a lot of inter-ethnic marriages. Thus, for ease of communication among people in the area, Pidgin developed as a common language and is spoken by everyone: young or old, rich or poor, literate or illiterate, urban or rural dweller. In fact, it has acquired mother tongue status for most Urhobo young people aged 25 years and below, irrespective of the educational or socio-economic status of their parents. Most embarrassing for me was that even in traditional courts conducted in the palaces of traditional rulers to settle disputes between locals, Pidgin was recognized as a medium of communication and freely used.

Some of the effects of the extensive use of Pidgin on Urhobo include the following:

a) Linguistically, rather than Urhobo interfering with Pidgin in the speech patterns of Urhobo youths, the reverse is the case. The following Urhobo sounds which are absent from the Pidgin inventory have been dropped from the speech of young Urhobo speakers and replaced by Pidgin equivalents:

   i) The voiceless palatal plosive /c/ spelt as 'ch' has been replaced by [ʃ] 'sh', so that a name like Ọchuko is now rendered as *[Ọshuko]
   ii) The voiced palatal plosive /ɟ/ spelt as 'dj' as in Odje 'personal name' is now replaced by [ʒ], so we now hear *[Oje]
   iii) The voiced velar fricative /ɣ/ spelt as 'gh as in Aghọghọ 'personal name' has been replaced by [g], so we now hear *[Agọgọ]
   iv) The voiced labio-dental approximant /ʋ/ spelt as 'vw' as in Rukẹvwẹ 'personal name' has been replaced by [w], so we now hear *[Rukẹwẹ]

Such sound replacements usually affect meaning. In the preceding examples, only the last one has some semblance of meaning but whereas 'Rukẹvwẹ' means 'blessed me', 'Rukẹwẹ' means 'blessed you'. The other three examples are meaningless.

Besides, Urhobo, like most Nigerian languages, but unlike Pidgin, is a tone language and tone has both lexical and grammatical functions, but many Urhobo youths have difficulty making such subtle distinctions. For example:

Ònànèfè meaning 'this is wealth'
Ònànéfè meaning 'this is more than wealth'
Ònànèfè meaning 'is this wealth?'

Failure to recognize such subtle distinctions often leads to ambiguity and causes misunderstanding.

b) The extensive use of Pidgin has led to the loss of the vast native literary, economic and technological knowledge of the people. Urhobo is well endowed with all sorts of literary resources such as poems, plays, proverbs folktales, praise songs, dirges, dance drama that are used to extol excellence and hard work or chastise laziness and bad behaviour. These are disappearing due to lack of use and promotion. I would like here to commend the efforts of Professors Tanure Ojaide and G. G. Darah in the documentation of some of the literature, but a lot still needs to be done. The native knowledge of the Urhobo in the areas of palm oil processing, boat building, gin distilling, setting of broken bones and so on, used to be legendary but most of it is now lost because the young ones do not understand the language of the older people for effective transfer of the knowledge.

Negative attitude towards Urhobo language and culture

From the foregoing, it is obvious that Urhobo people, like many Nigerians, have a negative attitude towards their language and culture. Attitude to a language is usually motivated by several factors such as the numerical strength of its speakers, its perceived socio-economic value, its upward social mobility potential, the roles and functions officially assigned to it by government, the political and economic power of its speakers as well as its educational value. Adegbija (2004) has rightly observed that a positive attitude, covert or overt, is developed towards a language that is perceived to have value in all these different areas while a negative attitude, overt or covert, develops towards a language that lacks such value. In Nigeria, even though English is a minority language since it is spoken by only about 20 per cent of Nigerians, it is a very powerful language as a result of its perceived utility value in virtually every domain of national and international life of the Nigerian.

In spite of several concerted efforts to make people think otherwise, most parents, educated and non-educated alike, still prefer that their children be taught in English from the first day at school. A good school in Nigeria today is measured by the facilities it has for teaching foreign languages, computer, mathematics and the sciences. Even if facilities for teaching local languages are available (and in most cases they are not), they may be appreciated by a few but they do not reckon when parents judge for quality. In fact, a school that carries 'international' along with its name is usually one in which English, French and/or German are taught, but not any Nigerian language. The thinking is that the latter has nothing to offer the international community. A lot of educated Urhobo and Africans in general believe that their languages have no place in science and technology, especially in this era of globalization defined according to standards set by the Western world through their languages. For this reason, the level of one's education and intelligence in Nigeria today is still measured by how well one can manipulate the English language or a European language, or whether titles such as engineer, doctor, professor are appended to one's name. To go to the university to study Urhobo is like committing academic suicide.

So much has been said about the problems besetting the Urhobo language and their effects. We now turn our attention to its revitalization.

Revitalization of Urhobo

Revitalization is an advocacy for a return to the era before the 1970s when Urhobo was a respected and respectable language whose owners took pride in using it extensively for their communication needs and people were eager to teach and learn it in schools. Urhobo must be made to function effectively in domains such as the home, education, government, politics, the mass media, business and commerce, medicare, technological advancement. These are domains where the language goes beyond the local to a wider audience and is used to carry out serious deliberations on matters relating to governance and development, to keep records and by so doing expand its vocabulary, standardize its writing system and make it feature in information and communication technology (ICT). Using Urhobo in these domains extends its utility value, opens up endless possibilities for jobs and wealth creation and enhances interest in its study and development.

To revitalize Urhobo, the following strategies have been suggested:

a) There must be an attitudinal change by Urhobo people towards their language and culture. A language is first appreciated and promoted by its owners before other people can appreciate it. English was once the language of the uneducated, but through the efforts of its native speakers, it is now a world language. Urhobo people, especially the elite, must change their negative attitude towards their language and be in the forefront of this advocacy for revitalization and it must begin from the home. The elites must give back to their children what they themselves received as children, that is using Urhobo at home, Pidgin in the community and English at school, which has made them competent users of all three languages yet they are successful in every field of human endeavour. The MT has been found to be very significant in a child's physical, mental, academic and social development because it enhances his or her creative and critical thinking ability, information storage and retrieval and appreciation of his or her environment. Modern parents must insist on the use of Urhobo at home and must create time to teach their children to appreciate aspects of Urhobo culture embedded in folktales, riddles, songs, festivals and so on, which emphasize virtuous life but which have now been replaced by home-videos, television and satellite programmes rendered mainly in English and based mainly on foreign culture.
b) We encourage multilingualism in Urhobo, Pidgin and English. In today's world, bilingualism and multilingualism are not an aberration but an asset and a necessity. There is no gainsaying that the Urhobo child needs Pidgin and English if he or she is to function well in the environment. Because of the heterogeneous nature of the environment, Pidgin is used as the language of wider communication, while English is the language for upward social mobility in Nigeria. However, acquiring these two languages should not be at the expense of the Urhobo. The three languages complement one another for a sound physical and mental development. Most Urhobo aged 40 years and above who have acquired a university degree have benefited from competence in the three languages. Pidgin and English can also be used to document and promote

aspects of Urhobo culture and native knowledge to reach a wider audience.

c) There must be a more serious use of Urhobo in the educational system and in the mass media. The current policy on indigenous language use in the polity must go beyond emphasis on the three major languages to genuinely reflect the multilingual nature of the country and encourage nonmajor languages like Urhobo to feature well especially in education and the mass media, two very important domains for language use and maintenance. It is a universal fact that MT competence enhances learning in all fields of study, which is why in the developed societies, even while they encourage people to learn other languages, they insist on the use of their own languages in their educational institutions. It is time for the developing world to imbibe this habit and ensure that our children are given the opportunity to develop their mental and intellectual capabilities to the fullest by being taught in their own languages.

To enable Urhobo to function well as a language of education, steps must be taken to produce learning materials for all levels of the school system and quality learners must be attracted to pursue academic programmes in Urhobo so as to produce quality teachers. One way of doing this is for government to formulate a policy that makes a certificate of proficiency in the language of the environment a requirement for certain categories of people, such as politicians seeking elective positions to represent the people at ward, local council, state and national levels; workers both in government and in private institutions who deal directly with community members, workers in community relations and customer care departments in oil companies, financial institutions, pharmaceutical companies, service providers for telephone network companies and others; workers in the state and local outlets of government parastatals, such as the Independent Electoral Commission (INEC), the National Action Committee on AIDS (NACA), and for the several nongovernmental agencies (NGOs) in Urhoboland. Such a requirement would ensure that people take the study of Urhobo more seriously.

Fortunately, the federal government recently constituted a committee to formulate a new language policy for Nigeria with membership that includes some seasoned linguists who are fully aware of the problems of language use in Nigeria. It is our hope that this committee will correct the anomalies in the present policy.

Socio-cultural organizations can also help by organizing holiday camps where Urhobo language and culture can be taught to the children, youths and adults who wish to be proficient. Such holiday programmes should teach all the communication skills of listening, speaking, reading and writing and be accompanied with interesting displays of art and drama so as to sustain the attention of the learners. Participants should also be taught aspects of indigenous science, technology and medicare. This will go a long way in making our children become more functional literates and purposeful leaders of tomorrow who are not strangers to their land and people.

In the mass media, more airtime must be given to programmes transmitted in Urhobo than what presently exists. Three radio and three television stations operate in Delta State, each with a broadcast time of about 18 hours a day but none of the ten indigenous languages of the state enjoys more than four hours total airtime a week, some even less. The programmes in which they feature include a five-minute news translation daily in five of the languages on both radio and television, a weekly one-hour musical request on radio and a fortnightly 30-minute discussion/magazine programme in each language on television. The rest of the time is devoted to English and Pidgin. There are no newspapers, magazines, posters that can enhance information dissemination and because of the low level of readership and poor economic returns, publishers are unwilling to publish manuscripts written in Urhobo. Consequently, the many programmes and discussions on topical issues such as HIV/AIDS, female genital mutilation, juvenile marriages, politics and electoral matters, poverty alleviation intervention strategies which affect the people are available only to the minority who can access them in English, thereby excluding the majority, especially women who make up the bulk of the illiterate population. As Bamgbose (2006) has also rightly observed, the various projects offered to alleviate poverty should be capable of being pursued through the medium of our indigenous languages such that existing practices in crafts, trade, agriculture, local industries and so on should be the basis of poverty alleviation intervention rather than some superimposed Western-oriented practices which inevitably have to be transmitted in English. It is very important that correct and up-to-date information be disseminated in the local languages to create better awareness and eradicate ignorance and avoidable deaths resulting from superstitious beliefs and taboos. The major languages have advanced considerably in this regard. Consequently, the illiterate Hausa woman in purdah in a village in Katsina State has access to more local, national and even international information than her Urhobo counterpart in the city of Warri. This is because while the former gets the news as it happens in her own language from her portable transistor radio, the latter has to wait for an interpreter who may be late, faulty or even unavailable.

d) The vast amount of native knowledge and skills that can be better transmitted in Urhobo needs to be understood, appreciated and documented to prevent their loss and enable them to be modernized and made available for global use. Unless we fully understand how the locals have managed their environment and merge that with modern trends, undiluted importation of foreign knowledge, skills and methods forced unto the environment are bound to fail. If traditional practices are understood, documented and modernized, we would not only be maintaining indigenous ways of managing the people and their environment but we would also be saving them from being lost.

e) Urhobo must become ICT-compliant. ICT resources such as the Yoruba computer keyboard called *konyin*, the font developed for Hausa, Igbo and Yoruba by the Nigerian Information Technology Development Agency (NITDA) and even India's simputer, a modified computer system used for providing information to local communities in local languages, can all be adapted for use in Urhobo.

Conclusion

It is clear from the foregoing that the use and study of Urhobo can be rewarding not only for the individual but also for local, national and international advancement. This fact needs to be appreciated so as to empower the language and attract quality teachers who would train quality learners who would participate more meaningfully in the affairs of the nation to move it to greater heights. A major asset is the high degree of language loyalty observed among the people, indeed most Nigerians, towards their language. Even though many may not speak it well or wish to study it as an academic discipline beyond the primary school level, they are eager to see measures put in place to ensure its survival. Therefore, with some concerted efforts, the advocacy strategies to revitalize Urhobo should work. The target is to emphasize and appreciate its utility value.

Although Urhobo has been the focus of this chapter, the findings from our research and the strategies proposed for revitalization are relevant to all nonmajor/developing languages. It is important that native speakers help to keep their languages alive for, in the final analysis, whenever a language dies, it is the native speakers who lose their identity and it is their culture and native knowledge that are irretrievably lost.

References

Adegbija, E. 2004. 'Language Policy and Planning in Nigeria', *Current Issues in Language Planning*, 5(3): web document. Retrieved from http://www.multilingualmatters.net.

Bamgbose, Ayo. 2006. *Linguistics and Social Responsibility: The Challenges for the Nigerian Linguist*. Port Harcourt: The Linguistic Association of Nigeria.

15 Itsekiri

Threatened and endangered

Tony E. Afejuku and Alero Uwawah

Introduction

The issue of threats to and endangerment of language has been the concern of many scholars in recent times. To make matters worse, globalization and its antecedents are daily drifting our youths far from their origin. Unfortunately, efforts by some persons to capture the essence of our indigenous languages are becoming more futile by the day. For instance, in some of the universities in Nigeria where we have departments of languages, the number of students admitted into them to study the indigenous languages is at times as low as one or none. Even then only a few of the languages are captured in these departments. Parents would rather wish their children to study English, French and Arabic in Nigeria than their indigenous languages. So from birth these languages are downplayed and the 'approved' languages such as English, French and Arabic are upheld. The significant question to ask is this: in the global world 'where is the place of the indigenous languages in the affairs of nations?' Major groups are not as much affected as the minority groups. Hence the fear of minority groups in contemporary times is that of how to exist in the next millennium. The Itsekiri ethnic nationality of the Niger Delta in Nigeria is one such minority group about whose continued existence beyond the millennium the people themselves are worrying.

Who are the Itsekiri(s)?

We shall begin this discussion in earnest with some remarks pertaining to the origin of the Itsekiri people, because doing so will enrich it and the conclusion (or anti-conclusion) we shall arrive at. Before we do so, however, we need to state that the word *Itsekiri* serves as both the language and the name of the people. Hence both the language and the culture are somehow inseparable. Journeying through the culture, we shall explain in relative terms how the inappropriateness of one is instrumental to the threatening and endangerment of the other. In other words, the language of the people is so intertwined with their culture (and even history) that a 'loss' of the language will clearly lead to the extinction of the people and what they stand or exist for. Language serves as an identity of a people, introduces the culture of a people, describes a people and localises a people.

The origin of the Itsekiri people

The above being said, we now draw attention, as our starting point, to some aspects of the historical origin of the people known as Itsekiri. Through the length and breadth of the coast of West Africa the Itsekiri are known for their graceful and charming disposition. Hence the European traders in the early fifteenth century were able to trade and settle with them.

The origin of the Itsekiri people can be grouped into two – the Ugborodo angle and the Itsekiri line, as many authorities have stated it from their respective standpoints. The myths surrounding this ethnic nationality have been themes of discourse over many generations. We shall, however, confine ourselves in this chapter to the position of foremost historian, John Sagay who argues in his book, *The Warri Kingdom* (1980: 1–13) that 'the people who constitute the tribe called Itsekiri have diverse origins'. Omoneukanrin (1935) argues that though there are a thousand and one myths surrounding the origins of the Itsekiri people, yet the most accepted and authentic is that of Iginua and his entourage. Of course, this is debatable since African mythology has been a thing of oral relay. However, we are in agreement with Okpewho (1998) who states that the element of subtraction and addition present in oral tradition when presented in the native form does not make it less authentic since the documented African history, in the process of translation for documentation purposes, is also filtered completely, thereby leaving us with incomplete history. It is on this premise that both the oral and documented myths on the origin of the Itsekiri people are herewith presented side by side.

As stated earlier, there are two schools of thought. The first (the 'Ugborodo' angle) believes that the migrants from Yorubaland formed part of the first settlers in Itsekiriland. According to Chief J. M. A. Uwawah in evidence given in the High Court of Justice of Mid-Western State of Nigeria, Warri Division, Suit No. W/70/89/16,

> The people of Ugborodo are the descendants of the five ancestors which founded the area now known as Ugborodo. The original five founders of Ugborodo are – Olaja Orori, Eghare Kromini, Eghare Eloko, Eghare Ebome

> and Eghare Oyen. Olaja Orori, Eghare Ebome and Eghare Oyen were brothers. According to Ugborodo history, they came from Ife. The three brothers met Eghare Kromini at a place called Ode in Yorubaland. Eghare Eloko migrated from Aboh. He met the other four ancestors at a place called Kekemu. From there the people proceeded to a place called Oboghoro where they lived and died. Their descendants later moved and established the following towns – Ogidigben, Ugborodo, Ajudaibo and Madangho. However, the whole area is called Ugborodo – later coined Escravos Bar by the whites. This happened hundreds of years before the advent of Prince Ginuwa.
>
> (Unpublished Court Proceedings n.p.)

To further confirm this myth, Pa Omadeli (2001) (in an interview granted one of the researchers) added that these *Eghares* have long been deified as *Umale* (supernatural/immortalised beings). Ayomike (1988) also states that both Orugbo and Ugborodo communities agree that some of their founding fathers migrated at different points in time before the origin of the dynasty. Another school of thought (the 'Itsekiri' angle) believes that in the course of fishing the Itsekiri migrants from Olukumi (in Delta Igbo, Nigeria) migrated from Igala, south of Nupe country. While some settled in Ebu, others proceeded to found part of Itsekiriland.

Ayomike (1988) quotes Stride and Ifeka (1971: 336) as saying:

> The Itsekiri probably are a mixture of several people. The original inhabitants were called Umale, but they were soon absorbed by invading groups from the forest. If oral traditions are correct the hard core of the Itsekiri people of Warri were made of two parties of immigrants . . . it appears that a party of Ijebu from Yoruba country arrived and settled near the site of modern Warri. . . . Afterwards, another party of Edo are said to have moved from Benin . . . they were led by a Bini Prince.
>
> (3)

There is also the account about the group of immigrants from Edo, whose authenticity cannot be denied because it is recent, and whose arrival also occurred in an era when some parts of Africa were becoming enlightened in the area of documentation because of the influence of Europeans. In *A Short History of Benin* Egharevba (1949: 2) describes the Benin version as it relates to the Itsekiri Kingdom thus:

> Oba of Benin (AD 1473) knew that his son Iginua was hated by the Binis for the bad advice he had given against the people. He therefore decided to found a kingdom for him by the sea. Iginua accepted the offer gladly as he was aware of his unpopularity. The Oba did not wish the scheme to be known to his

> chiefs, in order that they might send their sons to accompany him as his subjects, so he cunningly asked them to send their sons with Iginua to sacrifice for him by the sea. Iginua was invested with the necessary regalia title **Odihina-me**, but he became known generally by the Jekiris as Olu after his father's name . . . Iginua became the first Olu or Odihiname and was the founder of the Jekiri (in modern parlance 'Itsekiri') Kingdom.

Omoneukanrin confirms the preceding text when he succinctly says:

> With mind devoid of the traditional magical Iroko box (into which a king and his numerous subjects were said to have been conveniently encased for days and months without suffocating them), [and] the *Umale-okun's* (sea-god's) deliverance [of them from danger], [they employed] the magic-spear, the dry cart charm, the contact with certain 'immortalised' beings (Umale) at Ale-Iwere (alias 'Ode-Itsekiri') and other mythical appendages [to reach safety . . .] ; the simplicity [of the tale] and some rays of truth in the following brief account of the origin of the people now called 'Itsekiri' but originally known as IWERE [are interestingly tantalizing].
>
> (1942: 2)

However, the name 'Itsekiri', according to myth, came as a result of the Olu's appreciation of a man called Itsekiri. Itsekiri was a successful businessman with many beautiful daughters. He was an immigrant from Olukumi who helped the Benin immigrants to settle in Iwere-land from the beginning, and also married out his daughters to both the prince and his men. For his good deed, 'the Olu allowed the Iwere people or nation to be called Itsekiri, the same manner a Benin Oba permitted his country to be called Edo, after the name of his deified slave-friend'. Meanwhile, Omoneukanrin gives the following account as to the origin of the name as:

> Before this Ijijen (the first son of Ginuwa, who later became the second Olu) sighted a very large area of land with grown up leafs [*sic*] which he identified as 'EWERE-LEAFS'. This leaf signifies 'good luck and peace' in Edo land. Knowing the importance of this leaf and its ceremonial significance in Benin kingdom, he drew his host [*sic*] attention to this discovery . . . Itsekiriene (the host) was compelled to Christian [*sic*] the land IWERE . . .
>
> (1942: 1–2)

His second account is that the origin of 'Iwere', which is that

> the purported blessing of Okhienwere by the Oba and his chiefs (upon) the travelling royal team when they were leaving the kingdom, was continuously

> used by the group in wishing their leaders well as they journeyed on (through the sea kingdom) . . . Iwere (is a) mispronunciation of (Okhienwere) a word of Edo language – meaning a land of 'ewere' leaves – symbolically a land of peace.
>
> (1942: 2)

Another account that needs to be cited is P. C. Lloyd's:

> The Itsekiri call themselves Itsekiri or Iwere, and the Yoruba and Edo use the same names; the Urhobo call them Irhobo, a term sometimes said to mean 'those who float on the water', the Ijaw call them Selemo. In the English literature they are known as Warri or Jekri, though in the 19th Century, they were often referred to as Benin, since contact with them was first made on the banks of the Benin River.
>
> (1957: 2)

Finally, as regards the movement of the Prince and his entourage, he settled in Ijala and later Ode-Itsekiri. He died and was buried at Ijala, which has since then become the burial place for all Olus of the Itsekiri (Okorie 2012: 54; Okwurumgbe 2012: 11; Erikowa 2012: 19). This royal cemetery is a significant artefact which the Itsekiri nation has called on world archaeologists to investigate as one of the proofs of their existence and migration (Okoro 2012:15). The Itsekiri are today grouped into two main families, the *Oton-Olu*, royal descendants – princes and princesses and their offspring, and *omajaja*, free citizens who traditionally produced the *ojoyes* (chiefs) of the Warri kingdom.

It is worth stating here that beginning with the name and origin, distortion in both pronunciations and spellings are visible signs of endangerment. For instance, some of the aforementioned towns and names were badly affected during the recent interethnic wars (1997–2010), which will go into contemporary Itsekiri history as their *anni mirabilis*, between the neighbouring ethnic groups and the Itsekiri people. Second, the political boundary of Iwere land, which has since been converted to Warri, now encompasses many of the neighbouring ethnic nationalities that have gone beyond using the name as a landmark but rather use it as a claim of ownership. These neighbouring ethnic groups are bigger than the Itsekiri population-wise.

Physical characteristics

The Itsekiri are a beautiful people with generally well-built men and women. They are identified by tribal marks (a trait not common nowadays due to civilization and fear of easy identification during tribal wars), three small cuts on each side of the face, just below the eyes or, other fancy cuts like fowl legs (*ese-egbele*) incised at either the corners of the eyes or mouth. These marks are similar to those of the Benins and Ijebu-Ode Yorubas, and have since been copied by the Ijaws and Urhobos residing inside and around Itsekiri communities. However, the difference lies in the technique applied by the Itsekiri in designing their own, which makes them stand out from others. They are usually of average fair complexion, though their early association with the Europeans has introduced light-skins among them.

Occupation

The Itsekiri generally (and especially their females) are proficient traders. This inherent attribute was displayed in their association with the early Europeans, as they were known as wealthy middlemen in the past. Another occupation associated with the Itsekiri is fishing. This can be said to be aided by their environment, as they are a coastal people. They are also engaged in palm oil making (*ekpo firin-firin*) and salt-making (occupations especially females partake in).

Itsekiri society

The Itsekiri homeland can be found within the three Warri local government areas – Warri South West, Warri South and Warri North – of Delta State, Nigeria. As stated in Lloyd's description,

> The Administrative unit known as Warri Division (now Warri . . .) . . . whose area is 1520 square miles, is approximately co-terminus with the territory of the Itsekiri.
>
> (1957: 4).

> The Itsekiri homeland is bounded approximately by lat. 5°20' and 6° N and long. 5°5' and 5°40'E of the river Niger.
>
> (qtd in Ayomike, 3)

Warri as a contested space

The word Warri has faced heated contestations in recent years. But one thing is sure: never in history has the word been associated with any other tribe aside from the Itsekiri. In history, it has occurred as 'Ourre', 'Warre', 'Wari', 'Oue', and so on by the Europeans in their different documentations. Whether the word is Portuguese-derived (as the people aver) or not, it has only been used in history to refer to a particular ethnic group, the Itsekiri.

Democratic governance

The Olu is the head of all Itsekiri people. The throne is by inheritance. For good governance, the chiefs help in ruling the people. Every Itsekiri town has an Olaraja (village head) who administers the village in accordance with tradition. The village elders assist the Olaraja on behalf of the Olu to oversee the affairs of the community. In recent times, each community has an elders' council, youth executives and women executives to supervise the welfare of the community.

Philosophy/values

The Itsekiri are a gentle and peaceful ethnic group. They are an honest, sociable, kind-hearted, accommodating and democratic people. They are not known to be violent because, as Afejuku, puts it, 'the tribe was not founded by conquest and blood but with love and peaceful greetings from the great Bini Kingdom' (2009: 5). The royal blood that flows in them makes them stand out in character and charms. And thus, they are a proud nation. They see and refer to themselves as *Oton-Oloye* (meaning descendants of the royal family). They are a disciplined, well-cultured and well-bred people who abhor injustice and oppression. When they fight, it is for their rights. To them, a good name is better than riches, and thus, they do not covet others' properties, and are not greedy. Hence they have maintained their environment for centuries despite invasion by other tribes. One can say they are incorruptible and a highly principled people who hate nepotism, who appreciate good work and who are truthful. Whenever a good result is needed, call on an Itsekiri man and he will get the right answer. They are hardworking and clean. In fact, one of their philosophies is that cleanliness is next to godliness. They are not vengeful. To them, God is the final arbiter. This is as portrayed by their calmness despite the intrusion on their homelands and traditions, believing that one day God will vindicate them. They are not 'praise-praise', singers and they maintain their integrity at all times. For instance, as disclosed earlier, they have maintained and sustained their history of origin for centuries without addition, unlike some of their counterparts whose history of origin is being 'discovered' every day. Finally, they are good observers and are highly creative.

Ironically, all these positive attributes from their rich, undiluted, straightforward history to their mode of governance and moral philosophy and values are part of the real reasons that they incur the wrath of some of their envious neighbours who want their lands by any means, and who thus threaten the existence of the Itsekiri and endanger them, their language, their culture and all they live and stand for. There is no exaggeration in this remark.

The Itsekiri language

Itsekiri is a small nation with one tongue that is non-dialectical. Certainly, *en route* their exodus from Benin through the Yoruba area until they finally settled in their homeland, the Itsekiri took from the Yorubas and Benins, and perhaps also from the Ijaws certain words which form part of the spoken and written Itsekiri language. In addition to these languages are words and coinages from the Portuguese, their early European associates. However in contemporary times, the Itsekiri language is an entity of its own with its own unique identity. These are visible in the dialectical relationship with these other languages mentioned in terms of sound/pronunciation, spellings and usage of words. For instance, palm oil in Yoruba language is spelt *epo* but has the Itsekiri variant of *ekpo*.

Word similarities with other nations

Some Itsekiri words are similar to Yoruba, Benin and Portuguese. Examples are as follows: the Portuguese call shoe *sabatu*, spoon *kujere*, plate *esete* and a giant jug *kanakan* as the Itsekiri who borrowed them from the Portuguese do. Meanwhile, Benin words like *lele* (to follow), *akaba* (stool or bench), *aga* (chair) are the same as in Itsekiri. There are also similar traditional names and titles, although they vary in terms of diction and spelling: Iyase *Iyatsere*, Oshodi *Oshodin*, Ologbosere *Ologbotsere* (the italicized are Itsekiri variants while the roman are Benin's). Also, Benins call a glass cup *itobele* while Itsekiris call it *tobele,* although there is the belief in both Benin and Itsekiri circles that the word is Portuguese-derived. Furthermore, Itsekiris share with Yorubas words like *gba* (take), *aga* (chair), *ere* (play), *ẹgbẹ* (mate), *wa* (come), *uli* (house). It is noteworthy to say here that there are other variations in Yoruba language which are also in the Itsekiri language. Although there are many examples to cite, the ones given here suffice.

Alphabet

The Itsekiri alphabet is generated from the Greek alphabet with additions and omissions in some cases as follows:

Aa	Bb	Dd	Ee	Ẹẹ
Ff	Gg	Ii	Jj	Kk
Ll	Mm	Nn	Oo	Ọo.
Pp	Rr	Ss	Tt	Uu
Vv	Ww	Yy	Zz	Ş ş
GHgh	Kpko	GBgb		

According to (Ogharaerumi 2010: 1), 'Itsekiri orthography is made up of thirty-five letters comprising twelve vowels and twenty-three consonants.'

Pronunciation (*kpíkpè*)

Vowels known in Itsekiri language as *Éghàn-ábidí* are: Aa Ee Ẹẹ Ii Oo Ọọ Uu as in /a/, /e/, /ẹ/, /o/, /ọ/, /u/. These are usually oral. They are capable of being nasalized in a contiguous environment. Ogharaerumi further says that 'while there are seven phonemic oral vowels, there are only five phonemic nasalized vowels /ã/ (an); /ẽ/ (en); /ĩ/ (in); /ộ/ (ọn); /ũ/ (un). The difference in the numbers here is because nasalized /e/ becomes /ệ/ (ẹn) and /ō/ becomes /o/ (ọn)' (2010: 2–3). He also attests to the reason behind this being the interplay of the vocal and nasal organs which happens in speech, stating that the occurrence of the feature on /e/ and /o/ could be said to be language specific.

With consonants (*Igbásá ábidí*), there are two types – primary consonants which are 18 and secondary consonants (Digraphs), which are 5. Altogether we have 23 consonants. While the primary consonants are of English equivalents, the primary consonants have no English equivalents because they are a combination of two letters in a symbolic relationship.

Primary consonants are /b/, /d/, /f/, /g/, /h/, /j/, /k/, /l/, /m/, /n/, /p/, /r/, /s/, /ş/, /t/, /v/, /w/ and /y/ (2010: 3–5).

Secondary consonants are /kp/, /kw/, /gb/, /gw/ and /gh/ (2010: 5).

Unfortunately, these are not being taught (as they should be) in schools and colleges in Nigeria – for reasons ranging from politics to the nonchalant attitude of even educated and academically minded Itsekiris themselves. Politically, they are not in control of the administration of their own affairs even though an Itsekiri is currently the executive governor of the state (Delta) they inhabit. There is no single university within the Itsekiri three local government areas of Warri South West, Warri South and Warri North.

They trained to be lawyers, doctors, bankers, engineers, administrators and others and can speak excellent Queen's English. But Itsekiri scholars, who one might expect to write books, poetry, novels, dramas or plays, and short stories, do not do so. Their argument from our several interactions with them is that it is a 'bloody waste' of their time to write in a language that does not enhance their economic power. They also argue that there are no publishing avenues for the publication of works in the Itsekiri language since the average publisher publishes works that will guarantee economic gains; it is bad business to publish works in the Itsekiri language. Very painfully, there is no publishing house owned by an Itsekiri person. Perhaps the only exception is Vanguard Media Limited which publishes a highly successful daily newspaper called *Vanguard*, one of the widest circulating newspapers in Nigeria. The proprietor and owner is a veteran Itsekiri journalist, but his interest does not go anywhere near educational publishing that would accommodate publication of works in the language of his people. Again very painfully, those who run *Vanguard* – from the general manager to editors of all kinds and even reporters – are generally not from his Itsekiri ethnic nationality. Simply put, Itsekiri are drastically and blatantly underrepresented in the *Vanguard* establishment. The reasons are obvious and are linked to the question of economics and business, which makes no allowance for the kind of patriotism that would promote the well-being and continued existence of the Itsekiri language. What a tragedy for the Itsekiri ethnic nationality! If gold should rust, what will iron do? What a tragedy! Indeed, it is no exaggeration to say that the Itsekiri language is endangered and threatened. For such a highly creative and well-schooled, well-educated people (as noted in numerous historical accounts as well as colonial records), their general lukewarm attitude towards their language is a huge paradox.

The endangered and threatened Itsekiri language

In 1929 Captain Pender wrote of the Itsekiri in his intelligent report thus: 'It is commonly supposed that they (Itsekiri) are a dying race . . . ' (qtd. in Ayomike 1990: 14). It may not be out of place to ask how a language is threatened and endangered. Threat and endangerment, as mentioned earlier, could come as a result of political instability, war, ecological mishap and socio-economic needs, among others.

In the political terrain, Nigeria as a country has been plagued with mediocre people as leaders for many years. Once upon a time, within the space of one year, it experienced three heads of state. These leaders, unfortunately, concerned themselves more with looting the government treasury than with the welfare of its citizens. Femi Osofisan, a Nigerian playwright, captures it well when he says:

> Power . . . was merely an excuse to line their (the leaders') own pockets, and all the noisy programmes of 'development' announced with tedious frequency and fanfare . . . [are] convenient drainage pipes through which national wealth was greedily siphoned into private bank accounts.
>
> (1998: 13)

Ecologically, the Itsekiri as a nation are faced with serious problems which the Nigerian nation is unperturbed about. The Itsekiri are a coastal people. Each year, communities on the Atlantic coast experience uncontrollable oceanic erosion. For instance, the Ugborodos have been soliciting for help for over four decades and nothing is forthcoming aside from empty promises made by the government. (Ugborodo is an oil-rich town, and it is one of the Itsekiri towns on the Atlantic estuary of the Escravos River).

Their case is one of the numerous ecological crises in addition to that of gas-flaring confronting the people. Another injurious problem is that less than 5 per cent of the area is accessible by good roads. Thus, there are no other companies outside the oil multinationals and their service agents who employ outsiders rather than the indigenous people. Whereas, when employed, about 99.5 per cent are junior workers of whom 95 per cent are daily paid/contract staff, whose work can be terminated anytime without prior notice.

Unfortunately, the incidents of unrest and inter- and intratribal wars plagued the people from 1997 to 2010 (as already indicated, the *anni mirabilis* of the Itsekiri claimed lives and rendered hundreds of thousands of Itsekiri people homeless). Neighbouring communities in the bid to claim ownership of their land because of oil and gas exploration invaded Itsekiri communities, burning towns and villages, killing youths and the aged. Till date some of the land spaces are being occupied by these invaders because they are in the majority. A major example is Opuraja, a transient island for Ugborodo fishermen before the 1997 crisis, which is now an Ijaw megacity. To worsen the whole issue, oil and gas exploration has been identified as the root cause of the Itsekiri crises in recent times. The effect is now felt both in the environment and in the lives of the people. The more exploration, the bleaker the environment, the more pain the people bear and the more they depart their traditional homes for new homes where they and their children imbibe new lifestyles and learn new languages which they speak and even write to the detriment of their own.

As of today, in the electronic media within the Itsekiri environs there are about ten television houses and about eight radio stations – that is, within three states (Edo, Ondo and Delta) we have the presence of the Itsekiri people but none of these stations reads news in Itsekiri language or has a functioning Itsekiri language magazine programme like other nations. The reason is not far to seek. There is no Itsekiri newscaster to anchor it. During the crises, the fear of being identified as Itsekiri led many to hide their identity. Such an avenue to preserve and promote the language and to serve the cause of the people at a significant point in their lives and history became nonexistent.

In the preface to his *Moonlight Plays in Itsekiri*, Eyeoyibo says that 'in the last forty to fifty years, most Itsekiri youths have moved to other parts of the country as a result of social and economic changes in certain parts of their homeland' (1994: vii). In his view, "such youths, who are adults today, have grown "outside", without imbibing the cultural values of their traditional home-land' (1994: vii). Thus, his fear lies in the fact that vital areas of their cultural development would sink to oblivion.

Certainly, movement, no matter the reason for it, leads to the dropping of one habit and the picking up of another. Eighty per cent of Itsekiri students interviewed on University of Benin campuses are a proof of this. Disappointingly, not only those who grew away from their hometowns are unable to speak the language. Those brought up within Warri metropolis are worst hit on this issue. When questioned on their inability to speak their mother tongue, their responses were 'nobody taught us' and 'our parents never spoke it to us'. When asked if their parents do speak the language at home, about 92 per cent of them said 'Yes, they speak it between themselves but not to us'. Ogharaerumi (2010: iii) posits that 'if you do not use your language, it will gradually die and so goes your tribal identity'. In 'You and Your Language' (iii), he says 'the language of a people is the singular inalienable evidence of their history and corporate existence'. Thus, the upcoming youths have been denied the right to learn, understand and speak the language, and this may transfer (if it has not transferred already) to the next generations.

Efforts made at preserving the language so far

Despite these highlighted negatives, some efforts have been made and are still being made by some organizations and patriotic Itsekiri to save the language from annihilation. Credit will be given to the Bible Society of Nigeria who in their bid to evangelise the people translated and printed the four Gospels of the *New Testament Bible*, viz: *Iyen Rire Ni Ubara Jisos Kraist Ti Mak Ya* in 1974, the *Holy Bible* (*Baibol Fifen*)) and the *Itsekiri Hymn Book* (*Iwe Erin N'ohun Itsekiri*).

Another authority is Macaulay Oma Eyeoyibo. He is, ironically, of sparse education, a writer, news analyst and columnist. He belongs to various social and professional organizations such as the Nigerian Institute of Public Relations, the Museum Friends Committee, the Iwere Cultural Group, and he has tried to establish himself as a public educator. He has to his credit over nine published books on Itsekiri, which include *Moonlight Plays in Itsekiri* (1988); *Itsekiri Games and Sports* (1988); *304 Proverbs in Itsekiri*; *Book of Quotations in Itsekiri* (1996); *Cottage Industries in Itsekiri*; *Dictionary of Itsekiri Names* (2000); *How to Study: Itsekiri Gbe Onuwe (Itsekiri for Today)* (2002), among others yet to see the light of day.

Mark O. Ogharaerumi is another authority on Itsekiri language. He was a pupil in the extramural classes for Itsekiri language in Warri Urban in the late 1950s under the aegis of the then Western Region where he learnt the basic elements of the language. He holds a BA in theology from Washington Bible College, Maryland, USA, an MA in linguistics from the University of Texas in Arlington, Texas, USA and a Ph.D. in applied linguistics and missiology from the University of Aberdeen, Scotland. He has served as a Bible Translation Consultant for the Nigeria Bible Society, the Evangel Bible Translators in the USA and is currently with the Seed Company, an arm of the Wycliffe Bible Translators, a worldwide Bible translation agency. He is the director of the Centre for Itsekiri Studies, Warri and the current chaplain of Warri Kingdom. He has engaged in several Christian evangelistic missions in Nigeria and other parts of the world. He is the author of *A Handbook on Itsekiri Language: Ikoni Owun Itsekiri*.

In the film industry is Alex Eyengho, the president of the Association of Nollywood Core Producers (ANCOP). He is a film producer and director. He won the award for the most outstanding indigenous movie at the 2011 African Audio-Visual Awards (TAVA). He is also the president of the Association of Itsekiri Performing Artists (AIPA). He has to his credit indigenous movies in Itsekiri language of which two, *Oma tsen-tsen* and *Suara la*, have won him national awards in recent times.

In their respective works, these Itsekiri patriots are doing what they can to save the Itsekiri language from going into extinction, but it seems they are racing against the tide on account of the small population and the current political circumstances of the Itsekiri, as indicated earlier. It is significant to note that the majority of these publications and documentations were self-sponsored ones akin to vanity publications that circulated (and still circulate) among a few persons only. Consequently, they do not make the expected or envisaged impact on the lives of the people.

Efforts to rejuvenate the Itsekiri language

What Eyeoyibo and other authors have done is to document as many as possible of our indigenous day-to-day affairs in written form in order to arouse the interest of contemporary youths and to preserve the language. Others like Eyengho and members and crew of the musical group called *Ogono for Jesus*, among others, have been able to do audiovisual documentations. What the group *Ogono for Jesus* has achieved is to use indigenous beats to produce Christian music/songs in order to attract youths who have tilted towards Westernization back to their roots. However, there are challenges that cannot and must not be overlooked.

Challenges

Foremost among the challenges facing the efforts of those who wish to save the Itsekiri language is that of pronunciation. Some within the Yoruba ethnicity mix Yoruba language with Itsekiri when speaking. Eyeoyibo and Ogharaerumi have tried to alleviate the strain of this in their respective books *A Handbook on Itsekiri Language: Ikoni Owun Itsekiri* and *Mofe's Dictionary in Itsekiri (Iwe Umofo)* (2010), yet how many of our youths are interested enough to pick up such books to read in this era of the internet?

The advent of information and communication technology (ICT) is another form of endangerment to the language. Whether we like it or not, ICT has come to stay and most of our youths are glued to it. It is no longer the issue of literacy or illiteracy; almost everybody is interested and hooked to it. And the culture now is more individualistic than communal. Thus, moonlight plays and games are being taken over by the internet or GSM or computers, while the younger ones especially are glued to computer games and animations (popularly called cartoons).

Another prevailing problem with ICT is the dying culture of reading among our youths. They would rather chat online or via their handsets, watch films, and, in a few cases, read novels than 'waste' their time on indigenous movies or musicals. So if they do not hear it, how will they speak it? This may be a global problem, but a small ethnic group like the Itsekiri cannot afford this luxury that is riding their language to extinction.

Careerism, an offspring of Westernization, is another major challenge. In many families, both parents go to work while the children go to school. Oftentimes when these children are back at home their parents are still at work. So they employ house-helps who do not speak the Itsekiri language, and the children resort to toys and cartoons as playthings. Once the parents are back from work, the best and fastest way to communicate is the English language because they are in a hurry to get things done. There is no room to chat with the children in Itsekiri. Many do not even have time to watch the Itsekiri home videos, or to read or narrate the bedtime indigenous stories-cum-moonlight games as documented by Eyeoyibo to the children.

There is also the challenge posed by educational theatre. Of course, educational theatre is the art of the theatre within an institution of learning, that is, theatre sponsored by an institution. Clifford (1980) in *Educational Theatre Management* posits that one of the purposes of educational theatre, after entertainment, is to preserve cultural heritage. This would have been possible with dramaturgy, music, dance, scenic designs and costumes (as courses being handled by many universities and colleges within Nigeria). For instance, Mike Agbeyegbe's *The King Must Dance Naked* (1987) and Umuko's *Princess Esilokun* (1993) are plays based on the Itsekiri world view. These plays are richly packaged to reflect the culture and traditions of the Itsekiri. Ironically, in most of our institutions of learning, this culture has been bastardized, or should we say misrepresented? The plays and the culture they project are handled with levity and without passion. In-depth research into the culture of the people is not carried out, either for selfish reasons, or as a result of ignorance or laziness. Even with historicity and dramaturgy we see falsehoods in the offerings of some playwrights and critics, non-Itsekiri, who in the bid to project some lies, formulate their own stories which they dish out to these young scholars as truths. It is unfortunate that many persons who engage in these unwholesome acts and practices are professors who suddenly discover truth that is less than 100 years old. In dramaturgy, the language employed is an instrument of communicating the culture and tradition; and bastardization, or alteration in any form, as it relates to pronunciation, cannot but endanger the language. If properly articulated, educational theatre and its art would go a long way in an effort to preserve the language. Furthermore, the works would have served the interest of the Itsekiri if they were translated into the Itsekiri language. But who would pay the cost of publishing them and even of taking responsibility for their marketing? This is a valid question to ask. In this connection, the experience of Professor Tony E. Afejuku, a co-author of this chapter, is worth citing. A few years ago, Afejuku, in his academic zeal to promote the Itsekiri language, decided to translate some classics into Itsekiri. He thought of beginning with Chinua Achebe's *Things Fall Apart* which he called *Ita Okonkwo* (*The Story of Okonkwo*). He contacted several publishers who *ab initio* discouraged the venture for marketing and economic reasons. Even some wealthy Itsekiri persons he approached to support the venture gave him answers that traumatized him and his academic enthusiasm on behalf of his people. Sadly, very sadly, he gave up the venture – which, to put it mildly, suffered still-birth.

Conclusion (and anti-conclusion)

This chapter has discussed extensively Itsekiri as a threatened and an endangered language. It has touched on issues affecting the existence of the people and especially as they relate to the people's culture and language. It has been argued that the Itsekiri people are threatened culturally, politically, ecologically, and economically with the consequence that their language which gives them the distinction as an ethnic nationality is being endangered. The Itsekiris' fear of extinction is real, and is not an exaggeration. Because 'the language of a people is the singular inalienable evidence of their history and corporate existence', to quote Ogharaerumi (2010: iii), there is no doubt that the Itsekiri ethnic nationality will cease to exist as such unless it wins the battle of survival of its language. How to do this is the contention of this chapter. It is our wish that this conference will help provide solutions to the Itsekiri dilemma and problem. Of course, the chapter dwells on various aspects of the Itsekiri quagmire and efforts to circumvent it. But it is our contention that the efforts of various individuals to rescue the language from extinction appear to be too little or too insignificant to rescue the Itsekiri language from imminent annihilation. What a seeming anti-conclusion to this chapter which participants should rescue it from! What a seeming anti-conclusion as we stare at the mayhem facing the Itsekiri nationality, which we are requesting participants and readers of this chapter to help us tackle squarely and fittingly![1]

Note

1 We wish gladly to note here that the seriousness and enthusiasm with which Indian participants at the conference went about the enterprise of developing their respective languages, from the least to the largest, in terms of their respective population sizes, did not escape our notice. Already we are at work with some caring Itsekiri political leaders of thought to provide necessary stimulus along our Chotro experience.

References

Afejuku, Helen Doris. 2009. 'Itsekiri Arts & Culture: Its Relevance in the 21st Century', *22nd Atuwase II of Warri Kingdom Coronation Anniversary (Oyo Ekoro)*, 1 May: 9.

Agbeyegbe, Mike. 1987. *The King Must Dance Naked*. Lagos: Malthouse.

Ayomike, J.O.S. 1988. *A History of Warri*. Benin: Ilupeju Press.

———. 1990. *The Itsekiri at a Glance*. Benin: Mayomi Publishers.

Clifford, J.E. 1980. *Educational Theatre Management*. Chicago: Steekie National Textbooks Company.

Egharevba, J.U. 1949. *A Short History of Benin*. Lagos: Church Missionary Society Bookshop.

Erikowa, Henry. 2012. 'Falcorp Mangrove Park, Ijala-Ikeren, Warri', *The Guardian*, 28 April 19.

Eyeoyibo, Macaulay Oma. n.d. *Mofe's Dictionary in Itsekiri (Iwe Umofo)*. Benin City: Mofe Press.

———. 1988a. *Itsekiri Games and Sports*. Benin: Mofe Press.

———. 1988b. *Moonlight Plays in Itsekiri*. Benin: Mofe Press.

———. 1996. *Book of Quotations in Itsekiri*. Benin: Mofe Press.

———. 2000. *Dictionary of Itsekiri Names*. Benin: Mofe Press.

———. 2002. *How to Study: Itsekiri Gbe Onuwe*. Benin: Mofe Press.

Lloyd, P.C. 1957. *The Itsekiri*. London: International African Institute.
Ogharaerumi, Mark O. 2010. *A Handbook on Itsekiri Language: Ikoni Owun Itsekiri*. Warri: Centre for Itsekiri Studies.
Okorie, Uguru. 2012. 'Delta Community Where Kings Never Die', *The Nation*, 21 July: 54.
Okoro, Richard. 2012. 'Warri Cemetry to Become World Heritage Cite—Ayomike', *Urhobo Times*, 31 May: 15.
Okpewho, Isidore. 1998. *Oral Performance in Africa*. Ibadan: Spectrum Books.
Okwurumgbe, Uche Henry. 'The Place of Ijala in Warri Kingdom: History, Development', *The Pointer*, Saturday, 4 August 2012: 11.
Omadeli, Pa. 2001. *Burial Rites in Itsekiriland: Origin of Itsekiri People*. Alero Uwawah, 15 December.
Omoneukanri, C.O. 1942. *Itsekiri Law and Custom*. Lagos: Ife-Olu Printing.
Osofisan, Femi. 1998. '"The Revolution as Muse": Drama as Surreptitious Insurrection in a Post-Colonial Military State', in Richard Boon and Jane Plastow (eds), *Theatre Matters: Performance and Culture on the World Stage*, pp. 11–35. Cambridge: Cambridge University Press.
Sagay, J.O.E. 1980. *The Warri Kingdom*. Sapele: Progress Publishers.
Stride, G.T. and C. Ifeka. 1971. *Peoples and Empires of West Africa*. New York: Africana Publishing Corp.
Umuko, Eni-Jologho. 1993. *Princess Esilokun*. Lagos: Uto Enterprises.
Uwawah, J.M.A. 'The Evidence Given in the "High Court of Justice of Mid-Western State of Nigeria" Warri Division, Suit No. W/70/89/16.' n.d. Unpublished Court Proceedings, n.p.

16 Kikuyu phonology and orthography

Any hope for continuity of indigenous languages?

P. I Iribemwangi

Introduction

This chapter investigates the phonology and orthography of Kikuyu language. Kikuyu is a Western Bantu language spoken by the Agikuyu people of central Kenya. It is spoken predominantly in the central region and in other parts of the country where the Kikuyu people have settled. Kikuyu native speakers are arguably the most decentralized people in Kenya and are found in virtually every part of the country partly owing to the fact that the language has the highest populace in Kenya today. According to the 16th edition of *The Ethnologue* (Lewis 2009), the language has a speaker population of about seven million. There is a significant number of this populace in Nairobi, the Rift Valley and along the Kenyan coast.

Mutahi (1983) classifies Kikuyu language as having seven geographical dialects, namely Ki-Embu, Gi-Gichugu, Ki-Mbeere, Ki-Mathira, Ki-Ndia, Southern and Northern dialects spoken in Kiambu and Murang'a, respectively. As Wachera (2008) states, these geographically and politically motivated dialects of Kikuyu have since reduced in number with Ki-Embu first and Ki-Mbeere afterwards gaining the status of fully fledged languages. The geo-political boundaries separating the dialects have also changed drastically since Mutahi's (1983) classification and Kikuyu is now a predominant central Mount Kenya language divorced from Eastern Mount Kenya where Ki-Embu and Ki-Mbeere are spoken.

The Kikuyu dialects that are the subject of this study are Southern Kikuyu (spoken in Kiambu and Southern Murang'a), Ndia (Southern Kirinyaga), Gichugu (Northern Kirinyaga), Mathira (Karatina) and Northern Kikuyu (Northern Murang'a and Nyeri). The language is used in homes, social gatherings, and business transactions as well as in print and broadcast media (Kihara 2010). The language is also supposed to be taught in the elementary classes in Central Province.[1] The chapter explores the phonemes and orthography of these five dialects and posits a uniform phoneme matrix for the language. It also describes the syllable divisions and phoneme patterns found in the language as well as points at the shortcomings that cause the language to be viewed as underdeveloped in its written form.

Reading Kikuyu: the problem

According to current studies, the level of reading Kikuyu has gone down drastically. Piper (2010: 3) indicates that 7.4 per cent of children in Class 3 in Central Province are unable to read a single word in Kikuyu. This is quite worrying given that the policy of the Ministry of Education is to have Kikuyu both as a subject and as a language of instruction at the lower levels. Kikuyu is used as a medium of instruction only in 33.5 per cent of the instruction time. The study shows that English and Kiswahili are given more preference in total disregard to government policy. While use of Kikuyu is only 14.1 per cent, that of Kiswahili is 27.9 per cent and English 58.1 per cent. This is very different from Uganda where vernacular use in elementary level is 71.1 per cent compared to 28.9 per cent use of English. The levels are even more appalling when it comes to reading ability. While 59.6 per cent and 29.5 per cent of Class 3 pupils can read English and Kiswahili, respectively, only 10.8 per cent of the same pupils in central Kenya can read Kikuyu. These figures indicate that the situation of written Kikuyu is dismal and is therefore an area of concern especially given that this written form is still not fully developed. It is with these figures in mind that this research describes Kikuyu orthography and phonology as well as the problems associated with reading the language.

Kikuyu vowels

Banda (2002) states that it is generally said that most Bantu languages have a five-vowel system, a view he says that is both simplistic and misleading. His argument is that most Bantu languages have more than five vowels. Kikuyu is a case in point as it has 14 vowels; seven short vowels and seven long vowels. As Mutahi (1983) stated, vowel length is a distinctive feature in Kikuyu; hence there is the distinction between short and long vowels. In a vowel quadrilateral, the 14 vowels may be represented thus:

Figure 16.1 Vowels evident in Kikuyu

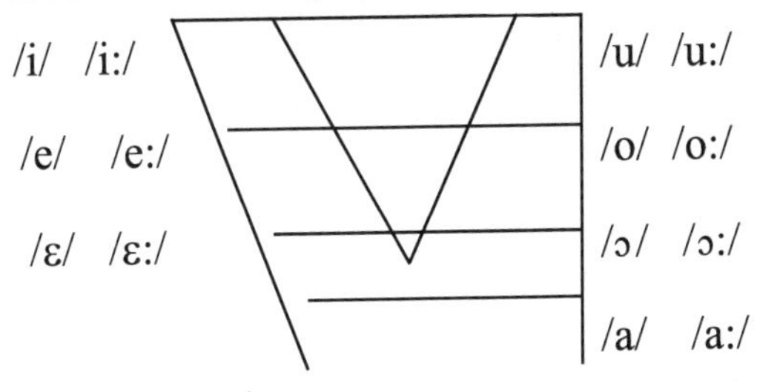

In words, the features for the short vowels may be stated as follows:

/i/ is a front high un-rounded vowel
/u/ is a back high rounded vowel
/e/ is a front mid-high un-rounded vowel
/o/ is a back mid-high rounded vowel
/ɛ/ is a front mid-low un-rounded vowel
/ɔ/ is a back mid-low rounded vowel
/a/ is a front low un-rounded vowel

The long and short vowels do form minimal pairs. This means that vowel length causes difference in meaning between word pairs, for example:

/tata/ means *aunt* while
/ta:ta/ means to *trickle in drops*

/ðaka/ means *good, smart, beautiful* while
/ða:ka/ means *play*

/kana/ means the *fourth* in the three languages while
/ka:na/ means a *baby* or to *deny* depending on the tone.

/rika/ is to *dip into water* while
/ri:ka/ means *age group*[2]

Drawing from proto-Bantu therefore, Kikuyu vowels are easily discernible.

Kikuyu consonants

While all the five Kikuyu dialects have a similar vowel inventory, the same may not be said of the consonants. These dialects have different consonant inventories. The thesis of this chapter is that the differences evident in the consonant inventory are a result of sound changes that have occurred diachronically arising from different reasons which vary from geographical to social. Reference to the proto-Bantu phonemic inventory does, at least, suggest this.

In laying down consonant matrices, we shall have two divisions of Kikuyu dialects. These divisions are born out of phonological and orthographical similarities of the dialects. The first division has two dialects, Gigichugu and Kindia. These two dialects neighbour each other geographically and are therefore in close proximity. The consonant matrix of these two dialects is given in Table 16.1.

A major distinction of these two dialects is in phoneme /β/. The proto-Bantu phonemes /p/ and /β/ are both realized as /β/ in Kindia and Gigichugu. What this means is that in all the cases, the proto-Bantu /p/ weakens. Both Kindia and Gigichugu do not have phonemes /ʃ/ and /tʃ/ but the alveolar fricative /s/ is realized in their place. It is worth noting that these two dialects have 17 consonant phonemes.

The other set comprises Kimathira, Northern and Southern dialects. Kimathira is spoken mainly in Mathira Division. The Northern dialect is spoken in Murang'a and the larger Nyeri (excluding Mathira). The Southern dialect is spoken in the larger Kiambu region. These three dialects of Kikuyu are quite similar and the minor differences that exist are actually negligible, as is evident in Table 16.2.

The seemingly major difference between this last group and the previous one is the presence and use of the glottal fricative /h/ which is

Table 16.1 Consonant matrix for Kindia and Gigichugu dialects of Kikuyu

Place of articulation	*Categories according to manner of articulation*					
	Obstruents			*Sonorants*		
	Stops		*Fricatives*			
	Plosives	*Affricates*		*Nasals*	*Trill*	*Glides*
Bilabial	/mb/		/β/	/m/		/w/
Labiodental						
Dental			/ð/			
Alveolar	/t/ /nd/		/s/	/n/	/r/	
Palatal		/ɲɟ/		/ɲ/		/j/
Velar	/k/ /ŋg/		/ɣ/	/ŋ/		
Total	5	1	4	4	1	2 **(17)**

Table 16.2 Consonant matrix for Kimathira, Northern and Southern dialects of Kikuyu

Place of articulation	*Categories according to manner of articulation*					
	Obstruents			*Sonorants*		
	Stops		*Fricatives*			
	Plosives	*Affricates*		*Nasals*	*Trill*	*Glides*
Bilabial	/mb/		/β/*	/m/		/w/
Labiodental			/f/ *			
Dental			/ð/ ▪			
Palatoalveolar			/ʃ/ •			
Alveolar	/t/ /nd/		/z/ ▪	/n/	/r/	
Palatal		/ɲɟ/ /tʃ/•		/ɲ/		/j/
Velar	/k/ /ŋg/		/ɣ/	/ŋ/		
Glottal			/h/			
Total	5	1	5	4	1	2 **(18)**

* /f/ is usually used in the Kimathira and Northern dialects, while /β/ is used in the Southern dialect.

▪ /ð/is used in both Northern and Southern dialects while /z/ is used in Kimathira.

• /tʃ/ is used by some speakers of the Northern dialect.

absent in the other group. However, within the dialects, there are other minor differences. For example, while Kimathira and Northern dialects use the labio-dental /f/, the Southern dialect uses the bilabial fricative /β/. Another difference is that Kimathira uses the alveolar fricative /z/ in place of the dental fricative /ð/ used in the Northern and Southern dialects. All the other phonemes are the same.

While this chapter suggests the realization of 18 consonants in the three dialects, it is noted that some other scholars suggest the existence of more consonant phonemes. Mutahi (1983) for example indicates that there are four other phonemes, namely /b/, /d/, /ɟ/ and /g/. In contrast, our research indicates that all these stops are pre-nasalized in the three dialects. What is apparent is that individual speakers articulate some of the phonemes differently. However, the idiosyncrasies that exist do not suggest a deletion of the nasal. The articulation of the nasal may be weak but in all cases native speakers always articulate it. As a result, in our view, the examples given by Mutahi (1983: 126) are articulated as shown in Table 16.3.

Table 16.3 Pre-nasalization

Mutahi (1983)	*This chapter*	*Proto*	*Gloss*
bata	Mbata	nβata	duck
boto	Mboto	nβoto	battalion
ɟanɔ	ɲɟanɔ	nsana	a mark
garjɔ	ŋgarjɔ	nkario	guava
garokɔ	ŋgarokɔ	nɣarokɔ	the other side

The dropping of the nasal in these cases does not seem to be motivated by any particular reason. The explanation given by Mutahi (1983: 126–127) does not seem adequate since there are more exceptions to his rule than the forms following it. Such exceptions include /mbea/ (rat), /ɲɟɔja/ (feathers) and /ngare/ (leopard). It is for these reasons that the four sounds have not been included in our matrix. We, however, note that this is one of the problems arising in the orthographical and phonetic representations of the language which arises out of lack of a standardized written form.

Orthography and phoneme matrix of Kikuyu

In this subsection, we posit the harmonized phonemes and graphemes that may be used in Kikuyu. The phonemes cut across the dialects leading to one form. It is noted that these phonemes are either familiar or recognizable to the speakers of all Kikuyu dialects.

From our analysis therefore, Kikuyu has *seven* short vowels. Phonetically represented, the short vowels are:

/a, ɛ, e, i, ɔ, u, o /

Orthographically, these vowels may be written as:

a, e, ĩ, i o, u and ũ

It is, however, noted that Kikuyu has both short and long vowels. The long vowels correspond to the short ones. The long and short vowels form minimal pairs. Phonetically stated, the long vowels are:

/a:, ɛ:, e:, i:, ɔ:, u:, o: /

That is:

aa, ee, ĩĩ, ii, oo, uu and ũũ

The code also has two semi vowels:

/j, w/

orthographically written:

y and w

Kikuyu consonants are:

/ β, ʃ, ɤ, h, k, m, n, r, t, ð, ŋ, ɲ/

whose orthographic graphemes are:

b, c, g, h, k, m, n, r, t, th, ng' and ny

The language also has four pre-nasalized consonants which are:

/nd, ng, mb, ɲɟ/

that is:

nd, ng, mb and nj

The long vowels should be indicated in written language sparingly; in fact, it is advisable to write long vowels only for words that are one of a complementary pair, that is, only when the use of the short vowel in a word would cause a different meaning. Long vowels should also not be written in an environment neighbouring either a double vowel or pre-nasalized consonants. The issue of long and short vowels in Kikuyu, especially when to use double vowels in orthography, is yet another problem arising from lack of standardization which shows underdevelopment in the written form. For example, in orthography, one should write:[3]

waru (/waru/) *not waaru* (potato)	watho (/waðɔ/) *not waatho* (law)
mwaria (/mwaria/) *not mwaaria* (talkative)	yaku (/jaku/) *not yaaku* (yours)
rũthanju (/roðaɲɟu/) *not rũthaanju* (rod)	mũndũ (/mondo/) *not mũũndũ* (a person)
baba (/βaβa/) not baaba (father)	ngingo(/ngingɔ/) *not ngiingo* (neck)

In morphology, vowels are quite dominant in Kikuyu and as a result, the preferred syllable structure is that of consonant vowel (CV). Although there are other syllable structures, such as (C½VV), (V) and (CVV), the (CV) structure is the most widespread. Furthermore, all words in Kikuyu carry open syllables and words with closed syllables would therefore appear grossly unfamiliar.

Loan words adapted into Kikuyu undergo various modifications that allow them to acquire the preferred syllable structure. Phonemes that do not exist in Kikuyu are substituted with those close to them available in Kikuyu. The following loan words are modified in this way.

Table 16.4 represents Kikuyu consonant phonemes. While most of the phonemes stand alone in their positions in words, some do change depending on different parameters such as geographical or social position. Sounds that may be used in variance without causing a change in meaning should be viewed as allophones of the same phoneme or as sounds that occur in free variation where there are major differences among the sounds concerned. Consequently, [β] and [f] should all be understood to be allophones of /β/. These sounds are close phonetically and cause no change in meaning when used. Similarly, [ð] and [z], which are allophones of /ð/. /tʃ/, /ʃ/ and /s/, may also be used in free variation as variants of the same phoneme. None of the sounds in either of the above sets would form a complementary pair, and as a result, this is a clear case of allophony. This issue of allophony, where a phoneme sounds different in different dialects without causing a change in meaning, forms the third problem in the phonology of Kukuyu.

Source word	*Orthography*	*Phonetic representation*	*Gloss*
pastor (English)	Bathita	βaðita	
police ,,	borithi	βɔriði	
bus ,,	mbathi	mbaði	
queen ,,	kwini	kwini	
Africa ,,	Abirika	aβirika	
page ,,	bĩnji	βeɲɟi	
thank you ,,	thengiũ	ðɛŋgio	
account ,,	akauti	akauti	
katiba (Kiswahili)	gatiba	ɣatiβa	constitution
chupa ,,	cuba	ʃu βa	bottle
kalamu ,,	karamu	karamu	pen
mzungu ,,	mũthũngũ	moðoŋgo	European

Table 16.4 Consonant matrix for Kikuyu

Place of articulation	*Categories according to manner of articulation*					
	Obstruents			*Sonorants*		
	Stops		*Fricatives*			
	Plosives	*Affricates*		*Nasals*	*Trill*	*Glides*
Bilabial	/mb/		/β/*	/m/		/w/
Labiodental			/v/* /f/ *			
Dental			/ð/ ▪			
Palatoalveolar			/ʃ/ ●			
Alveolar	/t/ /nd/		/s/● /z/ ▪	/n/	/r/	
Palatal		/ɲɟ/ /tʃ/●		/ɲ/		/j/
Velar	/k/ /ŋg/		/ɣ/	/ŋ/		
Glottal			/h/			
Total	5	1	5	4	1	2 (18)

* [f], [β] and [v] should be viewed as allophones of /β/.

▪ [ð] and [z] are allophones of /ð/.

● [tʃ], [ʃ] and [s] are allophones of /ʃ].

Kikuyu syllable divisions

Another phonological feature worth description in this chapter is the division of Kikuyu syllables. While issues concerning the structure of syllable in terms of onset, nucleus and coda as well as syllable weight (heavy and light syllables) may be of interest, they are not core to the discussion here.[4]

As Iribemwangi (2010) notes, syllables are constructed by combining phonemes together in neighbouring environments and forming a pattern that is articulated as one. Linguists such as Crystal (1991) assert that the understanding of the syllable structure of a language is important in the analysis of its phonology and that this involves combining sounds in individual languages to produce typical sequences. Katamba (1989) for his part posits that the syllable is the basic unit in terms of which phonotactic rules are best stated. These are the rules that control the language users in terms of the possible sound combinations of the given language. It is the syllable that dictates which sounds combine (or do not combine) in a given language. In this subsection, the various syllable divisions evident in Kikuyu words are explored. The data used are drawn from what is commonly referred to as 'Standard Kikuyu'.[5]

The first structure is what is usually referred to as the preferred syllable structure: that of a consonant–vowel cluster (CV). As in many Bantu (and indeed many world) languages, this is the structure that forms the bulk of syllables in Kikuyu.

There are words like:

/motito/	forest	(CV $ CV $ CV)
/karamu/	pen	(CV $ CV $ CV)
/moraja/	tall	(CV $CV $ CV)

The structure in all these lexical items is CVCVCV. It is important to note that the pre-nasalized phonemes bear this structure, for example:

/ɲɟara/	hand	(CV$CV)
/ndεru/	beard	(CV$CV)
/ŋgamera/	camel	(CVCVV)
/mboga/	vegetable/cabbage	(CV$CV)

The other structure is C½VV. Various consonants are used in the initial position and are then followed by a semi-vowel. A vowel takes the final position of the syllable. There are quite a number of words with such syllables, for example:

/mwεne/	owner	(C½VV$CV)
/kɔβja/	copy	(CV$C½VV)
/mbwε:/	jackal	(C½VV$V)
/orja/	ask	(V$ C½VV)
/ŋgwerε/	I tell you	(C½VV $ CV)

In each of these forms, one of the two semi-vowels in Kiswahili, /w/ and /j/, is used in the medial position.

Kikuyu also has the vowel syllable (V). Such syllables have a single vowel and have a high prevalence. They can occur in any position in Kikuyu words. Examples are:

/ima/ deny (V$CV)
/ando/ people (V$CV)
/kanua/ mouth (CVCVV)
/aito/ our (people) (VVCV)
/ao/ their (people) (V$V)
/amba/ crucify (V$CV)

Another syllable structure is that of a consonant and double vowel (CVV). As mentioned earlier, vowel length is very important in Kikuyu as it has direct bearing on meaning. This structure is widespread in Kikuyu and examples include:

/ta:ta/ trickle in drops (CVV$CV)
/ða:ka/ play (CVV$CV)
/ri:ka/ age group (CVV$CV)
/mɛ:rɛ/ tell them (CVV$CV)
/ʃu:ra/ toilet cleaner (CVV$CV)

As is evident, Kikuyu does not exhibit many syllable structures.[6] As noted, the CVCV structure is quite dominant. Kikuyu also uses an open syllable structure and as a result there are no examples of closed syllables in the language. Even when such syllables occur in borrowed words, they are immediately blocked through vowel insertion, which then creates the preferred structure.

Phoneme patterns in words

So far, this chapter has mainly focused on sound segments found in Kikuyu. It is apparent that the code has 14 vowels and 18 consonants, bringing the total to 32 phonemes. It has also been noted that some of these phonemes have more than one variant which have no bearing on the meanings of the words concerned. A further observation is that if the long vowels are ignored, the total number of phonemes would be 25. However, to ignore the long vowels would be quite misleading in the case of Kikuyu since vowel length is a distinctive feature.

Although this is a phonological study, it is necessary to briefly exemplify how the various phonemes combine to form word patterns, particularly for the allophones. The purpose of the information in Table 16.5 is to

Table 16.5 Sound patterns in words[7]

No.	*Kimathira*	*Northern*	*Southern*	*Kindia*	*Gigichugu*	*Gloss*
1	huanana	huanana	huanana	βanana	βanana	resemble
2	hiða	hiða	hiða	βiða	βiða	hide (smt)
3	hɛhɔ	hɛhɔ	hɛhɔ	mbeβɔ	mbeβɔ	cold
4	ʃoʃo	ʃoʃo / tʃotʃo	ʃoʃo	soso	soso	grandmother
5	mbirifiri	firifiri	βiriβiri	mbiriβiri	mbereβere	pepper
6	mo:ru	mo:ru	mo:ru	mo:ru	mwe:	bad
7	aneka	aneka	aneka	aneka	aneka	spread out
8	itu:nda	itu:nda	itu:nda	itu:nda	etu:nda	fruit
9	ɲɛki	ɲɛki	ɲɛki	ɲɛki	ɲaki	grass
10	ndinɔhɔ	ndinɔhɔ	ndinɔhɔ	ndinɔ:	erumbwa	snail

show how those allophones form words that are mutually understandable to all speakers of the harmonized language. As a result, the various sounds can be considered to be merely different forms of the same sound.

The data in Table 16.5 show that the differences[8] are minimal and that all these sounds belong to one language. The minor differences evident may be seen as a manifestation of dialectical differences. Furthermore, the differences are predictable depending on the particular dialect used.

Other related languages

There are five other languages that are closely related to Kikuyu. These languages include Kiembu and Kimbeere.[9] The other three are Kikamba, Kimeru and Kitharaka. All these codes fall into what Heine and Mohlig (1980) refer to as the 'Central Kenya Group'. This is Group 3 in their classification where subgroup 3.1 (Kamba-Gikuyu) includes Kikamba, Kiembu, Kikuyu and Chuka.[10] Subgroup 3.2 has the Meru-Tharaka codes which include Kimeru, Igoji Nithi and Tharaka. Classifications by other Bantuists such as Guthrie (1948, 1967/1970/71) and Hinnebusch *et al.* (1981) indicate similar groupings with Guthrie (1967) actually stating that Kikuyu, Kimeru, Kikamba, Kitharaka, Kiembu and Kimbeere all belong to the Central Bantu Group.

Conclusion

This chapter has explored the sound segments of Kikuyu at both the phonetic and orthographic levels of representation. It has shown that the language still has major phonological and orthographical aspects that need to be standardized in order for the written language form to be fully developed. Kikuyu is one of the languages said to be more advanced in terms of academic research and study. It is therefore plausible to state that other Kenyan languages are in dire need of study if written Kikuyu still has the aforementioned shortcomings. One of the shortcomings that have been explored concerns the dropping of the nasal in some cases. This chapter has suggested that this does not seem plausible in Kikuyu and that in fact, the reverse, pre-nasaliztion, is a more natural process in the language. Another problem involves the use of double vowels in orthography. We have suggested that these be used only where a minimal pair can be formed; that is where use of single or double vowels causes a change of meaning in the formed lexical items. The other problem arises from allophony, where a phoneme sounds different depending on speakers without causing a change in meaning. This has been said to be a result of dialectical variances in a language that does not have a standard written form.

Notes

1 However, the fact on the ground is that in most schools Kikuyu is not taught and Kiswahili takes its place; see Piper (2010) for more information and data. This writer participated in this research by Piper and the outcome is heavily relied on below.

2 For more examples of such minimal pairs, see Mutahi (1983: 137).

3 The gist of this exposition has been drawn from Dr Cege Gĩthiora's unpublished manuscript entitled *Kwandĩka* Gĩkũyũ *Kĩega.*

4 It is, however, noted that Wachera (2008: 29–37) deals with the issues of structure and weight of Kikuyu syllables in a more comprehensive manner.

5 This is Kikuyu as spoken in Kiambu and it is referred so by linguists such as Njuguna (1992) although no linguistic justification has been offered for the reference.

6 For example, contrast this with Kiswahili (another Bantu language not too distant from Kikuyu). Iribemwangi (2008: 69–77) identifies nine syllable structures in the language.

7 Most of the data in this table has been picked at random from Mutahi (1983: 267–272). However, the data has been reconfirmed and some of it altered.

8 The sound differences are as stated in Tables 16.1 and 16.2.

9 Some scholars, *inter alia* Mutahi (1983), classify the two as Kikuyu dialects.

10 It is important to note here that presently Chuka is associated more with Kimeru than Kikuyu and is actually identified as a Kimeru dialect.

References

Banda, F. 2002. 'Towards a Standard Bantu Orthography: The Harmonization and Standardization of the Orthographies of Zambian and Malawian Languages', in K.K. Prah (ed), *Writing African: The Harmonization of Orthographic Conventions in African Languages*, pp. 43–54. Cape Town: CASAS.

Crystal, D. 1991. A *Dictionary of Linguistics and Phonetics*, 3rd ed. Oxford: Blackwell.

Gĩthiora, Cege. n.d. *Kwandĩka Gĩkũyũ Kĩega*, Unpublished manuscript.

Guthrie, M. 1948. *The Classification of the Bantu Languages*. London: International African Institute.

———. 1967/1970/71. *Comparative Bantu*, Vols. 1, 2, 3 & 4. Farnborough: International Publishers.

Heine, B. and W. Mohlig. 1980. *Language and Dialect Atlas of Kenya*, Vol. 1. Berlin: Dietrich Reimer Verlag.

Hinnebusch, T., Derek Nurse, and Martin Mould. 1981. *Studies in the Classification of Eastern Bantu Languages* (SUGIA, Sprache und Geschichte in Afrika—Beiheft 3). Hamburg: Helmut Buske Verlag.

Iribemwangi, P.I. 2008. 'A Synchronic Segmental Morphophonology of Standard Kiswahili', Unpublished Ph.D. dissertation, University of Nairobi, Nairobi.

———. 2010. *The Structure of Kiswahili: Sounds, Sound Changes and Words*. Saarbrücken: VDM Verlag.

Katamba, F. 1989. *An Introduction to Phonology*. London: Longman.

Kihara, P.C. 2010. 'A Role and Reference Grammar (RRG) Analysis of the Morphosyntax of the Gikuyu Simple Sentence', Unpublished Ph.D. dissertation, University of Nairobi, Nairobi.

Lewis, M. Paul, (ed). 2009. *Ethnologue: Languages of the World*, 16th ed. Dallas, Texas: SIL International. Retrieved from http://www.ethnologue.com/16.

Mutahi, K.E. 1983. *Sound Change and Classification of the Dialects of Southern Mt. Kenya*. Berlin: Dietrich Reimer Verlag.

Mwangi, J.W. 1992. 'A Typology of Empty Categories (ECs) in Kikuyu', Unpublished MA thesis, University of Nairobi, Nairobi.

Njuguna, M. 1992. 'Mofofonolojia ya Kiswahili Sanifu na Kikuyu Sanifu: Mathalani Kikuyu cha Kabete: Ulinganishi', Unpublished MA thesis, University of Nairobi, Nairobi.

Piper, B. 2010. *Kenya Early Grade Reading Assessment Findings Snapshot*. Research Triangle Park: RTI International. Retrieved 30 December 2011, from http://

www.google.co.ke/#hl=en&site=&q=Kenya+Early+Grade+Reading+Assessment+Findings+Snapshot+july+2010&btnK=Google+Search&oq=&aq=&aqi=&aql=&gs_sm=&gs_upl=&bav=on.2,or.r_gc.r_pw.,cf.osb&fp=afde180cc1d684a&biw=1024&bih=551.

Wachera, S. K. 2008. 'Tone as a Distinctive Feature in the Lexicon of Gi-Gichugu Dialect, Gikuyu language', Unpublished MA thesis, University of Nairobi, Nairobi.

17 Endangered!

The Igbo language dilemma in Nigeria

Chinenye Nwabueze and Ezinwanne Okoli

Uses and gratifications of English and Igbo language programmes among radio listeners in Awka metropolis

Introduction

Communication is the cord that binds any society. It lubricates the existence and coexistence of people within and across cultures. Language is the channel through which communication activities – sharing of ideas and information, value exchange and others – are conveyed. Language is to communication what blood is to the human being. Odinye and Odinye (2010) write that man is incomplete without language and that language is an indispensable tool for human communication and national development. It is the medium through which a people's identity is expressed. It is part of a people's culture.

Toure (cited by Omego 2007: 16) notes that language constitutes the basis of a people's personality and if people renounce the use of their language it is doomed to stagnation, retrogression and possibly, extinction. Language is a very important tool for thinking and concept formation (Okoye 2007: 79). 'It is the key to the heart of the people. If we lose the key, we lose the people' (Nwadike 2008 cited by Odinye and Odinye 2010: 1). The indispensability of language in communication and, indeed, in the life of man is not in doubt. Igbo is a language spoken by people in the south-eastern states of Nigeria – Enugu, Ebonyi, Anambra, Imo and Abia – and some parts of Rivers and Delta states. It is one of the three constitutionally recognized major languages in Nigeria (the others being Hausa and Yoruba). It is a language generally believed by Nigerians, including some Igbos, to be endangered largely due to a declining level of acceptability and usage of the language by Igbo people.

This perception received credence from the forecast of UNESCO on endangered indigenous languages in the world which listed Igbo as one of the languages at risk of possible extinction in the next 50 years if nothing was done to reverse the level of decline (Odinye and Odinye 2010).

Unlike the other two major Nigerian languages (Hausa and Yoruba) which are enjoying a level of development and acceptability, the Igbo language is grossly threatened by the official foreign language in the country – English. Igbo-speaking people are said to prefer and communicate more in English than in Igbo language, when compared with the attitude of Yoruba- and Hausa-speaking people to their language. After a study of language shift among Igbo-English bilinguals, Njemanze (2007) found that whereas a greater percentage of parents and spouses communicate more in Igbo than in English among themselves, children, and grandchildren communicate more in English than in Igbo language and Igbos communicate more in English language among themselves in the workplace than in Igbo language.

This study sets out to ascertain whether the perceived declining level of acceptability of Igbo language or preference for English over the Igbo language is reflected in audience exposure and preference for Igbo and English language programmes. Since research evidence has shown that broadcasting, particularly radio, is most effective in transferring information on social change programmes from government and other institutions to the masses living in developing nations of the world (Nwuneli 1985), language is therefore an intrinsic part of goal-oriented development communication.

Igbo and English language programmes are aired by broadcast stations in the south-east geopolitical zone and some other parts of the country. These indigenous language programmes assist in localizing broadcast media content for audience consumption, especially with a view to adapting broadcast media content with local audience. This work is a media use study which seeks to examine the exposure to and uses of Igbo and English language programmes by Igbo-English bilingual audiences of Purity FM (radio) Awka who reside in Awka metropolis.

The problem

The audiences in the south-east geopolitical zone are exposed to different programmes packaged in English and Igbo languages. Emphasis is not only on the exposure to those programmes, but also more on their consumption. Someone could be exposed to a programme without a prior motive of satisfying a need.

However, there must be a reason why audiences willingly expose themselves to certain programmes and as well make use of certain programmes, whether packaged in English or Igbo. It could either be to gratify a need or as a habit. It could also be as a result of the language used in packaging a specific programme.

This study therefore seeks to determine the level of exposure to English and Igbo language programmes on radio by the audience, including gratifications derived from such programmes. This is against the backdrop of research findings showing a preference for English language more than Igbo language by Igbo-English bilinguals (Njemanze, 2007; Odinye and Odinye, 2010). Could it be said that the perceived preference for English language by Igbo-English bilinguals is also reflected in their preference and exposure to English and Igbo programmes on radio? This is what this study basically seeks to ascertain.

Research questions

The following questions guided this study:

1. What is the level of audience exposure to English and Igbo language programmes on radio?
2. What are the gratifications the audience derive from English and Igbo programmes on radio?
3. Is there a relationship between ages of respondents and their level of exposure to English and Igbo programmes?
4. Is there a relationship between respondents' level of education and their level of exposure to English and Igbo programmes?

Research hypotheses

The study tested the following hypotheses:

H_{01}: There is no significant relationship between respondents' level of education and their level of exposure to Igbo programmes on radio.

H_{02}: There is no significant difference between young and old adults' level of exposure to Igbo programmes on radio.

Theoretical framework: uses and gratifications theory

The uses and gratifications theory says that the audience's media use is based on certain satisfaction, needs, wishes or motives. These needs primarily include those for information, relaxation, companionship, diversion or escape (McQuail 2005). Marghalani *et al.* (1998) observe that the uses and gratifications approach depicts the audiences as the primary elements in understanding the mass communication process. They further note that it presents a coherent explanation of how the audience actively use the media to gratify their own needs and motivations.

McQuail (2005: 424) lists the basic assumption of the uses and gratifications approach which according to him was rediscovered and elaborated in the 1960s and 1970s as follows:

- Media and content choice is generally rational and directed towards certain specific goals and satisfactions (thus the audience is active and audience formation can be logically explained).
- Audience members are conscious of the media-related needs which arise in personal (individual) and social (shared) circumstances and can voice these in terms of motivations.
- Broadly speaking, personal utility is a more significant determinant of audience formation than aesthetic or cultural factors.
- All or most of the relevant factors for audience formation (motives, perceived or obtained satisfactions, media choices, background variables) can, in principle, be measured.

The uses and gratifications theory would help in understanding what motivates exposure to English and Igbo programmes on Purity FM by audiences in Awka, Anambra State.

Understanding degrees of language endangerment: where does the Igbo language fall?

Language endangerment simply talks about the possibility of a language going into partial or total extinction. It is either that the language is spoken by a very negligible number of persons as opposed to the relatively large number that used to speak it, or that the language is no longer spoken by any person especially as a daily means of communication.

Odinye and Odinye (2010) define language endangerment as a condition whereby the socio-economic, political, technological, cultural and religious ecologies have altered to a point where some language species cannot survive or thrive in them. Odinye and Odinye, citing Aikawa in UNESCO (2001), further list six degrees of endangerment with regard to intergenerational language transmission as follows:

1 Extinct: When there is no one who can speak or remember the language.
2 Critically endangered: Where the youngest speakers of the language are in the great–grandparents' generation and the language is not used for everyday interactions.
3 Severely endangered: Where the language is spoken only by grandparents and other generations. While the parents' generation may still understand the language, they typically do not speak it to their children or among themselves.
4 Definitely endangered: Where the language is not learnt as the mother tongue by children in the home. Though the parents speak the language to their children, these children would not respond in that language.
5 Unsafe: Where most children speak their parental language as their first language but this may be restricted to specific social domains such as the home where children interact with their parents and grandparents.
6 Safe: Where the language is spoken by all generations (parents and children) with uninterrupted intergenerational transmission of the language (Odinye and Odinye 2010).

Brenzinger and de Graaf (2012) write that a language is in danger when its speakers no longer pass it onto the next generation. They further observe that such endangerment may be caused primarily by a combination of certain external and internal forces – external forces such as military, economic, religious, cultural or educational subjugation; internal forces such as a community's negative attitude towards its own language or by a general decline of group identity. Internal pressures often derive from external pressures and they jointly halt the intergenerational transmission of linguistic and cultural traditions.

While stressing the significance of ecological factors in bringing about language endangerment, Grenoble and Whaley (1998) cited by Mufwene (2003) write that speakers abandon their native tongue in adaptation to an environment where use of that language is no longer advantageous to them. This shows how different ecological factors are weighted relative to each other and further point out the greater significance of socio-economic factors in language endangerment.

Available statistical data related to language use illustrate the extent of the problem of language endangerment across the globe. About 97 per cent of the world's people speak about 4 per cent of the world's languages; and conversely, about 96 per cent of the world's languages are spoken by about 3 per cent of the world's people (cited in Brenzinger and de Graaf 2012). Approximately 85 per cent of the almost 7,000 languages of the world are spoken in only 22 countries. According to Brenzinger and de Graaf, some of these countries are home to large numbers of different languages: Papua New Guinea (almost 900 languages), Indonesia (almost 700), Nigeria (about 500), India (almost 400), Cameroon (almost 300), Mexico (almost 250), Zaire (about 200) and Brazil (above 200).

With specific reference to the Igbo language, the degree of endangerment of this language could be explained using the degrees of language endangerment given earlier in this section. Odinye and Odinye (2010) say that the degree of Igbo language endangerment is in between 'Definitely Endangered' and 'Unsafe'. They buttress their point by observing that 50 per cent of Igbo children cannot speak the Igbo language and most parents (not every parent, as they wrote) encourage their children to speak English.

Odinye and Odinye further write that speaking of Igbo language is not encouraged anywhere in Igbo land – schools, churches, meetings, campaigns, conversations and homes. This observation may be too extreme, harsh and not entirely true. The trend has changed probably because Igbos are beginning to realize that their language is endangered, especially by one of the major 'killer' languages – English. Today, some states in Igbo land (south-east Nigeria) have a day officially set aside for speaking of Igbo language in offices and schools and wearing traditional Igbo clothes. Some of the states are Anambra, Abia and Imo. Some Igbo-speaking parents (though very few) attempt to speak Igbo to their children who, of course, are often encouraged to reply in English. But the direction still tends towards gradually shoving aside of the Igbo language by the English language especially among children of Igbo parents in contemporary society.

Radio programmes and the promotion of the Igbo language

Programming basically means determining what programmes to put on air and at what points in the programme schedule (Chester *et al.* 1978: 49, cited in Agbanu and Nwammuo 2009: 160). It is a decision-making process concerning the purpose, arrangement and content of all the programmes of a broadcasting station. Large audiences are won by a radio or television station through its programming, likewise, advertisers.

Programming is a serious venture that deals with searching out and acquiring programme materials and planning a coherent sequence. Programming, according to Agbanu and Nwammuo (2009: 160), involves not only choosing programmes and scheduling them in a meaningful order but also the evaluation of the degree of success or failure of the programmes.

Dunu defines programming as 'the determination of a particular programme type that will run in a broadcast channel. It entails the search and selection of quality and appropriate programme materials that best suit a homogeneous pre-determined target audience' (2002: 136). As a product of broadcasting, programming is the strategic design and act of selecting programme materials and the placement of such programme content or items (scheduling) at a particular period on the air which is suitable to a particular segment of a predefined audience.

The importance of programming is not just the placement of these programmes on air, but it is also the capability of such placement to factor in the nature of its target audience. For example, placing/scheduling 'Kiddies Corner' programme by 10 am Monday morning when children (target audience) are in school. Thus, even when such programmes may appeal to the audience, poor/wrong programming may prompt them to tune to other stations whose programming appeals to their working nature or daily activities.

Igbo language programmes could serve as channels for popularizing the Igbo language. Since radio is unarguably one of the most common channels of information dissemination especially in developing nations, the use of Igbo language programmes to encourage Igbo language use in daily communication could be effective. Igbo language programmes have to be interesting and should be scheduled to reach specific target audiences for such programmes to attract and keep a large audience. Such programmes should encourage Igbo-speaking people to develop positive attitudes towards their language.

Negative attitudes towards a language have been identified as one of the basic internal factors responsible for language endangerment (Odinye and Odinye 2010; Brenzinger and de Graaf 2012). Interesting Igbo language programmes rightly scheduled could make more speakers of the language want to associate with and speak the language (though there may be need for empirical studies to determine if a significant relationship exists between exposure to Igbo language and willingness to speak the language). What this study dwelt on was determining exposure and preference of Igbo language programmes by Igbo-speaking audiences in south-eastern Nigeria. Do these people prefer English language programmes to Igbo language programmes? If yes, what reasons could be responsible for this development?

Methodology

The survey research method was used in studying radio listeners in Awka South metropolitan area of Anambra State, south-east Nigeria. A structured questionnaire was self-administered by 384 respondents, while the interview and discussion group techniques were used to elicit data from another 30 Igbo-English bilinguals who also listen to radio programmes.

The survey method was adopted because the researcher was interested in finding out the preference and patterns of exposure of respondents to English and Igbo programmes aired on Purity FM, Awka. The population of this study consisted of listeners of Purity FM Awka, in Awka South metropolis. Since the exact population of listeners of Purity FM Awka in Awka South metropolis was not available, the population of Awka South local government area was used to arrive at a sample size. According to the National Population Census official *Gazette* (2006: B180), the population of Awka South is 189,049.

Having considered the population of the study, a sample size of 384 was arrived at using a sample size determination table by Cozby (2004: 130). According to Cozby, if the size of population is over 100,000, the sample size should be 384. Out of the ten communities that make up Awka South metropolis, the researcher selected five densely populated communities, using discretion. They are as follows: Agu-Oka (70), Amawbia (60), Awka (120), Nibo (64) and Okpuno (70). Purposive sampling technique was used in this work to ensure that respondents are those exposed to English and Igbo programmes on Purity FM, Awka.

The interview technique was also adopted to provide an opportunity for respondents to freely discuss their views on Igbo language endangerment and preference for English language programmes to Igbo Language programmes or vice versa. Some respondents were interviewed one-on-one, while the majority was engaged in group discussion which included discussions on how to move the language forward and possibly get the language out of the list of endangered languages of the earth.

Results

The first phase of the study involved the distribution of copies of a structured questionnaire to 384 respondents, while the second phase involved the interview and group discussion techniques. The result of the first phase would be presented first.

Out of the 384 copies of the questionnaire distributed, none was lost or found unusable because the researcher distributed them on a face-to-face basis and collected them from respondents. Demographic data of respondents show that female respondents dominated the sample by 210 accounting for 54.7 per cent, while male respondents were 174, representing 45.3.

The respondents cut across diverse age groups. Many of them were aged between 18 and 25 years old (140) representing 36.5 per cent; 32 per cent (123) of the respondents said they were 26–35 years old. The age group 36–45years old accounted for 17.7 per cent (68) of the respondents. The respondents who fall between the age bracket of 46 years old and above were 13.8 per cent (53).

On the marital status of the respondents, the data indicate that 40.4 per cent (155) were married, while 59.6 per cent (229) were still single. The data on the level of education of the respondents indicate that 61.7 per cent (237) attended a higher institution. This was followed by those who attended post-primary school (92), accounting for 24 per cent. Next were those who attended primary school (17), representing 4.4 per cent. Then finally, those who had no formal education (38), representing 9.9 per cent.

Answers to research questions

Research question one

What is the level of audience exposure to English and Igbo language programmes on radio?

Number 5 of the questionnaire copy provides the answer to research question one.

Data collected and shown in Table 17.1 indicated that 39.1 per cent (150) of the respondents are exposed to Igbo programmes on Purity FM Awka at the interval of 1 hour and below; 30.2 per cent (116) of the respondents are exposed to Igbo programmes on Purity FM at the interval of 2–3 hours in a day; 18.2 per cent (70) of the respondents said they are

Table 17.1 Respondents' level of exposure to Igbo programmes on Purity FM, Awka

Responses	*Frequency*	*Percentage*
1 hour and below	150	39.1
2–3 hours	116	30.2
4–5 hours	70	18.2
6 hours and above	48	12.5
Total	384	100

Source: Field Survey 2010.

exposed to Igbo programmes on Purity FM at the interval of 4–5 hours in a day while 12.5 per cent (48) of the respondents are exposed to Igbo programmes on Purity FM Awka at the interval of 6 hours and above. This shows that greater percentages of the respondents (39.1) are exposed to Igbo programmes on Purity FM at the interval of 1 hour and below.

Data further showed that the majority of the respondents were exposed to English programmes for over 4 hours and above (4–5 hours: 190 respondents; 6 hours and above: 98 respondents, giving 75 per cent of total number of respondents). The remaining respondents were exposed to English programmes for 3 hours or below. This shows that most respondents were heavy listeners of English programmes on radio.

Research question two

What are the gratifications the audience derive from English and Igbo programmes on radio? Numbers 11 and 12 of the questionnaire copy provides the answer to research question two.

Data in Table 17.2 show that the majority of the respondents, accounting for 46.6 per cent (179), listen to English programmes on Purity FM Awka because they are interesting; 15.4 per cent (59) of the respondents were motivated to listen to English programmes aired on Purity FM Awka because of the good quality of production; 7.8 per cent (30) of respondents said they expose themselves to English programmes on Purity FM because English programme presenters are more informed than Igbo programme presenters; 15.9 per cent (61) of the respondents said they listen to English programmes on Purity FM because they understand programmes in English more than Igbo programmes; 14.3 per cent (55) of the respondents listen to English programmes because of the time they were scheduled.

Table 17.2 The gratifications the respondents derive from English programmes on Purity FM Awka

Responses	*Frequency*	*Percentage*
Because it is interesting	179	46.6
Because of the good quality of production	59	15.4
Because English programme presenters are more informed than Igbo programme presenters	30	7.8
Because I understand programmes in English more than Igbo programmes	61	15.9
Because the times English programmes are scheduled are convenient for me	55	14.3
Total	384	100

Source: Field Survey 2010.

Table 17.3 The gratifications the audience derives from Igbo programmes on Purity FM Awka

Response0073	*Frequency*	*Percentage*
Because of it is interesting	161	41.9
Because of the good quality of production	72	18.8
Because Igbo programme presenters are more informed than English programme presenters	25	6.5
Because I understand programmes in Igbo more than English programmes	42	10.9
Because the times Igbo programmes are scheduled are convenient for me	84	21.9
Total	384	100

Source: Field Survey 2010.

Data presented in Table 17.3 show that the majority of the respondents, 41.9 per cent (161), who listen to Igbo programmes on Purity FM Awka did so because the programmes are interesting; 18.8 per cent (72) of the respondents were motivated to listen to Igbo programmes aired on Purity FM because of the good quality of production; 6.5 per cent (25) of the respondents said they expose themselves to Igbo programmes on

Purity FM because Igbo programme presenters are more informed than English programme presenters; 10.9 per cent (42) of the respondents said they listen to Igbo programmes on Purity FM because they understand programmes in Igbo more than English programmes; 21.9 per cent (84) of the respondents listen to Igbo programmes because the times they were scheduled are convenient for them.

What this finding is saying is that the drive to listen to Igbo programmes is basically premised on how interesting the programme is. Though respondents may listen more to English programmes than Igbo programmes, when they listen to Igbo programmes they do so primarily because such programmes are interesting. However, the oral interview sessions revealed that FM radio stations lacked interesting Igbo programmes according to respondents. Most of the interviewees said Igbo programmes were boring and drab in presentation, mostly involving reading out of request cards sent in by some listeners.

Research question three

Is there a relationship between the ages of respondents and their level of exposure to English and Igbo programmes? Numbers 2, 7 and 8 of the questionnaire copy provide answers to research question three.

According to Table 17.4, 31.4 per cent (44) of the respondents in age group 18–25 years old are exposed to English programmes on Purity FM Awka at the interval of 1 hour and below; 33.6 per cent (47) of the respondents in age group 18–25 years old are exposed to English

Table 17.4 Relationship between the age of respondents and their level of exposure to English programmes

	Level of exposure					
Age group	*1 hour and below*	*2–3 hours*	*4–5 hours*	*6 hours and above*	*Total*	*Percentage*
18–25	44 (31.4%)	47 (33.6%)	23 (16.4%)	26 (18.6%)	140	100
26–35	40 (32.5%)	41 (33.3%)	22 (17.9%)	20 (16.3%)	123	100
36–45	29 (42.6%)	23 (33.8%)	8 (11.8%)	8 (11.8%)	68	100
46 and above	24 (45.3%)	15 (28.3%)	7 (13.2%)	7 (13.2%)	53	100
Total	137	128	60	61	384	100

Source: Field Survey 2010.

programmes at the interval of 2–3 hours in a day; 16.4 per cent (23) of the respondents in age bracket 18–25 years old are exposed to English programmes on Purity FM at the interval of 4–5 hours in a day; 18.6 per cent (26) of the respondents in age bracket 18–25 years old are exposed to English programmes on Purity FM Awka at the interval of 6 hours and above.

Then, 32.5 per cent (40) of the respondents in age group 26–35 years old are exposed to English programmes on Purity FM Awka at the interval of 1 hour and below; 33.3 per cent (41) of the respondents in age bracket 26–35 years old are exposed to English programmes at the interval of 2–3 hours in a day; 17.9 per cent (22) of the respondents, in age bracket 26–35 years old are exposed to English programmes on Purity FM at the interval of 4–5 hours in a day; 16.3 per cent (20) of the respondents in age group 26–35 years old are exposed to English programmes on Purity FM Awka at the interval of 6 hours and above.

In the age bracket 36–45 years old, 42.6 per cent (29) per cent of the respondents are exposed to English programmes on Purity FM Awka at the interval of 1 hour and below; 33.8 per cent (23) of the respondents are exposed to English programmes on Purity FM at the interval of 2–3 hours in a day; 11.8 per cent (8) are exposed to the programmes at the interval 4–5 hours in a day, while 11.8 per cent (8) of the respondents are exposed to English programmes aired on Purity FM Awka at the interval of 6 hours and above.

In the age group, 46 years old and above, 45.3 per cent (24) of the respondents are exposed to English programmes on Purity FM Awka at the interval of 1 hour and below; 28.3 per cent (15) are exposed to English programmes at the interval of 2–3 hours; 13.2 per cent (7) of the respondents are exposed to English programmes on Purity FM at the interval of 4–5 hours in a day; 13.2 per cent (7) of the respondents are exposed to English programmes on Purity FM Awka at the interval of 6 hours and above.

This shows that a greater number of the respondents 47 (33.6%) in age group 18–25 years old are exposed to English programmes more at the interval of 2–3 hours in a day.

According to Table 17.5, in the age group 18–25 years old, 54.3 per cent (76) of the respondents are exposed to Igbo programmes on Purity FM Awka at the interval of 1 hour and below; 23.6 per cent (33) of the respondents are exposed to Igbo programmes at the interval of 2–3 hours in a day; 11.4 per cent (16) are exposed to Igbo programmes at the interval of 4–5 hours in a day; 10.7 per cent (15) of the respondents in the

Table 17.5 Relationship between the age of respondents and their level of exposure to Igbo programmes

	Level of exposure					
Age group	*1 hour and below*	*2–3 hours*	*4–5 hours*	*6 hours and above*	*Total*	*Percentage*
18–25	76 (54.3%)	33 (23.6%)	16 (11.4%)	15 (10.7%)	140	100
26–35	66 (53.7%)	28 (22.8%)	18 (14.6%)	11 (8.9%)	123	100
36–45	28 (41.1%)	27 (39.7%)	8 (11.8%)	5 (7.4%)	68	100
46 and above	24 (45.3%)	15 (28.3%)	9 (17%)	5 (9.4%)	53	100
Total	194	103	51	36	384	

Source: Field Survey 2010.

same age group 18–25 years old expose themselves to Igbo programmes on Purity FM Awka at the interval of 6 hours and above.

In the age bracket 26–35 years old, 53.7 per cent (66) of the respondents are exposed to Igbo programmes on Purity FM Awka, at the interval of 1 hour and below; 22.8 per cent (28) of the respondents in the same age group 26–35 years old are exposed to Igbo programmes on Purity FM Awka at the interval of 2–3 hours in a day; 14.6 per cent (18) of the respondents are exposed to Igbo programmes at the interval of 4–5 hours; 8.9 per cent (11) of the respondents are exposed to Igbo programmes on Purity FM at the interval of 6 hours and above.

In the age group 36–45 years old, 41.1 per cent (28) of the respondents are exposed to Igbo programmes on Purity FM Awka at the interval of 1 hour and below; 39.7 per cent (27) of the respondents are exposed to Igbo programmes at the interval of 2–3 hours in a day; 11.8 per cent (8) of the respondents are exposed to Igbo programmes on Purity FM at the interval of 4–5 hours in a day; 7.4 per cent (5) of the respondents are exposed to Igbo programmes on Purity FM at the interval of 6 hours and above.

In the age group 46 years and above, 45.3 per cent (24) of the respondents are exposed to Igbo programmes on Purity FM Awka at the interval of 1 hour and below; 28.3 per cent (15) of the respondents are exposed to Igbo programmes at the interval of 2–3 hours in a day; 17 per cent (9) of the respondents are exposed to Igbo programmes on Purity FM at the interval of 4–5 hours in a day; 9.4 per cent (5) of the respondents in the same age group 46 years old and above are exposed to Igbo programmes on Purity FM Awka at the interval of 6 hours and above in a day.

This shows that greater percentage of the respondents, accounting for 54.3 per cent (76) in the age group 18–25 years old, are exposed to Igbo programmes more at the interval of 1 hour and below. This means young adults (18–25 years) are light listeners of Igbo language programmes.

Research question four

Is there a relationship between respondents' level of education and their level of exposure to English and Igbo programmes? Numbers 4, 7 and 8 of the questionnaire copy provide answers to research question four.

According to Table 17.6, 41.2 per cent (7) of the respondents that had primary education are exposed to English programmes on Purity FM Awka at the interval of 1 hour and below; 29.4 per cent (5) of the respondents in the same category are exposed to English programmes on Purity FM Awka at the interval of 2–3 hours in a day ; 11.8 per cent (2) of the respondents are exposed to English programmes on Purity FM Awka at the interval of 4–5 hours in a day, while 17.6 per cent (3) of the respondents that only had primary education said they are exposed to English programmes on Purity FM Awka at the interval of 6 hours and above.

According to the data on respondents that only had post-primary education, 31.5 per cent (29) are exposed to English programmes on Purity FM Awka at the interval of 1 hour and below; 37 per cent (34) of the respondents are exposed to English programmes on Purity FM at the interval of 2–3 hours in a day; 14.1 per cent (13) of the respondents are

Table 17.6 Relationship between respondents' level of education and level of exposure to English programmes

	Level of exposure					
Education	*1 hour and below*	*2–3 hours*	*4–5 hours*	*6 hours and above*	*Total*	*Percentage*
Primary	7 (41.2)	5 (29.4)	2 (11.8)	3 (17.6)	17	100
Post-primary	29 (31.5)	34 (37)	13 (14.1)	16 (17.4)	92	100
Tertiary	89 (37.6)	76 (32)	35 (14.8)	37 (15.6)	237	100
No formal education	19 (50)	8 (21.1)	7 (18.4)	4 (10.5)	38	100
Total	144	123	57	60	384	

Source: Field Survey 2010.

exposed to English programmes at the interval of 4–5 hours in a day; 17.4 per cent (16) of the respondents are exposed to English programmes on Purity FM at the interval of 6 hours and above.

According to the data on respondents that had tertiary education, 37.6 per cent (89) are exposed to English programmes on Purity FM Awka at the interval of 1 hour and below; 32 per cent (76) of the respondents are exposed to English programmes on Purity FM Awka at the interval of 2–3 hours in a day; 14.8 per cent (35) are exposed to English programmes at the interval of 4–5 hours in a day; 15.6 per cent (37) are exposed to English programmes on Purity FM Awka at the interval of 6 hours and above.

Then, 50 per cent (19) of the respondents that had no formal education are exposed to English programmes on Purity FM Awka at the interval of 1 hour and below; 21.1 per cent (8) of the respondents who had no formal education are exposed to English programmes on Purity FM at the interval of 2–3 hours in a day; 18.4 per cent (7) of the respondents in the same category said they are exposed to English programmes on Purity FM at the interval of 4–5 hours in a day while 10.5 per cent (4) of the respondents that had no formal education are exposed to English programmes on Purity FM Awka, at the interval of 6 hours and above.

Data in Table 17.7 show that 29.4 per cent (5) of the respondents that only had primary education are exposed to Igbo programmes on Purity FM Awka at the interval of 1 hour and below; 35.2 per cent (6) of the respondents that only had primary education are exposed to Igbo programmes on Purity FM at the interval of 2–3 hours in a day; 17.7 per cent

Table 17.7 Relationship between respondents' level of education and level of exposure to Igbo programmes

	Level of exposure					
Education	*1 hour and below*	*2–3 hours*	*4–5 hours*	*6 hours and above*	*Total*	*Percentage*
Primary	5 (29.4)	6 (35.2)	3 (17.7)	3 (17.7)	17	100
Post-primary	34 (37)	21 (22.8)	25 (27.2)	12 (13)	92	100
Tertiary	143 60.3)	63 (26.6)	16 (6.8)	15 (6.3)	237	100
No formal education	11 (29)	13 (34.2)	8 (21)	6 (15.8)	38	100
Total	193	103	52	36	384	

Source: Field Survey 2010.

(3) of the respondents in the same category said they are exposed to Igbo programmes on Purity FM at the interval of 4–5 hours in a day; then 17.7 per cent (3) of the respondents are exposed to Igbo programmes on Purity FM Awka at the interval of 6 hours and above.

According to the data on respondents under post-primary education in the preceding table, 37 per cent (34) are exposed to Igbo programmes on Purity FM Awka at the interval of 1 hour and below; 22.8 per cent (21) are exposed to Igbo programmes at the interval of 2–3 hours in a day; 27.2 per cent (25) of the respondents said they are exposed to Igbo programmes on Purity FM at the interval of 4–5 hours in day while 13 per cent (12) of the respondents are exposed to Igbo programmes on Purity FM Awka at the interval of 6 hours and above.

According to the data under tertiary education, 60.3 per cent (143) of the respondents are exposed to Igbo programmes on Purity FM Awka at the interval of 1 hour and below; 26.6 per cent (63) are exposed to Igbo programmes on Purity FM at the interval of 2–3 hours in a day; 6.8 per cent (16) of the respondents are exposed to Igbo programmes on Purity FM Awka at the interval of 4–5 hours in a day while 6.3 per cent (15) of the respondents said they are exposed to Igbo programmes on Purity FM Awka at the interval of 6 hours and above.

According to the data of respondents under the category of no formal education, 29 per cent (11) are exposed to Igbo programmes on Purity FM Awka at the interval of 1hour and below; 34.2 per cent (13) said they are exposed to Igbo programmes at the interval of 2–3 hours in a day; 21 per cent (8) of the respondents are exposed to Igbo programmes on Purity FM at the interval of 4–5 hours in a day; 15.8 per cent (6) are exposed to Igbo programmes on Purity FM at the interval of 6 hours and above.

This shows that a greater percentage of the respondents accounting for 60.3 per cent (143) in the category of tertiary education are exposed to Igbo programmes on Purity FM at the interval of 1hour and below. This shows they are mostly light listeners of Igbo programmes.

Test of hypotheses

Two hypotheses were tested in this study and the results are presented.

Hypothesis one

H_0: There is no significant relationship between respondents' level of education and their level of exposure to Igbo programmes on radio.

H_2: There is a significant relationship between respondents' level of education and their level of exposure to Igbo programmes on radio.

Table 17.8 Summary of chi-square test analysis of relationship between respondents' level of education and their level of exposure to Igbo programmes on radio

	Level of exposure									
Education	*1 hour and below*	*2–3 hours*	*4–5 hours*	*6 hours and above*	*df*	A	X^2*cal*	X^2*tab*	*Decislon*	*Remarks*
Primary	5	6	3	3	9	0.05	43.47	14.68	Null hypothesis rejected	Hypothesis significant
Post-primary	34	21	25	12						
Tertiary	143	63	16	15						
No formal education	11	13	8	6						

In testing this hypothesis, the chi-square test of independence was used. Degree of freedom (df) for the chi-square test of independence is calculated as follows:

df = (4–1) (4–1)
df = 3 × 3
df = 9
Alpha level significance = 0.05
X^2tab = 14.68

The decision rule states that if the chi-square calculated value is greater than or equal to the chi-square table value, reject the null hypothesis, otherwise do not reject. Since the calculated value of chi-square (43.47) is greater than the chi-square table value (14.68), we reject the null hypothesis.

The conclusion is that there is a significant relationship between respondents' level of education and their level of exposure to Igbo programmes on radio.

Hypothesis two

H_0: There is no significant difference between young and old adults' level of exposure to Igbo programmes on radio.

H_2: There is a significant difference between young and old adults' level of exposure to Igbo programmes on radio.

Table 17.9 Summary of *t*-test computation showing relationship between young and old adults' level of exposure to Igbo programmes on radio

Subject	*N*	*X*	*STE*	*A*	*df*	*t-cal*	*t-crit*	*Decision*	*Remarks*
Young adults	4	65.8	49.4	0.05	6	0.72	2.447	Null hypothesis accepted	Hypothesis not significant
Old adults	4	30.3							

In testing this hypothesis, *t*-test for an unrelated independent sample was used. The degree of freedom (df) for *t*-test unrelated independent sample is calculated as follows:

df = 4+4+2
df = 8–2
df = 6
Alpha level of significance = 0.05
t-tab = 2.447.

The decision rule states that if the calculated *t*-value is greater than or equal to the table *t*-value, reject the null hypothesis (H_0), otherwise do not reject.

Therefore, since our calculated *t*-value (0.72) is less than the table or critical *t*-value (2.447) we do not reject our null hypothesis (H_0) but accept it. The conclusion is that there is no significant difference between young and old adults' level of exposure to Igbo programmes on radio.

Discussion of findings

The findings show that the English and Igbo programmes aired on Purity FM Awka are relevant to residents of Awka metropolis, and they listen to certain progammes in order to fulfil specific gratifications. The findings showed that a greater percentage of the audience (75%) listened to English programmes for a higher number of hours (over 4 hours in a day) than Igbo programmes. It was discovered that some residents of Awka metropolis are exposed to English and Igbo programmes because of the good quality of production while some are exposed to the programmes because of the time they were scheduled. These observations go in line with what McQuail (2005: 430) said, that the media system, timing and presentation influence media content choice. McQuail opines that preferences and choices are influenced by the make-up of the media system and also the specific strategies of timing, scheduling, placement content as well as the media message design. This shows that programming is inevitable for the success of any programme.

Data from the group discussion revealed that respondents preferred English language programmes to Igbo language programmes because the English language programmes were more interesting and creative. According to one of the interviewees, 'The problem is not peculiar to Purity FM. In most FM stations, Igbo programmes are boring. They are not exciting and such programmes cannot attract attention of serious listeners who value their time'. This is a wake-up call to radio programme producers especially in Igbo-speaking areas of Nigeria. Igbo programmes should be made interesting to attract audience attention.

It was also found that residents of Awka metropolis choose certain programmes in order to satisfy their entertainment needs. This finding supports what Ojobor (2002: 20) said, namely that the uses and gratifications theory emphasizes audience needs as excitement, guidance, relaxation, tension release, identity, socialization and information acquisition. This is also in line with the postulation by Herzog (1944) cited by Wimmer and Dominick (2003: 404), who identified three types of gratification associated with listening to radio soap operas as emotional release, wishful thinking and obtaining advice. Igbo programme producers need to factor in these gratifications in their productions.

In this study, two hypotheses were tested to allow the researchers to arrive at authoritative empirical conclusions. The first hypothesis was tested to ascertain whether there is a relationship between respondents' level of education and their level of exposure to Igbo programmes. The null hypothesis was rejected. It was discovered that respondents' level of education affects their level of exposure to Igbo programmes. Thus, the people who had no formal education or did not proceed beyond the primary or post-primary level tend to expose themselves more to their indigenous (Igbo) language programmes. This could be because most of them understand Igbo programmes more than English programmes. Also, during the group discussion sessions, it was discovered that those who said they preferred listening to Igbo programmes more than English programmes were mostly those with little or no formal education. These respondents who preferred listening to Igbo programmes more than English programmes, however, observed that there were more English programmes than Igbo programmes on most FM radio stations. They called for more local language programmes on FM stations to encourage interest in the language. Most privately owned radio stations in Nigeria run most of their programmes in English; a good number do not even have any local language programme. This is not a good development in view of the need to encourage people to speak their local languages. This is in line with what Miller and Philo (2010: 2) said, namely, that a text will mean completely different things to different audiences, which could perhaps happen if the audience literally doesn't speak the language of the message, or if there are radical cultural differences between those who produce the message and those who receive it.

The second hypothesis was tested to ascertain whether there is a significant difference between young and old adults' level of exposure to Igbo programmes. The null hypothesis was accepted. The researcher discovered that there was no significant difference between young and old adults' level of exposure to Igbo programmes.

Though the survey research showed that a slightly higher proportion of young adults (aged between 18 and 35 years) were exposed to the English language than to the Igbo language, the hypothesis test showed that the difference was not significant. This means both young and old adults had more interest in English language programmes than Igbo language programmes, though the older adults encouraged exposure to Igbo programmes. The older adults said in the discussion sessions that there was need to encourage people to associate with and speak the Igbo language through production of more interesting Igbo language programmes.

Conclusion

Based on the findings of this study, it could be concluded that there is a preference for English language programmes to Igbo language programmes by radio audiences in the south-east zone of Nigeria. Both young and old adults (i.e. English–Igbo bilinguals) are exposed more to English language programmes on radio than Igbo language programmes. However, people who have less education (having little or no formal education) expose themselves more to Igbo language programmes than English language programmes. The general observation from the study revealed a preference for English language programmes over Igbo language programmes, thus confirming the observation by Odinye and Odinye (2010) that there is a dwindling interest in Igbo language. The broadcast media (both radio and television) ought to play more functional roles in encouraging interest in Igbo language. The recommendations in this study are made along this line.

Recommendations

Broadcast media in Nigeria should carry out research before conceptualizing any programme. This would lead to the conceptualization of better and relevant programmes that reflect the trends of the contemporary world. It would also ensure that programmes are packaged in the most appropriate language that would ease message assimilation by the audience. Preference should be given to the airing of entertaining programmes. However, this should not be done at the expense of informative and educative programmes.

Radio stations in the eastern region of Nigeria should allocate more time to the Igbo programmes that border on culture and arts. This would help in the transmission of cultural heritage. Programming should also involve research. The working nature of the audience should be considered so as to schedule programmes at convenient times for the target audience. Research should be carried out to determine the type of Igbo programmes that would appeal to a greater number of English-Igbo bilinguals and such programmes should be given priority in scheduling.

Radio stations in the eastern region should create a forum for the teaching of Igbo language on radio for the benefit of the younger generation and the foreigners who do not understand Igbo language. Similar studies on local language programmes should be carried out in other states and among non-Igbo speaking audiences to establish what the situation is regarding the acceptance of programmes in other languages in relation to English language programmes.

State governments that have a policy on the use of Igbo language in all activities within the state on specific days should ensure that adherence to such policy is monitored. Paying only lip service to such policies would not encourage the use of local languages among people. Igbo-speaking parents should encourage their children to always speak the language by communicating with their children in the Igbo language. This would not prevent the children from speaking the English language fluently. There is every need to implement these recommendations with a view to saving the Igbo language from extinction.

References

Agbanu, V.N. and A.N. Nwammuo. 2009. *Broadcast Media. Writing. Programming. Production Management*. Enugu: Rhyce Kerex Publishers.

Brenzinger, M. and T. de Graaf. 2012. 'Documenting Endangered Languages and Language Maintenance. A Contribution to the *UNESCO Encyclopedia of Life Support Systems* (EOLSS)'. Retrieved 17 October 2012, from www.mercator-researcheu/fileadmin.

Chester, G. Garrison and E. E. Willis. 1978. *Television and Radio*. Upper Saddle River: Prentice Hall.

Cozby, P. 2004. *Methods in Behavioural Research*. New York: McGraw-Hill.

Dunu, I. V. 2002. 'Broadcast Programming Strategies', in C.S. Okunna (ed), *Teaching Mass Communication: A Multidimensional Approach*, pp. 135–43. Enugu: New Generation Books.

Federal Republic of Nigeria Official Gazette, No. 24. Lagos, 15th May, 2007. Vol. 94.

Grenoble, Lenore A. and Lindsay J. Whaley (eds). 1998. *Endangered Languages: Current Issues and Future Prospects*. Cambridge: Cambridge University Press.

Herzog, H. 1944. 'What Do We Really Know About Day-Time Listeners?', in P. Lazarsfeld and F. Stanton (eds.), *Radio Research*, pp. 1942–43. New York: Duell, Sloan & Pearce.

Katz, Elihu, Blumler, J. and M. Gurevitch. 1974. 'Utilization of Mass Communication by the Individual', in J. Blumler and E. Katz (eds), *The Uses of Mass Communication: Current Perspectives on Gratifications Research*, pp. 19–35. Newbury Park: Sage.

Marghalani, K., P. Palmgreen and D. Boyd. 1998. 'The Utilization of Direct Satellite Broadcasting (DBS) in Saudi Arabia', *Journal of Broadcasting & Electronic Media*, 42(3): 297–314.

McQuail, Denis. 2005. *McQuail's Mass Communication Theory*, 5th ed. London: Sage.

Miller, D. and G. Philo. 2010. *The Active Audience and Wrong Turns in Media Studies*. Retrieved 25 January 2010, from www.icce.rug.nl.

Mufwene, Salikoko S. 2003. 'Language Endangerment: What Have Pride and Prestige Got to Do With It?' Retrieved 17 October 2012, from www.rnld.org.

Nwadike, I. U. 2008. 'Igbo Language and Culture! Whither Bound! (*Asusu na Omenala Igbo: Ije Anaa?*)', In R. N. Umeasiegbu (ed.), *Chief (Dr.) F.C Ogbalu Memorial Lectures* (1 & 3), pp. 5–59. Onitsha Varsity Publishing Co. Ltd in Association with Nnamdi Azikiwe University, Awka.

Njemanze, S. I. 2007. 'Language Shift Among Igbo-English Bilinguals', *Journal of Nigerian Languages and Culture*, 9(1): 109–13.

Nwuneli, O.E. (1985). 'Development News and Broadcasting in Nigeria: An Overview', in O. E. Nwuneli (ed), *Mass Communication in Nigeria: A Book of Reading*, pp. 103–9. Enugu: Fourth Dimension.

Odinye, I. S. and I. E. Odinye. 2010. 'Preventing the Extinction of Igbo Language', *Ogirisi: A New Journal of African Studies*, 7: 85–93.

Ojobor, I. 2002. 'Mass Communication Theories', in S. Okunna (ed), *Teaching Mass Communication: A Multi-dimensional Approach*, pp. 3–26. Enugu: New Generation Books.

Okoye, H.C. 2007. 'Parental Attitude Towards the Teaching and Learning of Igbo Language: The Dangers Ahead', *Journal of Nigerian Languages and Culture*, 9(1): 79–82.

Omego, C. 2007. 'A Survey of Language Use and Culture in Igbo Land', *Journal of Nigerian Languages and Culture*, 9(1): 168–77.

Wimmer, R.D and J.R. Dominick. 2003. *Mass Media Research: An Introduction*. Bangalore: Eastern Press.

18 Aspects of discourse structure

A case of particles

Maloba Wekesa

Introduction

According to Wilson and Keil (2001: 231) discourse can be characterized in three principal ways. First, we may think of discourse as a type of event in which humans engage in verbal exchange. Second, we may also think of discourse as the linguistic content of that exchange, an ordered string of words with their associated syntactic and prosodic structures. Last, we may characterize discourse as the more complex structure of information that is presupposed and/or conveyed by the interlocutors during the course of the discourse event in view of the explicit linguistic content of the exchange. For the purposes of this chapter, I will adopt this third view on discourse as its application diversely covers the scope of the argument I intend to make. The argument concerns the question of discourse organization.

The debate on discourse organization of texts or utterances has received varying responses among scholars. There are those who lean on the argument that receivers somehow indirectly impose an organizational paradigm on speakers who inadvertently find themselves imposing discourse text on this structure. Terms such as 'recipient design' are used to capture this concept. Recipient design is the adaptation of communicative behaviour to a particular addressee (Garfinkel 1967). The concept of recipient design in conversational analysis has been understood as involving aspects of talk that 'display an orientation and sensitivity to the particular other(s) who are the co-participants' (Sacks, Schegloff and Jefferson 1974: 42). Thus, conversational analysis takes recipient design as being for participant(s) in one particular conversation. Also, conversational analysis treats the ability to build recipient-designed turns as part of members' given competencies. However, there are those who find the reverse to be true; that speakers are responsible for the structure of discourse, that information structure is indexed by speakers. Scholars like Lewis (1979), Grosz and Sidner (1986) and Roberts (1996) are quoted by Wilson and Keil (2001: 231) as leaning towards this view. The gist of this chapter is to bridge these two views using the relevance theory while examining how the principles of politeness play a role in both the speaker-generated discourse design and the recipient design of utterances. An examination of the use of particles of Lubukusu gives us a glimpse at how both receivers and speakers each play a role in the organization of discourse.

About politeness and relevance theory

Politeness has been conceptualized especially as strategic conflict avoidance or as a strategic construction of cooperative social interaction (Eelen 2001: 21, Watts 2003: 47). Brown and Levinson (1987: 1) argue that the social role of politeness is its ability to function as a way of controlling potential aggression between interactional parties. Leech (1983: 17) contends that politeness is about avoiding disruption in communication and maintaining social equilibrium and friendly relations. Seen within the prism of these definitions, the argument for this chapter is that discourse structure is indeed a product of considerations in politeness as both speaker and audience strive for cooperative social interaction.

Relevance theory on the other hand is a theory about human communication. Relevance itself as a technical concept is defined by Sperber and Wilson (2006) in comparative terms. By the use of extent conditions, Sperber and Wilson characterize relevance in two ways: in terms of effect and effort. It is an inverse relation: the more contextual effects gained from the processing of an utterance, the more relevant it is and the less effort expended in the processing, the more relevant. Any act of ostensive (attention seeking) communication communicates a presumption of relevance defined as follows:

Presumption of optimal relevance

(a) The set of assumptions which the communicator wants to make manifest to the addressee is relevant enough to make it worth the addressee's while to process the ostensive stimulus.
(b) The ostensive stimulus is the most relevant one the communicator could have used to communicate (Sperber and Wilson 1986: 158).

In fact, there is no way of verifying part (b) of the presumption of optimal relevance, but as long as part (a) and part (b) are not falsified, there is sufficient confirmation for the hearer to proceed with the interpretation. The principle of relevance itself is simply stated:

Principle of relevance

- Every act of ostensive communication communicates the presumption of its own optimal relevance (Sperber and Wilson 1986: 158).

The measurement of relevance cannot take place in absolute cost counting terms and Sperber and Wilson argue that it is psychologically implausible that it should do so. To capture the intuition that we see relevance in comparative terms rather than absolute terms, and that we have no way of comparing the relevance of different information in different environments, they claim that our assessment of relevance is analogous to that of the cost benefit analysis of a business. We count the number of contextual effects gained from the utterance and weigh these against the cost of processing in terms of effort. The more the contextual effects outweigh the processing cost the more relevant we will judge the stimulus to be. It is against this kind of thinking about relevance that this chapter argues for the nexus between speaker-generated discourse organizations against receiver-imposed discourse structure. This chapter uses particles of Lubukusu for illustration.

About particles and the Lubukusu language

In any oral text, one soon notices the abundance of 'particles' in speech. In the English language for example the many occurrences of *well*, *oh*, *let's see* and others are a typical discourse phenomenon. The same applies in Lubukusu with words like *Syo! Pe!*, *ndii*, *nono*, *khane*. At first sight, particles seem to be innocent little words that contribute little to the propositional information conveyed; however, they do play important roles in steering the flow of the text and in conveying various attitudes and expectations of the speaker which are in turn influenced by the expectation of the recipient. Naturally, individual languages will differ in their use of particles while maintaining some generic functions that cut across the board.

According to Lenk (1997) particles of any kind are merely 'fillers' used in spoken language, or optional items empty of lexical meaning that were assumed not to contribute anything to the proposition of the utterance or sentence in which they occur. In this respect, examining particles means looking at elements that are purely non-propositional, elements that only indicate or mark discourse rather than what they describe. These elements include *interjections, expletives, verb particles* and *adjectival particles*. But there are elements in language that seem to also carry propositional content while acting as particles. These are the *particles indicating consequence, agreement,* and *negation and sentence connectors*. These particles have the added responsibility of carrying propositional content or what Lenk (1997) refers to as lexical meaning and this attribute separates them from particles in the strict sense of the definition. In this chapter, I focus on the examination of non-propositional particles purely for illustrative purposes. It should be noted that in no way does this chapter suggest a hierarchy of sorts in giving priority to non-propositional particles. Each particle conveys something distinct from another particle, something non-truth-conditional that helps the hearer know how to take what is being said. Because of the bound relationship of what a particle is to its function, a system of identification of Lubukusu particles in relation to what they do in the sentence and how hearers use them to process meaning is adopted in this chapter. An illustration of these particles based on the functions is discussed to validate the bound relationship they have with recipient design and speakers' imposing an organizational paradigm on the discourse. Blass (2006: 124) argues that since particles guide hearers towards an intended range of contextual effects, they also tend then to have surprisingly similar functions across quite unrelated languages. Blass suggests a possible way of grammaticalizing these functions to arrive at a given generic typology. To the extent of her work on Sisala language, Blass's work cannot wholly be rendered in this chapter but her methods are acknowledged. However, our definition of a particle is taken from Schiffrin (1994), who lists these criteria: they bear no grammatical relationship to other elements in the sentence; they are not inflectable; they may be phonologically ill-formed; they connect utterances as a kind of 'discourse glue'.

Lubukusu is one of the subgroups of a cluster of languages referred to as Luhya. The word Luhya is a cover term used to refer to 17 subgroups, some of which straddle the Kenya-Uganda border, though the majority live in Kenya. Unlike other ethnic groups in Kenya, such as the Kikuyu and the Maasai, the Luhya is not homogeneous. These subgroups, however, speak a fairly mutually intelligible common language and share cultural and ethnic traits that distinguish them from such neighbouring ethnic groups as the Nilotic-speaking Kalenjin group to the north and east, the Luo speakers to the south, and the Teso to the west.

The Luhya traditionally have occupied the area between the southern side of Mount Elgon and the easternmost shore of Lake Victoria. The Babukusu, language speakers of the Lubukusu language, fall within this Bantu-speaking people of the Niger-Congo language family. In the early classifications of African languages, one of the principal criteria used to distinguish different groupings was the languages' use of prefixes to classify nouns or the lack thereof. Greenberg (1963) mentions Koell's *Polyglotta Africana* (1854), Bleek (1911), and Meinhof (1932) as the scholars responsible for coining the word Bantu. Greenberg's work, although initially greeted with scepticism, became the prevailing view for most scholars. Makila (1978) acknowledges that the ethnonym 'Bantu' was invented for the purposes of classifying under one family group, tribes whose word for 'Man' ended with the suffix '-ntu', '-tu', '-ndu', '-to', namely '*Muntu, Umtu, Omundu, Omonto*' and others. Specifically, the Babukusu fall within the larger Luhya tribe that belongs to the 17 clustering Bantu clans within the Lake Basin of Lake Victoria and specifically of East Africa.

The Babukusu inhabit the Bungoma and TransNzoia districts of Western Province, but their dispersion goes far into Busia district. Statistics by the Joshua Project, a ministry of the United States Centre for World Mission as at April 2011, puts the population of Babukusu at 1,433,000 including those in the diaspora.

Non-propositional particles

According to Stede and Schmitz (2000) particles, especially as they are manifested in discourse, are defined as words that are uttered not because of their contribution to propositional content, but because of some pragmatic function for the ongoing discourse. More important, far from being meaningless pause-fillers, particles do not occur randomly in discourse. They tend to 'colour' preceding or even post-ceding discourse and in this colouring process, evidence of speaker intention can be seen. Among these non-propositional particles are interjections, expletives, verb particles and adjectival particles.

Interjections *pebe*! A*khoo, po*!

Generally, an interjection is a kind of lexical category that is used to explain a kind of emotion or when a speaker encounters a kind of emotion. In Lubukusu, interjections capture emotions of surprise, derision, joy, excitement, enthusiasm, irritation and the like. There is no clear agreement on how many interjections there are in Lubukusu. It is noted in Lubukusu that most interjections are found at sentence initial position. However, this is not always the case which sets up interesting pragmatic undertones when the particle was not at sentence initial position. The following are some of the examples of interjections in use in Lubukusu.

- *Pebe* – Pronounced /peβe/ this interjection is always associated with an expression of astonishment or amazement by a speaker when also mixed with confusion. An example is as follows:
- *Embusi yacha khundulo oli eyinya, yabona babana bewe. Pebe! khane yuno kerire babana base kakila naloma ali basilu basutane*!!

Gloss

The goat went to the side to check what it was carrying. (Interjection) shockingly it found out that its kids had been murdered!!! He said to himself, 'the leopard killed my kids that is why he is saying fools are carrying themselves'!!

The preceding example is taken from a narrative. The preceding interjection when used at sentence initial evokes emotions of shock and confusion. This shock and confusion is not only on the part of the 'goat' in the narrative but also of the listening audience. The shock is more intense to the part of the audience especially if it is immediately after a statement that seems nonchalant. The undertone would dramatically shift if the interjection was placed at sentence final achieving a sort of *déjà vu* feeling rather than shock. The placement of the interjection further switching from sentence medial to final creates a pragmatic undercurrent that seems noticeable each time this interjection is used. This sort of manipulation does not seem accidental owing to the pragmatic shifts which the speaker is aware are being evoked. In the context of this chapter, a conclusion can be made that these shifts in position of the interjection are a pointer to how both the speaker and audience are unconsciously engaging in compromise on the structure of the discourse. This tentative conclusion becomes clearer as more examples are considered. Take the example of an interjection with different use as follows:

- *Akhoo!* – Pronounced /axo:/ this interjection is used to evoke emotions of suspense and fear especially when one is recounting a story. An example of this interjection in use is in the following utterance:

Khacha khola niyo lukingi lwakamila, khalola enjofu sebonekha ta
He went all the way to the horizon till the elephant wouldn't spot him
khalola efubu mumechi sebonekha ta,
and checked on the hippo who also couldn't spot him
Akhoo!!!khapakho eyekhungaki yayinga, eyemuchi yayinga,
(Interjection), then he readied them, the one on land tugged, the one on water tugged

The preceding interjection is used to signal impending danger. Again, the sentence initial position of the particle is maintained. The audience is left in suspense and fear as it waits to hear what will happen when the two animals tug at each other. The pragmatic effect of this particle used in this manner creates the illusion that the speaker was in fact an active and present participant in the story. More often than not, the speakers in such instances, given how they control the discourse, are higher in social and even intellectual ranking to the audience, otherwise believability can be compromised and with it the communicative intention. Just as in /*peβe*/, this example shows how a speaker can manipulate intention by the relative position of the interjection. Even more clear is both how the speaker controls the structure of information and at the same time how the audience predictably expects the chunking of information. However, other examples of interjections exhibit a different shade of attribute in terms of the position they take in sentences. For such interjections, irrespective of where they were placed, it seemed that the same pragmatic undertone was realized. The following are two examples that illustrate this.

- *Po!* – Pronounced /po:/ this interjection is mostly used as a snort of derision. An example is:
- *Enjofu eli po!! wanakhamuna newe nganoluri ata yakhaba sikele siase siongene osuta?*

The elephant (interjection) scoffed!! 'With your stature you can't even pull my leg'!!!!

The preceding example of /po:/ is different from the earlier /peβe/ and /axo:/ in that while the latter two interjections shift position in sentences to create different pragmatic undercurrents in an utterance, the former two seem to evoke similar undertones irrespective of where they are placed in sentences of utterances. The general conclusion from these examples is that interjections, depending on the intention of the speaker, take relative positions in sentences that have a direct effect in creating the different pragmatic undertones realized. The pragmatic undertones have a direct effect in the type of text in use. These in turn mean that a speaker chooses how to use the interjection and by extension also chooses the structure of the text. This choice of text by the speaker is automatic while also the choice of discourse structure. From these examples, it can be argued that the type of discourse realized out of the use of interjections is one that is likely to be subjective with deep emotional attachment from the speaker – in this case, narrative texts. It can further be argued that the speaker is likely to be interested in being friendly and maintaining camaraderie as explained through Lakoff's communication calculus quoted by Tannen (2011: 18) in showing politeness. Another conclusion can be made that use of interjections in Lubukusu has a direct relationship to politeness. Further, this sort of communication can be interrogated in terms of the variant contextual effects that the different sentential positions of the particles seem to evoke. This is the purview of relevance theory.

Expletives

Linguistic taboos exist in most cultures and languages, tabooed words generally being culture-specific and relating to bodily functions or aspects of a culture that are sacred. Lubukusu is no different and such words are publicly avoided, considered inappropriate and loaded with affective meaning. According to Matthews (2007), expletives are not just kinds of 'fillers' or 'pads' as would be considered for interjections but in ordinary use they are also used as swear words. For the use reserved specifically for swearing, this chapter separates expletives from interjections in the Lubukusu language. However, there is no agreement how many of such words are in the language, but the examples here suffice for the argument.

- *riswa!* /riswa/ – This expletive is used mainly to implore a higher power and indicate an overwhelming situation especially within religious circles.
- *Aseeno!* /ase:no/ – This expletive is used mainly to indicate extreme disgust and impudence.

What can be inferred from the data for this chapter is that the use of expletives in Lubukusu follows power relations between participants and is further constrained within cohort groups. Whereas the intention of a speaker in using an expletive within his or her age group might be at times for nuanced comic relief, the reverse is true when addressing people of a higher social standing whereby it is frowned upon. However, when a person of a higher social ranking uses an expletive directed to one of a lower ranking, then it is mostly taken as a reprimand of some sort. What is clear though is that expletives are carefully chosen within the discourse types they fall in subject to the intention of a speaker. Interaction between people who do not enjoy equal status and power is based on a system of strategy selection which allows all participants to adjust their processes of utterance production and interpretation according to mutually manifest social rules. Argued in this manner, we can make a general conclusion that use of expletives in Lubukusu has a bearing on politeness. If one is to flout being polite, choose to ignore these manifest social rules and wish for a confrontation, then expletives can be employed in utterances to underlie the intention of this confrontation. But in using these expletives, speakers not only provide evidence of their intentions but also give a guide to the type of text in use and the structure of the text. In this case, the structure will be a function of the type of text chosen.

Verb particles – Syo!te!

These particles are used to modify verbs to show the extent or degree of completion in doing something. Consider the following sentence:

Omwana kalile syo!
The child has eaten PRT.

The modification of the verb *kalile* is to anticipate the extent or degree to how the eating was conducted and eventually concluded. Other related particles in similar function such as *syo* would include *te!*.

The verb particle *te!* is used mostly in greeting formulas. The rule in use for this particle is that it appears immediately after the greeting to show a level of cordial relations between speakers. When used in tautology, the emphasis is even greater and the pragmatic overlay is that of close affection. An example could be as follows:

Mulembe! Mulembe te! Mulembe te! te!
Hallo! Hallo PRT! Hallo PRT! PRT!!

As argued before, this type of compromise that speakers engage in with their respective co-participants in speech is a product of politeness strategies that are under employ. But it is through such cooperation that processing effort by the listeners is lessened even as the contextual effects are increased through the tautology of the particle. In effect, relevance is manifest in the communication.

Adjectival particles *ti*!, *pe*!, *chwe*!

Just like verb particles, these particles are used to modify adjectives in Lubukusu. Some of the examples are *ti! pe! chwe!*. This chapter did not venture to find out how many such particles are in use but those identified exhibited a similar pattern of occurrence: they appeared immediately after the adjective and could also be used in tautology to create extra emphasis.

Ti – In most cases, this particle is used in tautological form mostly to create emphasis, the more it is repeated the greater the effect. An example would be as follows:

Abele musilo etimbile ti!
It was a night of pitch darkness PRT!

The particle *ti* is used to emphasize the extent of darkness. If used in tautology, the extent of darkness is increased and the listener is encouraged to imagine a more pitch black night than before. The same use of this adverbial is sustained in the following examples:

Pe – This adverbial is used to indicate extent or degree. For example,

Lirofu lirobile pe!
The banana is ripe PRT.

Chwe – This adverbial could be said to be in contradistinction from the above adverbial which was an indicator of darkness. Example:

Engubo abele ewangie chwe!
The dress was white!

What is noted in the use of the preceding particles is how each is used sentence final. It is also possible to use these particles sentence medial but in each case, it must be immediately after the verb. The pragmatic undertones realized from the utterances will be dependent on the relative position of the verb and adjective in each sentence and the attendant context between the participants in the discourse. Either way, one conclusion is clear: the type of discourse text seems to be affected each time a verb particle is used. All these are done as automatic information processing by the speaker, albeit unconsciously, but it is dictated by the intention of the speaker and the expected reaction from the audience. Tracking this intention from the evidence of the use of the particle as embodied within principles of politeness and the type of discourse is realized. It is axiomatic that relevance equations are at play at this point.

Conclusion

A dominant observation about particles in Lubukusu is that they seem to interact with the syntax of the sentences they operate in leaving evidence on the type and structure of text and conveying a lot of information about the state of mind of the utterer. Whether the speaker wanted to convey suspense to his audience, or surprise, or was interested in joining ideas in a way that would project either subjectivity or objectivity, the choice of text became imperative, as was the structure. It is for this reason that this chapter found it relevant to use particles in identifying types of discourse and the structure they assume.

Since the use of particles indicated something about the mental state or mental processes of the speaker, using a particle implies that there is a mind behind the utterance. In this respect, using non-propositional particles in general created an impression that speakers were very ego-involved in the discourse because it easily betrayed the feelings of the speaker. The particles in this respect were the interjections, expletives, verb particles and adjectival particles. Expletives indicated a breach of polite behaviour or could even signal comic relief. Interjections showing hesitation or change of turn prompted a certain reaction from listeners. Verb particles and adjectival particles indicated intensity and overtly showed a personal touch. With the use of each of these particles, a clear indication of how structure is conceived became apparent; that both speakers and their audiences play an integral role in determining how the text eventually takes shape.

References

Blass, Regina. 2006. *Relevance Relations in Discourse*. Cambridge: Cambridge University Press.

Bleek, W. and L. C. Lloyd. 1911. *Specimens of Bushman Folklore*. Cape Town: George Allen Press.

Brown, P. and S.C. Levinson. 1987. *Politeness: Some Universals in Language Usage*. Cambridge: Cambridge University Press.

Eelen, Gino. 2001. *A Critique of Politeness Theories*. Manchester: St. Jerome Publishing.

Garfinkel, H. 1967. *Studies in Ethnomethodology*. Englewood Cliffs: Prentice Hall.

Greenberg, J.H. 1963. *Universals of Language*. Cambridge: MIT Press.

Grosz, B.J. and C.L. Sidner. 1986. 'Attention, Intentions and the Structure of Discourse', *Computational Linguistics*, 12(3) (July–September): 175–204.

Koell, S.W. 1854. *Polyglotta Africana*. London. Gregg International Publishers.

Leech, G. N. 1983. *Principles of Pragmatics*. London: Longman.

Lenk, John D. 1997. *McGraw Hill Circuit Encyclopedia and Trouble Shooting Guide*. New York: McGraw Hill.

Makila, F.E. 1978. *An Outline History of the Babukusu*. Nairobi: Kenya Literature Bureau.

Mathews, P.H. 2007. *The Concise Oxford Dictionary of Linguistics*. Oxford: Oxford University Press.

Meinhof, C. 1932. *Introduction to the Phonology of the Bantu Languages*. Berlin: Dietrich Reimer.

Roberts, C. 1996. 'Anaphora in Intentional Contexts', in Shalom Lappin (ed), *The Handbook of Contemporary Semantic Theory*, pp. 215–47. Oxford: Blackwell.

Sacks, H., E.A. Schegloff and G. Jefferson. 1974. *Lectures on Conversation*. Oxford: Blackwell.

Schiffrin, D. 1994. *Approaches to Discourse*. Oxford: Blackwell.

Sperber, Dan and Deirdre Wilson. 1986. *Relevance: Communication and Cognition*, Oxford: Blackwell.

———. 2006. *Relevance: Communication and Cognition*, 2nd ed. Hoboken, NJ: Wiley-Blackwell.

Stede, M. and B. Schmitz. 2000. 'Discourse Particles and Discourse Functions', *Machine Translation*, 15(1–2): 125–47.

Tannen, Deborah. 2011. *That's Not What I Meant! How Conversational Style Makes or Breaks Relationships*. New York: HarperCollins.

Watts, R.J. 2003. *Politeness*. Cambridge: Cambridge University Press.

Wilson, Robert A and F.C. Keil (eds). 2001. *The MIT Encyclopaedia of the Cognitive Sciences*. Cambridge, MA: MIT Press.

19 Mobile telephone communication and the Akan language

Perpetual Crentsil

Introduction

Mobile technology has grown in indigenous communities in non-Western societies. In Africa, the rapid adoption of mobile telephone technology from about the early 2000s and its dramatic benefits have frequently been described in unrestrained terms as 'staggering' and a 'revolution' (Etzo and Collender 2010: 659). The high cost of fixed-line services and their absence in many remote communities, combined with the deregulation of the telephone market, have fuelled the exponential growth in mobile usage in Ghana. The high growth has also seen people developing practices which overcome the challenges of the high cost of mobile telephones relative to average income and recharging issues where electricity supplies, for example, are limited (Sey 2011). Village entrepreneurs make a living by charging a fee from community members for the use of their mobile telephones.

With each new technology emerging from the developed nations, new hope arises as to how it can transform the fortunes of people in the developing world (Sey 2011: 376). Mobile phones have become ubiquitous, multipurpose devices that support initiatives in the social, economic, political and health sectors. Ghanaians have adopted the mobile telephone and made it their own in their local settings, appropriating it in innovative ways. The mobile telephone has been used to support micro-business entrepreneurship, and it has also become the latest tool for delivering information on healthcare services. Mobile phones have become a symbol of status and are associated with sex, especially as objects for transactional sex. Hence, the term 'mobile phone girls' has come to symbolize 'expensive' young women with high tastes who depend on male lovers for buying them mobile phones and other economic gains. Other descriptions depicting human attributes about the devices have crept into the everyday rhetoric in Ghana, demonstrating the stimuli felt by talkers and users of the mobile technology (Yankah 2007).

This chapter concerns itself with how certain words, symbolism and other referents associated with the mobile telephone (I generically refer to all these as 'mobile phone language') have found their way into the local lexicon when people communicate in the Akan language, even by people who do not speak the English language at all. As mobile telephone use has become an everyday life in Ghana, words, phrases and ideas such as 'missed call', 'out of coverage area', 'wrong number', 'moba' (mobile), 'engaged' that create particular images associated with the device are rife.

The literature of Africa (and of the African Diaspora) often employs vernacular elements and the 'Africanization' of European languages (McLaren 2009: 97) and this has attracted much attention; there has been little or no attention paid to the 'Anglicization' of non-European languages (how English words have infiltrated into the local lexicon).

In this chapter, I use 'mobile phone language' in the Akan lexicon and symbolic referents associated with the mobile technology as a mirror to social values embedded in culture and social relations (de Souza e Silva *et al.* 2011). The chapter both draws on and contributes to the understanding of the role of cultural meanings in language and technology studies. I start off with a discussion of the literature about the appropriation of technology, followed by ideas and practices associated with mobile telephones in Ghana, including gender, sex and sexual referents, as well as human attributes to the devices. This chapter argues that the adoption and appropriation of mobile technology in Ghana have brought about a range of innovative ways in which mobile telephones are used but have also created symbolic referents and contested discourses in the Akan lexicon. Moreover, the infiltration of the 'new' vocabulary into the Akan language does not indicate obliteration of the indigenous language but, rather, its enlargement or growth and a transformation engendered by the adoption and appropriation of mobile technology in Ghana.

Appropriation of technology and indigenous culture

The appropriation of technology as an analytical tool focuses on the social aspects of technology use, specifically on how people engage with technology and the patterns of behaviour that emerge in the process. Donner (2008) outlines three major trends in the studies of mobile phones in developing countries – the adoption of mobile phones, the impact of mobile phones and the interrelationships between mobile technologies and users (141). Frequently, these areas intermingle; studies of mobile phone adoption, for example, can include issues about impacts of mobile phones and the interrelationships between mobile technologies and users (de Souza e Silva *et al.* 2011: 3). The social shaping of technology highlights the active role of the user (Mackay and Gillespie 1992: 698) in shaping and defining a technology's meaning (Klein and Kleinman 2002).

Much of technology studies has focused on the domestication of mobile phones in everyday life and on the cultural appropriation of such technology. The domestication approach concentrates on questions of how technology is adapted to everyday life and how everyday life, in turn, is adapted to technology (Tenhunen 2008: 516). The approach makes it possible to grasp how society shapes technology and how, conversely, technologies can have effects on the organization of society. As Tenhunen (ibid.) has pointed out, the approach has its roots in Western epistemologies (e.g. the concept of domesticity itself); it has been developed to understand the acquiring of technology in Western societies and how users position technology while at the same time making it useful and meaningful (517). However, it is relevant since the mobile phone as a new technology has been adopted and is widespread in non-Western societies. Horst and Miller (2005) focus on social aspects of mobile phone communication in kinship and social relations in Jamaica.

Appropriation generally refers to how artefacts are used and how they are adapted in use and subsequently interpreted (Mackay and Gillespie 1992). Ling (2004), who has researched the appropriation of mobile phones in Norway, represents the mainstream in social studies of technology. Employing the domestication paradigm, Ling focuses on social and behavioural patterns of mobile phone usage but he does not discuss much about their meanings and the symbolic referents associated with the devices. This chapter focuses on mobile phone user practices in Ghana and the symbolism associated with the devices. Pfaffenberger (1988: 241) contends that 'any technology should be seen as a system, not just of tools, but also of related social behaviours and techniques'. For Giddens (1990: 18–19), the ability to foster relationships with absent others is a central facet of modernity's globalizing dynamism. To him, in conditions of modernity locales are penetrated and shaped in terms of social influences quite distant from those locales.

Scholarly attention to the use and appropriation of mobile telephones in Africa is growing although much of the studies of mobile technology has been dominated by appropriation for economic (business) purposes (e.g. Overå 2006; Donner 2008; Frempong 2009), social relations (Elegbeleye 2005; Hahn and Kibora 2008), and gender and poverty (Scott *et al.* 2004). Less attention has been given to images and symbolic referents created by mobile telephones. This chapter contributes to the body of research on mobile telephones and socio-cultural aspects of life. Technology and society can never be separated (Pfaffenberger 1988). Such symbolic fields as kinship/family, gender, power, status, sex and sexuality, health and language constitute values and enduring meaning structures which cannot be ignored or overlooked.

Mobile telephones in Ghana

According to the National Communications Authority, in November 2014 there are over 30 million mobile phone voice subscriptions in a population of about 26 million. We must however bear in mind that some people might have two or even three phones while others might have none. All the same, the mobile telephone is currently a near-universal phenomenon in Ghana, and it has caused transformations in many ways of life. A pre-paid card allows a user to call (the lowest rate is one Ghana cedi which was equal to $0.50 in 2010) until the budget has been depleted but the phone can still be used for receiving incoming calls until the card's expiry date (cf. Kaplan 2006). Acquiring mobile phones engenders ideas and symbolism about the devices in Ghana. While mobile phones can be purchased by the user and many people have two or three phones in order to reach through on different networks (cf. Overå 2006: 1305), they are also used as a statement of affluence and status. Again, mobile phones can be received as gifts from relatives and friends. As common gifts from abroad, mobile phones demonstrate Ghanaians' engagements with international migration and the global economy. Ghanaians in the Diaspora use mobile phones to communicate with relatives back home on family matters and about remittances – monies and goods – they send home. Those who do not have their own phones and cannot arrange sharing with relatives or friends can easily rent from roadside operators in kiosks, booths or under trees and large umbrellas (see Figure 19.1). Many small-scale business ventures have emerged in the booming mobile phone industry today, with the service providers being mostly foreign.

The phenomenal growth of mobile phones has been the most important change in communication devices. When multiple licences for mobile networks were awarded in 1992, Millicom, a subsidiary of Millicom International UK/Luxembourg, had started its operations in 1991 as the

Figure 19.1 A roadside 'umbrella' sales point

first mobile phone network operator and by 1998, it had over 22,000 subscribers. Mobitel (1992), Celltel (1993), Spacefon (1996), and Onetouch (the mobile phone arm of Ghana Telecom in the year 2000) followed suit. By 2003, Mobitel, Celltel, Spacefon, and Onetouch together had 600,000 subscribers (Overå 2006). In 2010, six mobile phone companies existed in Ghana: Kasapa, Vodafone, MTN, Tigo, Zain and Glo (which was yet to start operations).

At a time when urban Ghana is fast shifting towards the use of mobile phones and surfing the internet, most parts of rural Ghana still have neither electricity nor landlines. The mobile phone is currently a near-universal phenomenon in its use and has the potential as most used device because, unlike landline telephone networks, mobile phones are not centralized and at a fixed spot. The fact that mobile phones can be used even if an individual can neither write nor has an office, or is on the move most of the time has made them the most appropriate communication technology (Overå 2006: 1302). There is currently a mechanism in Ghana to solve the problem of fake medicines by checking the authenticity of a drug through sending a free short messaging services (SMS) text to a central number; mobile phones are also helping in the area of maternal health. For example, affordable handsets were provided for pregnant women in the Ashanti and Upper East Regions of Ghana to enable them to receive answers to common ante- and post-natal questions as well as reminders about check-ups and vaccinations. This reduced maternal deaths; there was no maternal death in 2008, which is important because according to UN figures, 560 out of 100,000 women in Ghana die each year during childbirth or from pregnancy complications (*Irin News* 2009).

Mobile phones in Ghana can be fashion statements, symbols of status and expression of identity. At the same time they can be a gadget of misfortune. The fear of theft and physical or psychological harm have constrained most people from publicly displaying their mobile phones (cf. Sey 2011). Most people hide their phones in their bags or, as with women, they cover them with their cloths like they do with babies.

Modern technology and Akan language

In Ghana, the fascination of modern technology dawned when the automobile was introduced at the beginning of the twentieth century. As Yankah (2007) has suggested, the reaction of the local people clearly demonstrated puzzlement with an invention that enabled someone to combine mobility with a sedentary posture. *Kar* (a corruption of the English name for car) or 'lorry' found their way into the local dialect but the Akan term *tseaseanam* (literally, 'that which allows you to be seated and in motion') indicated a fascination with the automobile – something that allowed you to be seated, yet paradoxically in motion – a combination of two otherwise irreconcilable postures. The aeroplane is referred to as *dadieanoma* (literally, 'iron bird').

The fixed (landline) telephone surfaced during the colonial period. The telephone was known as *tetefon*, and the fascination with this device, which enables two people to communicate at distant places, is not lost in the Akan name for telephone. *Ahomatrofo* (conversation line) captures this idea. The mobile phone, which has become so popular in Ghana after its introduction from about year 2000, is referred to as *moba* in everyday usage. But the wonder of mobile technology is expressed in the metaphor of not being fixed to a single place. *Megyina abonten na merekasayi* (I am talking [with you] from outside the confines of the home) refers to that notion and in contrast to the fixed (home) phone.

The Western (foreign) language and communication cannot substitute for pure and pristine indigenous Akan language. To speak a foreign (European) language is to *poto*, that is, to mix (adulterate) or improvise. Hence, on occasion when one has to speak English before elders, one may apologize by saying: *Mesrɛ mapoto kakra* (I crave your indulgence to adulterate my speech with a foreign language). People may even apologize in advance when they are about to speak in a foreign language, which is considered impure and which may displease others. Sometimes, the worry is that the English language is given priority over the indigenous languages in Ghana. The Akan language and others like Ga, Ewe, and Dagbani are taught in basic schools but English is the major language of instruction. The development and mastering of the English language over the local languages can be traced back to Ghana's colonial period, when as in Kenya (Kioko and Muthwii 2001) it was the key to access to white-collar jobs, European thought, and was associated with a lot of prestige and power. Today, the English language as a global (transnational) tongue is dominant – major textbooks, research reports and other types of information are all published in English. Hence, many pupils are forced to study and communicate frequently in English and are found wanting when speaking the indigenous language. I remember that somewhere in 1977, a school girl with a good command of the English language saw an Akan inscription (in the Fanti dialect) on a lorry that read: *Nyame bekyerɛ* (which translates into 'God will provide'). In her attempt to read it, she exclaimed: *Nayambakiri*, which is meaningless, drawing much laughter and teasing from her friends.

The attainment of Ghana's independence in 1957 also stripped English of some of the prestige it had enjoyed during the colonial period. A good command of the English language at the expense of the local language was seen as a colonial mentality and, therefore, was stigmatized. Post-colonial attitudes that anything Western is superior still persist. However, there is also the feeling that the indigenous culture is being adulterated; elderly people especially give a lot of cultural weight to the Akan language and present it as the best in the world. Perhaps, it is for this reason that the bulk of the many FM radio stations established in Ghana today are relayed in the Akan language. It may be that this measure is to encourage people to speak the local language frequently and also to whip up enthusiasm in communicating in it. There seems to be an 'Africanization' of education and forms of communication going on in Ghana.

Advanced communication technologies, suspicion and derision

Africans are generally and basically suspicious of advanced communication technologies and Western scientific breakthroughs. While there is usually admiration for Western technology and scientific breakthroughs, there is sometimes disdain towards Western science because of the danger to humanity. When man first landed on the moon in 1969, many people in Ghana felt sometimes apprehensive that such exploits by the Whiteman could one day cause the moon to fall on the earth and kill everyone. Why would the Whiteman not be content with what we have here on earth; why should the secrets of God's creation be searched for? When it comes to HIV/AIDS blame, suspicions and conspiracy theories abound in Ghana, as among Haitians (Farmer 1992), about the origin of the disease. Many blame Americans for creating the virus in their laboratories in an experiment that went wrong and spread worldwide, and others think that the virus was deliberately created to discourage Africans from procreating (Crentsil 2007).

There is a general mistrust for Western-mediated communication evinced by its perception and depiction by tradition in rather derogatory terms (Yankah 2007). For instance, the newspaper was called *kowaakrataa*, literally 'loose-tongued paper tabloid' and it is derived from *ka no waa* ('say it in jest' or 'not to be taken seriously'). The radio was simply described as *akasanoma* ('talking bird') and was regarded as mere frivolity. Similarly, the reference to the telephone as *ahomatrofo* concerns the idea that it is a 'liar', 'the tale bearing wire', 'wire that conveys lies or unverified information' and the like and is therefore unreliable and not to be trusted because it deals in falsehoods. This also implies that fast travelling news whose veracity cannot be checked is untrustworthy.

The advent of British colonialism in the mid-1800s saw the springing up of earlier electronic media. The telegraph was first established in Ghana (then Gold Coast) in 1881 (Allotey and Akorli 1999, cited in Overå 2006). This made possible the landline (fixed telephones) to be established and thus became an important communication device over long distances. Postal services were established as part of the communication processes, and telegrams were one of the important ways of communicating health messages. Such was the popularity of telegram messaging that a common joke is said about a funny telegram message: *Seriously Kwesimintsim, hospital the wife*, sent to a man whose wife was seriously ill at a hospital at Kwesimintsim, in a town in southwestern Ghana. Newspapers, radio, and later fixed telephones (landline) and television were major sources of information on health and social issues. Various audiovisual aids such as the cinema became popular, and information vans with loudspeakers mounted by the Information Services Department (ISD), the Red Cross, (and later the Red Crescent) also came into existence after independence in 1957.

In the year 2000 when mobile technology was catching up in Ghana and a considerable number of people began to use mobile phones, the sight of people talking to themselves, as it were, brought on ideas of schizophrenia about those engaged in such acts. People laughing in the company of none other than themselves while walking or driving, or those walking but swinging just one arm with the other hand held closely to the ear and apparently talking aloud to themselves used to draw laughter from others. Even more unusual was the sight of people driving, talking, and heartily laughing without the observer noticing the phone. Today, such practices and behaviours have become normal ways of life (Yankah 2007).

'Mobile telephone language' in Akan language

In this section, I present two separate informal conversations I chanced upon during fieldwork in 2010. I reproduce them to show how mobile telephone language has crept into the indigenous Akan language. The first conversation was between a grandmother and her granddaughter over the whereabouts of the old woman's mobile phone which had been bought for her by one of her sons residing abroad. The other conversation was between a man and a woman, who are apparently lovers, about problems concerning their mobile phone communication. I reproduce parts of the two conversations here in their original form as they were deployed in the Akan (the first in Fanti and the second in Twi) language which I put in bold letters. A rough English translation is in parenthesis in both cases. I have decided to italicize the two conversations to highlight them. For the same reason, the English or anglicized words are put in single quotes.

Case one

A grandmother questions her granddaughter in the Fanti dialect of the Akan language about the whereabouts of her (grandmother's) mobile telephone:

Grandmother: ***Me 'moba' no wo hen?***
(Where is my mobile telephone?)

Grand-daughter: ***Onnyi wo dan no mu hɔ?***
(Is it not in your room?)
Grandmother: ***Oho***
(No.)
Grand-daughter: ***ɔno dze mennhunii***
(Then I have not seen it.)

(After a while when both grandmother and granddaughter searched for the phone.)

Grandmother: ***Oh, meehu no wɔ egua a nna metse do no nkyɛn. Wo tsir nkwa. Nna mo dwen dɛ eyi edze rekɛyɛ 'call' dze ama wo 'boy' no.***
(Oh, now I have found it beside the chair I have been sitting on. You are lucky. I thought you have taken it to make a call to your boy [boyfriend].)
Grand-daughter: ***Mennyi 'boy' oh, na mennfrɛ 'boy' biara.***
(I do not have a boy [boyfriend] oh, and I do not call to any boy.)
Grandmother: ***ɔyɛ ampa? Na 'call' no a inyae wɔ 'phone' yi do ndeda no fir hen?***
(Is it true? So, from where came the call you got on this phone yesterday?)
Grand-daughter: ***Oh, dɛm 'call' no a? Nna ɔyɛ 'wrong number'. Ahyɛse no muhun 'miss call'. Dɛm ntsi, me frɛɛ hwɛɛ dɛ ɔyɛ woana a. Ekyir no, muhun dɛ ɔyɛ 'wrong number'.***
(Oh, that call? It was a wrong number. Initially, I saw a missed call. Because of that, I called back to see who had called. Later, I realized it was a wrong number.)
Grandmother: ***Aah.***
(Ok; I see.)———

Case two

A woman confronts a man in the Twi dialect of the Akan language:

Woman: ***Aden nti na mefrɛ wo 'moba' no abere biara a na ayɛ 'engage' anaa sɛ nne bi reka sɛ ɛyɛ 'out of coverage area' yi?***
(Why is it that any time I call to your mobile phone it is either engaged or there is a voice saying it is out of coverage area?)

Man: ***Mennim.Wo yɛ 'sure' sɛ wo frɛ me 'number' no?***
(I don't know. Are you sure you call to my number?)
Woman: ***Anne, ɛyɛ wo 'number' no a.***
(Yes, it is to your number.)
Man: ***ɛno deɛ ɛbɛyɛ sɛ ɛyɛ 'network problem'. Wo nim sɛ 'phone companies' no nyinaa wɔ 'customers' bebree nti sɛ 'load' no yɛ duru a, na 'lines' no ɛnnkɔ yie.***
(Then, it must be a network problem. You know these telephone companies have many customers so that if the load becomes too heavy the lines do not go through very well.)

As already mentioned, the infiltration of the 'new' vocabulary into the Akan language does not indicate obliteration of the indigenous language but, rather, a transformation engendered by the adoption and appropriation of mobile technology in Ghana.

Symbolic referents: 'mobile phone girls', sex, gender, and human attributes of mobile telephones

Some mobile phone language has also crept into other aspects of Ghanaian life, symbolizing the ubiquitous nature of mobile phones. The phrase 'out of coverage area' has now been appropriated in other domains. For example, at a wedding, the MC told friends of the bride that henceforth 'she is out of coverage area' to mean that she was not available for any other love relationship (see Yankah 2007). Words and phrases such as *bɔ me nkɔmɔ* (converse with me), *twa me kɛkɛ* (simply call me), and *kasapa* (good talk) have been accepted as part of the local lexicon and stock of expressions (ibid.). Mobile phone text messages are also being used as greeting cards with inspirational words. One message said:

> May all who seek your downfall get network problem, may the Devil be out of coverage area in your life, may problems that come your way be put on Call divert, may any call of death be your missed call, may your incoming calls be victory and prosperity. Stay Blessed! Happy New Year. . . .
>
> (Crentsil 2014)

Symbolic referents to mobile telephones happen in other ways, especially those associated with sex. Casual sex, pre- and extramarital relationships are common in Ghana and show the extent to which girls and women have to engage in sexual intercourse through necessity – to pass school examinations or obtain training placements, to get access to farming land, to get money and food for daily subsistence, to get jobs and stay in them and others (Oppong 1995: 1). Although it is somehow condemned, as in Madagascar (Cole 2010), sex as a way of building connections and gaining resources seems acceptable; sex with men for economic gain is seen as a necessary evil (Nabila and Fayorsey 1996). Individual successes in wealth or fame are almost equated with the honour of the lineage/family, and family members are happy that a relative owns a phone no matter how it was acquired. African societies have continued to subject the colonial gender-sex identities (Aniekwu 2006), and mobile phones have added an impetus to this situation. There is the constant charge in Ghana that mobile phones increase the conduct of illicit relationships. Since many people have difficulty in acquiring, owning or using a phone due to socio-economic factors, women may resort to transactional sex. Husbands, boyfriends, and 'Sugar Daddies' (elderly male lovers) give their wives or girlfriends mobile phones so they can directly be contacted regularly and at will, clearly with intentions of both control and surveillance (Slater and Kwami 2005: 12).

Mobile phones are helping women to assert their feminine status as well as widen their spaces and contacts but the acquisition and use fuel certain gender stereotypes concerning both reputable and disreputable behaviours (Sey 2011).Women have long used their sexual and reproductive capacities to create desirable economic and kin relationships (Cole 2010). Mobile phones are used as bait by young women before they agree to an intimate relationship with a man, while most women use their phones for monitoring their husbands and boyfriends. 'Mobile phone girls' symbolize 'expensive' young women with high tastes who depend on male lovers for economic gains. Such women are considered notorious for requiring the newest mobile phone models from their romantic partners, and rightly or wrongly, this belief usually tags young unemployed women who own mobile phones as disreputable (Slater and Kwami 2005; Sey 2011). It is thought that a man who enters a relationship with such women is bound to buy mobile phone units, and even the cost of electricity for charging the phone battery. A woman who owns a mobile phone must have a lover who bought it for her or have several of them who gave her monies that paid for the phone. A 45-year-old seamstress who saw a teenage girl talking on a mobile phone and telling her three friends about what she was discussing with what looked like the male caller commented thus: 'From where would a young girl get the money to buy a phone? It surely comes from a man in exchange for sex. Oh, modern-day Ghana. . . . May God himself forgive us for such immorality.'

People maintain their mobile phones as they would do humans. They recharge the devices with energy (electricity, solar energy or through car battery) and 'feed' them with units, which one woman refers to as 'food' (*edziban*) for her mobile phone.

Mobile phones in Ghana can be fashion statements, symbols of status and expression of identity. At the same time they can be a gadget of misfortune. The fear of theft and physical or psychological harm has constrained most people from publicly displaying their mobile phones (cf. Sey 2011). The fact that people hide their phones in their bags and women cover them with their cloths as they do with babies gives mobile phones human qualities. And when people try to notify mobile phone users about the fact that their phone has been ringing, they usually equate the sound of ringing with crying; they say the mobile phone has been 'crying' for so long (*phone no esu saa*).

Conclusions

The adoption and appropriation of mobile technology in Ghana have brought about a range of innovative ways in which mobile telephones are used but have also created symbolic referents and contested discourses. The infiltration of the 'new' vocabulary into the Akan language does not indicate an obliteration of the indigenous language, but rather a transformation engendered by the adoption and appropriation of mobile technology in Ghana. It is obvious that mobile language has become the latest infiltration of the English language and other 'foreign' cultures into the Akan cultural and communicative values.

Most of the mobile phone expressions come from the English language and people are forced to use them at the expense of the indigenous ones. As a global language, English will continue to dominate other languages, especially indigenous and less dominant tongues such as the Akan. There is little that can be done to reverse the situation. This chapter suggests that some of the mobile phone language (and English words) could be translated into the indigenous vocabulary because the local language better expresses the culture, myths, values, and identity of the people. This will also eliminate any conceptual antagonism between the two languages.

Acknowledgements

The research on which this chapter is based is part of the research project *Mobile telephony, gender and development in Africa, India and Bangladesh* funded by the Academy of Finland.

References

Allotey, Francis K. and Felix K. Akorli. 1999. 'Ghana', in Eli M. Naom (ed), *Telecommunications in Africa*, pp. 178–92. Oxford: Oxford University Press.

Aniekwu, N.I. 2006. 'Converging Constructions: A Historical Perspective on Sexuality and Feminism in Post-colonial Africa', *African Sociological Review*, 10(1): 143–60.

Cole, J. 2010. *Sex and Salvation: Imagining the Future in Madagascar*. Chicago and London: University of Chicago Press.

Crentsil, P. 2007. 'Death, Ancestors and HIV/AIDS among the Akan of Ghana'. Ph.D. dissertation. Research Series in Anthropology 10, University of Helsinki.

———. 2014. '"Kasapa": Mobile Telephony and Changing Healthcare Communication in Ghana', in G.N. Devy, Geoffrey V. Davis and K.K. Chakravarty (eds), *Knowing Differently: The Cognitive Challenge of the Indigenous*, pp. 106–24. New Delhi and London: Routledge.

de Souza e Silva, A., D.M. Sutko, F.A. Salis, and C. de Souza e Silva. 2011. 'Mobile Phone Appropriation in the Favelas of Rio de Janeiro, Brazil', *New Media & Society*, 1–16. DOI: 10.1177/1461444810393901.

Donner, J. 2008. 'Research Approaches to Mobile Use in the Developing World: A Review of the Literature', *The Information Society*, 24: 140–59. DOI: 10.1080/01972240802019970.

Elegbeleye, O.S. 2005. 'Prevalent Use of Global System of Mobile Phone (GSM) for Communication in Nigeria: A Breakthrough in Interactional Enhancement or a Drawback?', *Nordic Journal of African Studies*, 14(2): 193–207.

Etzo, S. and G. Collender. 2010. 'The Mobile Phone "Revolution" in Africa: Rhetoric or Reality?', *African Affairs*, 109/437: 659–68.

Farmer, P. 1992. *AIDS and Accusations: Haiti and the Geography of Blame*. Berkeley: University of California Press.

Frempong, G. 2009. 'Mobile Telephone Opportunities: The Case of Micro- and Small Enterprises in Ghana', *Info*, 11(2): 79–94. DOI: 10.1108/14636690910941902.

Giddens, A. 1990. *The Consequences of Modernity*. Cambridge: Polity Press.

Hahn, H.P. and L. Kibora. 2008. 'The Domestication of the Mobile Phone: Oral Society and New ICT in Burkina Faso', *Journal of Modern African Studies*, 46(1): 87–109. DOI: 10.1017/S002278X07003084.

Horst, N. and D. Miller. 2005. 'From Kinship to Link-up: Call Phones and Social Networking in Jamaica', *Current Anthropology*, 46(5): 755–78. DOI: 10.1086/432650.

Irin News. 2009. 'GHANA: Cell Phones Cut Maternal Deaths'. Retrieved 11 January2015, from http://www.irinnews.org/report/87261/ghana-cell-phones-cut-maternal-deaths.

Kaplan, W.A. 2006. 'Can the Ubiquitous Power of Mobile Phones Be Used to Improve Health Outcomes in Developing Countries?', *Globalization and Health*, 2(9): 1–14. DOI: 10.1186/1744-8603-2-9.

Kioko, A.N. and M.J. Muthwii. 2001. 'The Demands of a Changing Society: English in Education in Kenya Today', *Language, Culture and Curriculum*, 14(3): 201–13.

Klein, H.K. and D.L. Kleinman. 2002. 'The Social Construction of Technology: Structural Considerations', *Science, Technology, & Human Values*, 27(1): 28–52. DOI: 10.1177/016224390202700102.

Ling, R. 2004. *The Mobile Connection: The Cell Phone's Impact on Society*. San Francisco: Morgan Kaufman.

Mackay, H. and G. Gillespie. 1992. 'Extending the Social Shaping of Technology Approach: Ideology and Appropriation', *Social Studies of Science*, 22(4): 685–716. DOI: 10.1177/030631292022004006.

McLaren, J. 2009. 'African Diaspora Vernacular Traditions and the Dilemma of Identity', *Research in African Literatures*, 40(1): 97–111.

Nabila, J.S. and C. Fayorsey. 1996. 'Adolescent Fertility and Reproductive Behaviour in Ghana', in E. Ardayfio-Schandorf (ed), *The Changing Family in Ghana*, pp. 137–68. Accra: Ghana Universities Press (for Family and Development Programme, Department of Geography and Resource Development, University of Ghana, Legon).

Oppong, C. 1995. 'A High Price to Pay: For Education, Subsistence or a Place in the Job Market', *Health Transition Review*, 5(Supplement): 35–56.

Overå, R. 2006. 'Networks, Distance, and Trust: Telecommunications Development and Changing Trading Practices in Ghana', *World Development*, 34(7): 1301–15. DOI: 10.1016/J.worlddev.2005.11.015.

Pfaffenberger, B. 1988. 'Fetishised Objects and Human Nature: Towards an Anthropology of Technology', *Man, New Series*, 23(2): 236–52. Retrieved from http://www.jstor.org/stable/2802804.

Scott, N., K. McKemyey, and S. Batchelor. 2004. 'The Use of Telephones Amongst the Poor in Africa: Some Gender Implications', *Gender Technology and Development*, 8(2): 182–207. DOI: 10.1177/097185240400800202.

Sey, A. 2011. 'New Media Practices in Ghana', *International Journal of Communications*, 5: 380–405. Retrieved from http://ijoc.org.

Slater, D. and J. Kwami. 2005. 'Embeddedness and Escape: Internet and Mobile Use as Poverty Reduction Strategies in Ghana', (Information Society Research Group, ISRG Working Paper No. 4). Retrieved from http://zunia.org/uploads/media/knowledge/internet.pdf.

Tenhunen, S. 2008. 'Mobile Technology in the Village: ICTs, Culture, and Social Logistics in India', *Journal of the Royal Anthropological Institute* (N. S.), 14: 515–34. DOI: 10.1111/j1467-9655.2008.00514.x.

Yankah, K. 2007. 'Mobile Phones and our Cultural Values'. Paper presented as a Keynote Speech at the Seminar on Mobile Telephony Organised by Ghana Telecom. Source: *The Ghanaian Times*, 9 and 13 February, 2007. Retrieved from http://www.ghanaculture.gov.gh.

Index